Lecture Notes in Economics and Mathematical Systems

Managing Editors: M. Beckmann and W. Krelle

228

Nonlinear Models of Fluctuating Growth

An International Symposium
Siena, Italy, March 24–27, 1983

Edited by R.M. Goodwin, M. Krüger and A. Vercelli

Springer-Verlag
Berlin Heidelberg New York Tokyo 1984

Editors

Prof. Dr. Richard M. Goodwin
Department of Economics, University of Siena
Piazza S. Francesco 17, 53100 Siena, Italy

Dr. Michael Krüger
Fachbereich Sozialwissenschaften, Universität Osnabrück
Postfach 4469, D-4500 Osnabrück

Prof. Dr. Alessandro Vercelli
Department of Economics, University of Siena
Piazza S. Francesco 17, 53100 Siena, Italy

ISBN 3-540-13349-6 Springer-Verlag Berlin Heidelberg New York Tokyo
ISBN 0-387-13349-6 Springer-Verlag New York Heidelberg Berlin Tokyo

Printed in Germany

Printing and binding: Beltz Offsetdruck, Hemsbach/Bergstr.
2142/3140-543210

FOREWORD

This volume is the outgrowth of an International Symposium organized by the Department of Economics of the Economics and Banking Faculty of Siena University (Italy) in march 24-27, 1983.

The main task was that of contributing to the remarkable progress which went on in the study of fluctuating growth in recent years. The same Department had already organized a small and informal workshop on the same subject in spring 1981 (whose proceedings have been published in Economic Notes, 3 , 1982). The unexpected success of this initiative suggested the launching of the subsequent International Symposium.

The scientific level of the papers has been considered by the participants of a quality to merit publication. The resulting volume may perhaps be judged something more than a mere record of Conference Proceedings. The debate had been so lively and effective that all the authors produced, in the wake of the discussion, substantially revised drafts of their papers in an amazingly short spell of time. We found the new versions interesting and homogenous enough to be considered as almost natural articulations of a monograph on recent advances in fluctuating growth. This made our work of editors surprisingly quick and simple. We are grateful for that to all the authors and all the participants to the Symposium.

We wish to thank also all the people and institutions that made possible its happy implementation.

We have to mention, first of all, the Faculty of Economics and Banking of Siena University, in particular, the Dean Antonio Cristofaro, for vital financial and organizational support.

We are glad to acknowledge all our gratitude to the Department of Economics which has been the main coordinating center in all the long and troublesome gestation period.

We have to give a particular thank to Mrs. Silvana Allegri for her efficient and tireless secretarial assistance, and to Mrs. Viviana Pietrelli, Mrs. Lucia Pogialini and Mrs. Rina Burroni for their precious help.

We have moreover to address a warm thank to Mrs. Palma Trefoloni, director of the

Conference Office of Siena University, and her collaborators Miss Giuliana Pasquini and Miss Janet Donovan, who solved all the logistic problems with amazing efficiency and charm (among the successes no one will forget the wonderful concert in the chapel of the Certosa Di Pontignano).

Last but not least, we should mention the unfailing and valuable contribution of the stuff of the Certosa, beautiful ancient building in the delightful surroundings of Siena, where the Symposium happily took place.

The Editors

CONTENTS

INTRODUCTION

I. Fluctuating Growth in Capitalist Societies

Post-war experience, in almost all advanced capitalist societies, gave at first considerable support to the view that the capitalist economy would no longer exhibit serious business cycles or, better, growth cycles. The general attitude in those heydays is evident from the title of a book edited by Bronfenbrenner in the late sixties: "Is The Business Cycle Obsolete?" (see Bronfenbrenner, 1969)

The last ten years, characterized by economic stagnation and crisis, renewed the interest of economists in a theory of economic fluctuations and cyclical growth (where growth, of course, may be null or even negative). Business cycles would not be considered obsolete today, neither empirically nor theoretically, by most economists so that Bronfenbrenner's question would possibly not be raised.

There is increasing scepticism about the adequacy of describing the evolution of capitalism in terms of steady-state growth models. The more important macroeconomic variables such as GNP, the national income, distributive shares, the rate of growth of the capital stock, the degree of capacity utilization, the employment ratio, nominal and real rates of interest, and the rate of inflation, cannot properly be described, explained or forecast without taking account of their fluctuating paths of growth.

A simple superposition of fluctuations on growth trends is not satisfactory for analytic purposes, since fluctuations and growth interact in a crucial way.

There is no doubt that for different countries the empirical design of the time series of the relevant variables is not uniform or of a simple, say sinusoidal, form. But in fact no one, who is interested in growth cycles, would expect this kind of rather trivial empirical pattern. Different institutional arrangements, different internal conditions of production and accumulation, and different effects of international trade on each national economy ensure the enormous variety of empirical findings for each country. Nevertheless there seems to exist a need for general theories of fluctuating growth which may, or could, form a first step towards an understanding of accumulation and crisis in different countries.

At the center of the debate at our symposium was the viewpoint that economic fluctuations are the natural outcome of the capitalist economy itself, as a consequence of its internal dynamic structures and conflicts. This is to say that advanced capitalism would undergo fluctuations with or without state intervention. We have concentrated our attention on nonlinear formulations because, for all their attractive simplicity, linear models will not do. As Frisch pointed out long ago, such models either die away or burst their bounds and so can exist only in the minds of academics, never in reality. In other words, linear models may describe only very simple patterns of behaviour which cannot satisfactorily represent the very complicated nature of cyclical fluctuations.

II. Determinants of a Theory of Cyclical Accumulation

To some extent it really is a tragedy that two outstanding minds, who contributed perhaps more than anybody else a deep insight into the dynamic structure of capitalism and its tendency of fluctuating evolution, Marx and Schumpeter, have largely been considered as outsiders by professional economists. Our understanding of the principal determinants of fluctuating accumulation of capital would be less tentative, if economists had taken account of their contributions. For his part Marx stressed the class antagonism as one main source of conflicts within the sphere of production and distribution, and both Marx and Schumpeter considered technical progress to be of highest importance for a proper analysis of capitalist development. No doubt that there exist other fruitful and convincing theories of cyclical accumulation as well. Suffice it to recall some of the highly original contributions of the 1930's such as Harrod (see 1936 and his later work in 1948 and 1973), Frisch (1966), Hayek (1929, 1931 and 1939), Preiser (1933), Kaldor (1940), and Kalecki (1954, 1969 and 1971). A large part of prominent work can indeed be traced back to these, now about 50 year old, theories, compare Hicks (1950), Rose (1967, 1969), and Lucas (1981). Other theories stem from different strands of thought, for instance Samuelson (1939), Duesenberry (1958), Bergstrom (1962, 1967), Holländer (1973), Meade (1963), Solow and Stiglitz (1968), Wenig (1975), Akerlof and Stiglitz (1969), and Stein (1971). Some of the modern writers preferred to go back to Schumpeter (Goodwin 1955) and to Marx (Boddy and Crotty 1975, Sherman 1979, and again Goodwin 1967). Goodwin's model of cyclical growth turned out to be a rather influential starting point for further studies on Marx/Goodwin-cycles. Izzo (1971) published the first generalization of Goodwin's model. Further developments and applications followed by Desai (1973), Medio (1979), Wolfstetter (1977), Vercelli (1977), Glombowski (1979), Cugno and Montrucchio (1979, 1982), Velupillai (1979), Balducci and Candela (1982), Krüger (1982), and Pohjola (1981). This listing is by no means exhaustive....

Apart from the fascinating variety of approaches and underlying methods, it should be mentioned that the main macroeconomic variables of business cycles theories, which are widely held to be primarily responsible for the fluctuations, are the determinants of the profit rate (the share of profits and the degree of capacity utilization), and, as a third variable, the rate of interest. It should be recognized, however, that until now there exists no dynamic model of cyclical accumulation of capital, in which all three variables interact simultaneously. The major differences between the various theories stem from the fact that they concentrate on the degree of capacity utilization only or on the rate of interest. Sometimes two variables are taken into account but never all three together. This remains a subject for further investigation.

III. The Predator-Prey Story

Volterra developed the famous predator-prey model (Lotka analysed the model about the same time) to describe analytically the laws of cyclical growth of two competing species of fish. Since then the equations have been widely applied in biology, ecology, chemistry, and in economics. The first application to economics was worked out independently by Samuelson (1972) and Goodwin (1967). Both referred to the theory of cyclical growth although Samuelson's problem was rather different from that of Goodwin.

Since the model of Goodwin is a main reference for many papers of this volume, we will now briefly recall its basic features (a more extensive description of the model may be found, for instance, in Desai's article (this volume)).

The share of wages is determined by the reserve army of labour, or, more precisely, by the employment ratio. The pace of capital accumulation determines the demand for labour. If the rate of accumulation is rising sufficiently, so does the employment ratio. Beyond a certain value of the employment ratio (i.e., in the neighborhood of full employment) the vigorous accumulation of capital leads to a rising real wage and a rising wage share. This process goes on until the rise in the wage share is sufficient to reduce the rate of profit to the point where the accumulation rate slows down and unemployment begins to rise. The replenishment of the reserve army of labour yields a falling wage share, therefore a rising rate of profit and eventually an upturn in the rate of accumulation.

The two main variables of the system are the employment ratio and the wage share, which exhibit cyclical fluctuations around the equilibrium path of growth. In the phase space spanned by the two variables we get closed orbits around the non-trivial equilibrium point. In other words it is highly unlikely that the system will be in an equilibrium position of growth.

The Lotka-Volterra model of struggle for existence has been considered by many economists as a stimulating metaphor. There are many features that may have attracted their attention. First of all the analytical simplicity notwithstanding the nonlinear form. Moreover the biological analogy has stimulated many economists, e.g. Marx, a great admirer of Darwin's work, Marshall, who defined the biological science as the true source of inspiration for economists, Schumpeter, who considered social evolution as analogous to a biological process.

In addition, applications to economics along Goodwin's lines, suggested to some economists a sketch of an integration among three great traditions in economic dynamics: the Keynes-Harrod traditions which appears in the basic growth relations of the model, the Marxian tradition represented mainly by the crucial role played by the industrial reserve army, and the Schumpeterian tradition of essentiality of cyclical growth. This is considered by a few economists as a promising research program, able to synthesize traditional theory with modern mathematical methods.

IV. Notes on the Articles

It may be worthwhile to give some brief comments on the order of the contributions and their content.

In the first section we present papers which are devoted to extensions and generalizations of Goodwin's model of a growth cycle. Van der Ploeg considers effects of endogenous technical progress, endogenous supply of labour, depreciation, wealth effects, and takes the implications of differential savings into account. In Di Matteo's paper there is an introduction of monetary considerations, in order to analyse some of the interacting real and monetary factors of growth cycles. The impact of different unemployment insurance systems on the dynamics of the model is the main problem of Glombowski's and Krüger's article. A more general model allowing for unbalanced insurance budgets in disequilibrium is also presented. Balducci, Candela, and Ricci show that the social and economic behaviour of the two main classes in a capitalist society may be based on particular strategies of the two macroeconomic 'agents'. To model the respective strategies of the antagonistic classes they introduce some concepts of non-cooperative differential games. The models mentioned so far may quite rightly be blamed for their level of aggregation. In fact the subject under consideration is an economy producing only one real product in one sector. Goodwin's paper is devoted to the analysis of dynamic interactions within the framework of multi-sectoral models, which are studied by means of generalized eigenspaces.

The following section contains four papers in which other approaches to a theory of fluctuating growth are presented. To begin with there is the paper of Benhabib and Nishimura. Recalling that in every growth theory on neoclassical lines the maximising behaviour of the economic agents is explicitly taken into account the two authors demonstrate that even when firms base their behaviour on optimal decisions it is not unlikely to find a cyclical investment path (closed orbits around the optimal steady state path of growth).

Phases of economic decline and stagnation lead quite frequently to a rediscovery of the long waves discussion. In the paper by Bowles, Gordon, and Weisskopf the reader is offered an explanation of long economic swings based on series of reproductive and unreproductive cycles. The next contribution, by Flaschel, aims to show that some standard monetarist models, which stress the natural unemployment hypothesis, are rather unsatisfactory for explaining current economic problems such as stagflation. Finally Thio presents a discrete version of a nonlinear model of cyclical growth and analyses various effects of endogenous technical change (on Kaleckian lines) numerically.

Next comes the section on new mathematical methods and methodological concepts. Cugno and Montrucchio offer a compact survey on these new methods for analysing nonlinear dynamic economic models such as bifurcation theory (including the famous Hopf-Bifurcation in the continuous and in the discrete case; compare Arnold (1980) or Hirsch and Smale (1974) for a good presentation of the Hopf-Theorem) and chaos, i.e., they discuss the canonical form of a first-order nonlinear difference equation, which may give rise to a chaotic solution path. Medio's paper is devoted to the analysis of nonlinear dynamics in a multi-sectoral framework. One main idea of his article is taken from synergetics (Haken (1978)), i.e., the analysis of higher dimensional dynamical processes in the neighborhood of critical values of parameters, in which the evolution of the whole system is dominated by few variables.

The recent self-organization paradigm has been extensively discussed by the Brussels School (Prigogine and his followers, see Nicolis and Prigogine (1977)) as well. Silverberg applies these ideas to the problem of dealing more adequately with embodied technical progress. The process of replacement of an old method of production by a new one is described by means of structural fluctuations in a dynamic nonlinear model. The widespread application of newer concepts such as structural stability raises a number of methodological problems. Vercelli connects the idea of structural stability with the work of Keynes, Schumpeter, and Marx to suggest an analytical approach for reintegrating and developing some characteristic ideas of their visions of capitalist evolution.

The last section presents two econometric models, of the Italian and the British economies, respectively. Gandolfo and Padoan develop a nonlinear model of the Italian Economy, which gives rise to a stable path of cyclical growth. Their model is designed for an open economy including the various feedbacks of real and financial markets. Desai has reformulated Goodwin's growth cycle model in econometrical form (and an extended version as well) to face the problem of its empirical validity for the United Kingdom 1855 - 1965. Apart from tests for the whole period he has also tested the model for selected periods.

V. A Final Remark

In recent years we observe a growing interest in new mathematical concepts for dealing with complicated dynamic situations of physical, biological, and social systems. The most important contributions seem to be those concepts, which have been developed for analysing evolutionary processes. We think here of catastrophe theory (see Thom 1975), and the principle of l'ordre par fluctuation (see Prigogine 1980), which is connected with the self-organization paradigm of "synergetics" (see Haken 1978). These new approaches concentrate on important aspects of system dynamics, especially on irreversible structural changes. The integrated application of mathematical tools, like stochastic differential equations, global analysis, differential topology, bifurcation theory, and the modern (qualitative) viewpoint on dynamical systems, in models of economic growth cycles deserves continuing and increasing interest. Nevertheless it should be clear that modern methods which enable the economist to analyse more complex situations cannot be a substitute for economic theory and perceptive intuition for empirically valid relations.

Selective Bibliography

Akerlof,G.A./Stiglitz,J.E., 1969, Capital, Wages, and Structural Unemployment, Economic Journal

Atkinson,A.B., 1969, The Time-Scale of Economic Models. How Long is the Long-Run?, Review of Economic Studies

Arnold,V.I., 1978, Ordinary Differential Equations, Cambridge, Mass.

-----------, 1980, Geometrical Methods in the Theory of Ordinary Differential Equations, New York

Balducci,R./Candela,G., 1982, Contrattazione Salariale E Ciclo Economico, Roma

Bergstrom,A.R., 1962, A Model of Technical Progress, the Production Function, and Cyclical Growth, Economica

------------- , 1967, The Construction and Use of Economic Models, London

Boddy,R./Crotty,J., 1975, Class Conflict and Macro-Policy, Review of Radical Political Economics

Bronfenbrenner,M., (Ed.), 1969, Is The Business Cycle Obsolete?, New York

Cugno,F./Montrucchio,L./Jade,P., 1979, Structural Stability in a Goodwin Model, Istituto matematico del Politecnico di Torino, Preprints No. 16

Cugno,F./Montrucchio,L., 1982, Cyclical Growth and Inflation: A Qualitative Approach to Goodwin's Model with Money Prices, see Vercelli 1982

Debaggis,H.F., 1952, Dynamical Systems with Stable Structures, Lefschetz,S., (Ed.), Contributions to the Theory of Nonlinear Oscillations, Vol. II, Princeton

Desai,M., 1973, Growth Cycles and Inflation in a Model of the Class Struggle, Journal of Economic Theory

Duesenberry,J.S., 1958, Business Cycles and Economic Growth, New York

Frisch,R., 1966, Propagation Problems and Impulse Problems in Dynamic Economics, Gordon,R.A./Klein,L., (Eds.), Readings in Business Cycles, London

Glombowski,J., 1979, Ein überakkumulationstheoretisches Modell zyklischen Wachstums mit variabler Kapazitätsauslastung, Das Argument, Sonderband AS 35, Berlin

Glombowski,J./Krüger,M., 1983, On the Rôle of Distribution in Different Theories of Cyclical Growth, Research Memorandum, Tilburg

Goodwin,R.M., 1982, Essays in Economic Dynamics, London and Basingstoke

Goodwin,R.M., 1951, The Non-linear Accelerator and the Persistence of Business Cycles, reprinted in Goodwin 1982

------------, 1955, A Model of Cyclical Growth, reprinted in Goodwin 1982

------------, 1967, A Growth Cycle, reprinted in Goodwin 1982

Hajek,F.A., 1929, Geldtheorie und Konjunkturtheorie, Wien

----------, 1931, Preise und Produktion, Wien

----------, 1939, Profits, Interest and Investment, London

Haken,H., 1978, Synergetics: An Introduction, Berlin/Heidelberg/New York

Harrod,R.F., 1936, The Trade Cycle, Reprint New York 1965

-----------, 1948, Towards a Dynamic Economics, London 1948

-----------, 1973, Economic Dynamics, London and Basingstoke

Hicks,J.R., 1950, A Contribution to the Theory of the Trade Cycle, Oxford

Hirsch,M.W./Smale,St., 1974, Differential Equations, Dynamical Systems, and Linear Algebra, New York and London

Holländer,H., 1973, Ein Beitrag zur Konjunkturtheorie, Ott,A.E., (Hrsg.), Wachstumszyklen, Berlin

Ichimura,S., 1955, Toward a General Nonlinear Macrodynamic Theory of Economic Fluctuations, Kurihara,K.K., (Ed.), Postkeynesian Economics, London

Izzo,L., 1971, Saggi di analisi e teoria monetaria, Milano

Kaldor,N., 1960, Essays on Economic Stability and Growth, London

---------, 1940, A Model of the Trade Cycle, reprinted in Kaldor 1960

---------, 1956, Capitalist Evolution in the Light of Keynesian Economics, Kaldor 1960

Kalecki,M., 1969, Studies in the Theory of Business Cycles 1933-1939, Warszawa

----------, 1954, Theory of Economic Dynamics, Reprint New York 1969

----------, 1971, Selected Essays on the Dynamics of the Capitalist Economy 1933-1970, Cambridge

Kolmogoroff,A., 1931, Sulla teoria di Volterra della lotta per l'esistenza, Giornale italiano degli Attuari, Vol. III,2

Krüger,M., 1982, Aspekte einer Theorie zyklischer Kapitalakkumulation, Frankfurt a.M. und Bern

Lucas,R.E., 1981, Studies in Business-Cycle Theory, Cambridge

Marx,K., 1867, Das Kapital, Bd. I, Marx-Engels-Werke Bd. 23, Berlin 1969

Meade,J.E., 1963, Adjustment of Saving and Income in a Growing Economy, Review of Economic Studies

Medio,A., 1979, Teoria nonlineare del ciclo economico, Bologna

Nicolis,G./Prigogine,I., 1977, Self-Organization in Nonequilibrium Systems, New York et al.

Phillips,A.W., 1958, The Relation between Unemployment and the Rate of Change of Money Wage Rates in the United Kingdom, 1862-1957, Economica

Pohjola,M.T., 1981, Stable and Chaotic Growth: The Dynamics of a Discrete Version of Goodwin's Growth Cycle Model, Zeitschrift für Nationalökonomie

Preiser,E., 1933, Grundzüge der Konjunkturtheorie, Tübingen

Prigogine,I., 1980, From Being to Becoming, San Francisco

Rose,H., 1967, On the Non-Linear Theory of the Employment Cycle, Review of Economic Studies

-------, 1969, Real and Monetary Factors in the Business Cycle, Journal of Money, Credit, and Banking

Samuelson,P.A., 1939, Interactions between the Multiplier Analysis and the Principle of Acceleration, Review of Economics and Statistics

-------------, 1972, A Universal Cycle?, Merton,R.C., (Ed.), The Collected Scientific Papers of Paul A. Samuelson, Vol. III, Cambridge and London

Schumpeter,J., 1912, Theorie der wirtschaftlichen Entwicklung, Berlin 1952[5]

-------------, 1939, Business Cycles, New York and London

Sherman,H., 1979, A Marxist Theory of the Business Cycle, Review of Radical Political Economics

Solow,R.M./Stiglitz,J.E., 1968, Output, Employment, and Wages in the Short Run, Quarterly Journal of Economics

Stein,J., 1971, Money and Capacity Growth, New York and London

Thom,R., 1975, Structural Stability and Morphogenesis, Cambridge, Mass.

Velupillai,K., 1979, Some Stability Properties of Goodwin's Growth Cycle, Zeitschrift für Nationalökonomie

Vercelli,A., 1977, The Phillips Dilemma: A New Suggested Approach, Economic Notes

-----------, 1982, (Ed.), Proceedings of the Seminar on"Non-Linear Theory of Fluctuating Growth", Economic Notes

Volterra,V., 1931, Lecons sur la théorie mathématique de la lutte pour la vie, Paris

Weisskopf,Th.E., 1979, Marxian Crisis Theory and the Rate of Profit in the Post-War U.S.Economy, Cambridge Journal of Economics

Wenig,A., 1975, Beschäftigungsschwankungen, Einkommensverteilung und Inflation, Zeitschrift für die gesamte Staatswissenschaft

Wolfstetter,E., 1977, Wert, Profitrate und Beschäftigung, Franfurt a.M. und New York

IMPLICATIONS OF WORKERS' SAVINGS FOR ECONOMIC GROWTH AND THE CLASS STRUGGLE

Frederick van der Ploeg*
Department of Applied Economics
University of Cambridge
Sidgwick Avenue
Cambridge CB3 9DE, U.K.

1. Introduction

There has been an intense debate on what determines the distribution of income in advanced capitalist economies. Neo-classical economists have argued that the share of wages in value added depends solely on the technology of production. On the other hand post-Keynesian economists have tended to rely on differential savings patterns to explain the functional distribution of income. The influence of workers' savings on the long-run share of wages and profits has taken a prominent place in these discussions. A major drawback of this debate is that all the crucial characteristics of the economy are typically discussed for the balanced growth equilibrium only, so that issues of class conflict and fluctuations receive little attention.

One exception is the beautiful theory of Goodwin (1967), which discusses the symbiotic contradictions of capitalism in one complete model of economic growth and perpetual cycles. However, this dynamic theory adopts the classical savings hypothesis and the assumption of a fixed capital-output ratio. The debate on the relative importance of technology vis-à-vis differential savings and the implications of workers' savings can therefore not be held within this model.

This paper hopes to extend Goodwin's theory to allow for differential savings. This is done first by assuming that retained earnings in firms depends on profits earned rather than on who owns what proportion of the capital stock and then by explicitly allowing workers to own shares in firms and receive a dividend. It turns out that it is helpful to have a post-Keynesian theory of the direction of technological innovations, based upon Kaldor's (1957) technical progress function, since this aids the discussion of the case where workers' savings are sufficiently high to eventually take over the means of production completely and a workers' state is achieved.

2. Economic growth and the class struggle

2.1. A generalisation of Goodwin's theory of perpetual conflict

Consider a simple aggregate model of an advanced capitalist economy. The national accounts are summarised in Table 1. Total demand, consisting of consumption

---

* The author has benefited considerably from many exciting discussions with the participants of the Workshop on Non-linear Models of Fluctuating Growth: Theory and Empirical Evidence, 24-27 March, 1983, in Siena.

Table 1: A System of National Accounts

Incomings \ Outgoings	1	2	3	TOTALS
1. Production		C	I	Q
2. Income and outlay	WE + Π			Y
3. Accumulation	D	S		I
TOTALS	Q	Y	I	

by households (C) and gross investment by firms (I), is immediately produced (Q). The sales revenues yield net national income (Y), in the form of wages (W.E) and profits (Π), and depreciation (D). Note that there are no Robertsonian, Lindbergian or income-output lags, so that there is no unintended savings or investment in inventories. Net income is either consumed or saved (S). Accumulation of capital or wealth (K) follows from the balance sheet identity

$$\dot{K} = S = I - D \tag{2.1}$$

To close the accounts assume that depreciation occurs at a fixed rate of the capital stock, $D = \delta K$, and that savings are determined by the asset-adjustment hypothesis

$$S = \sigma Q - \gamma K = \gamma\{(\frac{\sigma}{\gamma})\ Q - K\} \quad , \quad \sigma, \gamma \geq 0 \tag{2.2}$$

where σ, γ and σ/γ denote the savings propensity, the speed of asset adjustment and the desired stock-flow ratio.

A post-Keynesian theory relies on changes in the functional distribution of income rather than on the smooth substitution between factors of production adopted in neo-classical theory. The crudest form of incorporating such a post-Keynesian approach is to have a fixed capital output ratio, say $\alpha = K/Q = \alpha^*$, and a differential savings hypothesis of the form (Kalecki, 1939; Kaldor, 1956; Robinson, 1956)

$$\sigma Q = \sigma_1\ (\Pi + D) + \sigma_2\ W.E, \quad 0 \leq \sigma_2 \leq \sigma_1 \leq 1 \tag{2.3}$$

The classical savings hypothesis, adopted by Goodwin (1967), corresponds to $\sigma_2 = 0$ and allows one to refer to capitalists, saving part of their profits, and workers, consuming all their income. The general case allows for the facts that profit-income is more likely to be used for internal finance of investment and wage-income may be partially saved to provide for a pension in the later periods of life. An alternative analysis of workers' savings may be found in section 3.

The level of employment (E) follows from the technical progress function (Kaldor, 1957)

$$\frac{\dot{Q}}{Q} - \frac{\dot{E}}{E} = f\left(\frac{\dot{K}}{K} - \frac{\dot{E}}{E}\right), \quad f(0) \geq 0,\ f' \geq 0,\ f'' \leq 0 \tag{2.4}$$

This formulation captures the idea of cumulative causation, since the growth in labour productivity depends upon the growth in the number of machines employed per worker. Investment benefits productivity mainly because it provides opportunities for learning new methods and exploitation of previously unused inventions (cf. Arrow, 1962). The hypothesis for explaining real wages (W),

$$\frac{\dot{W}}{W} = -\nu_0 + \nu_1 \frac{E}{L} + \nu_2 \left(\frac{\dot{Q}}{Q} - \frac{\dot{E}}{E}\right), \quad \nu_0, \nu_1, \nu_2 \geq 0 \tag{2.5}$$

incorporates the Marxian concept of the reserve army of unemployed, because a large number of unemployed diminishes the bargaining strength of the working class and therefore depresses real wages. In addition, bargaining strength is stronger in periods of high labour productivity as firms are then better able to pay increased wage claims. The model is closed with an assumption on the growth in the proportion of the population supplying labour

$$\frac{\dot{L}}{L} - \frac{\dot{N}}{N} = -\mu \left(\frac{\dot{K}}{K} - \frac{\dot{N}}{N}\right) \tag{2.6}$$

where the population (N) grows at a constant rate, η. Hence, the participation rate is a decreasing function of the amount of wealth owned per head of the population.

The model may be summarised by two nonlinear differential equations describing the distribution of income and the employment rate:

$$\frac{\dot{\theta}}{\theta} = -\nu_0 + \nu_1 \varepsilon - (1 - \nu_2)\omega^* \tag{2.7}$$

and

$$\frac{\dot{\varepsilon}}{\varepsilon} = (1 + \mu) \left[\left\{\frac{\sigma_1(1 - \theta) + \sigma_2\theta}{\alpha^*}\right\} - \gamma - \eta\right] - \omega^* \tag{2.8}$$

where $\theta = WE/Q$ and $\varepsilon = E/L$ denote the share of labour in value added and the employment rate, respectively, and $\omega^* = f(\omega^*)$ denotes the fixed point of the technical progress function. The equilibrium of (2.7)-(2.8) corresponds to

$$\varepsilon^* = \frac{\nu_0 + (1 - \nu_2)\omega^*}{\nu_1} \tag{2.9}$$

and

$$\theta^* = \frac{\sigma_1 - \alpha^*(\gamma + g^n)}{\sigma_1 - \sigma_2} \tag{2.10}$$

so that technical progress unexploited by workers gives rise to a higher equilibrium unemployment rate and an increase in the natural rate of growth ($g^n = \eta + \omega^*/(1+\mu)$), the speed of asset adjustment or the degree of differential savings depresses the equilibrium share of labour. Note that the natural rate of growth is less than the sum of growth in population and labour productivity, since the nation withdraws labour as it becomes more affluent. In the balanced growth trajectories real wages and productivity grow at the rate ω^*, capital, wealth and output grow at the rate g^n, and employment per head diminishes at the rate $-\mu\omega^*/(1 + \mu)$.

However, in this post-Keynesian view of a capitalist economy such a harmonious picture of balanced growth can only occur as a fluke. In technical terms (2.7)-(2.8) corresponds to the well known Volterra-Lotka model and is therefore a conservative system, not asymptotically stable, structurally unstable and follows closed trajectories around the equilibrium corresponding to a centre (Andronov et al., 1979). The economy perpetually oscillates around the equilibrium, although the appropriate distribution of income and balanced rate of employment are almost never simultaneously achieved. When the reserve army of unemployed (share of labour) is lowest the share of profits (unemployment rate) decreases most rapidly. The recession stops when the reserve army is largest, the return on capital increases most rapidly and the recovery sets in. The recession starts when employment has become too high to be lucrative. The perpetual cycle of conflict high-lights the symbiotic contradictions of capitalism, for the livelihood of each class in society depends on the existence of the competing class and at the same time workers and capitalists fight for their share in the national income. The time it takes to traverse a complete cycle of conflict in this predator-prey model is approximately given by $T = 2\pi i/\lambda_{1,2}$, where $\lambda_{1,2}$ denotes the conjugate pair of imaginary eigenvalues of the Jacobian of (2.7)-(2.8) evaluated at the equilibrium

$$\lambda_{1,2} = \pm \sqrt{(1 + \mu)(\sigma_1 - \sigma_2)\nu_1 \frac{\varepsilon^*\theta^*}{\alpha^*}}\, i \tag{2.11}$$

Hence, the period of the conflict cycle diminishes as the scope for bargaining (ν_1) increases, as savings become more differentiated, as the sensitivity of the supply of labour to wealth increases and as the equilibrium profit rate and unemployment rate diminish.

The special case $\delta = \gamma = \sigma_2 = f' = \nu_2 = \mu = 0$ was adopted in the classic article of Goodwin (1967), which illustrates the essential features of this beautiful model of class conflict and economic growth in advanced capitalist economies. The post-Keynesian system (2.7)-(2.8) is structurally unstable, so that small perturbations in the economic structure can dramatically alter the qualitative nature of the trajectories (Freedman and Waltman, 1975). The next sub-section discusses an interesting and relevant example of such a structural perturbation.

2.2. Induced innovations and conflict over the means of production

Perhaps the most doubtful assumption of the crude post-Keynesian theory of section 2.1 was the fixed capital output ratio. Although we do not wish to fall into the trap of the static neo-classical model of profit-maximising substitution between labour and machines, we feel there is scope for a dynamic theory of firms choosing the best type of innovations. Instead of firms maximising profits subject to a neo-classical production function, firms maximise the reduction in unit costs (UCR) subject to Kaldor's technical progress function. On the assumption that the real cost of capital equals the gross profit rate, the optimal solution for the best direction of technical progress is given by

$$\omega = f\{(f')^{-1}(1 - \theta)\} \tag{2.12}$$

or

$$\frac{\dot{\alpha}}{\alpha} = (f')^{-1}(1 - \theta) - \omega = \psi(\theta) \tag{2.13}$$

so that the slope of the technical progress function must equal the gross profit rate. The second-order condition requires $UCR'' = f'' < 0$, which corresponds to having decreasing opportunities for learning new techniques. Since $f'' < 0$ and $f' < 1$ (near the equilibrium), $\psi' > 0$ and therefore high costs of labour induce the implementation of labour-saving innovations.

The more sophisticated post-Keynesian model of economic growth, the class struggle and induced technical change may be summarised by three differential equations: (2.13),

$$\frac{\dot{\theta}}{\theta} = -\nu_0 + \nu_1\varepsilon - (1 - \nu_2)\, f\{(f')^{-1}(1 - \theta)\} \tag{2.14}$$

and

$$\frac{\dot{\varepsilon}}{\varepsilon} = (1 + \mu)(\frac{\sigma}{\alpha} - \gamma - \eta) - (f')^{-1}(1 - \theta) \tag{2.15}$$

The equilibrium of this economy follows from (2.9), (2.10) and $\theta^* = 1 - f'(\omega^*)$, so that the appropriate distribution of income now follows from the cost-minimising behaviour of entrepreneurs and the equilibrium capital-output ratio ensures the matching of the natural and warranted rates of economic growth. The Routh-Hurwitz conditions require

$$(1 - \nu_2)(1 - \theta^*)\psi'(\theta^*)\alpha^* > (1 + \mu)\theta^*\{\sigma_2 + \nu_2(\sigma_1 - \sigma_2)(1 - \theta^*)\} \tag{2.16}$$

for local stability near the equilibrium. Under the classical savings hypothesis $(\sigma_2 = 0)$ and no influence of labour productivity upon bargaining strength, firms always obtain dissipation of the class struggle by choosing cost-minimising technology. This special case may be compared with Shah and Desai (1981), who also obtained local stability of a similar model based upon the Kennedy-Weizsäcker invention-possibility frontier rather than Kaldor's technical progress function. However, conflict could escalate if, by saving a greater part of wages, workers obtain sufficient control over the means of production and therefore the choice of innovation. When workers exploit the introduction of more advanced machinery by increasing their wage claims $(\nu_2 > 0)$, the chances of explosive conflict cycles increase. Indeed if workers get full compensation for productivity gains $(\nu_2 = 1)$, this post-Keynesian model becomes unstable. Further details on this and other structural perturbations may be found in Desai (1973) and van der Ploeg (1982a, b).

3. Implications of workers' savings for the class struggle

3.1. The institutional framework

Pasinetti (1962) argued that Kaldor's (1956) analysis could not be used to analyse the distribution of income between capitalists and workers, since it assumed workers would hand-over their savings to capitalists without demanding a dividend. In other words the fact that workers owned part of the capital stock did not give rise to any interest payments. To a certain extent Pasinetti's criticism also applies to the two post-Keynesian models of section 2. However the separation between ownership and management in capitalist economies implies that retained earnings in corporations depend on profits earned rather than on who owns what proportion of the capital stock, so that the above criticism may be too serious. In defence of Pasinetti (1962) one could argue that management cannot implement savings against the will of shareholders indefinitely, since retention leads to stock appreciation and workers can consume the capital gains by selling shares. The purpose of this section is to obtain a truly post-Keynesian model by taking account of Pasinetti's point and explicitly modelling the loans of workers to capitalists.

Consider therefore the revised system of national accounts for an economy with two social classes presented in Table 2.

Table 2: A System of National Accounts for an economy with two classes

Incomings \ Outgoings	1	2a	2b	3a	3b	TOTALS
1. Production		C_w	C_c		I	Q
2. Income and outlay						
a. Workers	$W.E$		R			Y_w
b. Capitalists	Π					Π
3. Accumulation						
a. Workers		S_w				S_w
b. Capitalists	D		S_c			I_c
4. NAFA				$\dot{K}_w$	$-\dot{K}_w$	0
TOTALS	Q	Y_w	Π	S_w	I_c	

Profits (Π) minus the transfer of dividends to workers (R) constitutes net income of capitalists (Y_c), which is either consumed (C_c) or saved (S_c). Similarly, workers receive income (Y_w), consisting of wages and dividends, which is either consumed (C_w) or saved (S_w). Workers' savings augment their holdings of financial assets (K_w), held in the form of loans to capitalists, and capitalists' savings augment their wealth (K_c). Gross investment (I) is financed by capitalists (I_c), that is by depreciation and capitalists' savings, and borrowing from workers ($\dot{K}_w$). Finally, the stock of physical assets (K) consists of wealth owned by workers (K_w) and by capitalists (K_c).

3.2. The balance sheets for workers and capitalists

The revised accounts may be closed by introducing some behavioural assumptions. Firstly, assume savings by each class are determined by the relationships

$$S_i = \gamma_i\left[\left(\frac{\sigma_i}{\gamma_i}\right) Y_i - K_i\right] = \sigma_i Y_i - \gamma_i K_i, \quad i = w,c \tag{3.1}$$

where γ_i, (σ_i/γ_i) and σ_i denote the speed of asset adjustment, the desired ratio of the stock of assets to income and the marginal propensity to save of class i. Secondly, for simplicity ignore the effects of depreciation. Thirdly, assume that the rate of interest $(r = R/K_w)$ equals the rate of profit (Π/K) by ignoring risk and uncertainty.

With these assumptions the reduced form balance sheets become

$$\dot{K}_c \equiv S_c = \lambda_c K_c \tag{3.2}$$

and

$$\dot{K}_w \equiv S_w = \sigma_w \frac{\theta}{\alpha} K_c + \lambda_w K_w \tag{3.3}$$

where $\lambda_c = \{\sigma_c(1 - \theta)/\alpha\} - \gamma_c$ and $\lambda_w = (\sigma_w/\alpha) - \gamma_w$

denote the eigenvalues of the balance sheets. The warranted rate of economic growth (g^w), conditional on a fixed distribution of income and a fixed capital-output ratio, corresponds to the dominant eigenvalue of the balance sheets, i.e.

$$g^w = \lim_{t\to\infty}(\dot{K}/K) = \mathrm{Max}(\lambda_c, \lambda_w) \tag{3.4}$$

Two cases may be considered. The first case corresponds to $g^w = \lambda_c$ and, in the absence of possibilities for substitution, must rely on the distribution of income to equilibrate the warranted and the natural rate of economic growth. The corresponding equilibrium share of wages in value added equals

$$\theta^* = \frac{\sigma_c - \alpha^*(g^n + \gamma_c)}{\sigma_c} \tag{3.5}$$

and the corresponding profit or interest rate equals

$$r^* = (g^n + \gamma_c)/\sigma_c \tag{3.6}$$

A remarkable feature is that the long-run distribution of wages and profits and the return on capital are independent of the workers' propensity to save and the workers' speed of asset adjustment, because proper account is taken of the institutional framework. The amount of profits workers receive in the long-run is such as to make their total savings exactly equal to the amount that capitalists would have saved out of workers' profits if they received it (cf. Pasinetti, 1962). Note that a high speed of asset adjustment and a high ratio of wealth to income for capitalists depress the equilibrium share of wages. However, the long-run distribution of income between capitalists and workers does depend on workers' savings behaviour. This may be seen from the equilibrium share of workers in value added

$$(Y_w/Y)^* = \theta^* + (1 - \theta^*)k^* \tag{3.7}$$

which depends on the proportion of assets owned by workers $(k = K_w/K)$ in the equilibrium

$$0 \leq k^* = \frac{\sigma_w \theta^*}{\sigma_w \theta^* + \alpha^*(g^n - \lambda_w)} \leq 1 \tag{3.8}$$

A low proportion of workers' wealth implies a high share of capitalists in value added, which occurs when the natural rate of economic growth (g^n) is much larger than the workers' inherent speed of accumulation (λ_w). A high speed of asset adjustment and a high desired stock-flow ratio for workers gives them greater access to the means of production and increases their share in total wealth and income.

The second case corresponds to $g^w = \lambda_w$, so that eventually all capitalists' are removed by workers' savings $(k^* \to 1)$ and workers own all wealth. This is the case of a bloodless workers' revolt and has been coined the 'anti-Pasinetti' range (Meade, 1963; Samuelson and Modigliani, 1966). Since λ_w does not depend on the distribution of income, the establishment of such a workers' state must rely on the capital-output ratio to ensure equalisation of the warranted and natural rates of economic growth (cf. Pasinetti, 1964).

There has been a very heated debate on these two cases (e.g. Meade, 1963, 1966; Pasinetti, 1964; Meade and Hahn, 1965; Robinson, 1966; Samuelson and Modigliani, 1966), which is probably due to the immense ideological importance of the rôle of the class struggle *vis-à-vis* the rôle of neo-classical substitution and marginal productivity theory under perfect competition. An excellent survey of the debate may be found in Harcourt (1972, chapter 5).

3.3. Stability and multiple equilibria

The analysis of the composition of assets owned by workers and capitalists adopted in section 3.2 does not give the complete picture, because the functional distribution of income and the direction of technical progress were assumed to be fixed. In addition the economy was assumed to be in full employment. We now relax these assumptions and consider disequilibrium in the labour market and the dynamics of economic growth. We will drop (2.6) and instead assume that the supply of labour per head of the population follows from the relationship

$$\frac{\dot{L}}{L} - \frac{\dot{N}}{N} = - \mu\left(\frac{\dot{K}_w}{K_w} - \frac{\dot{N}}{N}\right) \tag{2.6'}$$

so that the supply of labour depends more realistically on the amount of wealth owned by workers.

The complete post-Keynesian model of economic growth with explicit class conflict is then defined by four differential equations: (2.13), (2.14),

$$\frac{\dot{\varepsilon}}{\varepsilon} = (1 + \mu)\left\{\left[\frac{\sigma_c(1 - \theta) + \sigma_w\theta}{\alpha} - \gamma_c\right](1 - k) + \lambda_w k - \eta\right\} + \mu\frac{\dot{k}}{k} - (f')^{-1}(1 - \theta) \tag{3.9}$$

and

$$\frac{\dot{k}}{k} = \sigma_w \frac{\theta}{\alpha}\frac{(1 - k)^2}{k} + (\lambda_w - \sigma_c\left(\frac{1 - \theta}{\alpha}\right) + \gamma_c)(1 - k) \tag{3.10}$$

in terms of the four state space variables α, θ, ε and k. Again, there are two possible equilibria for this economy. In the Pasinetti equilibrium the share of wealth owned by workers, k, is given by (3.8), but in the anti-Pasinetti equilibrium workers own all the means of production $(k^* = 1)$. In both equilibria the share of wages is given by $\theta^* = 1 - f'(\omega^*)$, the capital-intensity follows from (3.5), and the employment rate is given by (2.9). Let us now investigate the stability and feasibility of these rival equilibria.

The anti-Pasinetti equilibrium can be shown, with the application of the Routh-Hurwitz condition to the Jacobian of the system (2.13)-(2.14) and (3.9)-(3.10) and extensive use of the inequality $\lambda_c - \lambda_w = \lambda_c - g^n < 0$, to be locally stable as long as $\nu_2 < 1$. An initial situation of an excessive army of unemployed causes a falling share of labour, so that the diminished profitability of capital-saving innovations reduces labour productivity and causes the share of labour and the unemployment rate to recover. Since the dynamics of the share of wealth owned by workers has a life of its own, the anti-Pasinetti equilibrium must be stable. However, it is clear that excessive compensation for the increased profitability of capital-saving techniques $(\nu_2 > 1)$ gives rise to an ever-increasing share of labour and explosive trajectories. This result is not altogether surprising, because the anti-Pasinetti world relies (even in the post-Keynesian version adopted in this paper) on cost-minimising changes in the direction of technological progress to attain convergence towards the equilibrium.

The Pasinetti case is rather more difficult to analyse. Since in principle this case can rely on changes in the functional distribution of income alone to attain the balanced growth equilibrium, we first consider the special case of an exogenous growth in labour productivity ($f' = 0$). Application of the Routh-Hurwitz condition to the Jacobian of the system (2.13)-(2.14) and (3.9)-(3.10) and making extensive use of the inequality $(\lambda_c - \lambda_w) = g^n - \lambda_w > 0$ shows that the Pasinetti equilibrium is locally unstable. The rationale for this result may be explained by the following story. Imagine that the economy is in an initial position with an excessive reserve army of unemployed, so that the bargaining strength of workers is weak, their share in value added falls and eventually their share of total wealth falls. The fall in the share of capital owned by workers swells the reserve army of unemployed despite an improvement in the internal finance position for firms due to having to pay less dividend and having more profits, so that conflict eventually explodes. However, application of the Liénard-Chipart conditions suggests that allowing for cost-minimising directions of technological innovation might lead to local stability. The intuition behind this result depends on the weakened bargaining position of workers reducing the cost of labour and thereby causing firms to move away from labour-saving to more profitable capital-saving innovations. This tends to recover the share of labour, in as far as technical progress is unexploited by labour in the wage-bargaining process, and provides an additional reason for more job creation. If these effects are strong enough, the Pasinetti equilibrium of this post-Keynesian model might be stable.

4. Concluding remarks

This paper has extended Goodwin's (1967) pioneering article of the class struggle and economic growth to allow for an endogenous supply of labour, depreciation, wealth effects in savings decisions and implications of productivity gains on the wage bargain and to allow for some saving out of wages in accordance with Kaldor's (1955-56) theory of distribution. These extensions do not alter the qualitative result of perpetual class conflict cycles around a balanced growth equilibrium. However, when firms are allowed to minimise the reduction in unit costs subject to Kaldor's (1957) technical progress function the qualitative properties alter. Unless labour attains too much control over the means of production (either by saving too much out of wages or by achieving too much pecuniary compensation for productivity gains), class conflict will gradually die out and convergence towards balanced growth will be attained. The next step was to extend this post-Keynesian description of unemployment, distribution and growth in a capitalist economy in the light of Pasinetti's (1962) criticism. This meant explicitly allowing workers to receive a dividend, since their savings result in them owning shares in firms. An analysis of the dynamics of the balance sheets for workers and capitalists confirms the existence of two equilibria. In the anti-Pasinetti equilibrium workers eventually completely take over the means of production, so that capitalists are phased out by "euthanasia". Any deviations from this equilibrium are corrected, so that the workers' socialist state is locally stable. In the Pasinetti equilibrium workers own part of the capital stock, although the functional distribution of income between wages and profits is independent of workers' savings.

It turns out that this equilibrium is not tenable (unstable) unless the effects of shifting to more profitable directions of technological progress are strong enough. These results are interesting, because they indicate that cost-minimising directions of technological innovations are not only essential for the existence of the classless society without capitalists defined by the anti-Pasinetti world but are also necessary for ensuring the stability of class conflict in the Pasinetti world. This paper hopes that the post-Keynesian description of the choice of technical innovation provides a realistic alternative to neo-classical marginal productivity theories, because the dynamics of the functional distribution of income and the rate of profit are still determined by the capitalist savings behaviour, by population growth and most importantly by the endogenous rate of technological progress.

It would be interesting to extend the post-Keynesian models of this paper to allow for the financial behaviour of companies towards the issue of new securities (e.g. Wood, 1975) and to allow for overspending of dividend income and savings out of capital gains (very much according to some form of life-cycle hypothesis combined with overlapping generations). Kaldor's (1966) "Neo-Pasinetti Theorem" provides a very interesting approach, where the valuation ratio ensures the equilibriation of the demand for securities (determined by savings out of income) and the supply of securities (consisting of consumption out of capital or gains and issues of new securities). In other words there will be a valuation ratio which ensures just enough savings to mop up the issues of new securities, although Davidson (1968) has argued that this is rather akin to aspects of neo-classical theory as the rate of interest serves to maintain equilibrium in both the securities and goods markets. The advantages of Kaldor's (1966) exciting theory are that the stock market is modelled explicitly, that "it does not postulate a class of hereditary capitalists with a special high-saving propensity", and that therefore the anti-Pasinetti outcome of a socialist economy no longer occurs. An analysis of Kaldor's theory of pension funds and companies in a truly disequilibrium setting with changes in unemployment and in the distribution of income and wealth appears a very interesting item on the agenda for future research.

References

Arrow, K.J. (1962). "The economic implications of learning by doing", Review of Economic Studies, vol. 29, pp. 155-173.

Davidson, P. (1968). "The demand and supply of securities and economic growth and its implications for the Kaldor-Pasinetti versus Samuelson-Modigliani controversy", American Economic Review, Papers and Proceedings, vol. 58, pp. 252-269.

Desai, M. (1973). "Growth cycles and inflation in a model of the class struggle", Journal of Economic Theory, vol. 6, pp. 527-545.

Goodwin, R.M. (1967). "A growth cycle", in C.H. Feinstein (ed.), Socialism, Capitalism and Growth, Cambridge University Press, Cambridge.

Harcourt, G.C. (1972). Some Cambridge Controversies in the Theory of Capital, Cambridge University Press, Cambridge.

Kaldor, N. (1955-56). "Alternative theories of distribution", Review of Economic Studies, vol. 23, pp. 83-100.

Kaldor, N. (1957). "A model of economic growth", Economic Journal, vol. 67, pp. 591-624.

Kaldor, N. (1966). "Marginal productivity and the macro-economic theories of distribution", Review of Economic Studies, vol. 33, pp. 309-319.

Kalecki, M. (1939). Essays in the Theory of Economic Fluctuations, Allen and Unwin, London.

Meade, J.E. (1963). "The rate of profit in a growing economy", Economic Journal, vol. 73, pp. 665-674.

Meade, J.E. and F.H. Hahn (1965). "The rate of profit in a growing economy", Economic Journal, vol. 75, pp. 445-448.

Meade, J.E. (1966). "The outcome of the Pasinetti-process: a note", Economic Journal, vol. 76, pp. 161-165.

Pasinetti, L.L. (1962). "Rate of profit and income distribution in relation to the rate of economic growth", Review of Economic Studies, vol. 29, pp. 267-279.

Pasinetti, L.L. (1964). "A comment on Professor Meade's 'Rate of profit in a growing economy'", Economic Journal, vol. 74, pp. 488-489.

Ploeg, F. van der (1982a). "Predator-prey and neo-classical models of cyclical growth", Zeitschrift für Nationalökonomie.

Ploeg, F. van der (1982b). "Economic growth and conflict over the distribution of income", Journal of Economic Dynamics and Control.

Robinson, J. (1956). The Accumulation of Capital, MacMillan, London.

Robinson, J. (1966). "Comment on Samuelson and Modigliani", Review of Economic Studies, vol. 33, pp. 307-308.

Samuelson, P.A. And F. Modigliani (1966). "The Pasinetti paradox in neoclassical and more general models", Review of Economic Studies, vol. 33, pp. 269-301.

Shah, A. and M. Desai (1981). "Growth cycles with induced technical change", Economic Journal, vol. 91, pp. 1006-1010.

Woods, A. (1975). A Theory of Profits, Cambridge University Press, Cambridge.

ALTERNATIVE MONETARY POLICIES IN A CLASSICAL GROWTH CYCLE*

M. Di Matteo

Istituto di Economia — Università di Siena

Siena, Italy

The model I will present and comment on was derived from the paper A Growth Cycle which Goodwin presented at the First World Congress of the Econometric Society in Rome in 1965[1] and was subsequently elaborated by Izzo[2]. The latter is the first attempt to introduce monetary factors in Goodwin's model which underwent various modifications — none of which preserved the original features. The peculiarity of Izzo's presentation is that his model, due to various simplifications, does exhibit the same oscillatory behaviour as Goodwin's original model (henceforth OGM). This is because the influence of monetary factors on the working of the model is kept to a minimum. However, I think, it is profitable to scrutinize Izzo's model closely because it allows us to draw some reflections on the interplay between monetary and real factors in business cycle theory.

1. A Model with an Exogenous Rate of Money Supply Growth

1.1 The model

The model is made up of the following relations:

(1) $X/K = b$

(2) $X/L = A_o e^{\alpha t}$

(3) $I = X - (w/p)L + nK(\theta - \mu \dot{X}/X)$

(4) $I = \dot{K}$

(5) $N = N_o e^{\lambda t}$

* This is a revised version of the paper presented to the workshop: I am indebted to H. Frisch, L. Izzo, J. Steindl, A. Wörgötter and to the participants in the workshop for helpful suggestions.
Financial help from the University of Siena is gratefully acknowledged.

[1] Cfr. Goodwin , R.M., 1967, A Growth Cycle. In Feinstein, C.H., Ed., Socialism, Capitalism and Economic Growth (Essays presented to Maurice Dobb), Cambridge University Press, London.

[2] Cfr. Izzo, L., 1971, Saggi di analisi e teoria monetaria, F. Angeli Editore, Milano.

(6) $\dot{w}/w = - \varepsilon + z(L/N)$

(7) $\dot{p}/p = \beta/(1 + \beta)(\dot{w}/w - \alpha)$

(8) $S = S(X)$

(9) $M^d = F(p, X, \pi)$

(10) $p(I - S) + v(M^d - M) = 0$

where all parameters are positive and where

X = Product

L = Employment

I = Ex-ante investments

$\dot{K} = \partial K/\partial t$

K = Stock of capital

w = Money wage

N = Supply of labour

p = Price level

θ = Growth rate of money supply

S = Savings

π = Rate of interest

M^d = Demand for money

M = Supply of money

Eq. (1) maintains that there is fixed proportion between capital and product. In Eq. (2) we have the usual assumption about technical progress i.e. it is of the Harrod neutral type. According to Eq. (4) investment plans are always fulfilld. Eq. (6) is a linear Phillip's curve cast in money terms. As for the determination of the rate of inflation a cost determined formula is used. The implication of this particular formulation is that the rate of price increase is lower than the difference between the growth rate of money wages and the rate of productivity growth. Consequently when the difference is positive (negative) the profits per unit of output (and capital as well) lower (increase). Eq. (8) and (9) need no comment being the first one an usual Keynesian savings function and the second one a demand for money equation depending positively on the price level, the product and the stock of capital and negatively on the rate of interest.

The major difference with the OGM lies in Eq. (3) where we admit of the possibility that owing to the existence of the banking sector ex ante investments can be affected by the growth rate of the money supply. Investements will be higher the higher the difference between the growth rate of money supply and the growth rate of income: this discrepancy can be taken as an indicator of credit possibilities. It is assumed that firms wish to invest this amount in production[3].

---

[3] P. Sylos Labini provided empirical support for an investment function somewhat similar to Eq. (3), as far as the Italian economic system is concerned. Cfr. Sylos Labini, P., 1967, Prezzi, Distribuzione e Investimenti in Italia dal 1951 al 1965: uno schema interpretativo, Moneta e credito.

On the other hand for any level of ex ante investments we can have that investments differ (or are equal to) from savings. To have an equilibrium in the economic system it is required that any difference between the two be matched by a difference (of opposite sign) between flow demand for and flow supply of money as indicated in Eq. (10).

However, via Eq. (4) investments plans are always fulfilled. Firms which are short of funds sell 'bonds' to the banking sector. 'Bonds' can be thought of as call loans. It is also assumed that there is no bonds transactions except those between firms and the banking sector. Consequently savings are either directly invested or converted into bank deposits. The banking sector can be visualized as consisting of a single bank which issues (inside) money vis à vis purchases of 'bonds'. High powered money is made of loans to the bankings sector by the Central Bank; the money multiplier is the reciprocal of the reserve requirement ratio so that the money stock is under the control of the monetary authorities.

1.2 Analysis of the Model

From the set of equations 1-8 a pair of differential equations of the Lotka-Volterra type can be derived[4]. The monetary subsystem can be solved separately since it has no deedback on the real part. Therefore we have:

$$(11)\quad \dot{Y}_1/Y_1 = h_1 - \beta_1 Y_2$$

$$(12)\quad \dot{Y}_2/Y_2 = -\beta_2 + \sigma_2 Y_1$$

where Y_1 is the employment-labour ratio and Y_2 is the share of wages in the product and

$h_1 = [b + n\theta - (1 + n\mu)(\alpha + \lambda)]/(1 + n\mu)$

$\beta_1 = b/(1 + n\mu)$

$\sigma_2 = z/(1 + \beta)$

$\beta_2 = (\varepsilon + \alpha)/(1 + \beta)$

It is necessary for h_1 to be positive: therefore a lower limit to the growth rate of money supply is implicit[5].

A non trivial stationary solution to the model is given by

---

[4] Throughout the article we omit the simple but lengthy calculations which can be asked for to the Author.

[5] If it were negative both the wage share and the employment ratio would tend to zero in the limit; if it were zero the wage share would tend to zero again whereas the employment ratio would tend to a costant. Cfr. Volterra, V., 1927, Variazioni e fluttuazioni del numero di individui in specie animali conviventi, Reprinted in Volterrra, V., 1962, Opere Matematiche, Accademia Nazionale dei Lincei, Vol. V, I Part, Parr. 4-5.

$\overset{\circ}{Y}_1 = \beta_2 / \sigma_2$ $\qquad$ $\overset{\circ}{Y}_2 = h_1 / \beta_1$

In order to be significant solutions $0 < \overset{\circ}{Y}_1 \leqslant 1$ and $0 < \overset{\circ}{Y}_2 < 1$.[6]

Therefore we need that $\varepsilon + \alpha \leqslant z$ and that the growth rate of money supply lies in the open interval.

$$(13) \quad [(1 + n\mu)/n] \; (\alpha + \lambda) - b/n \; < \; \theta \; < [(1+n\mu)/n] \; (\alpha + \lambda)$$

The results do not differ greatly from the OGM: it can be shown that the stationary solution (it occurs if appropriate initial conditions are met) is characterized by a 'natural rate of growth'[7], zero rate of inflation and, in general, lapse from full employment. The major difference is that now the share of profits (and the rate of profits as well) depends on the value taken on by the growth rate of money supply: the higher the latter the higher the share of wages in the product. Since the rate of income growth associated with the stationary solution is exogenous then a higher rate of money supply growth has to be associated with a lower profit share so that accumulation is financed by debt.

Let us now comment on condition 13. It is apparent that if n tends to zero θ can take on any value: this is not surprising since the hypothesis implies an investment function where monetary factors do not play any role, whereas the interval shrinks as n grows larger and larger. If μ tends to zero then the interval shrinks since now the effectivness of monetary policy is quite large: indeed the greater μ the greater the difference between the growth rate of money supply and the growth rate of income has to be product a given effect on the accumulation rate. Henceforth we will assume μ equals 1, for simplicity.

Let us now have a look at the consequences on the monetary side of the model which are implied by the steady state solution. It can be shown that if the rate of interest is equal to the rate of profit and that there is equilibrium on the money market, then the rate of money growth has to be $\eta(\alpha + \lambda)$ where η is the elasticity of the demand for money with respect to real income. Being the rate of inflation nil, this condition would enable a continous equality to be maintained between the real rate of interest and the rate of profit. If η equals μ then monetary policy cannot affect the rate of profit. The condition that the money market is in equilibrium (and therefore investments equals savings) depends however on a particular hypothesis, i.e. that

$$(14) \quad [\partial S / \partial X] \, b = \alpha + \lambda$$

---

[6] We exclude a situation where the share of wages equals 1.

[7] By this expression I mean a growth rate equal to the rate of productivity growth plus the growth rate of labour force.

In other words, contrary to Harrod's model, the above equality does not ensure full employment but equilibrium on each market.

1.3 Analysis of the System off the Steady State Path

As it is well known the Lotka-Volterra equations give rise to a particular set of solutions as depicted in the following diagram[8]:

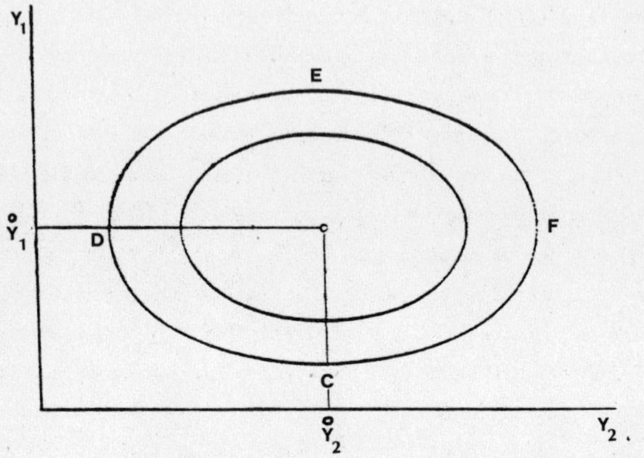

Fig. 1

To each set of initial conditions there corresponds a closed curve around the centre. The dynamics of the economic system when off the steady state path can be briefly described. In C the growth rate of income is the average one and the employment ratio is below its long run value. Therefore money wages grow at a lower rate than productivity letting the profit rate to rise. Starting from C consequently the growth rate of income rises too to get its maximum value at D where money wages growth equal the growth rate of productivity so that the rate of inflation is zero. Starting from D the rising employment ratio forces money wages to grow faster than productivity. Consequently prices rise at a lower rate than wages do causing the rate of accumulation to fall back to its average level in E. Then the system starts entering a recession wand the finally comes to C again where it statrs recovering again.

It is now time to analyse the behaviour of the rate of interest. It is appar-

---

[8] For a complete mathematical analysis cfr. Gandolfo, G., 1980, Economic Dynamics: Methods and Models, North Holland, Amsterdam, Part III, Chap. 3, Par. 5.3.

ent that we cannot say very much about it since it depends on the structure of the demand for money and on the pattern of evolution of the difference between investments and savings. As Izzo remarked if condition 14 is fulfilled investments equal saving at C and E whereas there is a positive (negative) excess of investment over savings at D (F). In this case starting from C if the demand for money (the rate of interest being steady) does not fall short of supply, then a rise in the interest rate is sufficient to create an excess supply of money at D as implied by Eq. (10). Starting from D the difference between investments and savings shrinks; if, the rate of interest being constant, the demand for money does not exceed the supply of it it is sufficient a fall in the rate of interest to get equality between the two at E as implied by Eq. (10). Mutatis mutandis the same argument between E and C will produce a pattern for the rate of interest similar to that of the rate of profits.

Though we emphasized that there is no feedback from the monetary subsystem to the real part it is our opinion that two requirements should be met if the pattern of the interest rate is not to be wholly inconsistent with the accumulation side of the model. First the interest rate should not exceed the rate of profit since debts are to be paid back out of profits. Secondly the rate of profits should not differ (greatly) from the real rate of interest. The first condition could be somewhat relaxed if it were easy to know in which part of the cycle firms will borrow: this however depends on the actual value of the growth rate of money supply and on the destination of savings. If we specify a particular demand for money equation, then it is in principle feasible for the monetary authorities to choose a level of the quantity of money that is consistent with the equality between the rate of profits and the real rate of interest at C.

The second requirement however cannot be fulfilled within the hypotheses already made since at C and E the rate of profits takes on the same values whereas the rate of inflation is negative at C and positive at E.

However it is possibile to reformulate the demand for money in a way that the second requirement can be fulfilled. In the case that the rate of money supply growth is rather low and the demand for money is rather sensitive to the level of income is perfectly plausible that even between points D and E the demand for money exceeds the supply of it and therefore a further rise in the interest rate is needed to have demand for and supply of money equal to each other at E. By essentially a similar argument we can imagine the rate of interest falling from E to C and therefore showing a pattern which resembles that of the employment ratio. For each cycle of this subset (of all admissible cycles) then it becomes possible to choose an appropriate stock of money (relatively to the maximum absolute value of the inflation rate) that it is consistent with a continuous equilibrium between the real rate of interest and the rate of profits. In this case the assumption that n does not depend on the relationship between the real rate of interest and the rate of profits is perfectly valid. Otherwise it would seem sensible to think that firms may be reluctant to invest the 'excess' liquidity in production if the real rate of interest is actually higher than the rate of profits (even in a classical model). Therefore in Izzo's presentation[9] one can see that between E and C it is perfectly possible that the rate of profits falls short of the real rate of interest depending on the value of the deflation (i.e. for a subset of all cycles). Therefore n could attain a lower value in the downswing than in the upswing and as a result a certain degree of stability could follow.

1.4 Effects of Alternative Values for θ.

It is now time to ask the following question: given the initial conditions by historical events what could have happened to the amplitude of fluctuations if the parameters had taken on different values at $t = t_0$, especially the parameters which are under the control of the Central Bank? Performing a linear approximation around the stationary solution and exploiting the well known fact that in this case fluctuations are ellipse like[10] one can show that when the centre moves northwest (southeast) the amplitude of fluctuations decreases (increases)[11]. In particular a lower (higher) θ means that, for any level of the share of wages, the rate of growth of the employment ratio is always lower (higher) so that the level of the employment ratio is permanently lower (higher): this in turn implies that the rate of growth of the share of wages too is lower (higher) and therefore the level of the share itself is lower (higher). It is also easy to see that if the rate of growth of the money supply equals the natural rate of growth the OGM and this model have the same centre but the amplitude of fluctuation is larger in the OGM.

Finally we would like to see if it is possible to get rid of cycles altogether. Let us imagine that the rate of money supply growth is not a constant over the cycle but it varies according to the following rule:

$$(15)\quad \theta = \theta' + \gamma(\overset{\circ}{Y}_1 - Y_1) - \delta(\overset{\circ}{Y}_2 - Y_2)$$

where γ, δ are non negative. This is tantamount to assume that the monetary authorities rise (lower) the growth of money supply whenever the level of employment is below (higher than) average and lower (rise) it whenever the rate of

---

[9] He presents the case where the real rate of interest and the rate of profits do differ over the cycle. Cfr. Izzo, L., 1971, <u>op. cit.</u>, pp. 203-5.

[10] Cfr. Volterra, V., 1962, <u>op. cit.</u>, p. 15.

[11] For southwest and northeast displacements of the centre the analysis is inconclusive depending on which parameter was responsible for the displacement.

income growth is higher (lower) than average. If this rule is adhered to the behaviour of the economic system changes quite a lot. Resorting to a linear approximation again, it can be shown that if δ is high enough the model is unstable and diverges monotonically, whatever the value of γ. If, on the other hand, $\delta < h_1 \sigma_2/n \beta_2$ then the system is stable provided γ is positive. The nature of the movement cannot be established for we lack quantitative information on the parameters. It has to be remembered that the overall value of θ has to satisfy condition (13) at any point in time and therefore we are limited to the small fluctuations case.

2. A Model with an Exogenous Rate of Interest

A similar exercise can also be worked out assuming a different hypothesis on the behaviour of the Central Bank. Let us suppose that the monetary authorities aims at controlling the money rate of interest rather than the money stock, as was the case with many countries during the 50's and the 60's. In this case we leave the model unaltered except for the investment function. We simply postulate that investments depend on profits and also on the difference between the rate of profits, r, and the rate of interest, π. Nothing important is modified with respect to the financial system except that now firms wish investing more than profits only when the rate of profits exceed the rate of interest. Suppose that Eq. (3) is replaced by the following:

$$(3') \quad I = X - (w/p)L + nK(r - \bar{\pi})$$

where $\bar{\pi}$ is the level at which the Central Bank pegs the money rate of interest[12].

By usual manipulations we get the Lotka-Volterra equations:

$$(16) \quad \dot{Y}_1/Y_1 = h_3 - \beta_3 Y_2$$
$$(17) \quad \dot{Y}_2/Y_2 = -\beta_2 + \sigma_2 Y_1$$

where $h_3 = b(1 + n) - (\alpha + \lambda) - n\bar{\pi}$

$\beta_3 = b(1 + n)$

For exactly the same reasons given above in note[5] it is necessary that h_3 takes on a positive value: therefore there is an upper limit for the rate of interest, i.e.

---

[12] The reason for that need not concern us. It is sufficient to say that it could be chosen for external reasons (e.g. balance of payments difficulties, etc.).

(18) $\overline{\pi} < [b(1 + n) - (\alpha + \lambda)] / n$

A non trivial solution to the model is given by

$\overset{o}{Y}_1 = \beta_2 / \sigma_2$ $\qquad\qquad$ $\overset{o}{Y}_2 = h_3 / \beta_3$

We note that the equilibrium value for the employment ratio is unaffected with respect to the previous model whereas in order to have a significant value for the share of wages we do not need any further restriction, except that π is positive. Even in the present model the stationary solution (it occurs if appropriate initial conditions are met) is characterized by a 'natural rate of growth', zero rate of inflation and, in general, lapse from full employment. The difference with the previous model is that the rate of profits is a linear and increasing function of the rate of interest[13]. This is not surprising since the higher the share of wages the lower the rate of interest has to be to finance an exogenously given growth rate.

Condition 18 states that the smaller n (i.e. the willingness of invest by firms when there is a discrepancy between the rate of profits and the interest rate) the larger the critical value for π has to be (in the limit it could approach ∞).

If we come to examine the monetary side of the model we are forced to remark that on the steady state where the rate of inflation is zero the monetary subsystem cannot exert any influence since the interest rate has to equal the rate of profits — they both take on the same value: the natural rate of growth. This traces a difference with the previous model where even on the steady state the accumulation can be financed by debt (provided $\eta \neq \mu$). If we start from a situation where there is equilibrium on the money market (as implied by condition 14) then continous equilibrium between the rate of profits and the rate of interest requires that the growth rate of money supply equal $\eta(\alpha + \lambda)$.

As for the solution other than the stationary one the model preserves its characteristics giving rise to the same pattern as depicted in diagram 1 above. As we have already remarked we know that investments equal savings at C whereas the latter fall short of investments at D. Since the rate of interest is to be pegged at a given level, the quanity of money, because of Eq. (10), has to grow since we need an excess supply of money (in real terms) at D. And presumably the stock of money will grow too between points D and E where the money market is again in equilibrium.

The problem now arises with the particular level of the interest rate which is chosen by the monetary authorities. With regards to first requirement stated in 1.3 we note that it is impossible for the rate of interest to be always less than the

---

[13] This has a Sraffian flavour. Cfr. Sraffa, P., 1960, Production of Commodities by Means of Commodities, Cambridge University Press, Cambridge, p. 33.

rate of profits (for the latter oscillates around an equilibrium values which depends on the level of the rate of interest) and that it is equally impossible for the real rate of interest to be continously equal to the rate of profits. Because of the latter, n should be treated as a variable rising (lowering) between points C(E) and E(C) (if we take into account a situation where the rate of interest equals the natural rate of growth at C) therefore contributing to a certain degree of instability.

The analysis can be carried on by means of the technique already employed in 1.4. It can be ascertained that when the centre of fluctuations moves nortwest (southeast) the amplitude of fluctuations decreases (increases)[14]. A lower (higher) level for the rate of interest means that, for any level of the share of wages, the rate of growth of the employment ratio is always higher (lower) so that the level of the employment ratio is permanently higher (lower): this in turn implies that the rate of growth of the share of wages is higher (lower) and therefore the level of the share itself is higher (lower). It can also be stated that if the rate of interest is pegged at a level equal to the natural rate of growth then the OGM and this model share the same centre but the amplitude of fluctuations is higher than in the OGM.

Finally even in this case we could analyse a situation where oscillations are removed in the end. We assume that the Central Bank varies the rate of interest according to the following rule:

$$(19)\quad \bar{\pi} = \pi' - \gamma(\overset{\circ}{Y}_1 - Y_1) + \delta(\overset{\circ}{Y}_2 - Y_2)$$

where γ, δ are non negative.

This is equivalent to assume that the Central Bank rises (lowers) the rate of interest whenever the level of employment is higher (lower) than average and lowers (rises) it whenever the rate of income growth is below (higher than) average. Resorting again to a linear approximation around equilibrium values we note that with a positive γ the system converges to the stationary statement as long as δ is less than $b(1 + n)/n$. The nature of the movement cannot be established and it has to be remembered again that at any point in time the rate of interest has to satisfy condition 18, so that we are limited to the small fluctuations case.

3. Some Final Remarks

The major conclusion which can be drawn from the exercises we performed above

---

[14] For southwest and northeast displacements of the centre the analysis shows that no change occurs.

is that it is not immaterial for the overall equilibrium of the system which rule of conduct the Central Bank chooses to adhere to, even in such a simplified financial structure.

First of all in a model with built-in fluctuations in income and employment stabilising the rate of interest (granted that is an easy matter) may come out to be inconsistent with the overall stability of the system leading possibly to changes in the value of behavioural parameters which would call for a complete reformulation of the model. On the other hand this result is not a necessary outcome of the other rule of conduct.

Secondly in both models by choosing an appropriate growth rate of money supply or level of the interest rate the monetary authorities can lead to a dissolution of the system where both the wage share and the employment ratio are zero — a situation that cannot arise in the OGM.

Thirdly in both models the system can be led to grow at the natural rate via a flexible rule of conduct by the Central Bank.

Fourthly initial conditions do play an important role in estabilishing the third conclusion which indeed is valid only for the small fluctuations case. Moreover in the first model we require oscillations to be 'small' in order to get a behaviour of the interest rate consistent with the overall equilibrium of the system.

Finally it is pretty obvious that the above analysis is flawed by the lack of a theory of the behaviour of the banking sector which would lead to a more profound understanding of the interplay between the industrial and the financial capitalists[15].

---

[15] It is quite obvious that an extension of the analysis in this direction would necessarily increase the order of the system as remarked in Velupillai, K., 1982, When Workers Save and Invest: Some Kaldorian Dynamics, Zeitschrift für Nationalökonomie, p. 257.

UNEMPLOYMENT INSURANCE AND CYCLICAL GROWTH

Jörg Glombowski
Faculty of Economics
Tilburg University
The Netherlands

Michael Krüger
Department of Social Sciences
Osnabrück University
Federal Republic of Germany

1. Introduction

As Goodwin's famous model[1)] is built on a small set of rigorous assumptions it provides a large field for generalizations. Although quite a lot of different contributions have been made already, we have not seen any attempt to account, in its framework, for elements of the "welfare state" so far.[2)] From a theoretical point of view the incorporation into the model of unemployment benefits schemes seems to us highly relevant, because it allows to discuss the following questions: Will such schemes affect the cyclical characteristics of the model significantly or even abolish cyclical features? What difference will it make in which way those payments are financed and to which degree the burden of providing the necessary funds is divided between labour and capital? Will the payment of unemployment benefits affect the bargaining power of workers? What effects can be expected from attempts to "correct" the burden of contributions via wage negotiations? Can we allow for deficits and surplusses arising necessarily with certain assumptions about institutional rules? Although this list of questions is by no means complete, we cannot even fully work out the answers to them in the present article.

The plan for the remainder of the paper is as follows: Throughout sections 2-4 a basic simplifying device will be used, i.e. the assumption of a permanent equilibrium of the unemployment benefits fund. In section 2 we introduce the equations which describe the operation of the fund by specifying the institutional rules according to which contributions are collected and payments are made. Of course, there is a spectrum of possible arrangements, some of which will be mentioned as examples. Section 3 discusses the way in which unemployment payments will enter Goodwin's model, i.e. the interaction between (un)employment, wage formation and accumulation. In section 4 the consequences of one special hypothetical institutional setting are developed, while results with respect to other cases are referred to without proof. The possible

1) See Goodwin (1972)
2) Of course, this does not mean that there are no attempts to include such elements into other kinds of models. Our approach has been stimulated by Reuten (1979) and Roemer (1981), section 9.5.

feedback from contribution levels to wage formation is generally ignored.
In order to deal with the more realistic case of deficits and surplusses occurring during various phases of the business cycle we suggest to use a modified Goodwin model which has been described by us elsewhere.[3] In this model capacity utilization has been introduced as a variable which is determined along Keynesian lines via the intersection of investment and savings functions. Disequilibria of the unemployment benefits fund can then be allowed for as indicated in section 5. In doing so, however, we still impose a restriction, i.e. that the fund has to be in equilibrium for the steady state values of the profit share and the degree of employment, while it may be in disequilibrium otherwise.

2. The Model Subset Relating to Unemployment Benefits

We will assume throughout the paper that all unemployed are entitled to unemployment benefits at a certain uniform actual rate $\underline{w}$. Thus there are neither waiting periods nor maximum periods for which payments are made. As there are no wage differentials in a macro-model à la Goodwin, there is no obvious need to allow for differential levels of payments (although differentials according to age or seniority could be taken into account even there).
The level of benefits ($\underline{w}$) will be linked to the level of the net wage rate (w^*), that is net of (possible) contributions to the unemployment fund to be paid out of gross wages (w). Therefore, we can formulate the following two relations

$$\underline{w} = \gamma w^* \quad (2.1)$$

$$w^* = (1-c)w \quad (2.2)$$

While γ denotes the ratio of benefits to net wages, c stands for the share workers have to contribute out of their gross wage rate.
Unemployment payments (U) are the mathematical product of the benefit rate $\underline{w}$ and the number of unemployed persons, i.e. A-L (A = total labour supply, L = number of workers employed):

$$U = \underline{w}(A-L) \quad (2.3)$$

We now turn to the contribution side which has already been touched upon as far as working class contributions (C_w) are concerned. If all the employed are obliged to contribute, we obtain

$$C_w = cwL \quad (2.4)$$

Capitalists' contributions (C_π) could be institutionalised in at least two different ways, i.e. proportional to contributions raised from labour or in proportion to gross profits (Π), as a kind of unemployment tax. Combining both methods gives rise to

3) Cf. Glombowski/Krüger (1983)

$$C_\Pi = \delta C_W + t\Pi \qquad , 0 \leq \delta,\ 0 \leq t < 1 \tag{2.5}$$

As unemployment contributions are the only (possible) subtractions from profits in the present framework, net profits (Π^*) can be defined by

$$\Pi^* = \Pi - C_\pi \tag{2.6}$$

Contributions to and payments out of the unemployment fund must not necessarily match. But for the time being we postulate a permanent fund equilibrium:

$$U = C_W + C_\pi \tag{2.7}$$

As a consequence, not all of our parameters of the payments and/or the contribution side, respectively, i.e. γ, c, δ and t, can be considered as constants. At least one of them **will** have to be adjusted permanently to preserve the financial balance.

It is obvious that the subsystem described so far gives rise to quite a lot of different cases. For instance, the obligation to contribute to the fund can be imposed on one of the two classes only. If, however, both have to share in providing the financial means, there are still various possibilities according to which way is chosen to determine capitalists' contributions: either $\delta = 0$ and $t > 0$, or $\delta > 0$ and $t = 0$, or $\delta > 0$ and $t > 0$. Last not least, different cases are produced depending on whether the level of payments (γ) or the levels of contributions (c, δ and/or t) are adjusted.

Now that the basic ideas about the system of unemployment benefits are developed, we are prepared to discuss the ways in which it can be linked to Goodwin's model.

3. Unemployment Benefits and Goodwin's Model: Possible Links

In Goodwin's model profits are automatically reinvested. If, however, contributions have to be paid out of profits, accumulation has to be confined to net profits. This is the primary way in which unemployment contributions are linked to Goodwin's employment/accumulation/distribution system. The link is expressed by using (2.6) together with

$$\dot{K} = \alpha\Pi^* , \quad 0 < \alpha = \text{const.} \leq 1 \tag{3.1}$$

instead of Goodwin's assumption $\dot{K} = \Pi$.

A second link could be established by an appropriate extension of the wage-formation equation. We can conceive of the possibility that workers try to shift some part of the burden of rising unemployment contributions to capitalists and that they do so with some success. In this case we would have to substitute the well-known wage formation function

$$\hat{w} = -a_1 + a_2\beta \quad , \qquad a_1, a_2 = \text{const.} > 0 , \tag{3.2}$$

employed by Goodwin, by the more general

$$\hat{w} = -a_1 + a_2\beta + \psi(c,\hat{c}) \qquad \text{with} \qquad \partial\psi/\partial c \geq 0, \quad \partial\psi/\partial\hat{c} \geq 0 \tag{3.3}$$

Of course, the first link can only operate if the capitalists have to pay contributions at all. All unemployment insurance systems which are financed by workers' contributions alone, will not affect distribution and accumulation, at least not in a direct way. Therefore, Goodwin's results are compatible with any unemployment assistance scheme in which only workers pay contributions, especially with all schemes set up autonomously by working class organizations.

The second link will only work if workers have to pay contributions and if the contribution level is a variable, which means that it is adjusted according to financial needs.

Both links could be made to work at the same time. Here we restrict ourselves to the discussion of the first type only.

4. Two Cases

4.1 The Complete Model

The two cases to be worked out in some detail in this section have in common that both classes are supposed to pay contributions to the fund. In the case of paragraph 4.2 capitalists pay a constant percentage of their gross profits while the workers' percentage is adjusted to maintain the balance of the fund. In the case of paragraph 4.3 capitalists' payments bear a constant proportion to those of labour. As the latter is again adjusted to assure permanent equilibrium, capitalists' payments become a variable share of their gross profits.

Before entering into the details, the most general model of the present modification of Goodwin's model is written out in full:

$$\beta = L/A \tag{4.1}$$

$$y = Y/L \tag{4.2}$$

$$\pi = \Pi/Y \tag{4.3}$$

$$Y = \sigma K \tag{4.4}$$

$$\hat{A} = n \tag{4.5}$$

$$\hat{y} = m \tag{4.6}$$

$$\Pi = Y - wL \tag{4.7}$$

$$\hat{w} = -a_1 + a_2\beta + \psi(c,\hat{c}) \quad (4.8)$$

$$\dot{K} = \alpha\Pi^* \quad (4.9)$$

$$\Pi^* = \Pi - C_\pi \quad (4.10)$$

$$C_\pi = \delta cwL + t\Pi \quad (4.11)$$

$$c = \frac{\gamma(1-\pi)(1-\beta) - t\pi\beta}{\gamma(1-\pi)(1-\beta) + (1+\delta)(1-\pi)\beta} \quad (4.12)$$

$$\pi^* = \Pi^*/Y \quad (4.13)$$

The first three equations define the degree of employment, labour productivity and the (gross) profit share, respectively. Next, Goodwin's familiar assumptions of a constant capital productivity and constant growth rates of the labour force and of labour productivity are expressed, followed by the determination of gross profits as the surplus of net product over the wage bill. Equations (4.8) to (4.10) have been explained above. Substitution of (2.4) into (2.5) yields (4.11), and (4.13) is the definition of the net profit share. But (4.12) remains to be explained. It is derived from the budget equilibrium equation as follows: From (2.1), (2.2) and (2.3) we get

$$U = \gamma(1-c)w(A-L) \quad (4.14)$$

Substituting U together with C_W and C_π into (2.7), one obtains

$$\gamma(1-c)w(A-L) = cwL(1+\delta) + t\Pi \quad (4.15)$$

Using (4.1), (4.2) and (4.3) and solving for c yields (4.12).
In both cases to be analysed below we put

$$\psi(c,\hat{c}) = 0 \quad (4.16)$$

for the sake of simplicity. Both cases have in common that the respective equation systems boil down to two differential equations in the degree of employment and the net profit share. Moreover, the equation for the degree of employment is the same in both cases, i.e.

$$\dot{\beta} = \{\alpha\sigma\pi^* - (m+n)\}\beta \quad (4.17)$$

It is derived as follows: From (4.1) we have

$$\hat{\beta} = \hat{L} - \hat{A} \quad (4.18)$$

while (4.2) and (4.4) imply

$$\hat{L} = \hat{Y} - \hat{y} = \hat{K} - \hat{y} \quad (4.19)$$

Substituting $\hat{K} - \hat{y}$ for $\hat{L}$ and using (4.5) and (4.6), respectively, leads to

$$\hat{\beta} = \hat{K} - m - n \tag{4.20}$$

As $\hat{K}$ can be replaced by

$$\hat{K} = \alpha(\Pi^*/Y)(Y/K) = \alpha\sigma\pi^* \tag{4.21}$$

because of (4.9), (4.13) and (4.4), it becomes clear that (4.17) holds.

4.2 Capitalists Pay Unemployment Taxes

We assume in this paragraph that capitalists contribute a certain constant percentage (t) of their profits, i.e.

$$C_\pi = t\Pi \ , \qquad 0 < t = \text{const.} < 1 \tag{4.22}$$

Labour's contributions are determined by

$$C_W = cwL \tag{2.4}$$

We have to develop a second differential equation of the system, explaining the movement of the net profit share in time. From (4.22) and (2.6) we have

$$\Pi^* = (1-t)\Pi \tag{4.23}$$

Taking (4.2), (4.7) and (4.13) into account, we get

$$\pi^* = (1-t)(1-w/y) \tag{4.24}$$

By expressing this equation in growth rates we obtain

$$\dot{\pi}^* = (\hat{y}-\hat{w})(1-t-\pi^*) \tag{4.25}$$

Now we have to substitute (4.6) and the (unaugmented) wage formation equation (3.2) to arrive at the differential equation in π^*

$$\dot{\pi}^* = (m+a_1-a_2\beta)(1-t-\pi^*) \tag{4.26}$$

Obviously, the equilibrium values in the present case are the Goodwin ones (although the <u>net</u> share of profit replaces the gross share of Goodwin's model):

$$\beta_0 = (m+a_1)/a_2 \qquad \text{and} \tag{4.27}$$

$$\pi_0^* = (m+n)/(\alpha\sigma) \tag{4.28}$$

The partial equilibrium curves are straight lines starting at the equilibrium intercepts of the β- and π^*-axes, respectively. As the same happens to be the case in Goodwin's model, we may expect closed solution curves here as well.

Considering the equations (4.26) and (4.17), we find that time can be eliminated by division and the variables can be separated to give rise to

$$\frac{m+a_1-a_2\beta}{\beta}\,d\beta = \frac{\alpha\sigma\pi^*-m-n}{1-t-\pi^*}\,d\pi^* \qquad (4.29)$$

Integrating and taking anti-logarithms leads to the family of closed solution curves in π^*,β-space expressed by

$$\beta^{(m+a_1)}e^{-a_2\beta} = H(1-t-\pi^*)^{\{m+n-\alpha\sigma(1-t)\}}\,e^{-\alpha\sigma\pi^*}\;, \qquad (4.30)$$

where H is a constant of integration to be determined by initial conditions, i.e. by specifying a pair of initial values $\pi^*(0)$ and $\beta(0)$.

Figure 1 illustrates the method to derive a graph of the solution curve. While the left-hand side is independent of t and reaches its maximum for $\beta = \beta_0$, the right-hand side defines a family of curves for different values of the shift-parameter t. For reasonable values of t, curves for higher t will lie above those for lower t. Therefore, the closed curves for higher t will lie inside those for lower t. A numerical

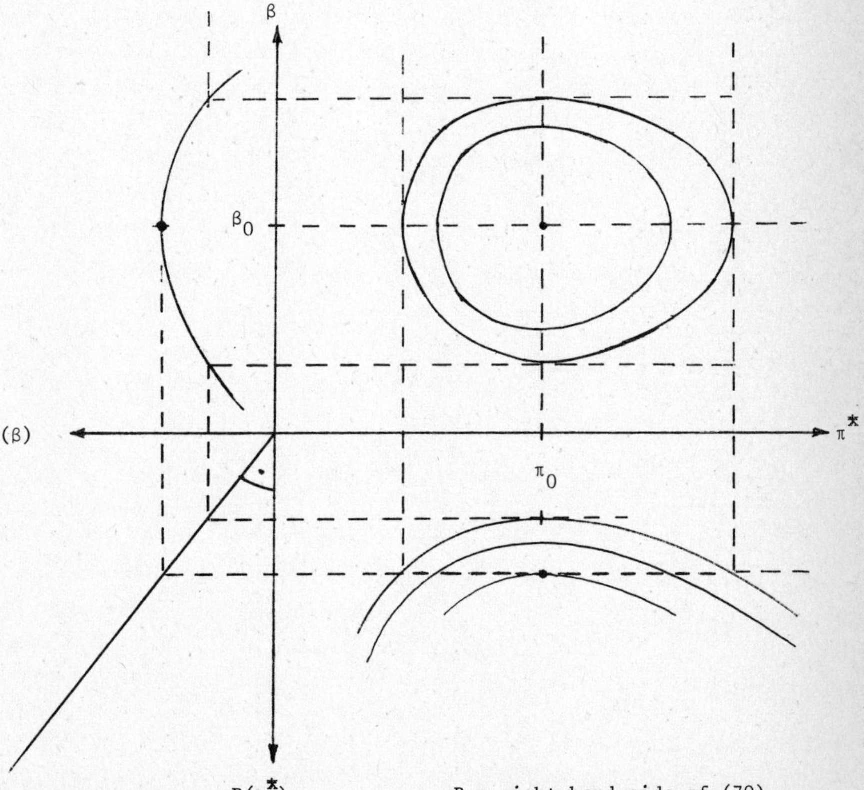

Figure 1

R = right-hand side of (70)
L = left-hand side of (70)

example has been calculated with the parameter values $m = 0{,}04$, $n = 0{,}01$, $a_1 = 0{,}9$ $a_2 = 1{,}00$, $\alpha = 0{,}3$ and $\sigma = 2/3$.

Fixing H such that for $t = 0{,}1$ the maximum of β will be unity, i.e. $H = 0{,}3656781225$, approximate maximum and minimum values of β and π^* for $t = 0{,}1$ and $t = 0{,}11$ are given by the following table.

	$t = 0{,}10$	$t = 0{,}11$
β_{max}	1,00	0,98
β_{min}	0,88	0,90
π^*_{max}	0,35	0,315
π^*_{min}	0,13	0,18

The closed curves degenerate into the equilibrium point if we insert β_0 and π^*_0 into the left-hand side and the right-hand side of (4.30), respectively, and determine t such that the equivalence between both sides is achieved. In our numerical example $t \simeq 0{,}11651$ will do. Of course, one should not interpret these results in policy terms, as if one could damp cycles by an adequate determination of capitalists' unemployment tax rate. Higher tax rates can give rise to cycles just the same if only "appropriate" initial conditions are "chosen" or "produced" by disturbing shocks.

There is still one minor point to touch upon, i.e. the development of c during the cycle. From (4.23), (4.3) and (4.13) we have

$$\pi^* = (1-t)\pi \tag{4.31}$$

Put δ equal to zero in (4.12) and insert into (4.31). After some manipulations one obtains

$$c = \frac{(1-t-\pi^*)\gamma(1-\beta) - t\pi^*\beta}{(1-t-\pi^*)\{\gamma+(1-\gamma)\beta\}} \tag{4.32}$$

We took $t = 0{,}10$ and $\gamma = 0{,}8$ to compute c for some critical points. The results are given below:

$c(\beta_{max}, \pi^*_0) \simeq -0{,}0385$ $\qquad$ $c(\beta_0, \pi^*_{max}) \simeq -0{,}0120$

$c(\beta_{min}, \pi^*_0) \simeq +0{,}0637$ $\qquad$ $c(\beta_0, \pi^*_{min}) \simeq +0{,}0325$

We conclude that in times of high employment and/or high profits contributions of workers may become <u>negative</u> as under the assumed institutional arrangements capitalists' contributions can exceed financial requirements in those periods. But in our example there are also phases of the cycle in which workers have to contribute a considerable percentage of their gross wages [4], that is when employment and/or profits are low, so that requirements are high while capitalists contribute little. The average level of workers' contributions can be calculated by taking the equilibrium point as a basis. This delivers $c(\beta_0, \pi_0^*) \approx 0{,}012$. It is positive, as it should be, although rather small. But this might be "improved" by calculating examples with somewhat lower tax rates for capitalists.

4.3 The Continental System

There is a wide variety of institutional arrangements as to the welfare state functions in different countries. Sometimes two broad different lines are distinguished, i.e. the "Continental" and the "Anglo-Saxon" system, respectively.[5] The Anglo-Saxon type would be characterized by tax-financed, government-managed minimum assistance schemes, while in the Continental system contributions to the fund as well as payments from it would depend on earning-levels and the fund would be self-managed by some committee of contributors. The model of paragraph 4.2 had some Anglo-Saxon flavour, because capitalists and workers paid some percentage of their respective incomes (although the latter percentage was made variable to allow for the budget restriction). With a constant percentage of workers' "taxes", government subsidies, and payments based on minimum requirements (fixed in absolute level or growing with a trend rate), the Anglo-Saxon character would become more pronounced.
In this paragraph we are going to follow a more Continental line by sticking to the assumption of earnings-related unemployment benefits and by assuming that capitalists' contributions are linked to those of workers. Net profits are once again given by

$$\Pi^* = Y - wL - C_\pi \tag{4.10}$$

Capitalists' contributions are a constant multiple of workers' contributions,

$$C_\pi = \delta C_W \quad , \tag{4.33}$$

while workers' contributions are described by

$$C_W = cwL \tag{2.4}$$

From these equations

$$\Pi^* = Y - wL - \delta cwL \tag{4.34}$$

is derived, which can be rewritten with regard to (4.2), (4.3) and (4.13) as

$$\pi^* = 1 - (w/y)(1+\delta c) \tag{4.35}$$

---

4) This percentage cannot exceed the degree of unemployment because such a percentage would be sufficient to pay all unemployed the net wage of the employed without using contributions from capitalists.
5) See for instance Gough (1979), p.57

From (4.35) it is clear that the unemployment benefits subsystem is going to exert a direct influence on the employment/accumulation/distribution system since c is involved in the determination of the net profit share and its rate of change. Rewriting (4.35) in growth rates leads to

$$\dot{\pi}^* = (1-\pi^*)\{\hat{y}-\hat{w}-(1+\widehat{\delta c})\} \tag{4.36}$$

In order to calculate the growth rate of $(1+\delta c)$, we have to make use of

$$c = \frac{\gamma(1-\beta)}{\gamma(1-\beta) + \beta(1+\delta)} \quad , \tag{4.37}$$

which follows from (4.12) if t is zero. Before doing so we would like to remark that making γ variable instead of c would cause much less trouble. In that case $(1+\widehat{\delta c})$ would vanish and we would be back on familiar Goodwin lines. But let us now proceed with our case of a variable c. We start by noting that

$$\frac{d(1+\delta c)}{dt} = \frac{dc}{d\beta}\delta\dot{\beta} \tag{4.38}$$

Next, $dc/d\beta$ is calculated as

$$\frac{dc}{d\beta} = -\frac{\gamma(1+\delta)}{\{\gamma(1-\beta)+\beta(1+\delta)\}^2} \tag{4.39}$$

Multiplication by $\delta\dot{\beta}$ and division by $(1+\delta c)$ leads - after some further steps - to

$$(1+\widehat{\delta c}) = -\frac{\gamma\delta\dot{\beta}}{\{\gamma(1-\beta)+\beta(1+\delta)\}\{\gamma(1-\beta)+\beta\}} \tag{4.40}$$

(4.40) can now be substituted into (4.36). At the same time we use

$$\dot{\beta} = (\alpha\sigma\pi^*-m-n) \quad , \tag{4.17}$$

which holds in the present model again to replace $\dot{\beta}$ in (4.40). Taking furthermore (3.2) and (4.6) into account, substitutions into (4.36) lead us to the second differential equation of the Continental system:

$$\dot{\pi}^* = (1-\pi^*)[a_1+m-a_2\beta + \frac{\gamma\delta\beta\ (\alpha\sigma\pi^*-m-n)}{\{(1+\delta)\beta+\gamma(1-\beta)\}\{\beta+\gamma(1-\beta)\}}] \tag{4.41}$$

Equilibrium values are the same as in paragraph 4.2. The same holds for the partial equilibrium curve $\dot{\beta} = 0$. In order to let $\dot{\pi}^*$ vanish, the term in square brackets on the right-hand side of (4.41) has to be put equal to zero. Making use of the equilibrium values, the partial equilibrium function may be represented as the tangens measured from the equilibrium point:

$$\frac{\beta - \beta_0}{\pi^* - \pi_0^*} = \frac{\alpha\gamma\delta\sigma\beta}{a_2\{(1+\delta)\beta+\gamma(1-\beta)\}\{\beta+\gamma(1-\beta)\}} \tag{4.42}$$

Obviously, its slope is positive. Moreover, it can be shown after some calculations that the slope will rise in the intervall $0 < \beta \leq 1$ if

$$\gamma > (1+\delta)/(2+\delta) \tag{4.43}$$

is fulfilled. Otherwise one turning point will exist in the interval to be calculated by

$$\beta = +\gamma\{(1+\delta-\gamma)(1-\gamma)\}^{-1/2} \tag{4.44}$$

Figure 2 shows the partial equilibrium curves and indicates the movements of the variables in the subsectors of the plane.

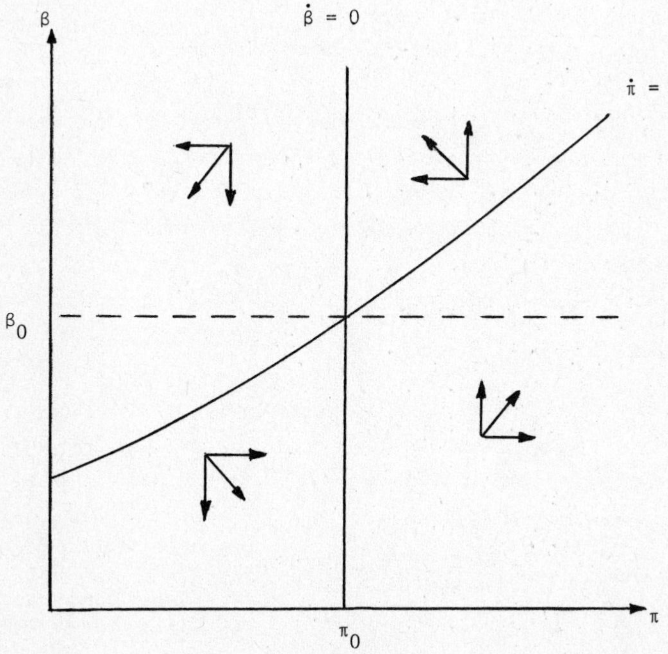

Figure 2

Linearization of the system (4.17) and (4.41) leads to

$$\begin{bmatrix} \dot{\beta} \\ \\ \dot{\pi}^* \end{bmatrix} = \begin{bmatrix} 0 & \alpha\sigma\beta_0 \\ \\ -a_2(1-\pi_0^*) & \dfrac{(1-\pi_0^*)\alpha\sigma\gamma\delta\beta_0}{\{(1+\delta-\gamma)\beta_0 + \gamma\}\{(1-\gamma)\beta_0+\gamma\}} \end{bmatrix} \begin{bmatrix} \beta - \beta_0 \\ \\ \pi^* - \pi_0^* \end{bmatrix} \tag{4.45}$$

Let us abbreviate the matrix of (4.45) by

$$\begin{bmatrix} 0 & B \\ C & A \end{bmatrix} \tag{4.46}$$

Obviously $A > 0$ holds, which means that the equilibrium point is locally unstable. Whether the expression $BC + (A/2)^2$ is positive or not depends on parameter magnitudes, since $(A/2)^2$ is positive while BC is negative. Take the numerical parameters from paragraph 4.2 and add $\gamma = 0{,}8$ and $\delta = 1$. For this numerical example $BC + (A/2)^2$ clearly is negative so that we obtain the result of an expanding spiral in the neighbourhood of the equilibrium point.

4.4 Remarks on the Results

Both models described above differ from Goodwin's model with respect to the equilibrium value of the profit share. It is the net share of profits in the presented models that equals the gross share in Goodwin's case. Therefore, the gross share in our models is higher than the Goodwin one and it is exactly as much higher as to allow the capitalists to pay their contributions without being off worse than in the Goodwin case. On the equilibrium path the accumulation of capital would not be affected, and the same assistance scheme for the unemployed could be secured if the gross share of wages would take on the Goodwin value and contributions would only be made by workers.

However, these results do not imply that the institutional arrangements have no consequences whatsoever for the accumulation process. As has been shown, the model of 4.3 differs from that of 4.2 with regard to its disequilibrium behaviour. While the latter produces Goodwin-like closed oscillations, the former is characterized by an unstable equilibrium point surrounded by spirals with a rising amplitude. How is this difference to be explained economically? In Goodwin's model the upswing of employment is decelerated and finally reversed by the decline of the gross profit share. If accumulation is governed by the net instead of the gross share, the process of deceleration and reversal may be affected, unless both behave in exactly the same way. The latter requirement is fulfilled in the model of 4.2, since the constant unemployment tax rate establishes a constant proportion between net and gross profits. In the model of 4.3 , however, the net share rises faster or diminishes slower whenever the degree of unemployment falls. As accumulation is governed by the net share, the alleviation of the burden of contributions prolongs and accentuates the upswing. Of course the analogous opposite argument applies to the downturn. This explains why the underlying institutional arrangement fosters instability. This feature may, of course, heavily depend on the assumption of a balanced budget of the unemployment benefits fund. It is this restriction that we are going to remove in the following section.

5. A Model Allowing for Disequilibria of the Unemployment Benefits Fund

5.1. The Main Modifications Introduced

The deficit (D) of the unemployment benefits funds is defined by the difference between payments and contributions, i.e.

$$D = U-(C_\pi + C_W) \qquad (5.1)$$

In which way can a deficit or an excess influence the level of economic activity? Looking back at our previous models, one recognizes that the approach followed so far leaves little scope for such influences: The level of production and income is governed by the size of the capital stock and a constant capital productivity. Unemployment insurance systems can only influence the level of income via accumulation, which is governed by distributive shares.

In the simplest Keynesian system demand determines production by the equilibrating operation of the multiplier. Domar's growth-theoretical generalization, which will be used below, accounts for capital stock growth as a consequence of investment, while on the other hand investment demand determines the whole of demand. The latter in turn determines the degree of capacity utilization. In order to have a simple relation between investment demand and the level of production, the multiplier may be assigned a constant value, and an instantaneous adjustment of production to demand can be assumed. Neither of the two simplifications seems justified and especially not in a business cycle setup. Yet, while we are going to remove the first one by allowing for a variable savings ratio, the second one is retained here for the sake of simplicity. The level of production and income will, therefore, be determined in a Keynesian way by the intersection of independent savings and investment functions to be introduced immediately. In doing so, we have to take our unemployment benefits arrangements into account. Demand (N) is defined by

$$N = C + \dot{K} + U \quad , \qquad (5.2)$$

where C is consumption out of net income. $\dot{K}$ represents capital accumulation, and unemployment benefits (U) are assumed to be spent completely. Income, being equivalent to production, is used for paying contributions as well as for savings and consumption out of net income, i.e.

$$Y = C + C_\pi + C_W + S \tag{5.3}$$

Instantaneous adjustment of production to demand implies

$$Y = N \quad , \tag{5.4}$$

from which we obtain

$$S = \dot{K} + U + C_\pi - C_W$$

or

$$S = \dot{K} + D \tag{5.5}$$

It remains to indicate how savings and investments are specified. We assume that the savings ratio depends on the (net) profit share with a constant elasticity (η),

$$S = a\pi^{*\eta}Y \quad , \quad a = \text{const.} > 0, \quad 0 < \eta = \text{const.} < 1 \tag{5.6}$$

Capital stock growth is assumed to depend on the (net) rate of profit, with a constant elasticity (ε) alike:

$$\dot{K} = b\rho^\varepsilon K \;, \quad , \quad b = \text{const.} > 0, \quad 0 < \varepsilon = \text{const.} < 1 \tag{5.7}$$

This may be considered as a specific form of the general investment function proposed by Kalecki.[7]
The (net) rate of profit (ρ) is decomposed into the capacity/capital ratio (σ), the degree of capacity utilization (θ) and the net share of profit (π^*), i.e.

$$\rho = \sigma\theta\pi^* \quad , \tag{5.8}$$

while the former two are defined by the relations

$$\theta = Y/P \qquad \text{and} \tag{5.9}$$

$$P = \sigma K \quad , \quad \sigma = \text{const.} > 0 \quad , \tag{5.10}$$

in which P denotes capacity output.
The remaining elements of the full model can be taken over from section 4. It will become clear in the discussion of the present model that capacity utilization cannot

---

6) It should be noted that by stipulating (5.6) the multiplier becomes a variable.
7) See, for example, Kalecki (1971), p.7

simply be determined by the intersection of the savings and investment functions, because the position of both depend on distribution, which is only determined by taking the labour market and the unemployment insurance sector into account. The latter, of course, also enters more directly, via its deficits or surplusses, into the equilibrium condition of the product market.

5.2 The Complete Model Specified

We will present the complete model in a slightly reduced form of only eight equations, which will later on be reduced to only two. The first equation summarizes the unemployment benefits subsystem. Define the function f as the ratio of the fund deficit to income, i.e.

$$f = D/Y \tag{5.11}$$

Taking (5.1) into account and making use of relations (2.4), (4.11), (4.14), (4.1) and (4.3), we arrive at

$$f = f(\pi,\beta) = \gamma(1-c)(1-\pi)(1/\beta-1) - (1-\pi)c(1+\delta) - t\pi \tag{5.12}$$

Obviously, the relative deficit is a function of both, the gross profit share and the degree of employment.
The second equation describes the growth rate of the degree of employment as folllows:

$$\hat{\beta} = \hat{\theta} + \hat{K} - m - n \tag{5.13}$$

It is derived in essentially the same way as (4.20). However, the variability of capacity utilization has to be taken into account here additionally.
The development in time of the gross profit share is determined in the same way as in section 4, i.e.

$$\dot{\pi} = (1-\pi)(m + a_1 - a_2\beta) \quad . \tag{5.14}$$

while the net profit share can be calculated from the gross share and the parameters of the unemployment benefits subsystem as

$$\pi^* = (1-t)\pi - \delta c(1-\pi) \tag{5.15}$$

Next, we rewrite the savings function by introducing the savings ratio (α) as a convenient new variable :

$$\alpha = S/Y = a\pi^{*\eta} \tag{5.16}$$

Moreover, the investment function (5.7) and the definition of the net rate of profit (5.8) are kept. The final equation of the reduced modified system is derived from the product market equilibrium condition. Dividing (5.5) by Y, we obtain

$$\alpha = \hat{K}\,(K/Y) + f$$

Substituting (5.9) and (5.10) makes it possible to rewrite (5.5) in the form

$$\theta = \hat{K}/\{\sigma(\alpha - f)\} \tag{5.17}$$

In essence, this is Domar's manner of determining the degree of capacity utilization with the proviso that $\hat{K}$, α and f depend on the remainder of the system.

5.3 Reduction of the Model to Two Differential Equations

The model which has just been specified can be reduced to two differential equations. It would take too much space to develop the whole procedure in full detail. Therefore, we decided to give only a rough sketch, which nevertheless should enable the interested reader to reconstruct the derivations.

First of all it is obvious that the gross share of profit can be replaced by the net share in the relative deficit function as well as in the differential equation for the profit share. The relative deficit function becomes

$$f(\beta,\pi^*) = \{\gamma(1-c)(1/\beta-1)-c(1+\delta)\}\frac{1-t-\pi^*}{1-t+\delta c} - \frac{t(\pi^*+\delta c)}{1-t+\delta c} \tag{5.18}$$

As the parameters c, δ and t occurring in (5.15) can be regarded as constants, the net-share equivalent to (5.14) is found to be

$$\dot{\pi}^* = (1 - t - \pi^*)(m + a_1 - a_2\beta) \tag{5.19}$$

This is the first one of the pair of differential equations we are looking for. Secondly, we substitute (5.7) and (5.8) into (5.13) and (5.17), which will then take on the new forms

$$\hat{\beta} = \hat{\theta} + b(\sigma\theta\pi^*)^{\varepsilon} - m - n \qquad \text{and} \tag{5.20}$$

$$\theta = b(\sigma\theta\pi^*)^{\varepsilon}/\{\sigma(\alpha - f)\} \tag{5.21}$$

The equations (5.18) - (5.21) plus (5.16) constitute a system in the five remaining variables α, β, π^*, θ and f. Thirdly, the degree of capacity utilization has to be eliminated. From (5.21) one obtains

$$\theta = a^{-1/(1-\varepsilon)}\, b^{1/(1-\varepsilon)}\, \sigma^{-1}\, \pi^{*(\varepsilon-\eta)/(1-\varepsilon)}\, \varphi^{-1/(1-\varepsilon)} ,$$

where

$$\varphi = 1 - f/\alpha = (\beta,\pi^*) \tag{5.23}$$

is used as abbreviation. The expression $b(\sigma\theta\pi^*)^\varepsilon$, which occurs in (5.20), can be replaced by

$$b(\sigma\theta\pi^*)^\varepsilon = i\pi^{*j}\varphi^{-\varepsilon/(1-\varepsilon)} \tag{5.24}$$

where i and j are short-hand expressions defined by

$$i = a^{-\varepsilon/(1-\varepsilon)}b^{1/(1-\varepsilon)} \quad \text{and} \tag{5.25}$$

$$j = \varepsilon(1-\eta)/(1-\varepsilon) \tag{5.26}$$

respectively. Still $\hat{\theta}$ has to be substituted into (5.20). From (5.22) we get

$$\hat{\theta} = (j-\eta)\hat{\pi}^* - \hat{\varphi}/(1-\varepsilon) \tag{5.27}$$

Therefore, (5.20) can be restated as

$$\hat{\beta} = (j-\eta)\hat{\pi}^* - \hat{\varphi}/(1-\varepsilon) + i\pi^{*j}\varphi^{-\varepsilon/(1-\varepsilon)} - m - n \tag{5.28}$$

Thus we are left with the two equations (5.19) and (5.28), the latter of which, however, contains expressions in φ and $\hat{\varphi}$, respectively, which have to be retranslated into α and f, or, in last instance, into π^* and β. With regard to φ this poses no problems. For $\hat{\varphi}$ we obtain

$$\hat{\varphi} = -\frac{f_\beta\beta}{\alpha-f}\hat{\beta} - \frac{f_{\pi^*}\pi^*-\eta f}{\alpha-f}\hat{\pi}^* \quad , \tag{5.29}$$

in which f_β and f_{π^*} denote the partial derivatives of the relative deficit function with respect to β and π^*. Substituting into (5.28) and solving for $\hat{\beta}$, or rather $\dot{\beta}$, gives rise to

$$\dot{\beta} = \frac{(j-\eta)g+f_{\pi^*}\pi^*-\eta f}{g - f_\beta\beta}\beta\hat{\pi}^* + \frac{g\{i\pi^{*j}\varphi^{-\varepsilon/(1-\varepsilon)} - m - n\}}{g - f_\beta\beta}\beta \quad , \tag{5.30}$$

where g is another abbreviation given by

$$g = g(\beta,\pi^*) = (1-\varepsilon)(\alpha-f) \tag{5.31}$$

Whenever wanted, one could replace the expressions $\hat{\pi}^*$, f_β, f_{π^*} and g by expressions in π^* and β. For our purposes this is not necessary: (5.30) can be used as the second differential equation in π^* and β, together with (5.19), being the first one.

5.4 Analysis of a Special Case

Up to now the unemployment insurance system has been formulated in rather general terms. From now on we are going to impose the condition

$$f(\beta_0,\pi_0^*) = 0 \qquad (5.32)$$

(5.32) states that an equilibrium of the system is to imply the equilibrium of the unemployment benefits fund, while positive or negative balances are allowed for whenever the degree of employment and/or the net profit share differ from their steady state values. It is assumed that (5.32) is made to hold by establishing appropriate combinations of the parameters of the subsystem. The underlying idea is, of course, that the unemployment insurance system is (or should be) set up in such a way as to guarantee a balance of the fund over longer periods of time or on the average. A straightforward implication of (5.32) is

$$\varphi(\beta_0,\pi_0^*) = 1 \qquad (5.33)$$

The equilibrium values of the crucial variables turn out to be

$$\beta_0 = (m + a_1)/a_2 \qquad (5.34)$$

$$\pi_0^* = \{(m + n)/i\}^{1/j} \qquad (5.35)$$

While (5.34) follows easily from (5.19) by putting $\dot{\pi}^*$ equal to zero, (5.35) follows if both, $\dot{\beta}$ and $\hat{\pi}^*$, are put equal to zero, if (5.33) is taken into account and if

$$g(\beta_0,\pi_0^*) - f_{\beta_0}\,\beta_0 \neq 0 \qquad (5.36)$$

holds. (5.36) is not at all restrictive, because from (5.18) we can show that f_β should be negative for relevant parameter values:

$$f_\beta = -\frac{(1-\pi^*-t)\gamma(1-c)}{(1-t+\delta c)\beta^2} < 0 \qquad (5.37)$$

Therefore, we may assume that the denominator of (5.30) is positive throughout. Having established the existence of a steady state solution, we now turn to the disequilibrium behaviour of the system. Here we restrict ourselves to the investigation of the stability properties of the linearized system around the equilibrium point. It is a rather tedious job to calculate the partial derivatives of the functions $\dot{\pi}^*$ and $\dot{\beta}$, although assumption (5.32) proves very efficient in reducing the complexity of expressions involved. Here we simply state the results, which read:

$$\left.\frac{\partial\dot{\pi}^*}{\partial\pi^*}\right|_0 = 0 \tag{5.38}$$

$$\left.\frac{\partial\dot{\pi}^*}{\partial\beta}\right|_0 = -\frac{a_2(1-\pi_0^*)\beta_0}{\gamma(1-\beta_0)+\beta_0} \tag{5.39}$$

$$\left.\frac{\partial\dot{\beta}}{\partial\pi^*}\right|_0 = ij\beta_0\pi_0^{*j-1}\;\frac{(1-\varepsilon)\alpha_0 + \varepsilon f_{\pi_0^*}\pi_0^*/j}{(1-\varepsilon)\alpha_0 - f_{\beta_0}\beta_0} \tag{5.40}$$

$$\left.\frac{\partial\dot{\beta}}{\partial\beta}\right|_0 = \frac{\beta_0[-a_2\{(j-\eta)(1-\varepsilon)\alpha_0 + f_{\pi_o^*}\pi_o^*\}(1-\pi_0^*-t)/\pi_0^* + \varepsilon i\pi_0^{*j} f_{\beta_0}]}{(1-\varepsilon)\alpha_0 - f_{\beta_0}\beta_0} \tag{5.41}$$

The linearized system can be written

$$\begin{bmatrix}\dot{\pi}^*\\ \dot{\beta}\end{bmatrix} = \begin{bmatrix} 0 & B\\ C & A\end{bmatrix}\begin{bmatrix}\pi^* - \pi_0^*\\ \beta - \beta_0\end{bmatrix} \tag{5.42}$$

where

$$A = \left.\frac{\partial\dot{\beta}}{\partial\beta}\right|_0 \quad , \tag{5.43}$$

$$B = \left.\frac{\partial\dot{\pi}^*}{\partial\beta}\right|_0 \quad \text{and} \tag{5.44}$$

$$C = \left.\frac{\partial\dot{\beta}}{\partial\pi^*}\right|_0 \tag{5.45}$$

Its eigenvalues are given by

$$\mu_{1/2} = A/2 \pm (A^2/4 + BC)^{1/2} \tag{5.46}$$

The system will be locally asymptotically stable if the real part of the eigenvalues is negative. Looking at (5.41), a general result seems difficult to establish. Indeed, a clear cut result would be rather surprising, as we have neither assumed a particular unemployment insurance system, nor have we indicated which of the two elasticities, ε and η, should be greater. Even then not only the signs but also the numerical values of our parameters may be important. Nevertheless, tentative conclusions can be reached for some cases. For instance, let

$$j - \eta > 0 \quad , \tag{5.47}$$

which is equivalent to $\varepsilon > \eta$. This means that the elasticity of the investment function is greater than that of the savings function. We have shown already that f_β is negative. Therefore, A will be negative, provided $f_{\pi_0^*}$ is nonnegative or negative but sufficiently small in absolute amount. From (5.18) we obtain

$$f_{\pi^*} = - \frac{\gamma(1 - c)(1/\beta - 1) - c(1 + \delta) + t}{1 - t + \delta c} \tag{5.48}$$

Making use of (5.32), the partial derivative in the equilibrium point becomes

$$f_{\pi_0^*} = - t/(1 - \pi_0^* - t) < 0 \quad ^{8)} \tag{5.49}$$

Substituting this expression into (5.41) it is evident that it works destabilizing in principle. If, however, institutional arrangements entail low values of profit-depending contributions or no contributions of this particular kind at all, then the equilibrium will be locally asymptotically stable.
Whether or not oscillations will occur is decided by the sign of the discriminant. A necessary condition for oscillations is $BC < 0$. As B is negative, C has to be positive to achieve that. The latter condition is more likely to hold, the smaller the parameter t happens to be. Of course, this is not sufficient to establish the existence of cyclical solutions.
Another way of characterizing the specific features of the present model is a comparison with the special case that is created if the unemployment insurance system is dropped while nothing else is changed. [9] We simply have to put the parameters γ, c, δ and t equal to zero, which, of course, implies

$$f = f_{\pi^*} = f_\beta = 0 \tag{5.50}$$

It will be found that the equilibrium values remain the same. But it should be noted that in the simplified model there is no difference between the gross and the net share of profits and that it is the equilibrium net share of profits of the enlarged

---

8) Implicit differentiation of the relative deficit function (5.18), subject to (5.32), shows that the slope of $f(\beta,\pi^*) = 0$ is negative in the equilibrium point. One only has to refer to the signs of the partial derivatives resulting from (5.37) and (5.49). Of course, $f(\beta,\pi^*) = 0$ is the locus of all points in β,π^*-space for which flows to and from the unemployment insurance system are balanced. Points above (below) it imply positive (negative) balances of the fund.
9) This model has been described in detail in Glombowski/Krüger (1983)

model which coincides with the equilibrium profit share of the simplified version. The elements of the Jacobian become much simpler, i.e.

$$\left.\frac{\partial\dot{\pi}}{\partial\pi}\right|_0 = 0 \tag{5.51}$$

$$\left.\frac{\partial\dot{\pi}}{\partial\beta}\right|_0 = -a_2(1-\pi_0) = B' < 0 \tag{5.52}$$

$$\left.\frac{\partial\dot{\beta}}{\partial\pi}\right|_0 = ij\beta_0\pi_0^{j-1} = C' > 0 \tag{5.53}$$

$$\left.\frac{\partial\dot{\beta}}{\partial\beta}\right|_0 = -a_2\beta_0(j-\eta)(1-\pi_0)/\pi_0 = A' \tag{5.54}$$

It is obvious that local stability in this simplified case depends only on the sign of $j - \eta$. Comparing A' with A, one cannot exclude a priori that a stable system is rendered unstable by the introduction of an unemployment insurance system, nor can one exclude the opposite. We are afraid that we have to deal with different institutional cases separately or even have to resort to numerical examples.

The necessary condition for oscillations, i.e. $B'C' < 0$, holds throughout in the simplified case. Yet, again, this is not sufficient. Unfortunately we have been unable to detect a meaningful economic interpretation of the inequality

$$A'^2 < 4\,|B'C'|$$

which would assure a negative discriminant, or, in other words, a cyclical process around the equilibrium solution. Therefore, the question of a rising (declining) likelihood of cyclical accumulation of capital due to unemployment insurance systems in general cannot be answered here.

6. Summary

In this article we have studied some implications of unemployment insurance systems within the theory of cyclical growth. Our starting point was an investigation of various insurance systems such as the "Continental" and the "Anglo-Saxon" types, which have then been implemented into Goodwin's model of a growth cycle. It has been shown that the disequilibrium solution of Goodwin's original findings is preserved in an institutional setting in which capitalists contribute to the unemployment fund proportionally to their income (profits). The Continental case, however, gave rise to a locally unstable equilibrium solution. We proceeded by establishing a more general model of cyclical accumulation, allowing for variability of the degree of capacity utilization as well as for unbalanced budgets of the unemployment insurance system.

Special emphasis was given to the situation of a budget which is (only) balanced in the economic equilibrium position. It has been argued that in this case the impact of the institutional setting and the size of the insurance parameters will allow a great variety of possible outcomes.

References

Glombowski,J./Krüger,M., On the Rôle of Distribution in Different Theories of Cyclical Growth, Research Memorandum, Tilburg University 1983

Goodwin,R.M., A Growth Cycle, in: Hunt,E.K./Schwartz,J.G., (Eds.), A Critique of Economic Theory, Harmondsworth 1972, pp.442ff.

Gough,I., The Political Economy of the Welfare State, London and Basingstoke 1979

Kalecki,M., Selected Essays on the Dynamics of the Capitalist Economy 1933 - 1970, Cambridge 1971

Reuten,G., Unemployment Payments and the Course of the Depression, Research Memorandum No. 7913, University of Amsterdam 1979

Roemer,J.E., Analytical Foundations of Marxian Economic Theory, Cambridge 1981

A GENERALIZATION OF R. GOODWIN MODEL WITH RATIONAL BEHAVIOR OF ECONOMIC AGENTS

R. Balducci*, G. Candela*, G. Ricci**

*Facoltà di Economia e Commercio, Università degli Studi di Bologna

**Facoltà di Economia e Commercio, Università degli Studi di Modena

1. Introduction

1.1. — In 1967, R. Goodwin put forth a mathematical model[1] aimed at capturing the fluctuating dynamics of the fundamental macroeconomic variables of a capitalistic system. From an economic point of view, the cycle is the natural effect of the intrinsic contradictions of capitalism[2], from a mathematical point of view, it is a property of the well-known Lotka-Volterra differential equations[3]. This model has brought about many theoretical contributions[4] and some empirical applications[5].

As is well known, Goodwin's model is based on technologic, demographic and economic hypotheses that generate an oscillating movement around a steady state equilibrium of the macroeconomic variables. These fluctuations are permanent and uniform; the model therefore gives us an endogenous explanation of both growth and cycle.

In this paper we mean to go back to the original content of Goodwin's model[6] studying whether the cyclical motion is caused by the myopic behavior of the agents

---

[1] R.M. Goodwin (6).

[2] We can say that Goodwin's model links K. Marx and J.A. Schumpeter's theories. The model is marxian because it is based on social conflicts (see R. Goodwin (6), p. 54: "This paper attempts to give more precise form to an idea of Marx's-that it can be explained by the dynamic interaction of profits, wages and unemployment", but it is as well schumpeterian because the cycle is not the pathological consequence of a conflictual system, but a physiological need for the survival of an evolutive system (again in Goodwin's work (7), p. 13 "La mia tesi è che la struttura propria del capitalismo costituisce un meccanismo omeodinamico che funziona in base a variazione delle quote distributive").

[3] V. Volterra (24), A.J. Lotka (14) and also L. von Bertalanffy (3).

[4] For a concise treatment of the literature see R. Balducci and G. Candela (1) and the listed bibliography.

[5] See A. Vercelli (23), C. Frateschi (5), R. Balducci and C. Candela (2), M. Desai (4).

[6] With J.M. Keynes (12), p. 277: "A study of the history of opinion is a necessary preliminary to the emancipation of the mind. I do not know which makes a man more conservative - to know nothing but the present, or nothing but the past", we think that periodically going back to the origin of an economic problem may be a significant and fruitful intellectual exercise.

that do not learn from experience the uselessness of the fluctuations around a constant mean value, or whether it occurs even under an assumption of rational behavior of the agents.

We shall look for the solution of this problem using the theory of non-cooperative differential games[7].

The analysis of optimal behavior within dynamic models can be found in literature either in growth models, as in Lancaster (13), Hoel (10), Pohjola (18), or in cyclical models as Selten-Güth (20), and Mehrling (16). In all these contributions the state variables paths are determined by some optimality criteria.

In particular Selten-Güth (20) analyze a problem very similar to ours (they determine optimal values for the parameters of a bargaining function[8]) using, however, a linear[9] dynamic model. On the contrary, Mehrling (16) considers (as we do) a non-linear dynamic model, but he does not determine endogenously the optimal values of the parameters which appear in the equations of the model.

The criterion functions we assume are unusual in economic literature: we will not maximize the consumption of the players, or some more general utility functions; we will rather formulate a preference function for each player based on the common target to drop off the undesirable periodic fluctuations. We will discuss extensively this point later on.

1.2. — The analytic structure of 1967 Goodwin model can be formalized by a system of non-linear differential equations describing the motion of the fundamental variables $U(t)$ = employment rate, and $V(t)$ = workers' income share:

$$\dot{U}(t) = \psi_1(V(t),a)\, U(t)$$

$$\dot{V}(t) = \psi_2(U(t),b)\, V(t)$$

where we indicate $dx(t)/dt$ by $\dot{x}(t)$ and were a and b stand for known, constant and exogenous vector of parameters.

---

[7] See K. Velupillai (22), p. 257: "An even more important, and perhaps more interesting direction in which to proceed would be to make explicit the nature of conflicting and complementary nature of the relationship between capital and labour. The most elegant way, within the framework of dynamical system, would be to use differential game".

[8] Selten-Güth contribution uses a dynamic system very similar to Hansen-Samuelson-Hicks multiplier-accelerator model; see J. Hicks (9) and P. Samuelson (19).

[9] For the mathematical differences among linear and non-linear dynamic models see H.R. Varian (21), and for the corresponding economic interpretations see A. Medio (15), p. 13: "In particolare, è noto che un sistema di equazioni differenziali lineari non può rappresentare fluttuazioni persistenti — cioè fluttuazioni che non siano né esplosive né smorzate. In altri termini un sistema dinamico lineare non può fornire una corretta idealizzazione matematica dei cicli economici reali".

The non-trivial critic point N of this system is a center and the integral curves are closed around N; these results derive from the fact that the trace of the Jacobian of ψ_1 and ψ_2 vanishes at N. This formulation presents both a problem and a fascinating property. The problem is that some component values of vectors a and b are constant and fixed from outside[10]. The steady state solution (U*, V*): $\psi_1(V, a) = 0$, $\psi_2(U, b) = 0$ and the qualitative form of the integral curves thus depend on some unexplained and constant parameters of the behavior equations, that can only be interpreted as simple rules of thumb (such as: all the profits are saved and reinvested) or better as hystorical categories[11].

But, if the decision makers, reacting to the oscillations above and below constant mean values, use strategies which are functions of the economic situation, the parameters will become either time varying or state factor dependent. The dynamic equations will be modified as

$$\dot{U}(t) = \psi_1 \,(V(t),\, a(U(t),\, V(t))\,) \,.\, U(t)$$

$$\dot{V}(t) = \psi_2 \,(U(t),\, b(U(t),\, V(t))\,) \,.\, V(t)$$

Therefore the coefficient matrix trace of the linearized part will be different from zero; the critic point will not be a center and the integral curves will not be necessarily closed orbits.

To see whether Goodwin's conclusions are robust, one must indicate precisely the decision process[12]. But in doing so we still want to keep the very convenient and fascinating property of the original structure, i.e. the possibility of obtaining explicitly the expressions of the integral curves[13].

---

10 "Yet the model and its extensions remain ad hoc since the underlying model of behavioural equations has not been elucidated", see P. Mehrling (16), p. 1.

11 For a similar interpretation of the parameters entering theoretical models see M. Kalecki (11), p. 117 "Da dove vengono presi questi valori? Le considerazioni svolte danno una risposta a questa domanda. Questi valori dei parametri sono il risultato di decisioni di periodi precedenti, grazie alle quali l'economia è stata indirizzata verso una intensità di capitale corrispondente al valore di k, o verso un periodo di utilizzazione corrispondente al valore di a. I parametri fondamentali, pertanto, sono categorie storiche: i loro valori dipendono da decisioni prese (...) molti anni prima" (italics are ours).

12 One can analyse the players behavior using two different points of view: a) look for the macroeconomic fundations of the aggregated model, assuming rationality both in workers and capitalists (see p. Mehrling (16)); b) consider as homogenous the two classes (see K. Lancaster (13)).

13 See A. Medio (15), pp. 16-17: "Un caso analiticamente piuttosto interessante è costituito dal modello di Goodwin del 1967, che nella sua forma matematica costituisce uno degli esempi molto rari di equazioni differenziali non lineari che possono essere integrate esattamente. Ciò ovviamente pone limiti piuttosto stretti alla possibilità di migliorare la qualità del modello da un punto di vista economico, senza distruggere la semplicità della sua soluzione matematica".

The aim of this paper is to establish conditions of robustness for Goodwin dynamic properties, maintaining most of the original algebraic structure, which to us represents a good compromise between reality approximation and analytic solvability.

We have used differential game tools in order to get qualitative and quantitative results for the parameters entering the two relationships wage-employment and saving-profits.

In section 2 we have performed a log change in the state variables. In section 3, a two-person non-cooperative differential game will be sketched out, defining two players: capitalists and workers; the strategic or control variables that the players have at their disposal; and the goals they pursue.

In section 4 a Nash solution is obtained and discussed. When the game is planned out in a finite time horizon, the optimal paths of strategic variables are defined by a system of four non-linear differential equations, which cannot be solved analytically. However, when the time horizon is extended to infinity and the extremal steady state is computed, the optimal paths of the strategic variables tend asymptotically to the players' desired paths. In this case a growth cycle still remains around a stationary equilibrium obtained taking only one target for each player.

Finally, the aim of section 5 is to compute a Stackelberg's solution of the differential game; i.e., a game in which one player is leader and plans out his strategy taking into account the possible reactions of the other decision-maker.

2. The model

To help reading, we give the list of variables and parameters:

Q = real aggregate output or income,

N = labor supply,

L = employment,

a = Q/L = average labor productivity,

w = real wage rate,

k = capital output ratio, exogenous and constant,

s = percentage of saving from profits,

S = parameter measuring the demand for real wage increase related to the rate of unemployment, and $S°$ is the increase demand independent of U,

U = $L/N = Q/aN$ = employment rate,

V = $wL/Q = w/a$ = workers share of income,

$x_1 = -\ln U$ and $\dot{x}_1 = -(\ln U)' = -\dot{U}/U$

$x_2 = -\ln V$ and $\dot{x}_2 = -(\ln V)' = -\dot{V}/V$

Further variables will be explained in the text when used.

By definition of the state variables U and V, we get respectively:

1 $\dot{U}/U = \dot{Q}/Q - \dot{a}/a - \dot{N}/N$

2 $\dot{V}/V = \dot{w}/w - \dot{a}/a$

Let's assume that workers do not save and capitalsts save and invest the percentage s of their profits, and that the capital output ration k is constant, then the rate of growth of the output will be:

3 $$\dot{Q}/Q = s(1-V)/k \sim \frac{s}{k}(-\ln V) = \frac{s}{k}x_2$$

Moreover we assume that the rate of change of the real wage depends on the labor's bargaining power, approximately measured by the unemployment ratio:

4 $\dot{w}/w = S° - S\,(1-U) \sim S° - S(-\ln U) = S° - Sx_1$

Assume that the rate of labor supply growth and the rate of labor augmenting change are constant:

5 $\dot{N}/N = n$

6 $\dot{a}/a = m$

then the substitution of the behavioral and technological equations 3, 4, 5, 6 in the definitions 1 and 2, leads to

1a $$\dot{x}_1 = -\frac{s}{k}x_2 + (m+n)$$

2a $$\dot{x}_2 = Sx_1 - (S°-m)$$

The system of two differential equations 1a, 2a is nothing else than the 1967 Goodwin model with the only difference of assuming the saving propensity smaller than or equal to unity. Then it describes conservative oscillations (closed orbits) around a stable equilibrium defined by

1b $x_1^* = (S° - m)/S$ with $S° > m$

2b $x_2^* = k(m+n)/s$

3. The dynamic game

3.1. — To give a complete formulation of a dynamic game one has to specify a) the dynamic state equations (as we did in the previous section); b) the number of players (2 in our case); c) the stategies set; d) the equilibrium or solution concept; e) the informations structure for each player (we shall assume that both players have access to an open loop σ-algebra of information to avoid any problem about informational non-uniqueness of solutions); f) a criterion function for each player.

3.2. — Since Goodwin's model is intended to formalize marxian dynamics of a competitive capitalism, the players are naturally identified in the two antagonistic classes: capitalists and workers; both will be considered as homogeneous groups with distinct targets[14]. From now on indexes 1 and 2 will indicate respectively workers and capitalists.

The dynamic system 1a, 2a contains two state variables x_1, x_2 and six parameters.

Among these the capital output ratio k, the productivity growth rate m and the labor force growth rate n are assumed constant and exogenously given. Furtermore, for the sake of simplicity, the intercept S° in eq. 4 is also assumed as constant.

According to Goodwin's interpretation of capitalism, the strategic variable of player 2 is the percentage of profits to be reinvested: $u_2=s$; while the strategic variable of player 1 is the intensity $u_1=S$ of claimed wages increase.

The model can be written in game format as

$$7 \qquad \dot{x}_1 = -\frac{1}{k}u_2x_2 + (m+n)$$

$$8 \qquad \dot{x}_2 = u_1x_1 - (S°-m)$$

The strategies for the two players are constrained by $0 < u_1$, $0 \leqslant u_2 \leqslant 1$.

The next step is to formalize reasonable targets for the "scenario" we are dealing with.

3.3. — In economic literature we can find several examples of differential games applied to aggregate dynamic models. We only mention here the original paper by Lancaster (13) and the subsequent contribution by Hoel (10) because they compare equilibrium solution obtained in a conflicting framework and in a cooperative one. They look for a Nash equilibrium of a finite horizon differential game where capitalists and workers behave in order to maximize their consumption. Compared to our

14 In this paper we agree with K. Lancaster (13), p. 1094, n. 1: "The approach of this paper is marxian in the sense that it treats workers as a homogeneous group with a common outlook and capitalists as another homogeneous group".
Under these assumptions the problem can be imbedded in a non-cooperative game framework.
One can also introduce coalitions but in this situation Goodwin model analytic structure has to be modified, see R. Balducci, G. Candela (1).

work, the main differences are the following. First of all Lancaster deals with only one differential equation in a model of pure accumulation with fixed technology, while we analyze a system of two differential equations generating a cyclical growth. Furthermore, in Lancaster (13) the workers control their share of income and, therefore, the maximum speed of accumulation, but they let capitalists decide the percentage of profits which is to be reinvested.

In equation 7 and 8 the accumulation process is correlated to the wage share because of the relationship (Phillips curve) between wage dynamics and unemployment rate.

Much closer to our work is an unpublished paper by Mehrling (16) where Goodwin's model is considered. One of Mehrling's main goals is to check whether the macroeconomic relations of the model (as Phillips curve and the assumption of complete profits reinvestment) are consistent with optimizing behaviors of the agents. He look for a Nash solution of a non-cooperative game where workers, assuming the employment rate as constant (but with a justification not fully convincing) and controlling the rate of change of income shares, maximize their consumption over an infinite time horizon; while capitalists, assuming the income shares as constant and controlling the employment rate, maximize their profits again over an infinite time horizon.

Turns out that the Nash solution implies the maximum wage rate increase (related to employment rate through the Phillips curve) and the maximum employment rate corresponding to complete profits reinvestment (s=1).

In other words, following optimal Nash strategies the economy moves according to the Goodwin equations which therefore can be interpreted as a result of agents' rational behaviors[15].

3.4. — However, it is well known that the constant amplitude of the periodic solutions of Goodwin's model depends upon the initial conditions.

Assuming diminishing marginal utility of consumption, it is easy to verify that orbits characterized by a small amplitude are better for both players than orbits with a large amplitude[16]. The center, being an orbit with null amplitude, is therefore the best of all possible situations. It is then interesting to investigate whether rational behaviors of the decision makers can lead the constant fluctuations of the model to a stop and guide the economy towards the steady state is Paréto optimal.

---

[15] However, in Mehrling's paper the two players do not use a same dynamic model and what generates the results is the differential structure of the strategies constraints.

[16] The same may be true when future consumption is discounted at a positive rate, in this case however the starting point of the cycle becomes decisive.

In other words, we shall assume that the players want to eliminate the fluctuations of the distributive shares and the unemployment rate. This goals is not only consistent with Mehrling's assumption of consumption maximization, but can be intended as a complement of that hypotesis.

3.5. — Therefore, given the desired steady state (x_j^i; i,j = 1,2), the objective functions of the i-th (i = 1,2) player are built up in terms of deviations between actual and desiderd values of the state variables.

We can approximate these deviations using the steady state relationships between state variables and control variables.

From 1b and 2b we have:

$$x_1^i = \frac{S°-m}{u_1^i}, \quad x_2^i = \frac{k(m+n)}{u_2^i}$$

From the identities

$$x_1 - x_1^i = x_1 \left(1 - \frac{x_1^i}{x_1}\right), \quad x_2 - x_2^i = x_2 \left(1 - \frac{x_2^i}{x_2}\right)$$

we easily get

$$x_1 - x_1^i = x_1 \left(1 - \frac{S°-m}{u_1^i} \frac{u_1}{S°-m}\right) = x_1 \left(\frac{u_1^i - u_1}{u_1}\right) \cong x_1 (u_1^i - u_1) = x_1 \ \phi_1^i (u_1)$$

$$x_2 - x_2^i = x_2 \left(1 - \frac{k(m+n)}{u_2^i} \frac{u_2}{k(m+n)}\right) = x_2 \left(\frac{u_2^i - u_2}{u_2}\right) \cong x_2 (u_2^i - u_2) = x_2 \ \phi_2^i (u_2)$$

Thus deviations in state variables can be replaced by deviations in strategic variables. Considering the squares of these deviations, we obtain the final structure of loss functions

$$9 \qquad J^i = 1/2 \int_0^T (x_1 \ \phi_1^i (u_1)^2 + x_2 \ \phi_2^i (u_2)^2) dt + F^i(x(T)) \qquad i=1,2$$

where the term $F^i(x(T))$ gives the cost associated by player i to final state.

4. The Nash solution

4.1. — Given the state dynamics 7, 8, the strategies u_1 and u_2 (with associated strategy sets U_1 and U_2) and the loss functions 9 we have got the following Nash solution[17]

10
$$u^*_1 = u_1^1 - p_2^1$$
$$u^*_2 = u_2^2 - p_1^2/k$$

where the costate variables p_j^i (i,j = 1,2) satisfy the system

$$\dot{p}_j^i = - \frac{\partial H^i}{\partial x_j}$$

Since the optimal Hamiltonians are affine functions w.r.t x_1 and x_2 we can find, for each player, a value function

11 $$V^i (x_1,x_2) = a_1^i x_1 + a_2^i x_2 + g^i \qquad i = 1,2$$

satisfying the Hamilton-Jacobi-Bellman partial differential equation

$$\frac{\partial V}{\partial t} = - H^i (x_1, x_2)$$

We observe that $p_j^i = \dfrac{\partial V^i}{\partial x_j} = a_j^i$ so that 10 take the form

12
$$u^*_1 = u_1^1 - a_2^1$$
$$u^*_2 = u_2^2 - a_1^2/k$$

The Hamilton canonical equation can be written as

---

17 We have used the Pontryagin minimun principle. the Hamiltonian functions for the problem are given by

$$H^i(x,p_1^i, p_2^i) = 1/2(x_1 (u_1^i - u_1)^2 + x_2 (u_2^i - u_2)^2) +$$
$$p_1^i (- 1/k\, u_2 x_2 + m+n) + p_2^i(u_1 x_1 - S° + m)$$

Therefore

$$\frac{\partial H^1}{\partial u_1} = x_1(u_1^i - u_1) - x_1 p_2^1$$

$$\frac{\partial H^2}{\partial u_2} = x_2(u_2^i - u_2) - x_2 p_2^1/k$$

$$\frac{\partial H^i}{\partial p_1^i} = \frac{\partial H^i}{\partial a_1^i} = \dot{x}_1 = -\frac{1}{k}(u_2^2 + \frac{1}{k} a_1^2) x_2 + (m+n)$$

13

$$\frac{\partial H^i}{\partial p_2^i} = \frac{\partial H^i}{\partial a_2^i} = \dot{x}_2 = (u_1^1 - a_2^1) x_1 - (S° - m)$$

and[18]

14 $$-\frac{\partial H^i}{\partial x_j} = \dot{p}_j^i = \dot{a}_j^i = f_j^i \, (a_1^1, a_2^1, a_1^2, a_2^2)$$

The four nonlinear differential equations system 14 cannot be solved explicitly but only numerically; thus we get functional form neither for strategies nor for state vector.

4.2. — In order to obtain some more qualitative informations about the time paths of the Nash strategies we let T go to + ∞. We need the following

DEFINITION[19]: "An extremal steady state (ESS) is a vector[20]

$$z = [\, x_1 \; x_2 \; a_1^1 \; a_2^1 \; a_1^2 \; a_2^2 \,]'$$

which is a stationary solution of Hamilton canonical equation, i.e.

$$\dot{x}_j = 0 \qquad\qquad j = 1,2$$

$$\dot{a}^i_j = 0 \qquad\qquad i = 1,2$$

In other words an ESS is a stationary equilibrium both for state and for co-

---

18 where

$$f_1^1 = 1/2\,(a_2^1)^2 - u_1^1 \, a_2^1$$

$$f_2^1 = -\left[1/2(u_2^2 - u_2^1)^2 + \frac{1}{k} a_1^2 (u_2^2 - u_2^1) + \frac{1}{2k^2} (a_1^2)^2 - \frac{1}{k} u_2^2 \, a_1^1 - \frac{1}{k} a_1^2 a_1^1 \right]$$

$$f_2^2 = \frac{1}{k} u_2^2 a_1^2 + \frac{1}{2k^2} (a_1^2)^2$$

$$f_1^2 = -\left[1/2(u_1^1 - u_1^2)^2 - a_2^1 (u_1^1 - u_1^2) + 1/2(a_2^1)^2 + u_1^1 a_2^2 - u_1^1 a_2^1 a_2^2 \right]$$

19 Cfr. A. Haurie-G. Leitman (8)

20 Remember that in our case $p_j^i = a_j^i$ $(i,j = 1,2)$

state variables[21].

It is easy to check that an extremal steady state exists and is unique; its components are given by

$$x_1 = \frac{S^\circ - m}{u_1^1}$$

$$x_2 = \frac{k(m+n)}{u_2^2}$$

15 $$a_1^1 = \frac{k}{2} \frac{(u_2^1 - u_2^2)^2}{u_2^2}$$

$$a_2^1 = 0$$

$$a_1^2 = 0$$

$$a_2^2 = -1/2 \frac{(u_1^1 - u_1^2)^2}{u_1^1}$$

The corresponding optimal strategies are

12 bis $$u_1^* = u_2^1 \qquad u_2^* = u_2^2$$

If we plug 12 bis in the dynamic system 1a, 2a we obtain

13 bis $$\dot{x}_1 = -\frac{1}{k} u_2^2 x_2 + (m+n) \qquad \dot{x}_2 = u_1^1 x_1 - (S^\circ - m)$$

We can note that each player's optimal strategy coincides with his desired stationary strategy so that the state equilibrium position

$$N^\circ \equiv \left(\frac{S^\circ - m}{u_1^1} ; \quad \frac{k(m+n)}{u_2^2} \right)$$

has its first component determined by player 1 and the second by player 2.

---

[21] Since state and costate variables are constant there is no reason for an economy to move from an ESS. We can say that a steady state is an equilibrium position while an extremal steady state is an optimal equilibrium position.

Going back to the original variables we can observe that the equilibrium value of the employment rate

$$U^* = e^{-x_1^*} = e^{-\frac{S^\circ - m}{u_1^1}}$$

is controlled by the workers; similary the equilibrium share of profits

$$1 - V^* = 1 - e^{-x_2^*} = 1 - e^{-\frac{S^\circ - m}{u_2^2}}$$

is controlled by the capitalists through their propensity to save. A tipical case is represented in Figure 1.

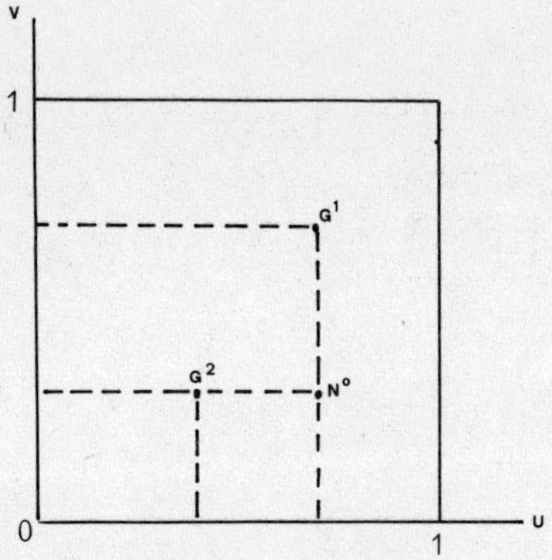

$G^1 \equiv (U^1, V^1)$
$G^2 \equiv (U^2, V^2)$
$N^\circ \equiv (U^1, V^2)$

Figure 1

Furthermore one can prove that ESS is not globally asymptotically stable. Finally, the dynamic system 13bis is linear and the trace of the coefficient matrix is equal to zero; therefore it has the same qualitative properties of the original model.

Thus we can conclude that fluctuations do not disappear but are centered at a point whose coordinates in state plane are rationally determined by using differential game tools.

Here are further properties of the fluctuations:

a) the oscillation period is given by

$$P = 2\pi \sqrt{k/u_1^1 u_2^2}$$

and depends upon the values of the target controls of the two players, the smaller these values are, the greater the period is;

b) the amplitude of the cycle is related to the distance between the initial position and the center $N^\circ(U^*,V^*)$, which implies that the amplitude will be smaller if the desired values of the classes are close to the initial values of the state variables.

4.3. — Taking as base of comparison the time paths of the optimal strategies and the state variables obtained for $T = +\infty$, it should be interesting to analyse how far or close the corresponding finite horizon optimal paths are.

Unfortunately we cannot prove any convergence result either for the optimal strategies or for the state vector time paths, but as a reasonable conjecture we can assume that such a limit behavior will occur. As a matter of fact, the trace of the system vanishes in both cases characterizing the critic point as a center. However such a critic point depends on time and so describes a curve in the phase plane.

We can also presume that there exists a band around the optimal integral curve $\mathcal{C}$ (namely, given an initial condition, the unique solution of the system 13bis), containing the solution of the system 13 for any T. These trajectories will eventually cross $\mathcal{C}$ more than once, as shown in figure 2. As the time t approaches T, the path will point towards or outwards the center depending on the relative weight of the final cost $F^i(x(T))$.

As a last comment we can observe that since the system 13 generates closed orbits, but around moving centers, we still have some sort of persistent ciclycity, which however is neither uniform nor constant.

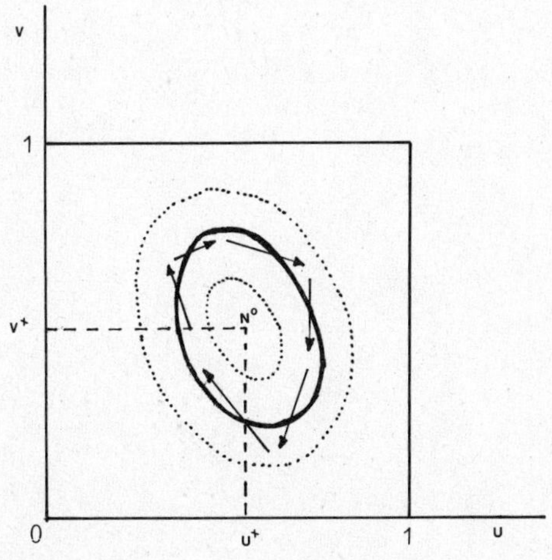

Figure 2

5. The Stackelberg solution

5.1. — So far we did not establish any hierarchy among the players qualifying the problem as a Nash game.

Even this assumption is common in a competing capitalistic system framework, we can list situations where hierarchycity is a more plausible hypothesis.

In order to complete our analysis of the non-cooperative differential game the Stackelberg equilibrium solution will be now determined and commented.

First we observe that the problem formulated in section 4 gives for the Stackelberg solution the same form obtained in Nash case; the reason has to be identified in the objective function structure, more precisely in the absence of cross terms between the strategies. The additive and separated form either in dynamics or in preference functions will not produce any difference between Nash and Stackelberg equilibrium solution.

5.2. — To obtain an autonomous Stackelberg solution we slightly modify the individual loss function introducing cross terms. However to keep the problem at a tractable analytic level we make two simplifying assumptions:

a) the leader expresses his preference function in terms of only one target value;

b) each control range is determined by the desired stationary values

$$0 \leq u_1^2 \leq u_1 \leq u_1^1$$

$$0 \leq u_2^2 \leq u_2 \leq u_2^1 \leq 1$$

Assumption a) allows to give a simpler formulation of leader criterion function; b) eliminates uncertainty in ϕ_j^i signs and permits to drop the squares in the differences. Because of a) the cross term in controls appears in the follower's criterion function.

If player 2 is leader[22] the loss functions take the following expressions[23]

18

$$J^1 = 1/2 \int_0^T x_2 \ \phi_1^1(u_1)^2 \cdot \phi_2^1(u_2)\,dt + F^1(x(T))$$

$$J^2 = \int_0^T x_2 \ \phi_2^2(u_2)\,dt + F^2(x(T))$$

---

[22] Since a symmetric situation occurs when player 1 is leader, we will not give the corresponding formulation.

[23] The square in the factor $\phi_1^1(u_1)$ is intended to differentiate its importance w.r.t. the deviation of the other player's strategy.

The meaning of these functions is quite simple; the leader (player 2) has an only explicit target: minimizing the difference between the realized and his desired profit share. On the other side, the follower (player 1) is trying to minimize either the wage share deviation and/or the employment rate deviation from their desired levels.

For any strategy announced by the leader the follower will chose his reaction minimizing his Hamiltonian function

$$H^1 = 1/2\ x_2 (u_1^1 - u_1)^2 \cdot (u_2^1 - u_2) + p_1^1(-u_2 x_2/k+m+n) + p_2^1(u_1 x_1 - S°+m)$$

getting

19 $$u_1 = u_1^1 - p_2^1 \frac{1}{u_2^1 - u_2} \frac{x_1}{x_2}$$

By assumption b) we conclude that p_2^1 can either vanish or be positive.

Case 1: $p_2^1 = 0$ [24]

The follower (being rational) will choose the constant strategy $u_1 = u_2^1$. Plugging this value in leader's Hamiltonian function

$$H^2 = x_2\ \phi_2^2(u_2) + p_1^2(- \frac{1}{k} u_2 x_2 + m+n) + p_2^2(u_1^1 x_1 - S°+m)$$

we observe that H^2 is linear w.r.t. u_2, it is decreasing if $p_1^2>k$ and this implies $u_2^* = u_2^1$; while if $p_1^2<k$ the function H^2 is increasing and therefore the optimal strategy for the leader becomes $u_2^* = u_2^2$.

Observing that p_2^2 is a not increasing[25] function of time we conclude that the

---

[24] The costate variable p_2^1 equal to 0 means that the follower gives null cost to variations of x_2; i.e. he is not interested in modifications of profit share. This conclusion does not seem reasonable but it is equally analysed because leads to the same results obtained in Nash solution.

[25] The Pontryagin necessary conditions for the leader's costate variable take the form

$$\dot{p}_1^2 = - \frac{\partial H^2}{\partial x_1} = - p_2^2 u_1^1;\ \dot{p}_2^2 = - \frac{\partial H^2}{\partial x_2} = - [(u_2 - u_2^2) - p_1^2 u_2/k]$$

and being p_2^2 greater or equal to 0 (to prove it one can use the same arguments for p_1^2) we get

$$\dot{p}_1^2 \leq 0$$

two alternatives will not exclude each other[26].

The Stackelberg equilibrium solution (u_1^1, u_2^1) is interesting because shows that being the leader is not always an advantage[27]. The other Stackelberg equilibrium solution (u_1^1, u_2^2) coincides with the Nash solution we obtained before. This is not surprising because the assumption $p_2^1 = 0$ cancels the correlation of players' strategies.

Case 2

The follower optimal strategy is defined by 19, which plugged in H^2 gives for the leader optimal strategy

$$20 \qquad u_2 = u_2^1 \pm \frac{x_1}{x_2} \sqrt{\frac{kp_2^1 p_2^2}{k - p_1^2}}$$

Taking $p_1^2<k$ [28] (to assure the square root to be real) and remembering assumption b) we obtain

$$21 \qquad u_2^* = u_2^1 - \frac{x_1}{x_2} \sqrt{\frac{kp_2^1 p_2^2}{k - p_1^2}}$$

We can see that the leader optimal strategy is expressed as a difference between follower desired value for u_2 and a term which is a function of state variables.

The corresponding follower optimal strategy takes the form

$$22 \qquad u_1^* = u_1^1 - p_2^1 \sqrt{\frac{k - p_1^2}{kp_2^1 p_2^2}}$$

which is not a function of state variables.

---

[26] The possibility of observing one or two constant strategies depends on the weight assigned to final state. If $F^2(x_1(T))>k$ we will necessarily have $p_1^2>k$, for any t, and therefore only one strategy will be feasible $u_2^* = u_2^1$; if $F^2(x_1(T))<k$ we will have, for t a neighbor of T, $p_1^2<k$ implying $u_2^* = u_2^2$, but for t sufficiently far from T we will have $p_1^2>k$ and thus $u_2^* = u_2^1$.

[27] In fact leadership does not necessarily means that one player is stronger but also that one player has to announce first his strategy giving more information to the follower.

[28] If $p_2^2 = 0$ then $u_2 = u_2^1$ and we get the results of case 1. The alternative $p_2^2<0$ is not realistic because it is equivalent to say that player 2 is not interested in the evolution of x_2 which is the only variable entering his criterion function. The assumption $p_1^2<k$ seems to be reasonable because x_1 does not enter player 2 objective function.

The dynamic system is now expressed by

$$\dot{x}_1 = x_1/k \sqrt{\frac{kp_2^1p_2^2}{k - p_1^2}} - u_2^1x_2/k + (m+n)$$

23

$$\dot{x}_2 = x_1 \quad u_1^1 - p_2^1 \sqrt{\frac{k - p_1^2}{kp_2^1p_2^2}} - (S^\circ - m)$$

The trace of the (linearized) system is equal to $\frac{1}{k} \sqrt{\frac{kp_2^1p_2^2}{k - p_1^2}} > 0$

and the determinant is equal to $u_2^1 \, (u_1^1 - p_2^1 \sqrt{\frac{k - p_1^2}{kp_2^1p_2^2}})/k > 0$;

the non-trivial critic point is an unstable point (node or focus). Thus, the peculiar property or original Goodwin's model of generating constant oscillations in state variables will disappear if we assume asymmetry among players.

Furthermore the critic point of the dynamic system depends on time and then it generates in phase plane a curve such that its points are repellors for the system trajectories. The situation which will occur is an irregular dynamics which has nothing to do with hypotheses of stationarity or almost stationarity.

We conclude this section by pointing out that, if effectively optimal strategies depend on the state vector, a more sophisticated hypothesis is possible. We can divide the positive orthant in four parts w.r.t. the Goodwin singular point, which we number I, II, III, IV moving clockwise from the origin.

In region I, both wage share and employment rate are low and in this part we could consider capitalists as leader; in region III, both wage share and employment rate are high and workers could be considered as leader; finally in region II and IV the two players could be both leaders (or followers) and then in these parts we need to look for a Nash equilibrium.

This exercise can produce further interesting results since it is carried out using an evolving model not only in the state variables but also in the strategic ones.

6. Conclusions

In this paper we have introduced a criterion of rationality in the decision process underlying Goodwin's model of 1967. This model has been proved to coincide with the ESS of a non-cooperative Nash game. This result has allowed to explicitly formulate two assumptions that were implicit in the original structure:

i) the model refers to a competitive capitalism with a symmetry among agents; if we disattend this condition, i.e. if we introduce a leadership among players, then the topological properties will be modified[29];

ii) the uniform cyclical motion is related to equilibrium and stationary values for the infinite horizon strategies.

Therefore the periodic and conservative fluctuation of Goodwin's dynamics is a property which is not dependent on irrational behaviors of players, but is rather a consequence of the conflicting elements proper of a pure capitalism. The cycle, then, seems to be a "modus vivendi" of bourgeoisie, generalizing in this manner Goodwin's original contribution.

Furthermore, our analysis gives an explanation of the mean values of the fluctuations (i.e. the coordinates of the critic point) and of the amplitude and period of the cycle, while in Goodwin's version those properties of the dynamics are functions of some parameters which only appear <u>criés par hasard</u>.

On the way we got some unexpected results. The 1967 model presents an economic dynamics with too high a degree of abstraction and simplification; this weakness has been emphasized by Goodwin himself during his present Italian period.

First of all, the "oscillating motion" generated by the differential equations do not have a conclusive empirical evidence. R. Goodwin says: "Si deve considerare il modello come una spiegazione elementare dei cicli durante il processo di crescita, ma non come una descrizione realistica dei cicli effettivi (...). Dal momento che la storia non si ripete, la teoria formale del ciclo non riesce a contenere tutta la verità"[30].

Moreover, Goodwin refers a second inconvenience of his model as regards to the irregular motion of a capitalist society: "Se dovessi riformulare la mia teoria (...) direi che non esiste alcun ciclo economico, il che è piuttosto sconvolgente, visto che si tratta del problema su cui ho passato la mia vita. Ma nessuna indagine statistica ha mai mostrato un ciclo economico. Tutto è così irregolare che non sopravvive ad alcun esperimento cui i matematici possono sottoporre i dati"[31].

In this line, the version of the model discussed in our paper presents two crucial properties.

i) If we do not consider any ESS situation, then the system dynamics does not show

---

29 As a matter of fact the Nash solution can be found as a particular case of a Stackelberg game formulation; but the condition leading to this situation is not really significant.

30 R. Goodwin (7), p. 15 and p. 18.

31 M. Palazzi (ed) (16), p. 38.

any cyclicity either constant or ripetitive; and even the singular point will behhave as a moving equilibrium point.

ii) Moreover abandoning the simmetry hypothesis among the agents, we end up in a completely irregular motion.

If we let the parameters wary w.r.t. time, then the "strait jacket" of the physic regularity of Goodwin's oscillations will get slack: the model parameters are endogenized becoming strategic variables in a non-cooperative differential game. This new setting make us find mathematical and economic justification for the corresponding structural changes.

REFERENCES

1. Balducci R., Candela G. (1982), Contrattazione salariale e ciclo economico, Roma, La Nuova Italia Scientifica.
2. Balducci R., Candela G. (1982), A model of Growth Cycle with its Applications to the Italian Case, in Economic Notes, n. 3.
3. Bertalanffy L. von (1977), Teoria generale dei sistemi, ISEDI, Milano.
4. Desai M., An Econometric Model of a Growth Cycle in the Share of Wages, U.K., 1855-1965, Forthcoming.
5. Frateschi C. (1979), Mercato del lavoro e distribuzione del reddito nella Germania Federale: un'applicazione del modello di Goodwin, in Note Economiche, n. 5.
6. Goodwin R. (1967), A Growth Cycle, in Socialism, Capitalism and Economic Growth, Essays presented to Maurice Dobb, edit., by C.H. Feinstein, Cambridge, pp. 54-58.
7. Goodwin R. (1982), Saggi di analisi economica dinamica, La Nuova Italia Scientifica, Roma.
8. Haurie A., Leitman G. (1981), On the global asymptotic stability of equilibrium solution for open loop differential games, Working Paper, Gerad, 8108, Montreal.
9. Hicks J. (1949), A Contribution to the Theory of Trade Cycle, Oxford University Press, N.Y.
10. Hoel M. (June 1978), Distribution and Growth as a Differential Game between Workers and Capitalists, in International Economic Review, pp. 335-350.
11. Kalecki M. (1963), Teoria dello sviluppo di un'economia socialista, Editori Riuniti, Roma, pp. 117; titolo originale: Zarys teorii wzrostu gospodarki socjalistycznej, PWN, Warsawa, 1963.
12. Keynes J.M. (1972), The End of Laissez-faire, The Collected Writing, vol. IX, Essay in Persuasion, Mac Millan Press, London.
13. Lancaster K. (December 1973), The Dymanic Inefficiency of Capitalism, in Journal of Political Economy, pp. 1092-1109.
14. Lotka A.J., Elements of Mathematical Biology, N.Y., Dover Pu., 1956.
15. Medio A. (1979), Teoria non lineare del ciclo, Il Mulino, Bologna.
16. Mehrling P., The game Theoretical Foundations of a Classical Model of Class Struggle, forthcoming, London School of Economics, March 1983.
17. Palazzi M. (a cura di), Intervista a un economista Richard M. Goodwin, Clueb, Bologna, 1982, p. 38.
18. Pohjola M. (March 1983), Workers' investment funds and the dynamic inefficiency of capitalism, in Journal of Public Economics, n. 2.
19. Samuelson P. (1939), Interaction between Multiplier Analysis and the Principle of Acceleration, in Review of Economic Statistic, pp. 75-78.
20. Selten R., Güth W., Game Theoretical Analysis of Wage Bargaining in a Sample

Business Cycle Model, in Journal of Mathematical Economics, n. 10, pp. 177-195.

21. Varian H.R. (1981), Dynamic System, in Handbook of Mathematics, K.J. Arrow and H.D. Intrilligator (edited by), North-Holland, Oxford.
22. Velupillai K, (1982), When Workers Save and Invest: Some Kaldorian Dynamics, in Nationalekonomie, n. 3.
23. Vercelli A. (1977), The Phillips Dilemma: A New Suggested Approach, in Economic Notes, vol. VI, n. 1.
24. Volterra V. (1928), Variations and Fluctuations of the Number of Individuals in Animals Species Living Together, in Journal du conseil International pour l'exploration de la mer, vol. III, n. 1.

DISAGGREGATING MODELS OF FLUCTUATING GROWTH

R. M. Goodwin
University of Siena

Aggregative models, including my own, are less than totally satisfactory; they are useful in helping to conceptualize and as preliminary skirmishes prior to elaboration in disaggregative form. Furthermore qualitative, as distinct from quantitative, analysis is desirable.

By the use of an economic potential one obtains a simple geometry of system dynamics. This can be further simplified by generalized coordinates. A single, aggregative, nonlinear labour market can then be used to drive all the sectors of the economy. A capital stock matrix provides an accelerator which makes the economy unstable for high levels of output. In this way it is possible to explain how more or less steady technical progress can become converted into fluctuating growth.

A fundamental necessity is a mechanism for the propagation of impulses to the various parts of the economy. As a transfer mechanism consider all sectoral transactions which are systematically dependent on the level of sectoral outputs: for large systems this dependence must be linear. Define an Economic Potential as a function of n prices and n quantities:

$$V(p,q) = \langle p \rangle [I - A] \{q\} = pq - pAq \,.$$

Thus, as different from classical mechanics, we have a bilinear form, with a matrix that is not symmetrical: it is a scalar equation yielding net national product; it also is a nonlinear function, a fact commonly, and with good reason, ignored by economists. Thanks to the ingenious vonNeumann, we can dissolve it into the dual linear forms:

$$\text{Supply less Demand} = \text{Gradient}_p V = [I - A]\{q\} \,,$$

and

$$\text{Price less Cost} = \text{Gradient}_q V = \langle p \rangle [I - A] \,.$$

A striking simplification arises if we transform to linear generalized coordinates, with n eigengoods, n eigenprices, n eigenvalues. Since the matrix is, in principle, empirical, none of the special problems arise, except for decomposability, which can be dealt with by solving for, in sequence, indecomposable subsets. Therefore an existing technology can be used to define a principal axis transformation h which yields the canonical form

$$[h][I - A][h]^{-1} = [\underline{I - \lambda}],$$

where the λ's are the n distinct eigenvalues, λ_1 to λ_r being real, and λ_s to λ_n complex. (Bar under indicates a diagonal matrix). Since the complex eigenvalues occur in conjugate pairs, $\alpha \pm i\beta$, we can transform to block diagonality in the purely real form $\begin{bmatrix} \alpha & -\beta \\ \beta & \alpha \end{bmatrix}$, where the α's determine stability, and the

β's the oscillations. If a system, not empirical, has the result of purely imaginary roots, then we get $\begin{bmatrix} 0 & -\beta \\ \beta & 0 \end{bmatrix}$. It was in this form that I defined, intentionally, my original model, with the questionable aim of clarifying the cyclical aspect, and leaving the more usual stability problem for elaboration of the model. Every physicist knows that this simple harmonic motion is best for explaining what oscillation is and how, why, and when it arises. He is also aware that it is never found in practice.

By separating variables, the complications of inter dependence have been removed, without being ignored, since when transforming back the solutions, they are taken account of. The result is the splendidly simple dual quadratic potentials:

$$V_p(p) = \tfrac{1}{2}p\left[\underline{I - \lambda}\right] p \quad ; \quad V_q(q) = \tfrac{1}{2}q\left[\underline{I - \lambda}\right] q,$$

yielding the basis for gradient dynamics:

$$\text{Grad } V_p = \langle(1 - \lambda_1)p_1, \ldots\ldots\ldots\ldots\ldots\ldots, (1 - \lambda_n)p_n\rangle, \text{ and}$$

$$\text{Grad}V_q = \begin{Bmatrix} (1 - \lambda_1)q_1 \\ \vdots \\ (1 - \lambda_n)q_n \end{Bmatrix}.$$

These two elliptic basins have always positive gradients, except at their unique equilibrium singular points. The gradients are all orthogonal (zero inner products) with all level surfaces for all constant economic potentials. Since all existing economies produce more than they consume in producing, we have, with the help of Frobenius, that $0 < |\lambda_i| < 1$ for all sectors. Therefore with the usual, simplest dynamical assumption, these are basins of attraction, providing the invaluable qualitative result that the transfer mechanism is asymptotically stable for both monotonic and oscillatory motions, i.e.

$$-\gamma\, \dot{q}_i/q_i = (1 - \lambda_i) = \delta\, \dot{p}_i/p_i \,.$$

There may be, but need not be, as many reversals of direction as there are real roots. So the system, undisturbed, goes skiiing down these slopes, zig-zaging and looping in a very complicated path, each sector following a different linear combination of all the constituent motions.

The point about this linear transfer mechanism is that it is what its name implies: it is equilibrium seeking (analogous to maximizing entropy) and thus transfers to each sector, in different ways, a tendency to the stationary solutions beloved of so many economists. Even though it may contain many constituent cycles, they are minor ripples, out of phase with one another, and rapidly dissipated amongst the sectors. What it does not do is to produce the generalized, alternating motions , affecting, though in varying degrees, all or most of the sectors: it is not an oscillator, a generator of cycles: for that we need other, nonlinear relations. Being stable, it will not generate growth either. Hence whilst we must disaggregate, since the economy consists of quite inhomogeneous parts, nonetheless it is necessary to search for macro-dynamic sources of growth cycles.

With valuation separated from output, there is no problem of invariant measure; eigenoutputs are meaured interms of own inputs, likewise wages, and eigenprices, so that profits are the differences between costs and prices in the same units. The meaurement of the real wage and rate of profit presents no problem. To reduce the system to simplest essentials, assume: constant prices, money wage rates being real, all wages and no profits consumed, operating profit, Π, equal to investment and growth. Then

$$\Pi_i = \dot{q}_i/q_i = 1 - \lambda_i - a_{\ell i} w_i = 1 - u_i - \lambda_i$$

where u_i is real unit wage cost and also share of labour.

$$\dot{u}_i/u_i = \dot{w}_i/w_i - \bar{g}_{ai}$$

where g_{ai} is the constant rate of decrease in labour input.

$\dot{w}_i/w_i = \bar{\mu}_i v_i - \gamma_i$ with $v_i = l_i/N_i$, the ratio of employment to labour force available, which grows at a constant rate $\bar{g}_{Ni}$, so that $\dot{v}_i/v_i = \dot{q}_i/q_i - (\bar{g}_{ai} + \bar{g}_{Ni})$. Hence

$$\dot{u}_i/u_i = \mu_i v_i - (\bar{\gamma}_i + \bar{g}_{ai});$$

$$\dot{v}_i/v_i = -u_i + (1-\lambda_i) - (\bar{g}_{ai} + \bar{g}_{Ni}).$$

Therefor we may write the whole system as

$$\begin{Bmatrix} \dot{u}/u \\ \dot{v}/v \end{Bmatrix} = \begin{bmatrix} [0] & [\underline{\mu}] \\ -[I] & [0] \end{bmatrix} \begin{Bmatrix} u \\ v \end{Bmatrix} + \begin{Bmatrix} -(\gamma + g_a) \\ (1-\lambda) - (g_a + g_N) \end{Bmatrix}$$

Thus, in deviations from equilibrium, there are n <u>pairs</u> of equations of the form $\begin{bmatrix} 0 & +\mu \\ -1 & 0 \end{bmatrix}$, which are easily recognizable as pure harmonic oscillators, stable but not asymptotically so. We may visualize the behaviour by considering any of the i pairs of equations and from them form a torus, the ensemble forming an n-fold torus. If the periods of one or more of these cycles form an irrational ratio, the motion of the system will be erratic, never repeating. It is of great importance that these cycles do not derive in any way from any complex eigenvalues of the productive technology: they derive from the whole set of interelationships. Thus all sectors will tend to move up and down together, though in highly diverse ways. Complicating the system by adding block diagonal terms will render it stable structurally and determine the dynamical stability. There are various relations which may make the system locally unstable, whilst global stability is guaranteed by, $v_i \leq 1$. This barrier or boundary will be approached gradually, thus constituting a nonlinearity.

A Related Alternative Model

It is quite likely that so complicated a system as the economy will not be capable of satisfactory explanation by any one model. In pursuit of this notion, I propose another model, shaped in a rather different way. One of the fundamental ways of conceptualizing an oscillator is to consider it as a frequency convertor. Many economists accept that Schumpeter's idea of innovatory technical progress is basic to capitalism. The problem is, however, how can technical progress, which consists not only of one centralidea but of thousands of smaller improvements, and hence approximates to a steady flow, how or why does it get bunched into 'swarms'. A good example of this is given by the ingenious, classical invention of the Roman fountain. It consists of a cistern fed by a stream or aqueduct with a steady but not necessarily constant, flow of water. In the cistern is implanted a syphon which feeds the fountain. When the cistern is nearly full, the syphon is primed and the cistern empties with a rapid flow , the flow ceasing until the cistern is refilled. The mechanism converts a steady flow into an oscillation of constant period, a period which, however, will vary if the rate of inflow varies.

Subject to restriction to constant prices, it is possible to determine from the capital stock-output ratio matrix B, a real demand function for each type of durable capital equipment by sector and per unit of all other sectors. Define $[p][B][p]^{-1} = [\beta]$. For any output vector this gives the required capital stock, $[\beta]\{q\}$, and hence desired capacity. Assuming the strict accelerator with capacity maintained equal to desired capacity, $I(t) = [\beta]\{\dot{q}\}$. Then the dynamical multiplier is given by

$$[\underline{\varepsilon}]\{\dot{q}\} = -[I - A]\{q\} + [\beta]\{\dot{q}\} + D(t),$$

where D(t) is all other real demands. B will have many zeros but some, and perhaps all, row sums multiplied by $\dot{q}_i$ will be larger than, ε_i, $0 < \varepsilon_i < 1$. Therefore the dynamical transfer equation is bifurcated from stable to unstable behaviour, since

$$[[\beta] - [\underline{\varepsilon}]]\{\dot{q}\} = [I - A]\{q\} - \{D(t)\}.$$

Because some or all $[[\beta] - [\underline{\varepsilon}]]\{\dot{q}\} > 0$, the motion becomes proportional to the gradients, thus being away from, not towards, the equilibrium point, $\hat{q} = [I - A]^{-1}D$. This is a disaggregated specification of the fundamental Harrod proposition that growth of the economy is inherently unstable, and hence <u>never</u> steady.

As $v = 1/n \rightarrow 1$, the economy is in a dynamical state which cannot persist, since v must be less than or equal to unity. The economy necessarily decelerates: however, the accelerator only operates with the expectation that future growth will be at least as great as present growth; any deceleration destroys the expectations upon which the accelerational investment is based. Therefore, in the pure case, as the economy decelerates, $\beta \dot{q} \to 0$ and the economy again becomes stable in a basin of attraction around $\hat{q}$.

The economy consequently descends in a complicated manner towards whatever level is determined by D(t), the exogenous real demands. There the economy remains until some exogenous change occurs. In economic cycle theory it is not difficult to explain the upper turning point; the real trouble comes with the lower one. Why should anyone invest when there is ample excess capacity in almost all sectors? The only satisfactory answer to this problem lies in Schumpeter's concept of innovational investment, which precisely is independent of existing capacity (some of which will be destroyed). The conversion of a steady stream of innovations into intermittent bursts of investment and subsequent relaxation, is to be explained by the feedback of effective demand through the transfer function, both in its stable and unstable forms. A small innovation may exhaust itself with little effect; a larger one may excite a stocks cycle and thus be somewhat expanded and prolonged. If, however, the innovational outlay is large, it may carry the economy back to the region of pre-existing capacity: then, independently of D(t), the economy will be swept up to the region of full employment. I should add that, in spite of prolonged efforts on my part, Schumpeter firmly and totally rejected this elaboration of his theory. He was deeply influenced by Marxian analysis, and, like Marx, made it plain that technical progress was not merely an influnce on the behaviour of the system, but was rather a transformation of its structure, so that not only did it enforce a change of direction, but the system itself emerged as a new and different organism. Thus the problem must be envisaged not only in terms of an altered effective demand but, much more fundamental, the creation of a new economic form---morphogenesis. It is not a simple case of parametric variation; a new good or a new process, like a new species, constitutes a different system. By contrast with previous economies, one of the differentia specifica of laissez-faire capitalism is the potent harnessing of human greed to the generation of new forms of production (fuelled and made possible, of course, by the extraordinary development of natural science). Capitalism enables such changes of inherited ways of working and living to be carried out in ruthless disregard of the effects on those involved.

The consequence is that we are not studying simply the impact on a given mechanism of repeated shocks: the transfer mechanism itself is altered. Consider, for example, a new method of energy production: if profitable, it will be carried out even with existing prices and capacities: the required investment will shift the equilibrium point and when that investment is completed, the new technology will also determine a different equilibrium, so that the system is in disequilibrium. The price and cost of power will fall, which means the prices and costs of many other things will also fall. These changes may, almost certainly will, lead to consequential changes in other techniques of production. The basin of attraction shifts and is deformed. To construct the new facilities and bring down prices, takes time. The favourable demand explains the bunching and the boom. From the upper turning point, the economy declines either to a lower level or to a slower growth rate.

Although such a model is more a pulsator than an oscillator, it has a number of specific advantages. Being a system built on the urge to accumulate by means of cost-reducing innovations, or new types of good, capitalism guarantees that sooner or later, a sufficient burst of expenditure always appears. This results in an irregular wave-like motion, which looks like a disturbed cycle, even if it is not one. No simple or sophisticated spectral analysis has ever revealed hidden cycles in economic time series. Furthermore it helps to explain why the great promise of econometrics has not been realized. If we are not analyzing a given structure but an ever-changing one, long run constants cannot be found. Then there is the unresolved question of the Kondratiefs. In any case there is no question of affirming or denying the existence of long cycles; the run of statistics is too short. Yet there is no doubt that some periods are buoyant and others stagnant. Economic history is obviously essential. When a major innovation becomes feasible, it will by no means be completed in one fluctuation. The recession phase inhibits further investment because of regressive market conditions, but once the bottom has been reached, the investment again becomes attractive. In such a case the trough will be short, and the booms vigorous and prolonged. On the other hand the opposite result, weak booms and prolonged depressions, may result if the innovations are minor, or follow on the completion of a major one, e.g. the motor car industry today.

Such a mechanism combines short-run formal analysis with long-run historicism of a distinctly non-analytic character. It produces an apparently irregular period and amplitude, requiring an exogenous explanation. It should be mentioned that there exists an alternative, endogenous explanation of irregularity — the theory of chaos.

CYCLICAL INPUT DEMANDS AND THE ADJUSTMENT COST THEORY OF THE FIRM*

Jess Benhabib
New York University
Department of Economics
New York, NY 10003

Kazuo Nishimura
Tokyo Metropolitan University
Faculty of Economics
1-1-1 Yakumo, Meguro-ku
Tokyo, Japan

I. INTRODUCTION

Various authors have investigated the dynamic theory of factor demands by considering the "costs of adjustment" faced by the firm. See Eisner and Strotz [5], Treadway [15], Lucas [8], Lucas and Prescott [9], Mortensen [12], Brock and Scheinkman [3] and Scheinkman [14]. In such models the firm maximizes the present value of its profit stream under the constraint that changing the levels of factor inputs involves costs of adjustment. One can then obtain optimal time paths for investments, that is for the accumulation or decumulation of the stocks of factor inputs. Under certain assumptions on the structure of the model, the optimal time paths of the stock of factors asymptotically approach some long-run equilibrium value. In particular Brock and Scheinkman [3] and Scheinkman [14] have studied conditions under which factor levels globally converge to some steady state equilibrium.

In this paper we are concerned with models that are "unstable," that is models where the optimal time paths of investment are such that factor levels do not converge to the steady state values. We will construct and analyze an example where the time paths of factor levels and of investments are, or approach, a closed orbit.[1] Let us stress that the orbital paths constructed will be completely endogenous: they will not depend on exogenous fluctuations in factor prices, the output price or technology, nor on money illusion or irrational behavior. The investment decisions of the firm will be optimal decisions. The possibility

---

*We are grateful to Professors W. A. Brock and M. J. P. Magill for suggestions and constant encouragement. Also, we would like to thank Cyrus Sorooshian for his help with the innumerable calculations in the paper.

[1]Recently Magill [10] has studied the causes of spiralling of optimal paths but not the convergence to closed orbits. See section III, footnote 4.

of such cyclical investment, derived from the optimal behavior of the firm, could form a basis for a new approach to business cycle theory.

In the following section we briefly sketch the model, essentially following Treadway [15]. In section III we construct an example where the steady state values of the factor stocks are totally unstable; that is it is never optimal to approach the steady state values if we do not start with them. In section IV we use bifurcation theory to show the existence of optimal paths for factor levels and investments that are closed orbits. We briefly discuss the stability of the orbits and the "structural stability" of the system. Then we generalize our results to the case of "perfect foresight equilibrium" by allowing prices to respond to the quantity supplied. Finally in section V we offer some heuristic explanations for our results.

II. THE MODEL

Following Treadway [15] we have a firm operating in competitive output and factor markets, facing a rate of interest r, a vector of factor prices g, and an output price of unity. It maximizes the present value of profits:

$$\text{Max} \int_0^\infty e^{-rt}(F[x(t),y(t)] - wx(t) - gy(t))dt \tag{1}$$

subject to

$$\frac{dx_i}{dt} = \dot{x}_i = y_i - n_i x_i$$

$$x_i(0) = \bar{x}_i(0) \qquad\qquad i = 1,\dots,n$$

where n_i is the rate of depreciation of the i'th factor, x is the input vector, y is the investment vector and w is a vector of "current account" costs which from here on we set equal to zero since it simplifies analysis without affecting any of our results. The output function F(x,y) satisfies the following:

(A.1) Let $\Omega = \{x \in R^n | x \geqq 0\}$ and let $\dot{\Omega}$ be the interior of Ω. Then

$$F : \Omega \times R^n \to R \text{ is of class } C^2 \text{ on } \dot{\Omega} \times R^n.$$

To solve (1) we write the Hamiltonian,

$$H = e^{-rt}(F[x(t),y(t)] - gy(t) + q(t)[y(t) - nx(t)])$$

and using the Maximum Principle we obtain the necessary conditions,

$$\dot{x}_i = y_i - n_i x_i \tag{2}$$

$$\dot{q}_i = -\frac{\partial F}{\partial x_i} + (r + n_i)q_i \tag{3}$$

$$0 = \frac{\partial F}{\partial y_i} + q_i - g_i \qquad i = 1,\dots,n \tag{4}$$

We define a steady state as a vector $(\hat{x},\hat{y},\hat{q})$ that satisfy (2), (3) and (4) such that $\dot{x}_i,\dot{y}_i = 0$ for $i = 1,\dots,n$. We make the following assumption:

(A.2) There exists a steady state solution $(\hat{x},\hat{y},\hat{q})$ to (2), (3) and (4) and $[\frac{\partial^2 F}{\partial y^2}]$ evaluated at $(\hat{x},\hat{y})$ is non-singular.

Using equation (4), the above assumption allows us to express y_i's as a function of the vector (q,k) in the vicinity of the steady state $(\hat{x},\hat{y},\hat{q})$ and we obtain from (2) and (3) a system of 2n differential equations in (x,q). Furthermore, using (4), we obtain

$$[\frac{\partial y}{\partial q}] = -[\frac{\partial^2 F}{\partial y^2}]^{-1} \tag{5}$$

$$[\frac{\partial y}{\partial x}] = -[\frac{\partial^2 F}{\partial y^2}]^{-1}[\frac{\partial^2 F}{\partial y \partial x}] \tag{6}$$

The local stability of the steady state can be studied from the roots of the Jacobian of equations (2) and (3) and is given by

$$J = \left[\begin{array}{c|c} [\frac{\partial^2 F}{\partial x \partial y}][\frac{\partial^2 F}{\partial y^2}]^{-1} + (r+n)I & -[\frac{\partial^2 F}{\partial x^2}] + [\frac{\partial^2 F}{\partial x \partial y}][\frac{\partial^2 F}{\partial y^2}]^{-1}[\frac{\partial^2 F}{\partial x \partial y}] \\ \hline -[\frac{\partial^2 F}{\partial y^2}]^{-1} & -[\frac{\partial^2 F}{\partial y^2}]^{-1}[\frac{\partial^2 F}{\partial y \partial x}] - nI \end{array}\right] \tag{7}$$

It is easily shown that the roots of J are symmetric around r/2 and that for r sufficiently "close" to zero the real parts of the roots come in pairs of opposite sign. (See Treadway [15], pages 850-851.) In the latter case the steady state is saddle-point stable and for any initial value of x(0) the firm can choose q(0) so that the optimal path returns to the steady state. The optimality of the path (q(t),k(t)) approaching the steady state is assured if the transversality conditions,

$$\lim_{t\to\infty} e^{-rt} q_i(t)[\tilde{x}(t)_i - x(t)_i] \geq 0 \qquad i = 1,\ldots,n \tag{8}$$

are satisfied where $\tilde{x}(t)$ is any non-negative feasible path, provided that $F(x,y)$ is concave. (See Pitchford and Turnovsky [13], pages 28, 29.)

In the next section we will give an example of a steady state that is not saddle-point stable. In the context of our investigation locally unstable steady states are not, as Treadway [15] puts it, "irrelevant"; in section IV we will show, using Hopf's Bifurcation Theorem, how the existence of closed orbits can be deduced from the local behavior of the optimal path in the neighborhood of the unstable steady state.

III. EXAMPLES OF INSTABILITY

We follow the notation of the previous section. The output function, subject to adjustment costs, is given by[2]

$$\begin{aligned} F(x,y) = {} & 0.5x_1^{1/2}x_2^{1/3} - 0.36x_1y_1^2 - 4x_1y_2^2 + 0.6x_2y_2 - x_1y_2 \\ & + 0.18x_2y_1 - 1.7469y_1 - 0.2885y_2 \end{aligned} \tag{9}$$

Note that the first term is simply strictly concave a Cobb-Douglas production function. Let the discount rate r_0 and the factor prices be as follows:

$$g_1 = 2.2037, \quad g_2 = 1.5222, \; r_0 = 0.06075 \tag{10}$$

Since it substantially simplifies calculation we follow Treadway [15] in setting the depreciation of each good equal to zero. We obtain the following steady state values:

---

[2]For all results that follow we require the output function $F(x,y)$ to have the form given by (9) only at the steady state $(\hat{y}_1,\hat{y}_2,\hat{x}_1,\hat{x}_2, \hat{q}_1,\hat{q}_2)$. At steady state values, it is easily shown that the function $F(x,y)$ is concave. To preserve concavity elsewhere, we can smoothly "bend" the output function in any manner we wish. This does not affect the results of the following sections which rely only on the properties of the steady state under consideration.

$$\hat{y}_1, \hat{y}_2 = 0, \quad \hat{x}_1 = (\frac{10}{9})^2, \quad \hat{x}_2 = (\frac{10}{9})^3, \quad \hat{q}_1 = -\frac{\partial F}{\partial y_1} = 1.5,$$

$$\hat{q}_2 = -\frac{\partial F}{\partial y_2} = 0.7, \quad \frac{\partial F}{\partial x_1} = 0.25, \quad \frac{\partial F}{\partial x_2} = 0.15$$

Let us note at this point that labor could be explicitly introduced into the model. We could write the Cobb-Douglas production function as $0.5x_1^{1/2}x_2^{1/3}\ell^{\gamma}$ where ℓ represents the amount of labor. If we assume that there are no adjustment costs to labor, then given the wage rate the amount of labor used at each moment would be determined by its marginal value product. If factor stocks $x_1(t)$ and $x_2(t)$ change through time so would the demand for labor.[3] However, for the results of this and the following sections we would only need the steady state value of labor. By proper choice of units we can set this value equal to unity and the steady state calculations would not be affected.

The values of the parameters have been chosen so that the Jacobian matrix J, given in (7), reduces to

$$\hat{J} = \left[\begin{array}{c|c} Q + rI & 0 \\ \hline -[\frac{\partial^2 F}{\partial y^2}]^{-1} & -Q' \end{array}\right] \qquad (11)$$

and where

$$Q = [\frac{\partial^2 F}{\partial x \partial y}][\frac{\partial^2 F}{\partial y^2}]$$

It can easily be shown that the roots of $\hat{J}$ are given by the roots of $Q + rI$ and $-Q$. Since the roots of Q, evaluated at the steady state, are $-0.06075 \pm 0.3109i$ and the discount rate is 0.06075, the roots of the matrix $\hat{J}$ are $\lambda_1, \lambda_2 = 0 \pm 0.3109i$, $\lambda_3, \lambda_4 = 0.06075 \pm 0.3109i$.

We constructed the above example with zero real parts for λ_1 and λ_2 so that we can apply it to the Hopf Bifurcation Theorem (see the next section). To obtain a totally unstable steady state we slightly modify the example and set $g_1 = 1.4814$, $g_2 = 1.1851$ and $r_0 = 0.1$. For these values the steady state vector $(\hat{x}, \hat{y}, \hat{q})$ does not change and in particular the roots of the matrix Q are the same. However, since r_0 is different, the roots of $\hat{J}$ become $\lambda_1, \lambda_2 = 0.03925 \pm 0.3109i$, $\lambda_3, \lambda_4 = 0.06075 \pm 0.3109i$.

---

[3]Alternatively, we could set the output function as $0.5x_1^{1/2}x_2^{1/3} + \ell^{\gamma}$ so that the amount of labor used, determined by its marginal value product, would be independent of the values of x_1 and x_2.

Now all the four roots of J have positive real parts. This implies that for any initial $(x_1(0),x_2(0))$ there is no choice of $(q_1(0),q_2(0))$ that would steer the system to $(\hat{x},\hat{y},\hat{q})$. The steady state is totally unstable.[4]

In the next section we will use our first example to establish the existence of a closed orbit solution to equations (2), (3).

IV. ORBITAL PATHS OF FACTOR ACCUMULATION

Theorem 1 (the Hopf Bifurcation Theorem)

Let $\dot{x} = F(x,\mu)$, $x = (x_1,\ldots,x_n)$ be a real system of differential equations with real parameter μ. Let $F(x,\mu)$ be C^r in x and μ for x in a domain G and $|\mu| < c$. For $|\mu| < c$ let $F(x,\mu)$ possess a C^r family of stationary solutions $\tilde{x} = \tilde{x}(\mu)$ lying in G:

$$F(\tilde{x}(\mu),\mu) = 0$$

For $\mu = 0$, let the matrix $F_x(x(0),0)$ have one pair of pure imaginary roots, $\alpha(\mu) \pm \beta(\mu)i$; $\alpha(0) = 0$, $\beta(0) \neq 0$ and $\alpha(0)/d\mu \neq 0$. Then there exists a family of real periodic solutions $x = x(t,\varepsilon), \mu = \mu(\varepsilon)$ which has properties $\mu(0) = 0$, and $x(t,0) = x(0)$, but $x(t,\varepsilon) \neq \tilde{x}(\mu(\varepsilon))$ for sufficiently small $\varepsilon \neq 0$. $x(t,\varepsilon)$ is C^r. $\mu(\varepsilon)$ and $T(\varepsilon)$, where $T(\varepsilon) = 2\Pi/|\beta(0)|$ is the period of the orbit, are C^{r-1}.

Proof

See Hopf [6] and section 2, pages 197-198, of "Editorial Comments" by Hopf's translators, N. L. Howard and N. Koppel in Marsden and McCracken [11]. Hopf states and proves the theorem for $F(x,\mu)$ analytic. Howard and Koppel revise Hopf's proof and provide the C^r version given above.

Theorem 2

Consider the optimal problem (1) with parameters given by (9), (10). Then there exists a continuous function $r = r(\varepsilon)$, $r_0 = r(0)$ and a continuous family of optimal paths $(x[t,r(\varepsilon)],q[t,r(\varepsilon)])$ that are non-constant closed orbits in the positive orthant for sufficiently small

---

[4] The analysis of Magill [10] shows that spiralling of optimal paths occurs because of the strong skew-symmetric forces at equilibrium. The skew-symmetric forces are represented by the off diagonal-matrices of the larger matrix [J] and are the causes of spiralling, though by themselves are not enough to give the existence of closed orbits.

$\varepsilon \neq 0$, and which collapse to the stationary point values $(\hat{x}(r_0), \hat{q}(r_0))$ as $\varepsilon \to 0$.

Proof

From equation (2) we observe that for any steady state, $y(r) \equiv 0$. Using the implicit function theorem we can also show that the stocks are locally differentiable functions of r, that is, $x = x(r)$ (see the appendix). It is shown in the appendix that the real parts of the pure imaginary roots of the Jacobian $\hat{J}$, given by equation (11), are not stationary with respect to r. Thus, we can apply Theorem 1 and obtain orbits in $(q(\cdot,r),x(\cdot,r))$.

Note from Theorem 1 that the amplitude of the orbit that bifurcates from the steady state is zero at the bifurcation value $r_0 = 0.0675$ and grows with the deviation of r from r_0. Since the steady state $(\tilde{q},\tilde{x})$ is positive, the orbits that bifurcate from it must also be in the positive orthant for r sufficiently close to r_0. This establishes the existence of positive orbits.

Finally, to establish that the orbit is an optimal path we simply note that the orbit $(q(\cdot,r),k(\cdot,r))$ is positive and bounded. Applying the transversality conditions given by (8) we establish optimality. Q.E.D.

Theorem 2 establishes that for some initial values of x, and appropriately chosen initial values of q, the optimal path is a closed orbit. To study the convergence of optimal paths from initial levels of stock in the neighborhood of the orbit we use the concept of stable manifolds.

Definition

Let the $dz/dt = h(z)$ possess a periodic orbit solution $z = \gamma(t)$ of least period p, $p > 0$, where $h(z)$ is of class C^1 on an open set. Let $C : z = \gamma(t)$, $0 \leq t \leq p$. Let the points z in the neighborhood of C, on solutions $z = z(t)$ of $dz/dh = h(z)$, and which satisfy $\text{dist}(C,z(t)) \to 0$ as $t \to \infty$ constitute a d-dimensional manifold. Then the periodic orbit is said to have a d-dimensional locally stable manifold.

The orbits that result from Hamiltonian systems are attracting if for any given initial values of the state variables $x(0)$ in the neighborhood of the orbit, there exists initial values for co-state variables $q(0)$ such that the path $(x(t),q(t))$ asymptotically converges to the orbit. In other words, a 2n-dimensional system has a "stable" orbit if there is an n-dimensional stable manifold in the neighborhood of the orbit. In our discounted Hamiltonian system this cannot be guaranteed and after the initial bifurcation we may end up with either an n-dimensional or an (n - 1)-dimensional stable manifold (see Benhabib and Nishimura [2], Theorems 3, 4, 5).[5] If the orbits exist for $r > \hat{r}$ (alternatively, $r < \hat{r}$) where r is the bifurcation value of the discount rate, then the stable manifold has dimension n (alternatively, n - 1). Whether the orbits occur for $\hat{r} > r$ or $\hat{r} < r$ depends on the interaction of the first and higher order terms of the Taylor expansion around the stationary point of the differential equations describing the motion of the system. There also exists the degenerate (non-generic) possibility; the effect of all higher order terms vanish at the bifurcation value of the parameter $\hat{r}$, in which case the family of orbits form a "center" and exist only for $r = \hat{r}$.

Let us also note that if we slightly perturb one of the parameters of the system, we can still obtain the existence of orbits by adjusting the bifurcation value of r. For instance consider a small change in n_i, the depreciation of good i. Let $a(r,n_i) + r \pm b(r,n_i)i$ be roots of the Jacobian $\hat{J}$ with $a + r = 0$, $b \neq 0$, for $n_i = 0$, as in our example of the previous section where non-constant closed orbits exist for $r + a \neq 0$. We would expect $a(n_i,r)$ to change with n_i. However, since $a/r + 1 \neq 0$, as shown in the appendix, the implicit function theorem implies that for n_i in the neighborhood of its initial value, there always exists a value of r such that $a(n_i,r) + r = 0$. However, to show the persistence of orbits for a general and unrestricted perturbation of all the parameters of the system requires more complex arguments in terms of "structural stability." (For "structural stability" arguments in relation to the Hopf Bifurcation see Arnold [1]. See also Hirsh and Smale [6], Chapter 16.) In general it can be shown that the subcritical orbits (those existing for $r > \hat{r}$) and the supercritical orbits (those existing for $r > \hat{r}$) that arise from the Hopf Bifurcation will persist under small perturbations of the system.

The results of Theorem 2 were derived under the assumption of fixed factor and commodity prices. We can now show that such an assumption is not necessary for our results. Suppose we have m identical firms in the industry, producing the same good and facing an aggregate demand curve, $p(x,y) = 1 - b(mF(x,y))$, $b \geq 0$. The representative firm's profit appearing in (1) will be $p(x,y)F(x,y) - wx - gy$. Following Lucas and Prescott [9], we define a "perfect foresight equilibrium" price path, $p : [0,\infty) \to [0,\infty)$, that equates demand and supply through time and that

[5](For the stability of orbits bifurcating from stationary points as they lose their stability, see Bruslinskaya [4] and also Marsden and McCracken [11], sections 4, 4A.)

is perfectly foreseen by the firms in the industry. The case analyzed earlier corresponds to $b = 0$, that is, $p = 1$. From the first argument in the previous paragraph we know that we can show the existence of closed orbits if we slightly perturb one of the parameters of our system. Thus for small positive values of b the results of Theorem 2 will hold. Note that in this case the price $p(x,y)$ will also follow an orbital path. A similar argument can be constructed to hold for the factor prices g. (See the discussion in the following section.)

V. FINAL REMARKS

Oscillations in the demand for factors with fixed output and factor prices may at first seem to be inconsistent with intertemporal profit maximization. We show that along an orbital path, the net marginal productivities of factors, that is, net of adjustment costs, will be fluctuating. It may appear that the firm can do better by shifting its purchases of factors towards periods where they have a high net productivity at the margin. But if the future is discounted, a larger output, and therefore a larger revenue, that only comes tomorrow may not compensate for the loss of the smaller revenue today.[6] In fact, persistent oscillations occur for discount rates above a critical bifurcation value that depends on technology. From Theorem 1 we see that the amplitude of the orbital path of factor levels is zero when the discount rate is equal to the bifurcation value and grows with the distance of the discount rate from the bifurcation value.

While a positive discount rate may be necessary to explain the orbital path of factor stocks it is by no means sufficient. The source of oscillatory behavior must be found in the asymmetrical effects of investments on the marginal productivities of the input stocks. This can be seen by considering the matrix J of the example in section III, given by (11). The submatrices Q, which determine the roots of J and therefore the nature of the motion around the steady state, contain the

---

[6] In fact one would have to compare costs and gains generated by the reallocation of investments not only between two points in time, t_1 and t_2, but along the orbital path at every instant between those two time points as well. A marginal change in one stock at t_1 affects the whole path up to t_2. We must also remember that the orbits are not necessarily symmetric; the path halfway along the orbit from $(\bar{x}_1, \bar{x}_2)$ to $(\hat{x}_1, \hat{x}_2)$ is not necessarily that from $(\bar{x}_1, \bar{x}_2)$ to $(\hat{x}_1, \hat{x}_2)$ in reverse.

cross-partial terms of the function $F(x,y)$. Thus technological conditions play a crucial role. (See footnote 4.)

Finally, let us consider the oscillatory behavior of factor stocks and output when we allow the output price to respond to the quantity produced, as we did at the end of the last section. If the output is not perishable and there are no storage costs (a possibility that we did not consider earlier), intertemporal arbitrage would dampen the cyclical variations in the price of output. A constant price level could emerge, while output and factor stocks continue along their orbital path as in the case previously considered. However, the fact that output is storable with zero costs does not guarantee a constant price level. A positive discount rate would induce the firms to accept a lower price today rather than wait until tomorrow for the higher price. Thus oscillations in price as well as output can be preserved in a market with rational, profit-maximizing firms.

APPENDIX

In this appendix, we will show by actual calculation that the real parts of the pure imaginary roots of the matrix $\hat{J}$, given by (11) in section III, are not stationary with respect to r. That is, if the roots of J are $(a + r) \pm bi$, $-a \pm bi$ (see sections II and III) and $(a + r) = 0$ at the steady state, we will show that $[d(a + r)]/dr \neq 0$. It is obvious that even if $[d(a + r)]/dr = 0$ turned out to be the case, a highly unlikely event, a small change in the parameters of the function $F(x,y)$, given in section III, would remedy the situation. Nevertheless, we carried out the calculations.

While labor does not explicitly enter the calculations below, we may think of the model as not involving any adjustment costs for labor and a production function with labor of the form $Ax_1^{\alpha}x_2^{\beta} + \ell^{\gamma}$. The production function, that is, the first term of $F(x,y)$ in section III, $0.5x_1^{1/2}x_2^{1/3}$, can then be replaced by $0.5x_1^{1/2}x_2^{1/3} + \ell^{\gamma}$. In such a case labor does not affect any of the calculations and its marginal value product is independent of the levels of x_1 and x_2. There is no conceptual difficulty in extending the calculations below to a production function of the form $x_1^{1/2}x_2^{1/3}\ell^{\gamma}$, where the level of labor would fluctuate together with x_1 and x_2. However, the calculations would get somewhat more tedious.

Consider steady state values $\hat{y}_1, \hat{y}_2 = 0$, $\hat{x}_1 = (10/9)^2$, $\hat{x}_2 = (10/9)^3$ for $r = 0.06075$. First we show that steady state values of $\hat{y}_1$, $\hat{y}_2$, $\hat{x}_1$ and $\hat{x}_2$ can be written as functions of r. Since depreciations are assumed to be zero, steady state values of $\hat{y}_1, \hat{y}_2$ are identically zero. Setting $\dot{q}_1 = 0$ in equation (3), we use the implicit function theorem to show that steady state values of $\hat{x}_1, \hat{x}_2$ can be written as differentiable functions of r in the vicinity of $\hat{x}_1 = (10/9)^2$, $\hat{x}_2 = (10/9)^3$. Solving for $d\hat{x}_1/dr$, $d\hat{x}_2/dr$, we obtain:

$$d\hat{x}_1/dr = -5.2610$$

$$d\hat{x}_2/dr = -11.2746$$

We would like to show that the real parts of the pure imaginary roots of the matrix $\hat{J}$, given by (11), are not stationary with respect to r. The calculations are tedious and we will provide a brief sketch below.

It can be shown that the roots of the matrix J given by (7), which becomes $\hat{J}$ with our specific parameter values of section III, has the same roots as the matrix

$$Z = \left[\begin{array}{c|c} F_{yy}^{-1}(Fxy - Fyx + rFyy) & F_{yy}^{-1}(Fxx + rFyx) \\ \hline I & 0 \end{array}\right]$$

(See Treadway [15], pages 850-851.) We know from section II that the roots will be $(a + r) \pm bi$ and $-a \pm bi$. We also know thay the algebraic product of the roots must be identically equal to the determinant of Z. If we differentiate this identity with respect to r we obtain one equation in da/dr and db/dr; the values of x_1, x_2, y_1, y_2, dx_1/dr, dx_2/dr that appear when we differentiate the determinant of Z are evaluated at the steady state values given above. Note also that steady state values for a and b are known; a = 0.06075 and b = 0.3109.

Unfortunately, to obtain a second equation in da/dr and db/dr we cannot use the equality of the sum of the roots and the trace, since the sum of the roots equals 2r and both a and b cancel out. So instead we use the fact that a restricted sum of principal minors of order 2 of the matrix Z always equals the restricted sum of the matrix Z always equals the restricted sum of the pairwise products of the roots:

$$\sum_{j>i} \begin{vmatrix} a_{ii} & a_{ij} \\ a_{ji} & a_{jj} \end{vmatrix} = \sum_{j>i} \lambda_i \lambda_j$$

where a_{ij}'s elements and λ_i's are the roots of Z. Fortunately, the zeroes in Z simplify the algebra. Differentiating the above identity, we obtain another equation in da/dr, db/br and we then solve to obtain

$$da/dr = -29.1491$$

$$db/dr = -0.3377$$

The rate of change with respect to r of the real parts of the pure imaginary roots of Z, (a + r), is

$$\frac{d(a + r)}{dr} = da/dr + 1 = - 28.1491$$

Thus $[d(a + r)]/dr \neq 0$ and the hypothesis of Theorem 1 holds for our example in section II.

REFERENCES

1. Arnold, V. I., "Lectures on Bifurcation and Versal Families," Russian Mathematical Surveys, 27 (1972), 54-123.

2. Benhabib, J. and K. Nishimura, "The Hopf Bifurcation and the Existence and Stability of Closed Orbits in Multi-Sector Models of Optimal Economic Growth," Journal of Economic Theory, 21 (1979), 421-444.

3. Brock, W. A. and J. A. Scheinkman, "On the Long-Run Behavior of a Competitive Firm," in Equilibrium and Disequilibrium in Economic Theory, ed. G. Schwödiauer, D. Reidel Publishing Company, Dordrecht, Boston, 1978.

4. Bruslinskaya, N. N., "Qualitative Integration of a System of n Differential Equations in a Region Containing a Singular Point and a Limit Cycle," Society Mathematics Doklady, 2 (1961), 9-12.

5. Eisner, R. and R. Stroz, "Determinants of Business Investment," in Impacts of Monetary Policy (Commission on Money and Credit), Prentice-Hall, Englewood Cliffs, N.J., 1963.

6. Hirch, M. W. and S. Smale, Differential Equations, Dynamical Systems and Linear Algebra, Academic Press, New York, 1974.

7. Hopf, E., "Bifurcation of a Periodic Solution From a Stationary Solution of a System of Differential Equations," in J. E. Marsden and M. McCracken, The Hopf Bifurcation and Its Applications, Springer-Verlag, New York, 1976.

8. Lucas, R. E., "Optimal Investment Policy and the Flexible Accelerator," International Economic Review, 8 (1967), 78-85.

9. Lucas, R. E. and E. C. Prescott, "Investment Under Uncertainty," Econometrica, 44 (1976), 841-865.

10. Magill, M. J. P., "On Cyclical Motion in Dynamic Economics," Journal of Economics, Dynamics and Contr l, 1 (1979), 199-218.

11. Marsden, J. E. and M. McCracken, The Hopf Bifurcation and Its Applications, Applied Mathematical Sciences, No. 10, Springer-Verlag, New York, 1976.

12. Mortensen, D. T., "Generalized Costs of Adjustment and Dynamic Factor Demand Theory," Econometrica, 41 (1973), 657-665.

13. Pitchford, J. D. and S. J. Turnovsky, Applications of Control Theory to Economic Analysis, North-Holland, New York, 1977.

14. Scheinkman, J. A., "Stability of Separable Hamiltonians and Investment Theory," Review of Economic Studies, 45 (1978), 559-570.

15. Treadway, A. B., "The Rational Multivariate Flexible Accelerator," Econometrica, 39 (1971), 845-855.

LONG-TERM GROWTH AND THE CYCLICAL RESTORATION OF PROFITABILITY

by

David M. Gordon, Department of Economics, New School for Social Research, 66 West 12th Street, New York, New York, 10012

Thomas E. Weisskopf, Department of Economics, University of Michigan, Ann Arbor, Michigan, 48104

Samuel Bowles, Department of Economics, University of Massachusetts, Amherst, Massachusetts, 01003

Macroeconomic theory today is marked by a curious hiatus: the study of long-term growth and the study of cycles are carried on almost entirely independently of one another, the central concerns of the one disappearing in the simplifying assumptions of the other, and conversely. Not surprisingly, the methodological distance between the two fields is associated with a division of labor among macroeconomists almost as rigid as that which at least until quite recently divided the practitioners of microeconomic theory from the macroeconomists.

The unfortunate consequences of this Balkanization of scholarship are nowhere more evident than in the study of long swings in economic activity. As the rapid and stable growth of the early post-World War II period was succeeded by the relative stagnation and instability of the 1970s and early 1980s, the "smooth growth" assumptions of the neoclassical long-term growth models became increasingly unacceptable scientifically and increasingly irrelevant from a practical political or policy standpoint. Yet the short-term models--driven by exogenous shifts in investors' "animal spirits" or "supply shocks" and marked by the assumed constancy of many variables whose change is central to longer-term dynamics--provided little coherent basis for understanding the shift from a long-swing expansion to the long-swing crisis.

Those long-term growth theorists who have sought to understand the growth slowdown of the 70s and 80s have followed the logic of their models, many seeking explanations in a retardation of the rate of technological progress. These explanations bear a strong resemblance to a much older interpretation of long swings in economic growth: that based on the bunching of technological innovations, deriving from the work of Schumpeter and others.

But little success has greeted efforts to identify a bunching of innovations, or to provide a compelling empirical account of the long-swing effects of major innovations, or to explain the current growth slowdown as the effect of a reduction of either innovation or research and development expenditures.

In this essay we offer, by contrast, what might be termed a social structural theory of long-swing expansions and crises, in which the functioning of the short-term cycle is essential to understanding the long-term dynamics of the economy. Our attempt to integrate long-term growth and cyclical analysis is distinct from much of the related literature in the following three ways.

First, long swings in economic growth are associated with discontinuities in the evolution of social institutions--the bunching of institutional innovation, rather than the bunching of technological innovations. To the extent that technical change plays a role in long-swing dynamics, it is endogenous in our model.

Second, the model is driven by the rate of profit: the level of investment depends critically on the expected rate of profit, which in turn depends upon the current and recent past profit rates. The current profit rate (and hence expected profit rates) depends on both the (Keynesian) aggregate demand and capacity utilization determinants and the (classical) cost and productivity determinants.

Third, the cost and productivity determinants of the profit rate depend critically upon the institutions regulating class conflict both in labor markets and in the production process itself.

These three characteristics point to the theoretical roots of this analysis in the Marxian (rather than Keynesian, classical, Sraffian, or neoclassical) tradition.

We cannot in this brief paper devlop a full model along these lines, although we have made progress in this direction in the works cited below. Rather we will focus on some empirically testable aspects of our model of the relationship of the cycle to long swings.

A notable and, we shall argue, defining characteristic of the current and prior long-swing crises is the failure of the business cycle, through its normal functioning, to restore conditions for rapid accumulation. It is precisely this failure of the self-correcting nature of the cycle which requires conscious social intervention--often state intervention--to restructure the accumulation process. This recurrent necessity for structural change warrants the designation of these periods as crises rather than simply cyclical downturns or episodes of economic stagnation.

Our approach thus implies that the most theoretically coherent basis for dating long swings in capitalist economies is not to be found in the movements of total output or investment, but rather in an investigation of what Gordon (1980) has called the social structure of accumulation and its ability to restore profitability during cyclical downturns.

This model of the relationship of cycles to swings not only clarifies the characteristic patterns of long swings; it may also help resolve a number of anomalies which have occasionally puzzled economists. The considerable <u>rise</u> in real wages under conditions of massive unemployment during the sharp cyclical downturns of the 1890s and 1930s in the U.S. is no longer anomalous, for example, but is rather an expected feature of business cycles in a period of long-swing crisis. (This does not explain, of course, why real wages rose.)

Further, the inconclusive Keynes-Dunlop exchange during the 1930s, and the continuing debate about the pro-cyclical or anti-cyclical behavior of real wages may be clarified by our observation that real wages tend to move pro-cyclically during long-swing expansions and anti-cyclically during long-swing crises. The prevailing debate is thus seen to be focused inappropriately on whether real wages are <u>generally</u> anti-cyclical (Keynes' position) or pro-cyclical (Marx's position). By contrast, the question arising from our analysis is: <u>under what conditions</u> will real wages move pro-cyclically or anti-cyclically.

Most studies of the relationship of the business cycle to long swings in economic activity have failed in part because of the absence of any theory of the relationship between these two forms of economic fluctuation. Recent Marxian analysis of the dynamics of long swings offer the possibility of overcoming this weakness.[1] These analyses have stressed the crucial importance of a periodically reconstituted set of institutions, called the social structure of accumulation, which provides the economic stability and moderation of political and economic conflict essential for favorable profit expectations and therefore for rapid capital accumulation. These institutions include, for example, systems of labor-management, the financial system, the international monetary system, and structures mediating raw materials supply. Their erosion sets the stage for a crisis of the accumulation process. Despite the promise of this approach, however, the operations of the business cycle have not been integrated into the broader analysis of the social structure of accumulation and long swings.

We begin our attempt to rectify this shortcoming by distinguishing the _reproductive_ (or well-behaved) _cycle_ from the _non-reproductive_ (or perverse) _cycle_. The reproductive cycle is one in which a downturn in economic activity is corrected by the functioning of the cycle itself. We call this cycle reproductive because it endogenously restores conditions for rapid accumulation without requiring fundamental changes in the structure of the accumulation process. The non-reproductive cycle, by contrast, is one in which a downturn does not correct itself endogenously and which therefore requires basic changes in the institutions which regulate the accumulation process and establish the conditions for profitability.

This distinction allows us to define the difference between long-swing expansions and crises in a particularly simple manner. Long-swing expansions are characterized by reproductive cycles, sustaining the effectiveness of the social structure of accumulation in promoting profitability, investment, and growth. Long-swing crises are characterized by non-reproductive cycles, leading to prolonged periods of economic stagnation or disaccumulation and eventually, if capitalism is to continue, to the construction of a new social structure of

----

1. See Gordon, Edwards, and Reich (1982), Ch. 2, for a review.

accumulation capable of restoring profitability, investment, and growth. The theoretical distinction between long-swing expansions and crises thus resides in the reproductive or non-reproductive nature of the business cycle; slower economic growth or reduced accumulation are therefore probable consequences of a long-swing crisis rather than its defining characteristic.

These definitions presuppose a specific set of interconnections among the social structure of accumulation, the expected profit rate, the cycle, and investment activity which we may now briefly summarize. The expected profit rate depends on the effectiveness of those institutions which make up a given social structure of accumulation. The level and pattern of investment depends upon the social structure of accumulation and the expected profit rate. Cyclical downturns are induced by a decline in the expected rate of profit. Reproductive cyclical downturns restore the expected rate of profit, and thus investment activity, while non-reproductive cyclical downturns do not.[2]

Why would a reproductive cycle become non-reproductive? We may examine the functioning of the reproductive cycle through an analysis of the determinants of the profit rate. Abstracting from taxes, we may represent the profit rate of the individual firm, r, as the product of the share of profits in firm value-added, s_r, the ratio of output to utilized capital stock, y_u and the ratio of utilized to owned capital stock, k^*, or

$$r = s_r y_u k^*, \tag{1}$$

where $r = R/K_o$; $s_r = R/Y$; $y_u = Y/K_u$; and $k^* = K_u/K_o$ and R is net output minus the wage bill, or profits, K_o is the value of the firm's owned capital stock, Y is firm value-added, and K_u is the currently utilized portion of the owned capital stock.

----

2. We provide some econometric evidence for these propositions in our book, Bowles, Gordon, and Weisskopf (1983a), in Weisskopf (1979) and in Weisskopf, Bowles, and Gordon (1983). One effort at explaining the emergence of the non-reproductive cycle in the post-World War II period is found in Bowles and Gintis (1982). The shift from pro-cyclical to anti-cyclical real wage movements in many European economies during the post-World War II period is documented in Schor (1984)

The expected profit rate, r_e, will by parallel reasoning depend on the expected profit rate on utilized capital stock, $s_{re}y_{ue}$, and expected capacity utilization, k^*_e, or

$$(2) \qquad r_e = s_{re}y_{ue}k^*_e$$

Expression (2) suggests that a cyclical downturn may restore expected profits in either of two principal ways, by raising the expected profit share, s_{re}, or by raising the expected ratio of output to utilized capital, y_{ue}.

We assume that expected values of s_r and y_u are formed in major part by reference to present values of their variables and recent changes in their values. The cyclical downturn may raise y_u by eliminating high cost firms and by inducing the non-use of high cost processes within surviving firms. The effect of the cycle on y_u is closely associated with the effect of the cycle on competitive pressures among business and, by implication, with the business failure rate.

The effect of a cyclical downturn on the profit share involves a somewhat more complicated set of connections. It may be investigated by representing the profit chare as unity minus what we call real unit labor cost , or

$$(3) \qquad s_r = 1 - \left[(w/p)/ed\right]$$

where w is the nominal wage, p is the price of output, e is output per input of labor effort and d is labor effort input per hour. (The term ed thus represents output per labor hour.)

A cyclical downturn <u>may</u> lower the product wage (w/p), raise output per unit of effort (e), or raise labor effort per hour (d). The effects on w/p and d are derived from the increased power of capital over labor associated with an increase in the size of the reserve army of the unemployed and the consequent increase in the cost to the worker of losing his or her job.[3] The effect of the downturn upon e

----

3. These effects are identified theoretically in Bowles (1981), (1983a) and (1983b) and estimated econometrically in Weisskopf, Bowles, and Gordon (1983) and in Schor and Bowles (1984).

may arise because of the elimination of inefficient firms and competitive pressure effects outlined above, or because of increased power of capital in determining work rules and technical changes, or for other reasons.[4]

The non-reproductive cycle is one in which these restorative effects of the downturn on the profit share and the ratio of output to utilized capital fail to operate. The failure of these effects signals an erosion of the effectiveness of the institutions of the social structure of accumulation and therefore the onset of a long-swing crisis. Under what conditions might they fail to operate?

The cyclical downturn might fail to raise the ratio of output to utilized capital stock if high cost firms and high cost operations were not eliminated, or if the downturn was characterized by an especially severe contraction in sectors with relatively high output/capital ratios, or if the reserve army effects failed to raise output per effort unit or effort per hour, or for other reasons.

The cyclical downturn might not raise the profit share if producer price cutting outweighed wage cutting, giving rise to an increase in the product wage, or if the contraction failed to have positive effects on output per unit of effort or effort per labor hour.

Considering first the product wage effects of the contraction, it is clear that price cutting might conceivably more than offset wage cutting, since both capital and labor face intensified competition in the downturn. Consider a simple monopolistic competition profit-maximizing pricing model in which price is a mark-up over marginal costs, c, or

$$p = Ec/(E - 1), \tag{4}$$

---

4. By letting d represent the units of both gross and net output produced per unit of effort, we are here abstracting from intermediate goods used in production. Were intermediate goods inputs to be considered we would need to consider the effect of the cycle on the "real price of intermediate goods" or their price relative to the output price (we assume that the amount of intermediate goods used per unit of output do not vary over the cycle.) Cyclical effects on the real price of intermediate goods may well be substantial, as there is no reason to expect output prices to exhibit the same cyclical amplitude as input prices (and particularly imported raw materials and fuel prices).

where E is the perceived elasticity of demand facing the monopolistic competitor. The perceived elasticity of demand is a negative function of both the degree of industry concentration and of the fraction of the firm's potential competitors who are perceived to be quantity-constrained and hence not engaged in or responsive to price competition. Assuming that the degree of concentration is not cyclically sensitive, which seems reasonable, price cutting will occur in the downturn for two reasons: the marginal cost function will shift downwards to the extent that wages and the prices of other inputs fall; and the mark-up will fall to the extent that the general reduction in capacity utilization gives rise to a smaller share of the firm's potential competitors being perceived to be operating under capacity constraints, and hence an increase in the perceived elasticity of demand facing the firm. (If marginal costs were a rising function of output levels prior to the contraction, as they generally would be in a profit maximizing optimum, and if the contraction is associated with production cutbacks, a third source of price cutting would obviously some into play.)

While this model of pricing would seem to imply an excess of price cutting over wage cutting in the downturn, David Kotz (1982) has pointed out that to the extent that monopolistic firms practice limit pricing to inhibit entry of competitors, and to the extent that entry is less of a threat during contractions when investment levels are relatively low, the negative effects of the contraction on product prices will be attenuated. The cyclical movement of product prices will also depend upon the degree of openness of the economy in question and the extent to which the cycles of the economy's major trading partners are synchronized.

The effect of the contraction on the other components of real unit labor costs--the nominal wage rate, output per effort unit, and effort per labor hour--may be derived from a microeconomic analysis of the capital-labor conflict over wage setting and work intensity and their macroeconomic consequences, as modeled in Bowles (1983a). For our purposes here, it is sufficient to observe that the effects of the cyclical downturn on the above determinants of real unit labor costs will be more favorable to capital, the more the contraction increases the expected duration of unemployment and the greater is the difference between the worker's current after-tax wage and the worker's expected level of unemployment insurance and other income-replacing payments from the government.

In an accounting sense, the effect of a cyclical downturn on the expected profit rate will obviously depend on the sum of the above contradictory effects. More substantively, the overall effect will depend on the manner in which the social structure of accumulation regulates product markets, labor markets, the labor process, international exchanges, financial markets, state expenditures, and so forth. Elaboration of an adequate model of these relations cannot be pursued in such a short essay.[5]

We confine ourselves, more simply, to a brief empirical demonstration that one of our central hypothesized relationships between the business cycle and long swings is quite strongly confirmed by the historical data. Because data on the capital stock and its utilization for the years prior to World War II are inadequate for cyclical analysis, we cannot explore the effects of cyclical downturns on the level of output per utilized unit of capital stock, y_u. But available data do permit investigation of the movements of real unit labor costs in the U.S. economy for the period from 1890 to 1982.

We use these data to classify cycles as reproductive or non-reproductive. A non-reproductive cycle is defined as one in which the ratio of the product wage to output per hour, or real unit labor costs --$[(w/p)/ed]$--rises rather than falls between the business cycle peak and the year following the trough. (We measure changes from peak to the year after the trough, to allow time for the restorative impact of the downturns.)[6]

Our results in column (3) of Table 1 are strikingly consistent with our hypothesis. Our data indicate alternating periods of non-reproductive and reproductive cycles, with the non-reproductive or crisis

----

5. Gordon, Edwards, and Reich (1982) provide this kind of analysis for the labor process and labor market. Gintis and Bowles (1982) analyse aspects related to state expenditures.

6. We use cycles rather than annual or quarterly time periods as our units of observations on the grounds that calendar time lacks theoretical coherence in a model of cyclical activity when the cycles are of varying length. We note below, however, that our results appear to be confirmed, at least for the recent time period, when estimated using annual data. We have not estimated analogous relationships using annual data for the earlier periods.

periods spanning the years 1890-1903, 1926-1937, and 1969 to the present--the cycles numbered, respectively, 1-4, 11-12, and 19-21.[7]

Table 1

The Restoration of Profitability in Cyclical Downturns, United States, 1890-1980

	Cyclical Downturn		Percentage Average Annual Change			
Cycle Number	Peak	Trough	(1) Product Wages	(2) Output per hour	(3) Real Unit Labor Costs	(4) Change in Unemployment Rate
1	1890	1891	0.78%	0.00%	0.78%	1.4
2	1892	1894	3.84	-0.70	4.54	15.4
3	1895	1897	1.63	-0.67	2.30	0.8
4	1899	1901	2.03	1.45	0.58	-2.5
5	1903	1905	-0.93	2.55	-3.48	0.4
6	1907	1909	-3.24	2.67	-5.91	2.3
7	1910	1912	3.05	4.66	-1.61	-1.3
8	1913	1915	-1.69	6.28	-7.97	4.2
9	1919	1922	5.87	10.83	-4.96	5.3
10	1923	1925	2.28	6.30	-4.02	0.8
11	1926	1928	4.29	3.32	0.97	2.4
12	1929	1933	1.50	1.35	0.15	21.7
13	1937	1939	2.40	3.72	-1.32	2.9
14	1944	1947	-2.94	-1.34	-1.60	2.7
15	1948	1950	3.92	4.46	-0.54	1.5
16	1953	1955	0.96	2.73	-1.77	1.5
17	1957	1959	2.57	3.13	-0.56	1.2
18	1960	1962	3.14	3.48	-0.34	0.0
19	1969	1971	2.33	2.17	0.16	2.4
20	1973	1976	1.17	1.07	0.10	2.8
21	1979	1980	0.85	0.45	0.39	1.3

Notes: Cycle peaks are those identified by the National Bureau of Economic Research (annual calendar year reference dates). Troughs designated here are one year after the NBER trough, except where this is another peak year, in which case the NBER trough is used. The NBER peak-trough-peak cycle of 1918-1919-1920 was ignored as a cycle, since the respective unemployment rates for these years were 1.4 %, 1.4 %, and 5.2 %; we designate 1919 as the peak instead. Pre-1948 data refer to manufacturing while post-1948 data are for the private business sector.

----

7. If the last cycle is considered to extend from a peak in 1979 to a trough in 1982, the entries in columns (1) through (4) of Table 1 become 1.25 %, 1.08 %, 0.17 %, and 3.9, results which are consistent with the remainder of the data, and particularly striking given the severity of the recession.

The Restoration of Profitability
in Cyclical Downturns
United States, 1890 - 1981

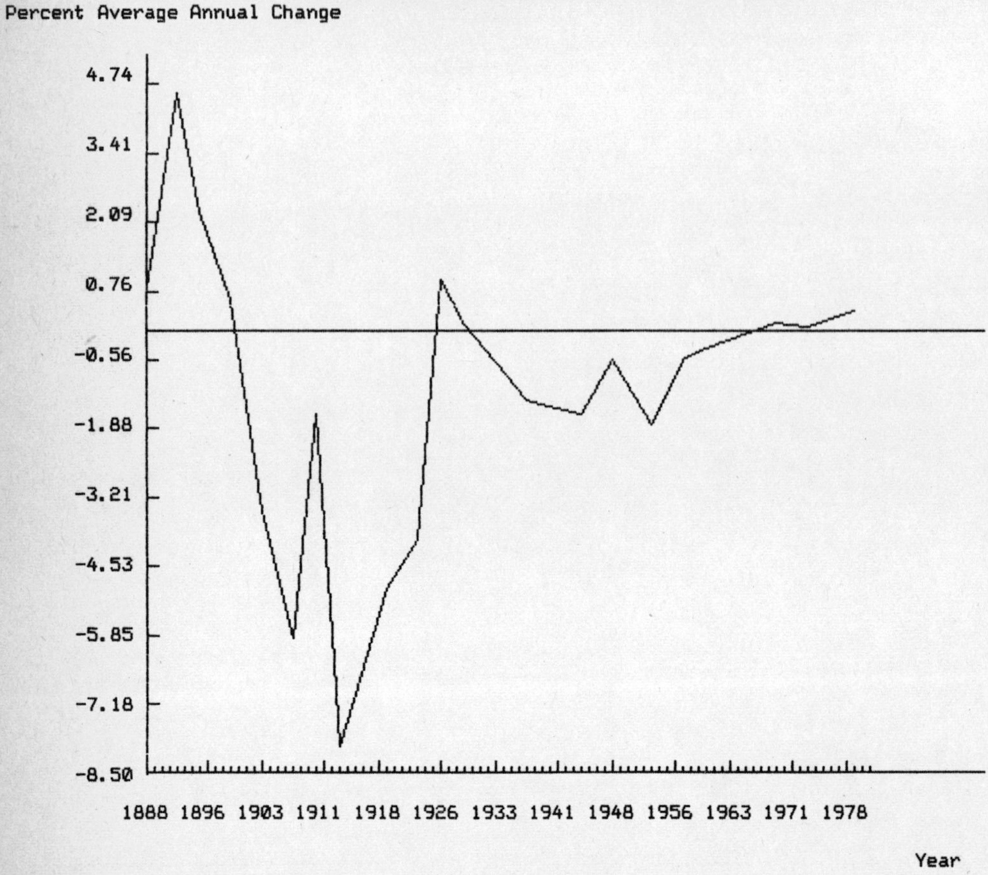

Source: Table 1, Col. 3

—— Percentage Average Annual Change in Real Unit Labor Costs

There is also a noticeable long-swing pattern in the date in column (3), as one can see by graphing its cycle values against time, as in Figure 1. This impression is sustained by evidence of autocorrelation when the data in column (3) are tested against the null hypothesis of constancy over time. The Durbin-Watson statistic for such a test is

0.90, significant at 5 % and substantially lower than for comparable tests on the between-cycle movements of data on producers' prices, aggregate output, or aggregate investment.[8] Our model of the effects of cycles on expected profits, in short, reveals clearer evidence of long-swing behavior than other macroeconomic indicators on which economists have previously concentrated.

Additional analysis supports our hypotheses about the differences between reproductive and non-reproductive cycles. In the reproductive cycle, we would expect a systematic inverse relationship between the peak-to-trough changes in unemployment and changes in real unit labor costs: the greater the increase in the size of the reserve-army, the larger the reduction in real unit labor costs during the downturn. In the non-reproductive cycle, given our hypothesized erosion of the SSA, we would expect a breakdown of this effect; we should therefore find no evidence of any systematic statistical relationship between the movements in unemployment and real unit labor costs. We have combined the reproductive cycles (5-10 and 13-18) in one group and the non-reproductive cycles (1-4, 11-12, and 19-21) in another. Regressing the data in column (3) on the data in column (4), we find a negative and statistically significant relationship for the group of reproductive cycles. By contrast for the non-reproductive group we find no significant relationship.[9]

We can next explore the relationship between the data in Table 1 and conventional hypotheses about long swings in economic activity. The first non-reproductive cycle in each sequence in column (3)

----

8. We performed these tests on data for the wholesale price index, gross private domestic product, and gross private domestic investment. The Durbin-Watson statistics for these tests were 1.28, 1.37, and 1.12, respectively.

9. Covariance analysis further confirms the hypothesis of differences in both intercepts and slopes between the two groups. Furthermore, using annual data for the years 1951 to 1966 we find a highly statistically significant negative relationship between the change in the unemployment rate (lagged one year) and the change in real unit labor costs, as defined here. For the years 1967-1979, by contrast, the relationship is positive and statistically insignificant. We have adopted the 1966 dividing line as the apparent turning point of a series of relevant indicators of long term economic performance, uncluding the rate of productivity growth, the level of net non residential fixed domestic investment (expressed as a ratio to net domestic product), and the after tax profit rate in the non-financial corporate business sector.

--cycles 1, 11, and 19--appears to precede by one cycle those periods which are generally characterized as crises or depressions.[10] We present in Table 2 the results of dating economic crises proper, as opposed to their onsets, as commencing after one non-reproductive cycle. (We have dated the end of the 1890s crisis at the NBER peak of 1899, discounting the non-reproductive nature of the 1899-1903 downturn, since the unemployment rate actually fell during this "contraction".) The data for aggregate output, industrial production, and aggregate investment presented in table 2 all demarcate distinct epochs of relative growth and stagnation.

Table 2

Growth of Output and Investment in the U.S. Economy, 1840s-1979[a/]

	I		II		III			
	Boom	Crisis	Boom	Crisis	Boom	Crisis	Averages	
	1840s to 1892[b/]	1892 to 1899	1899 to 1929	1929 to 1937	1937 to 1973	1973 to 1979[e/]	Boom	Crisis
Gross domestic nonfarm product[c/]	6.6%	2.9	3.7	-0.8	4.2	2.9	4.8	1.8
Industrial production	5.1%	3.4	4.5	0.4	4.9	2.7	4.8	2.2
Gross domestic private fixed non-residential investment[d/]	8.0%	1.3	2.4	-4.7	4.7	2.8	5.0	-0.2

Sources: Booms and crises are dated from peak to peak, using NBER cycle peaks.

a) All entries are average percentage annual rates of change in constant dollars.
b) The first boom begins in the 1840s, but data are not actually available until later: The nonfarm product series begins in 1874, the industrial production series in 1860, and the investment series in 1873.
c) The data for the years before World War II are for national rather than domestic product, and the post-1929 data are for gross domestic nonfarm business product.
d) The data for 1937 are for gross business fixed investment and before World War II for national rather than domestic investment.
e) We end this period at 1979, not 1981, in order to avoid over-stating the slowdown after 1969 and because of the disagreement among economists about whether or not 1981 constituted a business cycle peak. (The annual unemployment rates show a monotonic rise from 1979 through 1982).

Table 3 presents the average effects of cyclical downturns, averaging the data from columns (3) and (4) in Table 1, for crisis and expansion periods defined by this dating system. There are substantial and consistent differences between the crisis and expansion periods by these measures as well.[11] The extent to which long-wave expansions and crises are characterized by divergent cyclical behaviors of real unit labor costs appears, however, to have declined considerably over time. In the post-World War II period both the "well behaved" and the "perverse" effects, while consistent with our model, are quite small quantitatively.

Table 3

Average Effects of Cyclical Downturns[a/]

	Cycle Nos.	(1) Real Unit Labor Costs	(2) Unemployment Rate
Crises:[b/]	1-3	2.54%	5.9
	11-12	0.56	12.0
	19-21	0.22	2.3
	Crisis Average	1.18	6.1
Expansions:	4-10	-3.91	1.3
	13-18	-1.02	1.6
	Expansion Average	-2.58	1.4

a) Columns (1) and (2) represent the averages for the respective cycle groups of the data presented in columns (3) and (4) in Table 1.
b) We include for this comparison the cycle identified as the onset of the crisis, or the first nonreproductive crisis, whereas we excluded this cycle in our presentation of the data in Table 2.

----

10. Since we do not have comparable data for the years before 1890, we cannot be certain, of course, that the cycle beginning with the peak in 1890 was the <u>first</u> non reproductive cycle in this particular sequence.

We note, finally, that our dating identifies crisis periods which correspond to eras in which historians have identified major institutional innovation. What have been termed "key" presidential elections, those of 1892 and 1896 and of 1932 and 1936, fall within our first two crisis periods. All three crisis periods, defined by our method, have witnessed intensified class conflict and sharp debates over major economic policy issues.

We are curious to find out if similar patterns of reproductive and non-reproductive cycles may be identified in other advanced capitalist economies. We suspect, however, that in economies with less market-determined wage bargaining and more centralized or politicized labor-capital relations the cycle downturn may play a considerably less important role in restoring the conditions of profitability during long-wave expansions. Indeed, as we have seen immediately above, such a reduction of the centrality of the cycle appears in the post-World War II data even for the U.S.

We conclude that our empirical evidence, however provisional and country specific, establishes strong initial support for our model of the relationship between the business cycle and long swings. The data further suggest the potential fruitfulness of the Marxian analysis of long swings and the social structure of accumulation, and particularly of class conflict in labor markets and in the production process itself as essential aspects of models of cycles amid long-term growth alike.

----

11. Some readers may question our use of the NBER dating of peaks and troughs rather than a cycle dating by peaks and troughs in the unemployment rate. We think that the NBER dating makes sense since we are concerned with the effects of downturns in business activity in general, not simply with movements in unemployment. Indeed, there are two "false" business cycle downturns, during which the unemployment rate did not increase. Our results are robust if we use an analogous unemployment-based dating scheme: the numbers corresponding to the averages in column (1) of table 3 are +2.66, +0,94, +1.23, +1.55 and -1.93, -0.98, and -1.49 respectively.

REFERENCES

BOWLES, Samuel, "The Cyclical Movement of Real Wages, Labor Productivity and 'Overhead Labor' in a Competitive Non-Monetary Economy", mimeo, University of Massachusetts, December 1983a.

BOWLES, Samuel, "Long-Term Growth and Unemployment in Open, Competitive Capitalist Economies", mimeo, University of Massachusetts, 1983b.

BOWLES, Samuel, "Competitive Wage Determination and Involuntary Unemployment", mimeo, University of Massachusetts at Amherst, 1981.

BOWLES, Samuel and GINTIS, Herbert, "The Crisis of Liberal Democratic Capitalism: The Case of the United States", Politics and Society, Winter 1982, 11, 51-92.

BOWLES, Samuel, GORDON, David M., and WEISSKOPF, Thomas E., Beyond the Waste Land: A Democratic Alternative to Economic Decline, New York: Doubleday books (1983a).

BOWLES, Samuel, GORDON, David, and WEISSKOPF, Thomas, "The Social Structure of Accumulation and the Profitability of the Postwar U.S. Economy: A Quantitative Analysis", paper presented to December, 1983 conference of the Union for Radical Political Economics, San Francisco (1983b).

GORDON, David M., "Stages of Accumulation and Long Economic Cycles", in T. HOPKINS and I. WALLERSTEIN, eds., Processes of the World-System, Beverly Hills: Sage Publications, 1980.

GORDON, David M., EDWARDS, Richard, and REICH, Michael, Segmented Work, Divided Workers: The Historical Transformation of Labor in the United States, New York: Cambridge University Press, 1982.

KOTZ, David, "Monopoly, Inflation, and Economic Crisis", Review of Radical Political Economics, Fall 1982, Vol. 14.

SCHOR, Juliet B., "Changes in the Cyclical Variability of Real Wages: Evidence from Nine Countries, 1955-1980", mimeo, Columbia University, 1984.

SCHOR, Juliet B., and BOWLES, Samuel, "Conflict in the Employment Relation and the Cost of Job Loss", mimeo, 1984.

WEISSKOPF, Thomas E., "Marxian Crisis Theory and the Rate of Profit in the Postwar U.S. Economy", Cambridge Journal of Economics, December 1979, 3, 341-78.

WEISSKOPF, Thomas E., BOWLES, Samuel, GORDON, David M., "Hearts and Minds: A Social Model of Aggregate Productivity Growth in the United States, 1948-1979", Brookings Papers on Economic Activity, 1983:2.

DATA SOURCES

1. Business cycle peaks and troughs are the annual calendar year reference dates identified by the National Bureau of Economic Research (NBER) and presented on p.64 of U.S. Department of Commerce, Bureau of Economic Analysis, Long Term Economic Growth, 1860-1970, Washington, D.C., 1973 (LTEG), and in later editions of Bureau of Economic Analysis, Business Conditons Digest.

2. Product prices are the Bureau of Labor Statistics wholesale price series presented in column B-68 on p. 222 of LTEG for the period prior to 1948 and thereafter the gross domestic product deflator for the private business economy presented in Table B-41 of the Economic Report of the President, 1982, Washington, D.C., 1982. (ERP)

3. Nominal wages for the period prior to 1948 refer to production workers in manufacturing and are taken from the real wage series presented in column B-70 on p. 222 of LTEG, reflated to their nominal levels using the consumer price index used by Albert Rees to convert the original nominal values to real terms. For 1948 and after the nominal wage is the hourly compensation series for the private business economy presented in table B-41 of ERP.

4. Output per hour is the series estimated by John Kendrick for the manufacturing sector, presented in column A-175 on p. 210 of LTEG for the pre 1948 period. Thereafter output per hour refers to the private business economy series presented in table B-41 of ERP.

5. The data on the recent cycle and the regression analysis of annual data presented in footnotes 7 and 9 are from the Economic Report of the President, 1984, table B-41.

6. The aggregate economic data in table 2 are from LTEG and from the U.S. Bureau of Economic Analysis, National Income and Product Accounts, various years.

THE INFLATION-BASED 'NATURAL' RATE OF UNEMPLOYMENT AND THE CONFLICT OVER INCOME DISTRIBUTION*

by

Peter Flaschel
Freie Universität Berlin

1. Introduction

In reviewing modern inflation theory H.Frisch (198o) in particular presents a monetarist model which - in a way that is comparable with Vanderkamp's (1975) and Dornbusch and Fischer's (1978) treatment of monetarist ideas - allows an analysis of the interaction among the growth rate of money supply, the growth rate of real income and the rate of inflation. In a revised presentation of this model [see Frisch and Hof (1981, pp.158f.)] it is no longer maintained that this textbook version of inflation and unemployment is "exclusively'monetarist' because the quantity equation is linked with the real sector through the Phillips curve and Okun's Law." In contrast to this revised characterization of Frisch's model, we shall, however, continue to call it a 'monetarist standard model,' because its Phillips curve in particular is essentially 'monetarist' in spirit, since it is based on the so-called natural rate hypothesis. This hypothesis claims that there is a stable relationship between deviations from monetarist 'natural' unemployment (which is exogenously given) and unanticipated inflation. Furthermore Okun's Law as it is used in this model is based on a given growth trend of potential output, which is an important ingredient in proving several 'monetarist' assertions including the belief in the *asymptotic* stability of the private sector. Frisch and Hof's (1981) model thus not only summarizes some important results of the so-called 'monetarist debate,' but also includes important components of the monetarist view of the economy. This justifies our designation of this model, despite the fact that today's monetarists may prefer more complicated transmission mechanisms of monetary impulses as well as formally different structural equations - as e.g. a Lucas supply function - with regard to deviations from 'natural' unemployment to derive Frisch and Hof's results [cf. the end of section 2]

---

*The author wishes to thank K.Dietrich, M.Krüger and M.J.M.Neumann for helpful criticism and comments.

In the following investigation, we intend to show by means of simple modifications of Frisch's standard model that the main building blocks [which are responsible for its monetarist implications], i.e., the 'natural' rate of unemployment and the NUR-hypothesis built upon it as well as the exogenously given trend growth of potential output, must be rejected as overly simplified, misleading and irrelevant to a proper analysis of the current problems of stagflation. To show this, we will present in section 2 a generalized continuous version of Frisch's model and a brief survey of its possible implications. Section 3 then questions the usual interpretation of the inflation-neutral (natural) rate of unemployment by showing that a quite different and endogenous interpretation may be more plausible to explain the high 'natural' rates of unemployment observed in the recent past. Section 4 finally will show that skepticism is justified in respect to the assumed stable relation between 'unnatural' unemployment and unanticipated inflation and will question the sense of assuming a given growth rate of potential output. Both sections derive their new views concerning natural unemployment and its relation to inflation by integrating aspects of the conflict over income distribution into Frisch's model, aspects which are complementary to each other but will not be integrated into a consistent whole in this paper. It is beyond the scope of this paper to provide a convincing and complete alternative to Frisch's prototype monetarist model. Our more modest aim is to question radically the theoretical usefulness of starting from given rates of 'natural' unemployment and potential output growth by assuming certain stable relations with regard to these rates. The problems concerning that part of unemployment not due to unexpected inflation and concerning capital shortage and cyclical accumulation are too important to be treated as exogenous, even in a simple model of stagflation. Yet, endogenizing these significant aspects of real development in our view will imply that a stable relationship of the NUR-hypothesis type can no longer sensibly be assumed.

2. A generalized 'monetarist standard model'

Below we shall introduce a general non-linear version of the monetarist 'textbook' model of Frisch and Hof (1981) - derived from Frisch (198o, II.4) - in order to present the so-called NUR-theorem and other standard monetarist assertions based on the concept of a natural unemployment rate (NUR). The significance of this rate - and of the theorem named after it - will be examined critically in two further paragraphs (§3 and §4), where especially the Phillips curve utilized - the so-called NUR-hypothesis - will be shown to be of rather dubious nature. A final paragraph (§5) will provide mathematical details for various formal statements made in the text. In the interest of simpler mathematical procedure we will use - in contrast to Frisch and Hof's article - a continuous-time version of their model and its modifications throughout and shall employ only purely qualitative methods of treatment due to the non-linearities now allowed for. Including non-linearities in Frisch's 'standard model' is compelling, at least with respect to the Phillips curve, and is also of great use in any more detailed discussion of the dynamic process where it takes part in [compare Vanderkamp (1975, p. 121) for an example].

The following four equations represent the general version of Frisch and Hof's (1981) 'monetarist model' we shall work with [compare their equations (1),(2),(3) and (16) for a linear and discrete presentation of these equations]:

$$\bar{\rho} = \pi + g \tag{1}$$

$$\pi = \bar{\eta}\pi^* + f(U-\bar{U}) \tag{2}$$

$$\dot{U} = h(g-\bar{g}) \tag{3}$$

$$\dot{\pi}^* = k(\pi-\pi^*) \tag{4}$$

The functions f,h,k fulfill $f(o) = h(o) = k(o) = o$ and $f' < o$, $h' < o$, $k' > o$. We use ($\bar{\ }$) to signify exogenous variables and ($\dot{\ }$) for time derivatives (d/dt). Equation (1) is the well-known quantity relationship between the growth rate of the money supply $\bar{\rho}$ on the one hand and the rate of inflation π as well as the growth rate of real income g on the other hand. This equation will not be questioned in the context of this paper [see, however, the final section of this paragraph for a short review of a different approach to the NUR-theorem which does not employ the above crude transmission mechanism (1) for monetary impulses $\bar{\rho}$]. Equation (2) represents a general version of a Phillips curve on the basis of a given 'natural' unemployment rate (NUR): $\bar{U}$. The parameter $\bar{\eta}$ in front of π^*, the expected rate of inflation, need not be equal to 'one', as is often assumed by monetarists [despite the mixed empirical results surveyed in Santomero and Seater (1978 , VI.A); in fact, we shall see in §4 that $\bar{\eta}$ must be less than one if a classical modification of the above model should suffice the monetarist 'postulate of stability'].'Okun's Law' as given by equation (3) describes the change $\dot{U}$ of the unemployment rate U as a falling function of the difference $g-\bar{g}$ of actual and 'natural' growth $\bar{g}=\bar{\alpha}+\bar{\beta}$ [the sum of labour productivity growth $\bar{\alpha}$ and population growth $\bar{\beta}$; compare §4 for a more detailed application of these two component rates $\bar{\alpha},\bar{\beta}$]. The Phillips curve and Okun's Law regulate the breakup of exogenous monetary impulses into growth and inflation. They represent the field of possible modifications for the following paragraphs, while equation (4), the assumption of an adaptive formation of inflationary expectations, will only temporarily give way to other still simpler assumptions concerning the formation of such expectations.

Equations (1) - (4) can easily be reduced to the following autonomous, non-linear system of differential equations in the variables U, π^*:

$$\dot{U} = h(\bar{\rho} - \bar{\eta}\pi^* - f(U-\bar{U}) - \bar{g}) \tag{5}$$

$$\dot{\pi}^* = k(f(U-\bar{U}) - (1-\bar{\eta})\pi^*) \tag{6}$$

Evaluated algebraically this system implies the unique steady-state solution ($\dot{U} = \dot{\pi}^* = o$):

$$\pi_o = \pi_o^* = \bar{\rho} - \bar{g} \tag{7}$$

$$U_0 = \bar{U} + f^{-1}((1-\bar{\eta})\pi_0^*) \tag{8}$$

if $(1-\bar{\eta})\pi_0^*$ lies within the domain of definition of the function f^{-1}. [For the sake of simplicity and corresponding to the textbook character of Frisch and Hof's presentation, we will, however, generally not explicitly state such additional assumptions as, e.g., those which would assure the condition $o \le U \le 1$]. In the steady-state the economy grows with the given trend $\bar{g}$ and with constant inflation (or deflation) of rate $\pi_o = \bar{\rho} - \bar{g}$. This rate π_0 can be called the 'inflation ceiling'; i.e., higher inflation rates π are necessarily related with subnormal growth rates g, due to the assumed strict quantity theory of money [see Rowthorn (198o, p.17o) for further comments on this notion . It follows that the difference between the 'natural' unemployment rate $\bar{U}$ and the steady-state rate U_0 carries the same sign as the inflation ceiling π_0 if $\bar{\eta} < 1$[it is zero if $\bar{\eta} = 1$].

Dynamic development apart from the steady-state can easily be derived by means of Olech's Theorem [see §5] and is illustrated in the following phase diagram. According to Olech's Theorem, the system is globally asymptotically stable, when for the Jacobian J (or the linear part) of the right-hand side of (5),(6)

$$J = \begin{pmatrix} J_{11} & J_{12} \\ J_{21} & J_{22} \end{pmatrix} = \begin{pmatrix} -h'f' & -\bar{\eta}h' \\ k'f' & -(1-\bar{\eta})k' \end{pmatrix} \tag{9}$$

the conditions trace $J = J_{11} + J_{12} < o$, $\det J = J_{11}J_{22} - J_{12}J_{21} > o$ and $J_{11}J_{22} \neq o$ or $J_{12}J_{21} \neq o$ are valid everywhere in $\mathbb{R}^2$. These conditions are fulfilled due to the assumptions made in relation to (1) - (4) if $\bar{\eta} < 1$ holds true, in which case the trajectories of system (5),(6) thus all approach the steady-state values (7),(8) for $t \to \infty$. And utilizing the isoclines $\dot{U} = o$, $\dot{\pi}^* = o$, i.e., the curves $U = \bar{U} + f^{-1}(\pi_0 - \bar{\eta}\pi^*)$ and

$U = \bar{U} + f^{-1}((1-\bar{\eta})\pi^*)$, this situation can be depicted in a phase diagram e.g., in the case $\bar{\eta} = 1$ considered by Frisch and Hof (1981) as follows:

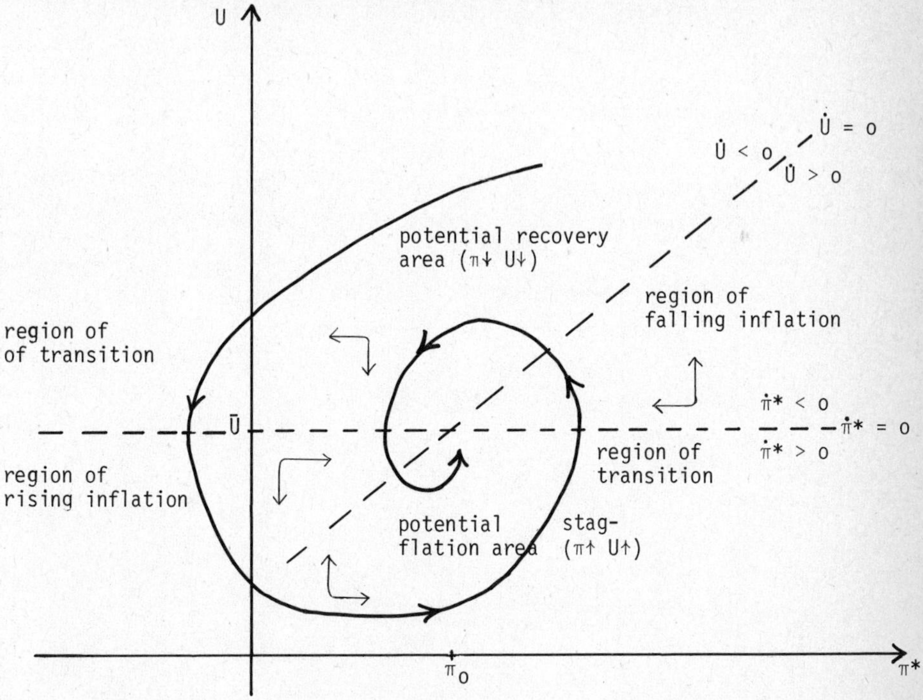

Figure 1: Convergence toward the steady-state values $\pi_0, \bar{U}$ for $\bar{\eta} = 1$, $\pi_0 > o$ [note here, that $\pi = \pi^* + f(U-\bar{U})$, i.e., $\dot{\pi} = \dot{\pi}^* + f'(U-\bar{U})\cdot\dot{U}$ provides the necessary information on the sign of $\dot{\pi}$ for two regions of this phase diagram].

The isoclines $\dot{U} = o$, $\dot{\pi}^* = o$ separate the four possible types of movement of system (5),(6) in the phase space (π^*,U) and seem to imply a cyclical behaviour of the variables π^*,U. An analysis of the eigenvalues of (9), however, demonstrates that, similar to the difference equations considered in Frisch and Hof (1981), locally cyclical behaviour (complex eigenvalues) will arise only under a further condition, namely $h'f' < 4k'$. Such cyclical dynamics implies that π^* and $-U$ cannot always run in phase, a fact which then must also hold true for $\pi = \pi^* + f(U-\bar{U}),-U$. The area in figure 1 beneath the curves $\dot{U} = o$, $\dot{\pi}^* = o$ shows the potential domain of a 'perverse' phase synchronisation (stagflation), which grows larger the steeper the curve f becomes.

To start the discussion on the NUR-hypothesis (2), the monetarist type of Phillips curve, let us reconsider this equation (2) in more detail. This NUR-hypothesis contradicts the conventional Phillips-curve trade-off in so far as it implies [for $\bar{\eta} = 1$, i.e., in the monetarist case] "that a fixed relation exists, not between economic aggregates and the rate of inflation, but between these aggregates and the difference between the actual rate of inflation and expectations about the rate of inflation" (Grossman, 198o, pp.6,7). The overly simplified Phillips-curve menu of Samuelson-Solow type is thereby modified to give a quite different kind of stable relationship. Roughly characterized, this new hypothesis is generally considered to derive from the assumption of a 'natural' rate of unemployment $\bar{U}$ ground out by the Walrasian system of general equilibrium equations if interpreted in terms of real world imperfections. Deviations of unemployment U from 'natural' unemployment $\bar{U}$ are then viewed to correlate negatively with deviations between actual and expected inflation π,π^* and are explained by (various types of) confusion prevailing among the agents of this economy. This general-equilibrium motivation of the NUR-hypothesis (2), $\bar{\eta} = 1$ goes back to the classic article of Friedman (1968) and might be called the *Speculative Walrasian Interpretation* (SWI) of the NUR-hypothesis. Disregarding this speculative background of the structural equation (2), however, this equation simply states that 'natural unemployment' prevails if and only if inflation is fully anticipated and that deviations from this unemployment rate correlate in a stable and predictable way with unanticipated inflation. We shall call this black-box type description of the 'natural' rate $\bar{U}$ the *Simple Inflation Approach* (SIA) to the definition of 'natural' unemployment. Finally, the 'natural' rate of unemployment may also be defined as that rate which is compatible with the steady-state development of a given macroeconomic system. This definition of 'natural' unemployment will be called the *Steady-State-Approach to 'Natural' Unemployment* (SNU) in the following. All three characterizations, the SWI, the SIA and the SNU are used interchangeably in Frisch (198o); compare in particular his page 51 and note that a partial justification of his formulations is provided by the NUR-theorem to be presented below. To my knowledge, however, no thorough and complete formal derivation of the SWI-approach à la Friedman has been presented to the date. Consequently this definition will only be of minor importance in examining the NUR, the NUR-hypothesis and the NUR-theorem to which this paper is devoted.

On the basis of the NUR-hypothesis (2), restricted to the case $\bar{\eta} = 1$, the following set of standard monetarist assertions very easily follows from the above model (1) - (4):

A. Short-term theorem: If a given steady-state is disturbed by a rising rate of monetary expansion $\bar{\rho}$, the actual unemployment rate will fall below the 'natural' rate, if expectations concerning inflation remain at the originally correct level.

B. Neutrality theorem: Every such disturbance of the steady-state moves, after the adaptive expectation adjustment process (4) sets in, toward a new steady-state and will consequently result solely in a rising rate of inflation.

C. Acceleration theorem: Every attempt to counter the neutrality theorem in order to perpetuate the employment effect of the short run requires an accelerating rate of monetary expansion $\bar{\rho}$ and implies accelerating inflation ($\pi \to \infty$).

D. Long-term theorem: If the expectations regarding inflation, in contrast to (4), are oriented toward the actual inflation ceiling π_0, then all adjustments to the steady-state $\bar{U},\bar{g}$ are monotonic and independent of the parameter $\bar{\rho}$, i.e., its variations.

E. NUR-theorem: If inflation is always fully anticipated, the economy (1) - (4) cannot depart from the steady-state.

These statements immediately follow from what has been shown for the system (1) - (4) if one observes that it suffices to discuss the differential equation (5) when considering A. and D. [in the latter case the movement of the unemployment rate U is governed by $\dot{U} = h(f(U-\bar{U}))$], that equation (5) is no longer in effect when C. is under consideration and that B. has already been treated in the stability analysis following (7) and (8).

Theorem E. - which is trivial in the context of the model (1) - (4) - specifically states that the SIA and the SNU-definitions of the 'natural' unemployment rate are in fact equivalent. This, however, is mainly due to what we consider an overly simplified hypothesis (2), the monetarist type of a stable Phillips curve relationship. Furthermore, the determination of 'natural' unemployment $\bar{U}$ is left completely unexplained in the context of the above model. Should this be 'standard' for the monetarist view on the dynamics of a capitalistic economy, it - and this view - can be criticized for at least two reasons. First, since the 'natural' rate $\bar{U}$ is exogenously given, we are still free to associate any interpretation with it which is consistent with the structural equations (1) - (4). We need not accept the SWI of Friedman and others, unless it is integrated into the standard model in an acceptable way. This, however, is a task which is neither easy nor has it been seriously approached, which is the reason why we designated the Friedman interpretation of the 'natural' rate $\bar{U}$ as 'speculative.' An alternative interpretation of the rate $\bar{U}$ will be considered - by way of its endogenization - in §3, and it may help to induce monetarists to express their ideas about their 'natural' rate in a similar prototype and explicit way. Secondly, the assumed stability of the NUR-hypothesis (2) bears close resemblance to the overly simplified stability assumption for the Samuelson-Solow modification of the original Phillips curve, which has justifiably been attacked by monetarists for its crude menu-view of the problem of unemployment cum inflation. We shall see in §4 that a simple classical model with an endogenous determination of the growth of potential income and th capital stock is sufficient to demonstrate that a stable relationship of type (2) cannot sensibly be assumed.

Summing up the discussion of this paragraph theorems A.-E. can be illustrated in the following manner:

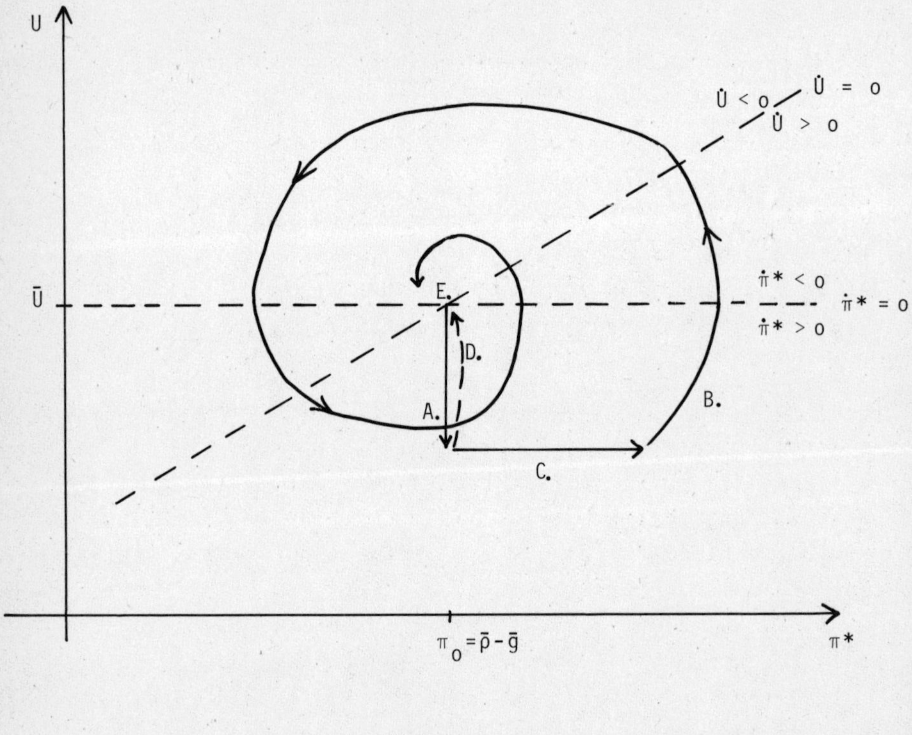

Figure 2: Short-term actions (A.), Neutrality (B.; on the assumption tha initially as well as in the end holds: $\rho = \bar{\rho}$), Acceleration (C.), long-term expectations (D.) and perfect foresight (E.).

This diagram proves again the futility, in the context of the present model, of wanting to operate for longer periods below the $\dot{\pi}^* = 0$-line, i.e., below 'natural' unemployment $\bar{U}$ [Note that during the process C. the $\dot{U} = 0$-isocline must continuously shift to the right, so that in giving up the goal of reaching 'unnaturally' low rates of unemployment the dynamic process is again left to itself at the unfavourable end of the stagflation area, see figure 1]. Furthermore, situations C.-E. very well illustrate the crucial role that the Phillips curve (2) plays in this model: Together with Okun's Law (3) it regulates the economy in such a way that temporary deviations from a given trend will always be corrected in the end; they indeed will be eliminated the quicker, the more foresight we introduce into the process by which inflationary expectations are formed.

A supplementary remark: This paragraph has provided a brief sketch of how to derive standard monetarist assertions from a very simple dynamic model. It has been argued, however [see Neumann (1983)], that the equations of this model - in particular the assumed strict quantity theory of money (1) - are not 'monetarist' in spirit, so that Frisch and Hof's model (1) - (4) should not be characterized as a 'monetarist standard model.' Though other authors exist who use similar equations to represent monetarist assertions, Neumann's claim nevertheless seems to be correct, since 'assets' are not really present in the model employed to date. However, even in Neumann's (1983) alternative monetarist model the ultimate effect of monetary policy on the behaviour of output and prices is very similar to that shown by Frisch and Hof - despite their use of only one asset of very dubious nature (helicopter money). The inclusion of various assets, various relative prices, and the change from a Phillips-Okun-type of dynamics to a (static) Lucas supply-function (based on labour market equilibrium) to treat unexpected price changes caused by a transmission process which leads from money supply changes to output price changes, thus does not fundamentally alter the two basic assumptions of monetarist constructions criticized here: the unexplained, since exogenous, nature of the 'natural' rate of unemployment $\bar{U}$ and the assumption of a stable relationship between prices, price expectations and output and employment in comparison to their natural levels $\bar{Y}, \bar{U}$ [see equation (6.b) in Neumann (1983)]. Hence, the following critique of the monetarist treatment of unemployment and its development over time essentially also applies to alternative presentations of the monetarist analysis of the phenomenon of stagflation.

3. Conflict over distribution and the 'natural' unemployment rate

We have shown in the last section how standard monetarist assertions can be derived from a very simple macroeconomic model. And in closing this section we have stressed the fact that these assertions will not be significantly altered if more flexible market mechanisms are allowed for to deal with aggregate demand shocks - as long as the essence of the NUR-hypothesis (2) is preserved, i.e., as long as deviations from a predetermined 'natural' (or equilibrium) rate of unemployment can only occur *in combination with* unanticipated inflation (or price changes).

The NUR and the hypothesis built upon it consequently represent the critical steps in the monetarist arguments against an active monetary policy - or other types of demand management to combat high unemployment rates - at least with regard to their 'natural' core [5 to 6 percent according to Tobin (1972)!]. This 'natural' core, in the words of Friedman (1968, p.8), "is the level that would be ground out by the Walrasian system of general equilibrium equations, provided there is imbedded in them the actual structural characteristics of the labor and commodity markets, including market imperfections, stochastic variability in demands and supplies, the cost of gathering information about job vacancies and labor availabilities, the costs of mobility, and so on."

In the light of existing Walrasian general equilibrium models, this idea of 'natural unemployment' must be regarded as being fairly speculative, not only because of the huge task involved in modelling this rate by means of the proposed extension of Arrow-Debreu theory, but also because "this theory has nothing simple to offer in answer to the question why is the share of wages, or of profits, what it is?...[because, P.F.] social class is not an explanatory variable of neo-classical theory. The latter is not formulated in terms of workers and capitalists but in terms of inputs and outputs. This lack of contact between the economic theory and sociological reality may well be the most damaging criticism of the neoclassical construction." (Frank Hahn, 1972, p.2).

The commonly employed identification of the noninflationary 'natural' rate of unemployment with a Walrasian equilibrium rate of unemployment consequently must be regarded as premature, unless some prototype and complete model is presented in which a thorough endogenous description of the NUR $\bar{U}$ is given. Otherwise, the SWI-view of the NUR-hypothesis (2) should rather be dismissed as being unfounded. There then remains only the SIA-attitude to justify the model (1) - (4) of section 2. This, however, is a black box description of the NUR, which not only allows a variety of monetarist interpretations of this behaviour, but also makes an interpretation admissable that is explicitly based on the existence of social classes, as stressed by Hahn. The spectrum of beliefs about the nature of inflation described in Laidler (1981, pp.7f.) indeed can be enriched by a version which sharply differs from any monetarist one without significantly changing the equations (1) - (4) on which Frisch's monetarist standard model is based. We shall demonstrate in this section that Frisch's standard model in fact allows such an extremely contradictory interpretation of one of its basic premises, the 'natural' rate of unemployment $\bar{U}$.

The following new interpretation of equations (1) - (4) has the decisive advantage that the determination of the rate $\bar{U}$ is now explained by the model itself. This eliminates a grave weakness from the monetarist model of the causes of unemployment, though it, of course, is but a small step in the critical evaluation of the NUR-hypothesis and of the monetarist theory of the business cycle built upon it (section 2). Further steps in this direction will be taken in section 4, where the NUR-hypothesis itself is criticized as representing a structural equation of too crude a type.

The variation of the 'standard model' (1) - (4) to be treated here closely follows some concepts developed in Rowthorn (198o). Equation (1), the 'budget equation' for inflation and growth, as well as equation (4), the adaptive process by which expectations about inflation are formed, will remain unquestioned in this model variant. Yet, in order to derive equations (2) and (3), which essentially determine the division of a monetary impulse $\bar{\rho}$ into inflation π and growth g, the following new assumptions about behaviour will be made. Instead of Frisch's Okun-Law (3), we will employ one of Okun's (197o) original approximations of this law [see his page 136]:

$$V/\bar{V} = (Y/Y_p)^{\bar{d}} = \Theta^{\bar{d}}, \; \bar{d} > 0. \qquad (1o)$$

Here, V represents the rate of employment, which according to this 'law' is positively correlated with the degree of capacity utilization Θ of the capital stock K. Logarithmic differentiation of (1o) then yields the equation by which we shall replace Frisch's equation (3):

$$\hat{V} = \bar{d}(\hat{Y}-\hat{Y}_p) = \bar{d}(g-\bar{g}_p) \qquad (11)$$

[note that Okun assumes $\bar{V} \equiv 0.96$, i.e., $\hat{\bar{V}} \equiv 0$]. As is evident from their formulation, these equations again assume a constant trend growth of potential output Y_p (of rate $\bar{g}_p$). Equations (11) essentially differ from (3) in that $\dot{V} = -\dot{U}$ has been replaced by $\hat{V}$. Our main deviation from Frisch's model (1) - (4) consequently will concern its Phillips curve (2), which here is derived from the following assumption about how the inflation rate is formed ($\bar{\eta} = 1$ again):

$$\pi = \bar{c}(\Pi^*-\Pi) + \pi^*, \; \bar{c} > 0. \qquad (12)$$

In this equation the symbols π^* and π signify expected and actual inflation rates as usual, while Π, Π^* denote the actual and the target profit share of capitalists. [cp. Rowthorn (198o, pp.15off.) for further details]. Equation (12) indicates that the expected inflation rate undergoes a correction that is proportional to the aspiration gap $\Pi^*-\Pi$ in its transmission into actual inflation π. In order to make this type of Phillips curve (12) analytically applicable, the determinants of the aspiration gap remain to be stipulated. Rival income claims, expressing themselves in the target share Π^* and in the momentary wage share $l = 1-\Pi$, can initially be seen as dependent on the demand for the commodities supplied by the respective party. That is, they can be viewed as dependent on the degree of utilization Θ of the capital stock and on the degree of 'utilization' V of the labour force, respectively:

$$\Pi^*(\Theta), \Pi^{*\prime} > o, \quad l(V), \quad l' > o \tag{13}$$

Income claims are therefore simply regulated by the respective utilization of capital and labour. But according to equation (1o), the employment rate V can be substituted for Θ in $\Pi^*(\Theta)$ without causing a change in the assumed mode of reaction $\Pi^{*\prime} > o$. The final form of the Phillips curve of this section consequently is

$$\begin{aligned}\pi &= \bar{c}(\Pi^*(V) - (1-l(V))) + \pi^* \\ &= \bar{c}(\Pi^*(V) + l(V)-1) + \pi^*,\end{aligned} \tag{14}$$

a form which, if one wishes to do so, can be interpreted as a specific explication of the Phillips curve (2) we used in section 2.

The analogy to equation (2) can be made even more obvious if one defines as 'natural' (in applying the SIA to determine 'natural' unemployment) that rate V_0 which implies a wage share $l(V_0)$ and a target share $\Pi^*(V_0)$ which are compatible with each other insofar as no additional inflation effects will arise above and beyond the inflationary expectations π^* in this case. This rate V_0 is defined by $l(V_0) + \Pi^*(V_0) = 1$ and it is uniquely determined [see (13)]. It will exist if $l(o) + \Pi^*(o) < 1 < l(1) + \Pi^*(1)$ holds true. Finally, by means of this rate we obtain from equations (14)

$$\pi = \bar{c}(\Pi^*(V) + l(V) - (\Pi^*(V_0) + l(V_0))) + \pi^* \tag{15}$$

which is the kind of Phillips curve we used in the preceding section [if V, V_0 are replaced by $1-U$, $1-U_0$].

The important point with regard to this curve is that its 'natural' rate V_0 [in general $\neq \bar{V}$, the rate which underlies the Okun curve (1o)!] is no longer exogenously given and of a SWI-type. Social classes and their particular interests - and no longer households and firms subordinated to them - are now at the center of the analysis. Conflict over income distribution is regulated by the respective power of the two classes, here measured in terms of the utilization rates Θ and V, and gives explicit content to the black box unemployment rate of the Simple Inflation Approach (SIA). Monetarists may - and surely will - not be content with the way we have filled the gap given by their black-box rate $\bar{U}$. Yet, they cannot disqualify the above additions to Frisch's monetarist model simply by pointing to the complex Walrasian character of their 'natural' rate $\bar{U}$. Complexity is no excuse which allows one to treat a rate of unemployment of more than 5 percent as exogenous in a complete model of macroeconomic interdependence. If a noninflationary 'natural' rate of unemployment of basically Walrasian type worth mentioning really exists in a monetary economy, then ways have to be found by which their essential determinants can be treated explicitly in a macroeconomic model of unemployment and inflation.

It should be obvious from our discussion that up to our endogenous determination of the rate $\bar{U}(= 1-V_0)$ Frisch's standard model (1) - (4) has undergone practically no revision. Equations (14),(11) now simply replace equations (2) and (3). Thus, equations (5) and (6) can be replaced by

$$\hat{V} = \bar{d}(\bar{\rho}-\pi^*-\bar{c}(\Pi^*(V) + l(V)-1) - \bar{g}_p) \qquad (16)$$

$$\dot{\pi}^* = k(\bar{c}(\Pi^*(V) + l(V) - 1)) \qquad (17)$$

In view of this formal correspondance, the entire analysis presented in section 2 is therefore also valid for the model considered in this section and need not be repeated here.

The 'natural' unemployment rate is estimated in Batchelor (1981) principally on the basis of the NUR-hypothesis (2). The result of his calculations can be roughly summarized in the following diagram

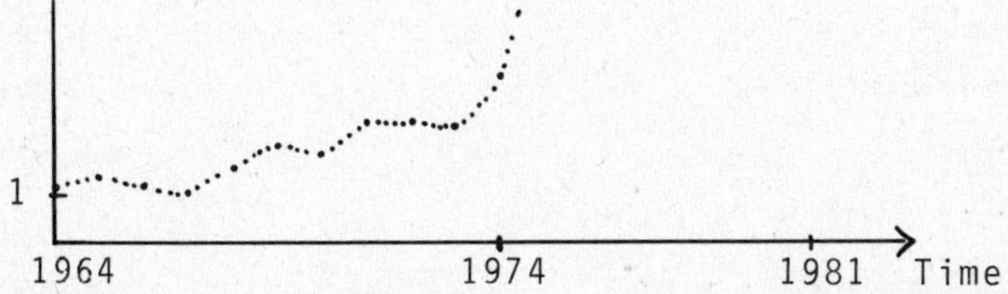

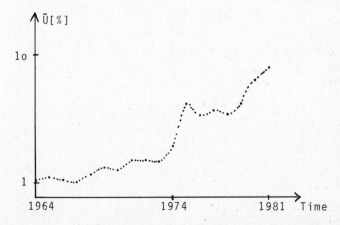

Figure 3: The behaviour of 'natural' unemployment in time

Should we conclude on the basis of this empirical evidence (which in its qualitative features is confirmed by other empirical studies) by employing Friedman's SWI that the Walrasian world we are suggested to live in has become progressively imperfect to ground out this steep rise in 'natural' unemployment? We do not think that such a conclusion - nor its basis - makes much sense. Our alternative interpretation of the observed behaviour of the 'natural' rate $\bar{U} = 1-V_0$ (on the basis of the above reformulation of Frisch's model) here is that situations of depressed growth $\bar{g}_p$ of potential output (the occurrence of which still requires explanation) may go hand-in-hand with upward shifts in the aggressiveness of capitalist' or labourers' income claims, due to the fact that there is now less (additional) income to distribute. Such upward shifts imply that the 'natural' rate $U_0 = 1-V_0$ will rise, and will cause further inflationary pressure at the current rate of unemployment $U = 1-V$. This additional inflationary pressure can be reduced - if the fight against inflation becomes of primary importance for the political decision maker - either by a wage-price freeze or (as is customarily the case today) by allowing for idle labour and capital, thus reversing the upward shift in income claims behaviour in the end. 'Natural' unemployment consequently should fall again after a certain period of high unemployment and low capacity utilization - at least if there are no severe social consequences like, e.g., the development of a hard core of unemployables because of the interstratified existence of large rates of unemployment. We conject that it is this view and not Friedman's speculative Walrasian view which implicitly underlies the anti-inflationary programs put into effect in the recent past. This is documented to some extent by the indifference of politicians towards the rapid rise of unemployment, an attitude which can hardly be justified on the grounds of wanting to break inflationary expectations π^* alone. The disciplinary function of the $U-\bar{U} = V_0-V$ term in the Phillips curve (14) is in our opinion fairly well-known, though it is seldom explicitly expressed. Less known, however, are the social consequences of these economic policies [see, e.g., Hargreaves Heap (198o) for a formalized approach to such consequences].

A thorough analysis of the views expressed above, however, cannot be supplied in the context of this paper, which mainly addresses a critique of a particular monetarist hypothesis by formulating simple alternative views, which are at least equally plausible as the monetarist constructions, but which nevertheless still need elaboration. A further step in this direction is the observation that the monetarist NUR-hypothesis (2) is still utilized (at least formally) in the above modification of

Frisch's 'monetarist standard model' and that potential output grows at a predetermined rate $\bar{g}_p$ in this variant, too. The weaknesses still present in this section's approach to unemployment and inflation also find expression in the fact that the development depicted above concerning the 'natural' rate $\bar{U}$ (figure 3) must be solely attributed to rising aggressiveness of income claims if one uses our revised form of Frisch's model to explain this development. Such a monocausal explanation of the rise in that part of unemployment, which cannot be attributed to erroneous expectations about inflation $\pi^*-\pi$, is not very convincing. We need further arguments to help explain this component of unemployment. Some such arguments will be supplied in the following section using a model which discusses the consequences of the conflict over income distribution with regard to 'natural' growth $\bar{g}_p$, now by neglecting the problems of capacity utilization Θ considered in this section. The result of this discussion will be that the NUR-hypothesis should be completely dismissed because it is not a sensible and stable relationship, which also implies that it should not be used to measure the core of the unemployed (however defined). The models of this and the following section stress different aspects of the conflict over income distribution which should be integrable (but are not integrated in this paper) by treating simultaneously the problems of the underutilization of existing capital and its varying growth over time.

4. A classical modification of the 'standard model'

We have seen in the last section how the interpretation of the 'natural' unemployment rate of the Simple Inflation Approach (SIA) can be radically changed and why it will depart from Okun's (197o, p.137) exogenous benchmark rate of 4 percent unemployment. The results obtained question Okun's procedure to identify this benchmark rate with a reasonable target for anti-inflationary politics, since this latter target rate heavily depends on developments in the conflict over income distribution which should not be included in an output-unemployment relationship of mainly technological nature.

Okun (197o, pp.132ff.) qualifies his treatment of the technological relationship $V = o.96(Y/Y_p)^{\bar{d}}$, however, by means of a variety of additional observations, which are normally ignored when this 'law' is used for economic model building. For example, Okun (197o, p.137) remarks that the growth rate g_p of potential output Y_p was not uniform throughout his sample period 1947-6o and that "the failure to use one year's potential fully can influence future potential GNP: To the extent that low utilization rates and accompanying low profits... hold down investment..., the growth of potential GNP will be retarded." [see p.134].

However, profits and thus investment may also vary even if actual output always coincides with its potential level - due to changes in income distribution! Such a possibility is ignored in the models of sections 2,3 where the growth rate of potential output g_p is treated as exogenous, not subject to a retardation process at all. It is not possible in this paper to present a thorough extension of the model of section 3 which would incorporate the type of retardation mentioned in Okun (197o). Instead, we shall ignore problems of the underutilization of capital below and will concentrate our interest on a further mechanism - the profit-squeeze mechanism - by which fluctuations of potential output may be generated. This choice has the advantage that it can be treated in an analytically well-established way. Furthermore, this influence on potential output growth is of a sufficiently sweeping character to question radically the NUR-hypothesis of section 2 (and its implications), the main intention of this paper. And finally, the classical investment cycle derived from it solely abstracts from the problems of deficient demand and idle capital and therefore does not exclude a later integration of these effects into its dynamics, e.g., along the lines we have sketched in the preceding section.

The two models we have considered so far do not allow the possibility that potential output growth g_p varies with actual output Y and its rate of growth g. The dynamics considered above thus should only be applied to an analysis of the short-run. In the medium run it is no longer possible to assume the rate g_p as given. To endogenize this rate we shall - as has already been stated - start from a simple classical view of capital accumulation, namely Goodwin's (1967) classical growth cycle model. This model will now be appropriately modified to make it comparable to Frisch's monetarist standard model, i.e., to allow equally well for the discussion of the impact of exogenous monetary impulses on real growth and inflation. Goodwin's (1967) model, which discusses the interaction between profitability and capital accumulation, is meanwhile well established in the literature and has been extended into various directions [see, e.g., Malinvaud's (198o, pp.72f.) classical unemployment dynamics for a recent contribution which is in the spirit of this growth cycle model]. The following description of our modification of Goodwin's original model therefore can be brief and will be concentrated on its implications in the main.

Assume as given a conventional aggregate production relationship in the fixed coefficient form which is subject to Harrod neutral technical change. Assume furthermore a Kaleckian classical savings function $S = s_p P$ with $o < s_p \leq 1$, where P denotes profit income [see Jones (1975, Ch.2) for details]. Assume finally that ex-ante investment is identical with ex-ante saving, so that the Keynesian difficulties of deficient demand (and of idle capital, see section 3) can be ignored. On the basis of these standard assumptions of growth theory, we get from the tautological relation

$$V = Y_p/[(Y_p/N)\cdot N^s]$$

[see section 3 with regard to the content of its symbols] the following set of relationships between the rate of change of the employment rate $\hat{V}$, the growth rate of the potential output g, labour productivity growth $\bar{\alpha}$, labour force growth $\bar{\beta}$ and the share of wages l:

$$\begin{aligned}\hat{V} &= g - \bar{\alpha} - \bar{\beta}\\ &= \hat{K} - (\bar{\alpha}+\bar{\beta})\\ &= s_p(1-l)Y_p/K - (\bar{\alpha}+\bar{\beta})\\ &= s_p(1-l)/\bar{\sigma} - (\bar{\alpha}+\bar{\beta})\end{aligned} \qquad (18)$$

These equations immediately follow from our above assumptions of a constant capital-output ratio $\bar{\sigma} = K/Y_p$ and a Solowian investment behaviour $\dot{K} = I \equiv S$ based on earned profits $P = (1-l)Y_p$ and a constant savings propensity s_p [note that the above symbols $\bar{\alpha},\bar{\beta}$ in addition indicate that we - in line with common practice in this field of investigation - proceed from given rates of growth of labour productivity and of the labour force]. Equation (18) replaces Okun's Law (11) by endogenizing capital stock accumulation $\hat{K}$ in the place of capacity utilization Θ. And instead of the NUR-hypotheses (2),(15) we here return to Phillips' original money-wage specification of his curve, now also augmented by a term which reflects inflationary expectation (m the money wage):

$$\hat{m} = \bar{\eta}\pi^* + \tilde{f}(V), \quad \tilde{f}' > o \qquad (19)$$

As in section 2 and 3 these two equations are again supplemented by the strict quantity theory of money

$$\bar{\rho} = \pi + g = \pi + s_p(1-l)/\bar{\sigma} \qquad (2o)$$

and by an adaptive mechanism of inflation rate expectations

$$\dot{\pi}^* = k(\pi-\pi^*), \quad k' > o \qquad (21)$$

Utilizing the definitional relation $\hat{l} = \hat{m} - \pi - \bar{\alpha}$ these four equations form a complete model in the four unknowns V,l,π,π^* [when the Phillips curve (19) is reformulated as $\hat{l} = \bar{\eta}\pi^* + \tilde{f}(V) - \pi - \bar{\alpha}$ by means of the above definitional relationship].

The modification region of Frisch's monetarist model (1) - (4) is thus, as in section 3, here again only the form of division of a monetary impulse $\bar{\rho}$ into inflation π and growth g, now by means of the following dynamic equations (18),(19):

$$\hat{V} = s_p(1-l)/\bar{\sigma} - (\bar{\alpha}+\bar{\beta}), \quad \hat{l} = \eta\pi^* + \tilde{f}(V) - \pi - \bar{\alpha}$$

instead of (2) and (3). Since we have restricted our attention in this section to the case where capital is fully utilized, it is no longer possible to include implicitly or explicitly a mark-up pricing procedure in the present model. This is only admissable when the degree of capacity utilization is allowed to vary (to reconcile the double determination of the inflation rate through the quantity theory and the chosen theory of mark-up pricing), an additional complication which will not be treated in this paper, since it will not alter the negative conclusions found out below.

With regard to the curve (19) it is assumed that there exists $\bar{V} \in (o,1)$ which fulfills $\tilde{f}(\bar{V}) = \bar{\alpha}$. Note, that this is not equivalent to the assumption of a 'natural' unemployment rate $\bar{U}$ as it underlies hypothesis (2). Instead, this rate $\bar{V}$ rather resembles the rate V_o derived in section 3, despite the different types of dynamics considered in this and the preceding section. The unique steady-state values of system (18) - (21) can easily be calculated and they fulfill the equations

$$l_o = 1 - \bar{\sigma}(\bar{\alpha}+\bar{\beta})/s_p$$
$$\pi_o = \bar{\rho} - s_p(1-l_o)/\bar{\sigma} = \bar{\rho} - (\bar{\alpha}+\bar{\beta}) = \bar{\rho} - g_o = \pi_o^*$$
$$V_o = \tilde{f}^{-1}((1-\bar{\eta})\pi_o + \bar{\alpha}), \ \bar{\eta} \text{ close to } 1$$

With regard to the theorems A.-D. of section 2 we may now briefly state, that A. and D. will again be true, since the dynamics of system (18) - (21) can then be reduced to only two differential equations which fulfill the assumptions of Olech's Theorem [expectations π^* are treated as exogenous (short-term theorem) or are given by $\pi^* = \bar{\rho} - \bar{\alpha}-\bar{\beta}$ (long-term theorem)]. The proof of global stability of the whole dynamic system (18) - (21), which by means of $\pi = \bar{\rho} - s_p(1-l)/\bar{\sigma}$ can be reduced to three nonlinear equations in the three variables l,V,π^*, is now no longer straightforward. What can be shown by means of Routh's criterion, however, is that this system is locally asymptotically stable. This restricted assertion leaves everything concerning *practical* stability open and thereby greatly reduces the power of the neutrality theorem B. Finally, the acceleration theorem D. now largely falls from consideration since a stabilization of the employment rate V, e.g., above its steady-state value V_o annuls at once the whole dynamic structure of the system, which means that this theorem requires a more extensive model specification for its sensible discussion in our new setting.

Though a more careful treatment of these four theorems may reveal further differences in comparison to the results obtained in section 2, these differences are not of primary concern in this paper. Our interest lies in the NUR-hypothesis and in the theorem E. derived from it. If we abstract - as is demanded by this theorem - from unanticipated inflation ($\pi^* \equiv \pi$), the above system (18) - (21) of differential equations is again reduced to only two equations, namely

$$\hat{l} = \tilde{f}(V) - \bar{\alpha} - (1-\bar{\eta})(\bar{\rho} - s_p(1-l)/\bar{\sigma}) \qquad (22)$$

$$\hat{V} = s_p(1-l)/\bar{\sigma} - (\bar{\alpha}+\bar{\beta}) \qquad (23)$$

which imply the same steady-state values as before. For the dynamics of this system with fully anticipated inflation we now, however, get:

<u>Theorem</u>: The dynamic system (22),(23) is globally asymptotically stable (totally instable) if $\bar{\eta} < 1$ ($\bar{\eta} > 1$). And for $\bar{\eta} = 1$ system (22),(23) only exhibits closed orbits around its steady-state values l_o, V_o, i.e., the monetarist case $\bar{\eta} = 1$ is not asymptotically stable.

<u>Proof</u>: The first part of this theorem is an immediate consequence of Olech's Theorem, appropriately reformulated for the two situations under consideration [see the mathematical appendix]. And its second part is at least plausible, since it must be the limit case between the two situations $\bar{\eta} < 1$, $\bar{\eta} > 1$ already considered [see Flaschel (1984) for a more detailed proof].

Represented in a phase diagram we obtain for the monetarist case $\bar{\eta} = 1$:

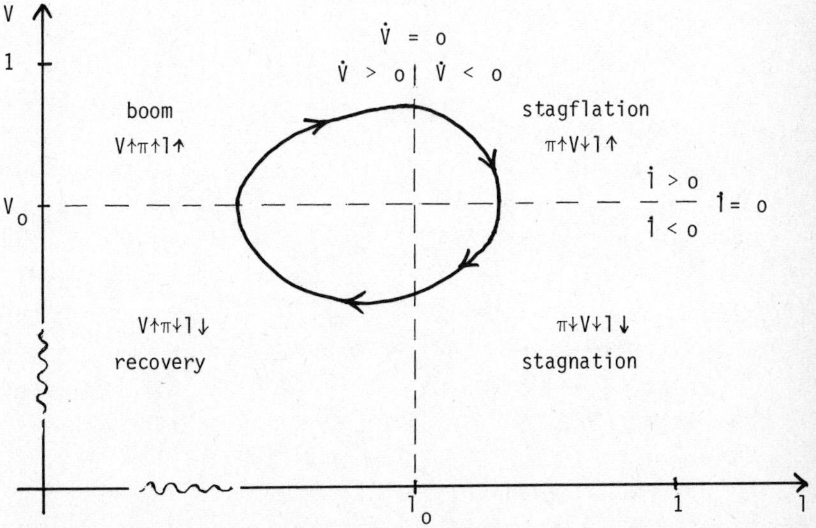

<u>Figure 4</u>: The 'Lotka-Volterra' case of system (22),(23)

On the basis of this diagram and the preceding theorem the following important economic conclusions can now be drawn (for the case $\bar{\eta} = 1$):

a.) There is no fixed relation â la Grossman (see section 2) between economic aggregates and the difference between actual and expected inflation in the context of this system of endogenous capital growth.

b.) Such a fixed relation can only be ensured if mark-up pricing of the type $p = \bar{R}(mN/Y)$ implying $\pi = \hat{m} - \bar{\alpha}$ is introduced into the above model. However, such an extension of system (18) - (21) - in addition to the capacity utilization problems it will cause - has the unpleasant feature that it implies $\widehat{m/p} = \bar{\alpha}$ and $\hat{l} = o$, facts which can sensibly be assumed solely for the short-run, yet not for the intermediate-run that is considered here.

c.) Assuming $\hat{l}=o$ [$\widehat{m/p} = \bar{\alpha}$] and $\bar{\alpha} = \widehat{Y/N}$ (also in the case of idle capital) allows to transform system (18) - (21) into the following system of differential equations

$$\hat{V} = g - (\bar{\alpha}+\bar{\beta}),\ g = \hat{Y}$$
$$\pi = \pi^* + \tilde{f}(V) - \bar{\alpha}$$
$$\bar{\rho} = \pi + g$$
$$\dot{\pi}^* = k(\pi-\pi^*)$$

because of $V = N/N^S = Y/[(Y/N)\cdot N^S]$. This result indicates to some extent how the standard model (1) - (4) of section 2 can be obtained by ignoring the effects of a changing income distribution [$\hat{K} = s_p(1-\bar{l})/\bar{\sigma} = \bar{g}_p$ is then exogenously determined (and equal to $\bar{\alpha} + \bar{\beta}$ if $\bar{l} = l_o$) due to the restrictive assumption $l = \bar{l}$].

d.) In the context of the above model the SIA and the SNU (see section 2) are no longer equivalent, i.e., the neutrality theorem E. of section 2 now fails: The SIA now implies that each actual unemployment rate has to be characterized as 'natural', while only the rate V_o can be 'natural' with regard to the SNU. Similarly, there now holds $g = g_p$ with regard to every actual growth situation, yet $g_p = \bar{\alpha} + \bar{\beta}$ will in general be false! The two stable curves (2),(3) of section 2 thus become of very dubious nature in the frame of this simple classical model of capital accumulation. The commonly believed equivalence between a Walrasian, a perfect-foresight, and a steady-state characterization of the 'natural unemployment rate' is completely absent from this classical variation of Frisch's standard model (1) - (4) and therefore cannot be considered to represent a very robust proposition of economic theory.

e.) Any measurement of the 'natural' unemployment rate which is based on the NUR-hypothesis (2) as, e.g., in Batchelor (1981), compare figure 3 in section 3, can be completely misleading if the dynamics considered above is of some relevance. Considering for example figure 4, its actual unemployment rates U would then all be measured as 'natural' by this procedure - if measurement errors are neglected - which in part explains the steep rise of 'natural rates' that has been observed by Batchelor. If the steady-state $U_o = 1-V_o$, the only unemployment rate which allows for constant rates of inflation, is to be estimated, unanticipated inflation therefore is by no means a sufficient starting-point to determine its complementary part $U-U_o$.

f.) In the context of the above model, also the Keynesian approach of structuring unemployment into frictional, structural and demand-deficient components must be looked at in suspicion [see Armstrong and Taylor (1981) for such an approach]. Such attempts, based on Hansen's U-V-methodology - classify all unemployment U exceeding the number of vacancies as demand deficient. This last, unquestionably important component of unemployment has, however, been excluded by assumption from the above model, which leads us to the absurd conclusion that in this Goodwin-type model open positions and job hunters always balance each other out. Capital shortage, too little capital to employ the entire workforce, seems to play no role in the above Keynesian classification of unemployment.

g.) The above model finally implies that the private sector can only be asymptotically stable if the growth rate of money supply $\bar{\rho}$ exercises some influence on the development of 'natural' unemployment V_o, which, of course, is a trade-off not very favourable to the monetarist view of the economy.

The above conclusions [drawn from a simple variant of Frisch's (198o) as well as Goodwin's (1967) model] should not be regarded as being well-established propositions derived from a framework that is also already acceptable to a monetarist inclined reader. They should be viewed rather as a starting point for discussion, which on the one hand must integrate problems of effective demand, price setting behaviour, risky financial assets, etc., but which, on the other hand, should not return to the crude view of a given 'natural' unemployment rate and a given trend growth of potential output [to which short-term deviations will adjust in the end]. It is our conjecture that the above depicted cyclical development of the wage share l and the employment rate V (which here follow each other with a quarter phase displacement) at least partially will remain intact in the above proposed extensions of the model. Capital shortage (and abundancy) - relative to the trend $\bar{\alpha}+\bar{\beta}$ - is an important macroeconomic problem and not only a logical possibility which allows to conjecture the disappearance of available jobs without a deficiency of total demand. The economic system may not function so regularly as the ideal case depicted in figure 4 suggests [see Malinvaud (198o) for a more diversified dynamics, which in part, however, relates to the above described dynamical behaviour]. Yet, endogenizing that part of unemployment which cannot be attributed to misconceptions of the economic agents with regard to price behaviour and also endogenizing potential output growth, e.g., along the lines here suggested (or along different lines), will in any case preserve the basic conclusion of this article, namely that the NUR-hypothesis and the NUR-theorem cannot be maintained in an economic model which truly investigates these two types of complications. After correctly criticizing the crude descriptions of the unemployment-inflation trade-off developed in the sixties, monetarists have established alternative stable relationships, which in the end, however, will suffer from the same type of critique, because they take components and structures of the economic system as exogenous and stable which are too important to be treated in this way.

5. Mathematical appendix

The original version of the theorem of Olech which we have used in section 2 reads as follows [compare Ito (1978, p.312)]:

Theorem 1: Given an autonomous differential equation system

$$\dot{x} = f(x,y),\ \dot{y} = g(x,y),\ (x,y) \in \mathbb{R}^2 \tag{24}$$

with continuously differentiable functions $f,g: \mathbb{R} \to \mathbb{R}$, which possesses exactly one stationary point $(x_0,y_0) \in \mathbb{R}^2$, i.e., a point where $\dot{x}$ and $\dot{y}$ are zero. This equilibrium point (x_0,y_0) is globally asymptotically stable if the Jacobian J of (24) fulfills the following three conditions:

(a) trace $J = f_x + g_y < o$ for all $(x,y) \in \mathbb{R}^2$

(b) $\det J = f_x g_y - f_y g_x > o$ for all $(x,y) \in \mathbb{R}^2$

(c) Either $f_x g_y \neq o$ for all $(x,y) \in \mathbb{R}^2$ or
$f_y g_x \neq o$ for all $(x,y) \in \mathbb{R}^2$

In place of Ito's (1978) generalization of this theorem the following modification suffices for the purposes of § 3 and 4:

Theorem 2: Take as given an autonomous differential equation system of kind (24), the left side of which, however, is based either on time derivatives $\dot{x}(\dot{y})$ or on growth rates $\hat{x}(\hat{y})$ and which again exhibits a unique equilibrium solution (x_0,y_0) [> o in so far as growth rates appear] and for which one of the two products in (c) is identically zero. The conditions for global asymptotic stability of the equilibrium point (x_0, y_0) are then the same as in Theorem 1 [whereby for variables which relate to growth rates the restriction to the interval $(o, +\infty)$ is possible and necessary].

Proof: Instead of $\dot{x} = f(x,y)$ take as given the equation $\hat{x} = f(x,y)$. The transformation $z = \ln x$ then yields $\dot{z} = f(e^z, y) = \tilde{f}(z,y)$, which brings about no change in the conditions (a) - (c). The intervall $(o, +\infty)$, which includes by assumption x_0, will be mapped onto the entire real line $\mathbb{R}$ through the above transformation of the variable x, so that the fully transformed system is again defined on the entire $\mathbb{R}^2$.

Corollary: If in theorem 2 in place of trace $J < o$ the condition trace $J > o$ holds, then the equilibrium (x_0, y_0) is totally instable in the large, i.e., the reversed solution curves of this system all converge to the equilibrium (x_0, y_0).

Proof: The system $(-f,-g)$ then satisfies the conditions of theorem 2. Its solution curves $(\tilde{x}(t), \tilde{y}(t))$ fulfill $(\tilde{x}(t), \tilde{y}(t)) = (x(-t), y(-t))$ with respect to arbitrary initial conditions $(x(o), y(o))$ and corresponding curves (x,y) of the system (f,g).

References

Armstrong, H. and J.Taylor (1981): The measurement of different types of unemployment, in: J.Creedy (ed.): *The Economics of Unemployment in Britain*. London: Butterworth, 99 - 121.

Batchelor, R. (1981): A natural interpretation of the present unemployment. Paper presented to the City University Conference on 'Monetarism in the United Kingdom'. London: The City University.

Dornbusch, R. and St.Fischer (1978): *Macroeconomics*. New York: McGraw Hill.

Flaschel, P. (1984): Some stability properties of Goodwin's growth cycle. A critical elaboration. *Zeitschrift für Nationalökonomie*, Bd.44.

Friedman, M. (1968): The role of monetary policy. *American Economic Review*, Vol. 58, 1 - 17.

Frisch, H. (198o): *Die neue Inflationstheorie*. Göttingen: Vandenhoeck u. Ruprecht.

Frisch, H. und F.Hof (1981): A "textbook" model of inflation and unemployment. *Kredit und Kapital*, Bd. 14, 159 - 179.

Goodwin, R.M. (1967): A growth cycle, in: C.H.Feinstein (ed.): *Socialism, Capitalism and Economic Growth*. London: Cambridge University Press, 54 - 58.

Grossman, H.I. (198o): Rational expectations, business cycles, and government behaviour, in: St.Fischer (ed.): *Rational Expectations and Economic Policy*. Chicago: University of Chicago Press, 5 - 22.

Hahn, F. (1972): *The Share of wages in the National Income*. London: Weidenfeld and Nicolson.

Hargreaves Heap, S.P. (198o): Choosing the wrong 'natural' rate: accelerating inflation or decelerating employment and growth? *Economic Journal*, Vol. 9o, 611 - 62o.

Ito, T. (1978): A note on the positivity constraint in Olech's Theorem. *Journal of Economic Theory*, Vol. 17, 312 - 318.

Jones, H.G. (1975): *An Introduction to Modern Theories of Economic Growth*. London: Thomas Nelson and Sons.

Laidler, D. (1981): Monetarism: An interpretation and an assessment. *Economic Journal*, Vol. 91, 1 - 28.

Malinvaud, E. (198o): *Profitability and Unemployment*. Cambridge: Cambridge University Press.

Neumann, M.J.M. (1983): Monetaristische Theorie der kurzen Frist und die Rolle der Erwartungen, in: G.Bombach et al. (Hrsg.): *Makroökonomik Heute: Gemeinsamkeiten und Gegensätze*. Tübingen: J.C.B.Mohr (Paul Siebeck), 183 - 2o9.

Okun, A.M. (197o): *The Political Economy of Prosperity*. Washington, D.C.: The Brookings Institution.

Rowthorn, B. (198o): Conflict, inflation and money, in: B.Rowthorn: *Capitalism, Conflict and Inflation. Essays in Political Economy*. London: Lawrence and Wishart.

Santomero, A.M. and J.F.Seater (1978): The inflation-unemployment trade-off: a critique of the literature. *Journal of Economic Literature*, Vol. 16, 499 - 544.

Tobin, J. (1972): Inflation and unemployment. *American Economic Review*, Vol. 62, 1 - 18.

Vanderkamp, J. (1975): Inflation: a simple Friedman theory with a Phillips twist. *Journal of Monetary Economics*, Vol. 1, 117 - 122.

CYCLICAL AND STRUCTURAL ASPECTS OF UNEMPLOYMENT AND GROWTH IN A NON LINEAR MODEL OF CYCLICAL GROWTH

K.B.T. Thio
Faculty of Economics
University of Amsterdam
Jodenbreestraat 23
1011 NH Amsterdam
Netherlands.

§ 1. Introduction

The aim of this paper is to make a contribution to the theory of cyclical growth by considering the possible effects of technological change on economic growth and employment in the context of a non-linear model of cyclical growth. Generally, theoretical models of cyclical growth are of small size in order to allow for analytical solution (see Allen, ch. 20).

I present a medium size model of the product and labour market, which can be solved numerically, in order to capture some more aspects of economic development. It builds upon existing theories of the business cycle (Goodwin 1951) and of technical change (Kalecki 1972) in order to study the interaction of growth and cycles in output and its impact on structural and cyclical (or : capacity- and demand determined) unemployment. Paragraphs 2 and 3 develop the cyclical and growth aspects of the model, paragraph 4 shows its working by some numerical illustrations.

---

* I would like to thank the Stichting voor Economisch Onderzoek, which permitted the use of its computer programma for the solution of dynamic models, Coen Teulings, whose aid with the implementation of this programma has been indispensable, Wim Driehuis, with whom I discussed a number of aspects of the model, Hans Amman and Casper van Ewijk who made comments on a first draft of this paper. The responsibility for the result is, of course, my own.

§ 2. An extended non-linear model of the business cycle

As a starting point for the study of cyclical movement of the economy, the model which has been designed by Goodwin (1951) provides important principles. The introduction of a non-linear investment function opens the possibility to describe oscillations with a stable amplitude. There is no need for exogenous and unexplained factors to put the cycle into motion , the form of the cycle will not depend on initial conditions, and the resulting cyclical movement will (in general) not die away or explode into ever wider movements.

Of course one could maintain that in the short run the occurrence of shocks in autonomous expenditure, in international trade, or in prices of raw materials, are of great significance for the amplitude and length of the business cycle. No empirical study of actual cycles is possible without taking account of such exogenously generated impulses.

In order to study the interaction of cyclical and structural factors in the longer period, however, it seems preferable to start with a model which is able to generate regular cyclical patterns of an endogenous nature.

Otherwise, the causes of cyclical behaviour and those governing economic growth would be separated from the outset.

In the model of cyclical growth that is developed here, the basic features of Goodwin's model are retained.

A few modifications are made, which will be explained below. The analysis in terms of continuous time is abandoned and replaced by period analysis, in order to make numerical solutions more easy.

The cyclical behaviour of the economy, as far as it is determined by the demand side, is based on the following set of equations.

$$K_t = K_{t-1} + I_t \tag{2.1}$$

$$Y^c_t = \frac{1}{g} K_t (1 + \alpha)^t \tag{2.2}$$

$$I_t = \min \left[g(Y_{t-1} - Y^c_{t-1}),\ \phi\, Y^c_{t-1} \right] \qquad \text{if } Y_{t-1} \geq Y^c_{t-1} \quad (\phi > 0) \tag{2.3}$$

$$I_t = \max \left[g(Y_{t-1} - Y^c_{t-1}),\ \chi\, Y^c_{t-1} \right] \qquad \text{if } Y_{t-1} < Y^c_{t-1} \quad (\chi < 0)$$

$$C_t = a + b\, w_t \left[L_t + \zeta(L^s_t - L_t) \right] + c\, r_t K_t \tag{2.4}$$

$$\Delta Y_t = \frac{1}{\tau}\left[Z_t - Y_t\right] \qquad (2.5$$

$$Z_t = C_t + I_t \qquad (2.6)$$

$$r_t = \left[Y_t - w_t\,\{L_t + \zeta(L_t^s - L_t)\}\right]/K_t \qquad (2.7)$$

$$L_t = q_t^{\psi}.Y_t^c \qquad (2.8)$$

$$w_t = \text{constant} \qquad (2.9)$$

$$q_t = Y_t/Y_t^c \qquad (2.10)$$

$$u_t = \left[L_t^s - L_t\right]/L_t^s \qquad (2.11)$$

The variables are :

K_t = real capital stock at the end of period t
Y_t^c = capacity of production
I_t = volume of net investment during period t
C_t = volume of consumption
Z_t = volume of expenditure
Y_t = volume of output
r_r = rate of profits
w_t = real wage rate (taken as constant here)
q_t = rate of capacity utilization
L_t = volume of employment
L_t^s = labour supply
u_t = unemployment (as a fraction of labour supply)

Equation 2.1 explains the formation of capital stock by accumulation.
Equation 2.2 shows the amount of production capacity incorporated in the capital stock. Capital requirements increase when α is negative and decrease when α is positive.
The investment function 2.3 is a modified version of the one used by Goodwin (see figure 2.1).

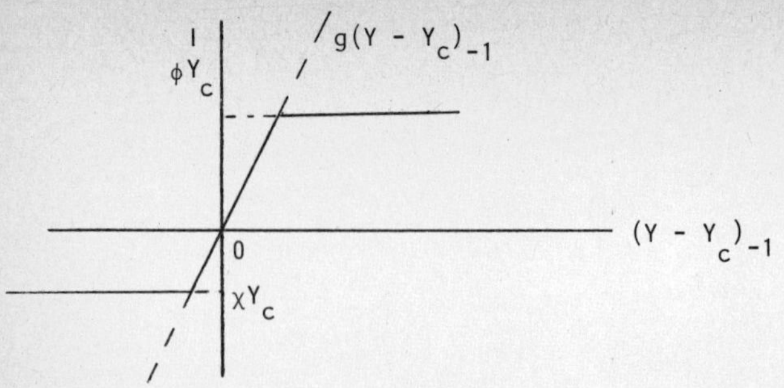

Fig. 2.1 investment function.

The acceleration coefficient g is equal to the capital-output ratio in equation 2.2. Net investment behaves according to a capital stock adjustment mechanism, which makes capital stock adapt to desired capital stock as is also the case in Goodwin's simple model.

The upper and lower limit of investment are not taken as constant now; they move parallel to production capacity, because these limits are supposed to depend on the production capacity of the capital goods industry.

This may be more realistic, especially when the economy is allowed to grow.

A lag in investment behaviour is assumed, which takes account of the fact that investment expenditure lags behind the decision to invest. The length of the investment lag is about one half of the average construction time of investment goods (see Kalecki, 1971 p. 2-4).

For the sake of simplicity, the investment lag is assumed to be the unit of time in the model.

The form of consumption function 2.4 implies differential saving behaviour for incomes from wages and profits respectively. If, however, b equals c, the consumption function reduces to its simple form.

This consumption function is assumed not only for the sake of realism, but also because it enables us to take account of the effect of changes in the wage rate upon the cycle.

Moreover, a term $\zeta w_t \left[L_t^s - L_t\right]$ is added to the sum of real wages as a determinant of consumption. This term is included as a simple approximation to the influence of social security benefits on secundary wage income. We interpret ζ either as the ratio of the level of unemployment benefit to the wage rate, or - given that ratio - as the extent to which the cost of benefits is shifted upon wage income. If ζ is lower than the ratio of the level of unemployment benefits to the wage rate, benefits are partly financed by a deduction from gross real wages. As ζ approaches

1 from below, total disposable real wage income (and consumption) are less affected by changes in employment, and determined to a greater extent by labour supply (L_t^s). We may write the consumption function as

$$C_t = a + \zeta b\, w_t\, L_t^s + (1-\zeta)\, b w_t\, L_t + cr\, K_t$$

Therefore it is clear that - given the wage rate w_t - ζ acts as an automatic stabilizer.

The autonomous part of consumption - institutionally or exogenously determined - increases with ζ.

In the extreme case $\zeta = 1$, $c = 0$, consumption is a constant. The value of the multiplier of wage income upon demand - and thus the form of the cycle - is strongly influenced by ζ.

The form of the cycle is typically asymmetrical (nonsinusoidal) just as in Goodwin's model (see fig. 2.2)

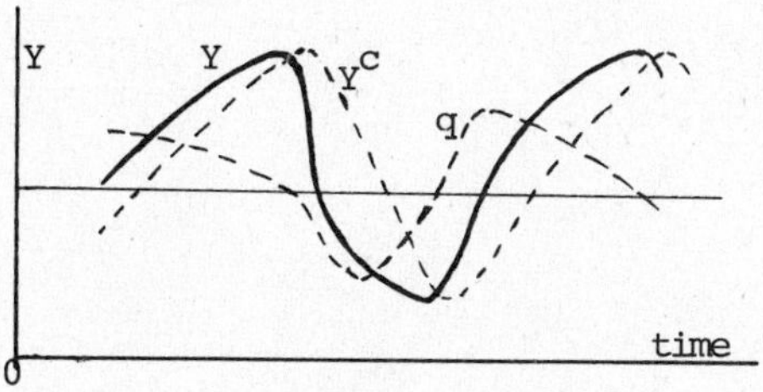

The turning points of output coincide with normal or 'average' values of the rate of capacity utilization.

Fig. 2.2

As long as we take the output lag $\tau = 0$ and consumption from profits as zero ($c = 0$), we may (approximately) calculate the length T of the upswing from

$$\left(1 + \frac{\phi}{g}\right)^T = 1 + \frac{\phi - \chi}{1 - bw\,(1-\zeta)} \qquad \text{or}$$

$$T = \log\left(1 + \frac{\phi - \chi}{1 - bw\,(1-\zeta)}\right) / \log\left(1 + \frac{\phi}{g}\right)$$

whereas the amplitude of the cycle during the upswing is determined by the value of

$$1 + \frac{\phi - \chi}{1 - bw(1-\zeta)}$$

A few remarks may now be made on the characteristics of the model.

1. The present model, like that of Goodwin (1951) describes business cycles of an endogenous character. Generally, the economy moves according to a limit cycle along the boundaries of the investment function. The possibility of damped cycles within those boundaries remains, however, if the working of the dynamic multiplier - flexible accelerator is sufficiently stabilizing.

2. The model describes a wide variety of cyclical patterns as to period and amplitude, depending on the width of the (dis)investment boundaries, on the value of the acceleration/capital coefficient, and on the specific features of the consumption function.

3. The fixed boundaries of the investment function in Goodwin's model are replaced by moving boundaries, because this seems more adequate to describe economic growth.

4. An obvious limitation of the model is that economic growth may only be generated either by introducing an autonomous trend in demand, or by technical change of the capital using type. In the latter case there will be growth of the capital stock without growth of output : the upswing is lengthened relative to the downswing. Goodwin interpretes that situation as spurts of investment caused by innovation (Goodwin 1982, p. 87).
If we do want to explain cycles and growth simultaneously, it is necessary to extend the model by a theory of technical change and by mechanisms that translate productivity change into additional demand.
Moreover, it seems preferable that the occurrence of growth in output should not be uniquely connected with increasing capital requirements per unit of output. Different kinds of technical change, capital using as well as capital saving, should be compatible with growth of output. We turn to such an extension of the model in the next paragraph.

§ 3. A theory of endogenous technical change

Up to this point, possible changes in the capital-output ratio are entirely of an exogenous nature (see equation 2.2). The ratio of capital stock to production capacity is either constant or changing at a given rate. Only the ratio of capital stock to output changes according to the rate of capacity utilization, and there is no room for the choice of a different capital intensity of production. We need two steps to extend the model in order to make this possible: firstly, a formalization of the consequences of a change in capital-output ratio for the labour coefficient (or, inversely, labour productivity), and secondly a behavioral mechanism which describes how changes in the capital coefficient take place.

In order to meet the first requirement we choose to elaborate a theory of technical change that has been put forward by Kalecki (1972, especially ch. 7) and which is rather close to post-Keynesian theories of technical progress.

Kalecki assumes that labour requirements per unit of output (λ) will vary inversely with capital requirements per unit of output (κ).

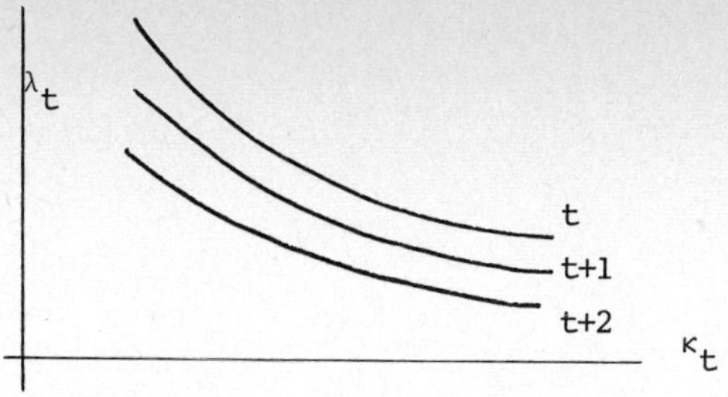

fig. 3.1

Technical change is called 'uniform' if it proceeds at a constant relative rate through time, so that for a given level of the capital coefficient (κ) labour productivity increases at a constant rate.

Technical change is called neutral, when this rate of progress is the *same* for all levels of the capital output ratio. It is called 'encouraging capital intensity' when the rate of progress of labour productivity is greater as the level of the capital output ratio is higher, and 'discouraging capital intensity' in the reverse case. In this way, technical change becomes an endogenous factor. By a change to a particular level of capital intensity, a qualitative change in the method of production may be attained, while each method of production entails a particular range and pace of technical improvements. When technical change encourages capital intensity, accumulation of investments towards a higher level of capital intensity is 'rewarded' by a faster change in labour productivity. We have formalized this idea in the following equations :

$$\lambda_t = \left[\kappa_t/\kappa_o\right]^{-\beta} \cdot \left[1-\gamma \left\{\frac{\kappa_t}{\kappa_o}\right\}^{\delta}\right]^{t}$$

$$\kappa_t = K_t/Y_t^c \qquad (3.2)$$

$$L_t^P = \lambda_t Y_t^c \qquad (3.3)$$

in which λ_t is the labour coefficient of production at a 'normal' level of output, as indicated by equation 3.3. Potential employment is determined by capacity and the labour coefficient.Equation 3.1 implies that λ moves from an initial value: $\lambda_0 = 1$ as κ_t moves away from its initial value. We may (approximately) rewrite 3.1 in terms of relative changes ($\hat{}$ over a variable denotes a relative rate of change) :

$$\hat{\lambda}_t = -\beta\, \hat{\kappa}_t - \gamma\{\kappa_t/\kappa_o\}^{\delta} \qquad 0 < \beta < 1 \qquad (3.1a)$$

It is clear that β indicates a rate of substitution between labour and capital inputs analogous to a production function.

Technical change is of the uniform kind, proceeding at a neutral rate γ if $\delta=0$.

If, however, δ is positive, technical change is encouraging capital intensity. For if the capital output ratio is above its initial level the rate of increase of labour productivity will be higher than γ.
The reverse is true if δ is negative.

Following this method, an exogenously given rise (α) in the capital output ratio (as in equation 2.2) will give rise to a substitution effect on labour productivity ($\beta\alpha$), complemented by a gain in labour productivity from technical change if γ is positive. This theory may be considered as a variation on the theme of a technical progress function as introduced by Kaldor, because the rate of change of labour productivity depends both on a change in the level of capital intensity and on a rate of technical change which is initiated thereby. The two are not separated from each other, as would be the case in a neoclassical approach.

The second step we have to take is to incorporate the possibility of changes in methods of production into investment behaviour.
Until now, investment depends entirely on capacity utilization and is directed towards expansion of production capacity. We would propose to distinguish a second kind of investment, directed towards a change in the technical structure of the capital stock. It means that worn out or obsolete capital stock is replaced by capital stock that makes a different (or more modern) method of production available, or that existing capital stock is rebuilt or transformed for this purpose. Thus, a change in the technical structure of capital stock is presented not as a costless operation, but as requiring a certain amount of investment. We may call this kind of investment replacement investment I_t^r as opposed to investment in expansion of capacity I_t^c which is investment as conceived of before.
Replacement investment thus defined is a part of replacement investment in the usual sense: it is that part which is not used to replace worn out production capacity. Hence, I_t^r could also be called net investment in replacement and modernization. It may assume positive as well as negative values.
Replacement investment as used here represents a particular application of the concept as it is introduced (with varying interpretation) by e.g. Tinbergen and De Wolff (1939), Feldstein and Foot (1971), Eisner (1972) who provide also a number of considerations as to the determinants of replacement and modernization.
Formalizing the distinction between I_t^c and I_t^r, we get the definitions:

$$I_t = I_t^c + I_t^r \tag{3.4}$$

$$K_t = K_{t-1} + I_t \tag{3.5}$$

$$K_t^c = K_{t-1}^c + I_t^c \tag{3.6}$$

So total net investment is divided between investment in expansion of capacity and in replacement and modernization. Total capital stock is the accumulation of all net investments, while K_t^c is defined as the accumulation of all net investment that is destined to expand capacity. Thus, K_t^c will become the determinant of production capacity. Equation 2.2 will from now on be read as

$$Y_t^c = \frac{1}{g} K_t^c e^{\alpha t} \tag{3.7}$$

In all cases to follow it is assumed that $K_o^c = K_o$. Thus, the structure of capital stock is supposed to be in a position of 'equilibrium', in which the capital-output ratio κ_o conforms to the technical relationship g between K^c and Y^c initially after a period in which - by assumption - the capital-output ratio has not been subject to change by impulses to make production more or less labour-intensive.
The impuls to change the labour intensity of production by adaptation of the capital-output ratio through investment in replacement and modernization will now be formulated as follows:

$$I_t^r = \rho\{r_{t-1}^e - r_{t-1}\} \cdot Y_{t-1}^c \tag{3.8}$$

in which ρ is a positive constant, and

$$r_t^e = r_{t-1}^e + \mu\{r_{t-1} - r_{t-1}^e\} \tag{3.9}$$

in which r_t^e represents the expected rate of profits, derived from the actual rate of profits r_t according to a mechanism of adaptive expectations. In what follows it will be assumed that $\mu = 1$, since the effects of different lag structures are not our primary interest here. Therefore, 3.9 reduces to $r_t^e = r_{t-1}$.
In effect, I_t^r as a fraction of production capacity is determined by $-\rho\Delta r_{t-1}$, a relationship that is encountered in the literature (f.i. Kalecki 1954, ch. 9), but which is applied now to a specific aspect of investment. The cycle in the rate of profit, which arises from the non-linear model of the business cycle (par. 2), produces in its turn a cycle in replacement investment. Thereby a cyclical movement of the capital-output ratio is introduced which causes changes in the labour intensity of production. In effect, when the rate of profit starts to decline during the upswing, and profit expectations are disappointed while output is still rising but the growth rate declining, a part of net investment will be dedicated to increase the capital intensity of production and to reduce labour input thereby. Thus, replacement investment 'competes' with investment for expansion increasingly within the limits set for investment as a whole.*

* We could make I^c and I^r make additional to each other by determining I^c instead of I by investment function 2.3. This seems to contradict, however, the idea that total net investment is restricted by the capacity of the investment goods sector.

The rate of profit declines quickly during the crisis, intensifying thereby the process of substitution of capital for labour. Thus, as long as the rate of profit is declining, attempts at reducing variable costs and 'capital deepening' are going on. During the second half of the downswing profit expectations improve while actual profit rates increase, and the process starts to move in the other direction. Net replacement investment becomes negative so that capital intensity diminishes by disinvestment and more labour is used per unit of output.

From the lower turning point of output, the rate of profit increases quickly and I^r moves further in negative direction. Thus, as long as the rate of profit increases, no 'capital deepening' takes place. The capital structure is 'enshallowing' . *

When the equations, developed in this paragraph, are combined with the model of paragraph 2, we arrive at a more complicated model of cyclical growth. Two essential features are added to the model.

Firstly, in the absence of technical change (α=0, γ=0) the capital-output ratio is not merely changing by the influence of the rate of capacity utilization (the capital stock adjustment mechanism), but additionally by the movement of replacement investment. Apart from the 'cyclical' variation of the capital-output ratio, a 'structural' variation is now included, which makes the technical coefficients of production vary through the cycle.

Secondly, technical change may cause a long run movement of the technical coefficients of production, which may cause economic growth.

The various effects on the technical ratio's may be illustrated by an approximative representation in relative changes. The ratio of capital stock to <u>actual</u> output is distinguished in

$$K_t/Y_t = (K_t/Y^c_t) \cdot (Y^c_t/Y_t) = K_t/q_t \rightarrow \widehat{\left[K_t/Y_t\right]} = \hat{\kappa}_t - \hat{q}_t$$

Furthermore, the capital coefficient κ may be expressed as

$$\kappa_t = \left[K_t/K^c_t\right] \cdot \left[K^c_t/Y^c_t\right] \rightarrow \hat{\kappa}_t = \left[\hat{K}_t - \hat{K}^c_t\right] + \left[K^c_t\hat{/}Y^c_t\right] = \left[\hat{K}_t - \hat{K}^c_t\right] - \alpha$$

with

$$\hat{K}_t = I_t/K_t \simeq I_t/K^c_t \quad \text{and} \quad \hat{K}^c_t = I^c_t/K^c_t$$

---

* So our presentation is quite in conformity with Kaldor's view of the matter in his "Capital intensity and the Trade Cycle" (1939) (cited from Kaldor (1960)), where it is argued - contra Hayek - that the capital deepening process is not the <u>cause</u> of cyclical fluctuations and that capacity creating investment is the decisive factor in this respect. It is not capital scarcity which causes the boom to collaps. Moreover, it is seen that capital deepening occurs predominantly during the depression under the influence of declining profit rates. See Kaldor (1960, p.137 a.o.).

so that

$$\hat{K}_t - \hat{K}^c_t \underset{-}{\sim} (I_t - I^c_t)/K^c_t = I^r_t/K^c_t = -\frac{\rho e^{\alpha t}}{g}\ \Delta r_{t-1}$$

The relative change of the capital coefficient and that of the labour coefficient (to be derived from 3.1a) are then approximately

$$\hat{\kappa}_t \approx -\frac{\rho e^{\alpha t}}{g} .\Delta r_{t-1} - \alpha$$

$$\hat{\lambda}_t \approx \beta . \frac{\rho e^{\alpha t}}{g} .\Delta r_{t-1} + \alpha\beta - \gamma \left[\kappa_t/\kappa_o\right]^{\delta}$$

So, apart from the cyclical influence of the rate of capacity utilization q on the divergence of K/Y and κ, a cycle in both capital and labour coefficient is introduced by replacement investment. The amplitude of that cycle is determined by the amplitude of the profit cycle, by ρ and g, and - for the labour coefficient - β. This amplitude diminishes when technical change is of the capital using type (α negative). In that case, the labour coefficient decreases in the long run by $\alpha\beta$ and the capital coefficient rises by $-\alpha$, so that apart from cyclical movement the capital-labour ratio increases by a rate $(-\alpha(1+\beta))$.

Additional labour saving technical change occurs when γ is positive. This rate of labour saving is accentuated when δ is positive , so that technical change is encouraging capital intensity, but held in check when δ is negative.

Finally, it is necessary to complete the model with a few equations describing labour market conditions. We have determined potential employment before by 3.3 as

$$L^p_t = \lambda_t . Y^c_t \tag{3.3}$$

Actual employment as determined by 2.8 in paragraph 2 : $L_t = q_t^{\psi} . Y^c_t$

has to be replaced now by

$$L_t = q_t^{\psi} . L^p_t \tag{3.10}$$

because there is no longer a proportional relationship between L^p and Y^c.

The supply of labour is determined by a fixed rate of change

$$L^s_t = L^s_o . (1+n)^t \tag{3.11}$$

The distinction of potential and actual employment enables us to divide unemployment u_t in a 'cyclical' and a 'structural' component (u^c_t and u^s_t), though as we will see, structural unemployment runs through cycles, too.

$$u^c_t = \left[L^p_t - L_t\right]/L^s_t \tag{3.12}$$

$$u^s_t = \left[L^s_t - L^p_t\right]/L^s_t \tag{3.13}$$

It follows that cyclical and structural unemployment add up to u_t.

The model may be closed by replacing the constant wage rate of paragraph 2 by a relationship that links the real wage rate to productivity change and to the unemployment rate:

$$w_t = \left[\pi/\lambda_{t-1}\right] .\exp\left[-\xi u_{t-1}\right] \qquad (3.14)$$

in which π is the share of the real wage per unit of labour in the product per unit of labour in the initial situation. In relative changes, this relationship implies

$$\hat{w}_t = -\hat{\lambda}_{t-1} - \xi \Delta u_{t-1}$$

The specification of the labour market is kept rather simple. For future research it seems interesting to extend this part of the model by taking into account nominal wage and price movements, so that the conflict over distribution of the product is incorporated into the analysis.

The model is summarized in the appendix. It gives rise to a wide variety of cyclical growth paths. A full exploration of possibilities by mathematical solution would be very difficult. The characteristics of the model are studied by its numerical solution; a few examples are given in the next paragraph. We may review some of the features of the model as it has been presented as a close to this paragraph.

1. We have taken up the old problem of explaining the business cycle and economic development or growth by the same mechanism. Economic growth is not like a trend, superimposed on the cycle. Rather, we have introduced some 'development factors' (see Kalecki (1954), ch.15), which have to work their way through the cyclical development of the economy. In this respect we have concentrated on changes in technology, that may change the capital structure. Higher capital requirements per unit of output, representing investment opportunities arising from innovations, or lower capital requirements representing rationalization of production, both combined with different varieties of labour saving technical change.
   Hence, the cyclical characteristics of the model are connected with its possibilities to describe economic growth. Growth of output and capital stock are analysed not as a succession of equilibrium situations in a steady state solution, but as a succession of cyclical movements with changing boundaries over time.
   In this context, we refrain from explanation of growth by given changes in autonomous investment or consumption demand, because we like to see how growth may arise endogenously from the interaction of demand and supply factors. This is not to say that trends in autonomous demand could not play a significant role in determining the shape of actual growth paths.

2. In this respect the model is different from the multiplier-accelerator type of growth theory. The weak points of that theory are, as Goodwin (1953, p.115) indicates, that in trying to explain growth only the possible existence of an unstable growth path is uncovered, while

"in adapting the theory to explain fluctuations, we lose any explanation of trend". On the other hand, the model differs from the neoclassical way of explaining growth as a state of moving equilibria in product, labour and capital markets, movement being generated by changes in the data of the system (labour supply and technology). In our model, such development factors will not generate output growth per se, but only by particular interactions of the supply and the demand side. Growth depends on the extent to which productivity change is translated into additional demand, especially via the labour market.

3. Growth of the capital stock is caused, basically, by a lengthening of the boom relative to the depression through an increase of the desired capital-output ratio. That leaves open for explanation why and how output growth may occur, because the level of output is unaffected by a lengthening of the boom. For output to grow, demand has to increase through the cyclical movement of the economy. Labour market conditions play a decisive role in this respect.
   When labour saving occurs and the real wage rises proportionally with labour productivity, this will not be a sufficient condition to generate an upward trend in consumption demand. Taken by itself, labour saving will cause structural unemployment; labour income will be distributed over a shrinking number of employed. Only when demand is sustained by income grants or redistribution of income to the growing number of structurally unemployed (with ζ positive in terms of the model), demand and output are allowed to grow. In that case, a further growth of capital stock is induced by the increase in desired capital stock. When unemployment or other factors make the real wage lag behind productivity, this will affect the rate of growth negatively.

4. Hence, according to this model, economic growth is unsure even in the presence of technological progress; it occurs only when and to the extent that demand adapts to changing supply conditions. The importance of income flows to the unemployed, or alternatively, to those who cannot be employed by the private sector of the economy, is a striking feature of this model. They act not only as stabilizing device in the cyclical context, but also as a condition for economic growth. If this would be applicable to the experience in the past decades, we would have to explain high rates of economic growth by the building of welfare state arrangements and, more broadly, by an economic policy that permitted the absorption of labour supply in the service or public sector, which generates income and employment without labour saving. As soon as these processes come to an end for whatever reason, labour saving technical change starts to generate structural unemployment without economic growth, and the cycle predominates over the trend.

5. The characteristics of the model are accentuated by the cycle in replacement investment, which is superimposed on the profit cycle that arises from changes in capacity utilization. Any downward trend in the profit rate, either by increasing ca-

pital requirements or by relative increases in labour income, will induce net investment in replacement and modernization, strengthen the labour saving tendency and increase structural unemployment.

6. It should be mentioned that, although all variables are endogenous, and initial conditions are unimportant in the longer run, the course of the economy and its possible rates of growth are significantly influenced by the data of the model, especially the trends in technological change and the boundaries of the investment function.

§ 4. Some illustrations: fluctuations and growth in output, technical conditions and unemployment

This paragraph illustrates the working of the model by showing two examples of its numerical solution and gives an indication of the effects of changes in some of the coefficients (some more examples are to be found in Thio (1983)). In particular, it is shown how cyclical growth is generated by endogenous mechanisms and to what patterns of structural and cyclical unemployment this may lead. Figure 4.1 represents the time paths of output, unemployment and the technical coefficients over 50 periods of time for two cases, that will be commented upon below.
Case 1 is based on the following set of coefficients:

$\alpha = 0, \quad \beta = .5, \quad \gamma = 0, \quad \delta = 0, \quad \phi = .05, \quad \chi = -.06,$

$a = 30, \quad b = 1, \quad c = 0, \quad g = 2, \quad n = 0, \quad \tau = 1,$

$\rho = 4, \quad \zeta = .5, \quad \psi = 1, \quad \xi = 0, \quad \mu = 1, \quad \pi = .7 .$

The initial conditions are:

$K_0^c = K_0 = 190; \; \kappa_0 = 1.9; \; \lambda_0 = 1; \; Y_0 = 100; \; r_0 = r_0^e = .15; \; L_0^s = 100.$

So, in case 1 no technical change is assumed, whereas in case 2 we assume instead:

$\alpha = .005$ and $\gamma = .01$

which means that technical change is capital as well as labour saving.

Case 1

Under these assumptions a regular business cycle in output develops, much the same as in Goodwin's (1951) model. The size of the cycle as to period and amplitude has been cut down by the assumption $\zeta = .5$, so that the period of the cycle is about 8 time units (or years). The main difference with Goodwin's model is the introduction of the fluctuations of replacement investment, which leads to a cyclical movement of the capital and labour coefficients. Otherwise, these coefficients would be constant through the cycle (or, in the case of economic growth, they would follow a smooth path).
A positive ρ slightly shortens the cycle because in the downswing net replacement in-

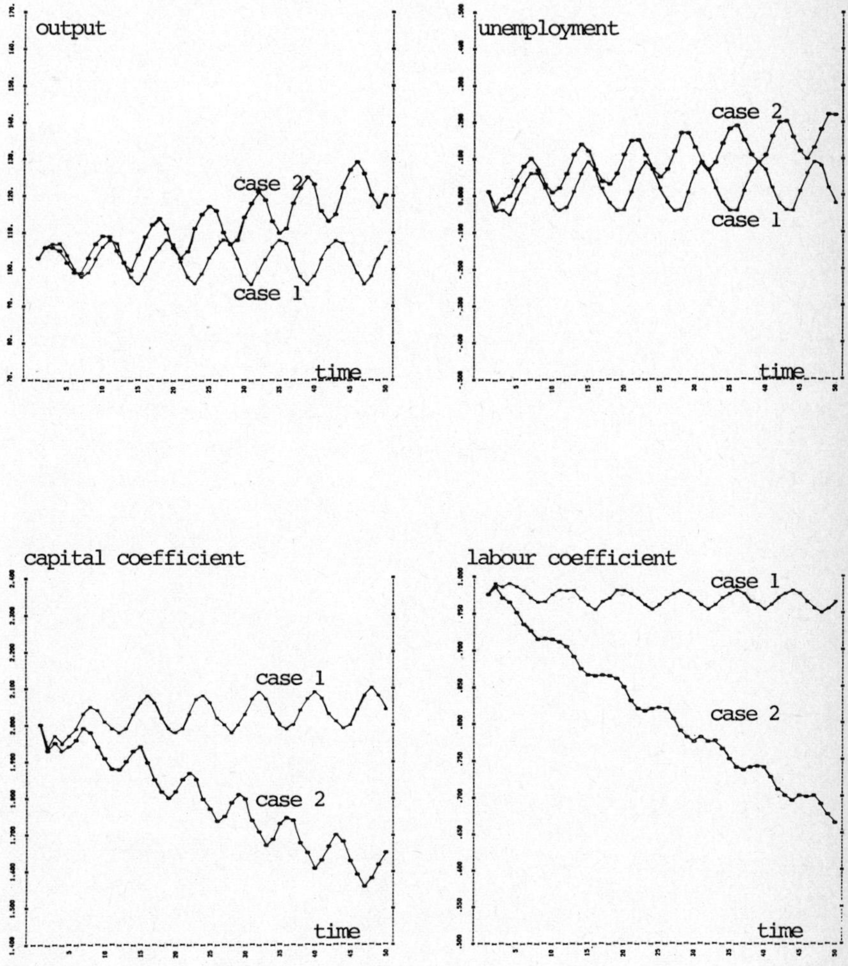
output
case 2
case 1
time
unemployment
case 2
case 1
time
capital coefficient
case 1
case 2
time
labour coefficient
case 1
case 2
time

Figure 4.1

vestment is positive and so net investment in capacity is more negative than it would otherwise be. So capital stock adjustment takes place somewhat faster.
The typical movement of both types of investment is illustrated in figure 4.2 below (see also paragraph 3).

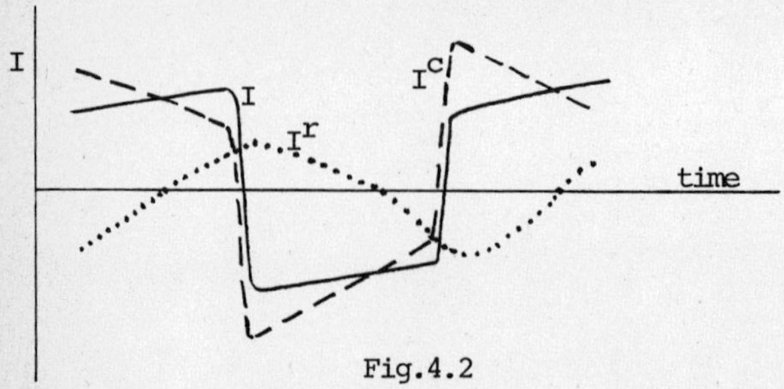

Fig.4.2

The movement of unemployment is the mirror image of the output cycle as is clear from figure 4.1. It is interesting to distinguish unemployment in its 'structural' and its 'cyclical' component, or, more correctly, in its capacity-determined and its demand-determined part (u^s and u^c respectively). Then typically a pattern like the one designed in figure 4.3 is found. u^c, or demand-determined unemployment, is in phase with the rate of capacity-utilization (q), whereas u^s is roughly in phase with capacity output (Y^c). *

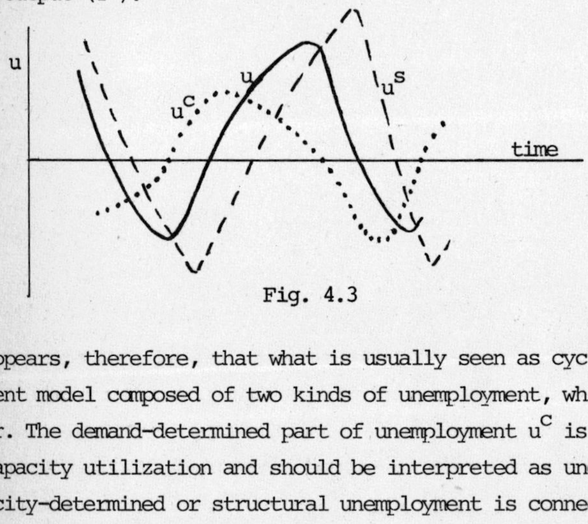

Fig. 4.3

It appears, therefore, that what is usually seen as cyclical unemployment, is in the present model composed of two kinds of unemployment, which are not in phase with each other. The demand-determined part of unemployment u^c is connected with the fluctuation of capacity utilization and should be interpreted as underemployment of available jobs. Capacity-determined or structural unemployment is connected with the movements of capacity output and labour coefficient. So it reflects changes in potential demand for

* Note that in this model utilization of capacity and of labour are considered relative to 'normal' values, i.e. the rate of capacity utilization q is allowed to cycle around 1 and the rate of unemployment u is allowed to cycle around zero (when there is no trend). Thus we find values of q above 1 and of u below zero. This could be changed, if so wished, by introducing explicitly a normal rate of capacity utilization in the investment function with a value below 1, so that q and u are kept within limits. It changes the argument in no way.

labour or numbers of jobs available (L^p). Even if the labour coefficient is a constant, structural unemployment u^s shows fluctuations, corresponding to the cycle of capacity output. The cycle of u^s can be made more pronounced by the cycle of replacement investment.

The fact that a substantial part of 'cyclical' unemployment is determined by 'structural' factors seems at first sight to reduce the importance of demand factors in the creation of unemployment. The former are, however, influenced by the latter; changes in the multiplier, in the wage function, or in ζ , affect the form and size of the output cycle and thus the movement of structural unemployment. So, structural unemployment u^s is not a centre of gravitation or trend value of unemployment, but subject to growth cycles itself.

<u>Case 2</u>

Now a slow rate of technical change is assumed with decreasing capital and labour requirements (.5 and 1 percent per period of time respectively). The trend in labour productivity is therefore $\alpha\beta-\gamma$ or .75 percent per unit of time (see par.3). Under the present assumptions, it is equal to the trend of the real wage rate. Wage income per head (per unit of labour supply) rises less, however, since $\zeta = .5 < 1$. Therefore, growth of output (nearly .5 percent on average per unit of time) is less than the growth of labour productivity. Thus, labour saving leads to some growth of output, which absorbs part of the labour 'set free', but insufficiently to prevent structural unemployment from rising to higher levels.

It could be shown that when ζ approaches zero, growth of output disappears altogether so that the supernumerary labour force is not absorbed at all and labour saving is translated into structural unemployment to the full. On the other hand, if ζ approaches 1, the growth rate converges to the trend in labour productivity and the upward trend of structural unemployment disappears.

Along a different road, such variations in the rate of growth may come about by changes in the coefficients of the wage function, but this matter is not pursued here.

The kind of economic development that is described by this model entails an increase of aggregate wage income (direct and redistributed) that encroaches upon profits, or that, at least, implies a shift of relative shares from disposable profits to wage income. We may have to conclude that, under labour saving technical change, economic growth and stable average levels of unemployment are only sustainable by such distributional shifts - and that otherwise and in so far as it does not take place, 'compensation' in employment for those who are 'set free' by capital will not occur. When the balance of class forces does not bear such distributional change any longer, the pattern of growth and unemployment has to change.

In the present case 2, with diminishing capital requirements per unit of output (see figure 4.1), the rate of profit - not shown here - remains roughly constant on the average, because the shift in aggregate income distribution is offset by a decreasing capital coefficient. But when instead a technical change with constant or increasing capital requirements is assumed, the profit rate has to decline in the long run. Then, even if output growth would be sufficient to offset the effects of labour saving on employment, structural unemployment would rise. For the decline of the rate of profit would cause a permanent shift of investment in capacity towards investment in replacement and modernization, which entails a rise in the capital coefficient and in labour productivity. The effect on labour productivity and unemployment would be stronger as technical change would be non-neutral and of the type that encourages capital intensity (δ positive), and smaller in the opposite case.

§ 5. Concluding remarks

The model presented here combines a non-linear accelerator model of the business cycle with a theory of technical change into a rather complete model of growth and fluctuations in real variables (output, technical coefficients, employment, real wage and profit rates). There are essentially three principles of movement in the model:
firstly, the extended dynamic multiplier - flexible accelerator mechanism of the business cycle accounts for persistent cyclical movements;
secondly, the specification of production relations and technical change, which may take various forms and the rate of which is partly endogenously influenced, provides necessary (but not sufficient) conditions for economic growth and shapes the trends in employment and unemployment;
thirdly, investment in replacement and modernization, depending on profit expectations provides a link between techical change and income distribution on the one hand and capital structure and unemployment on the other hand. This mechanism interacts with the other two.
The model makes no use of purely exogenous factors to explain either fluctuations or growth (such as autonomous trends or shocks in demand).

As prominent features emanating from this analysis of cyclical growth we may sum up:

- The occurrence of economic growth does not depend on the existence of technical change alone, but is also crucially dependent on demand and labour market conditions especially the link between employment, population (labour supply) and real labour income.
- Economic growth tends to be mutually interdependent with increasing structural unemployment.
- The technical production coefficients show cyclical as well as trend movements, thereby inducing cyclical and trend movements in structural unemployment, quite apart from the purely demand - determined movements in cyclical unemployment.
- The cyclical component in economic development is not superimposed upon the trend,

but is codetermining the path and rate of economic growth. The persistence of cyclical movement is an essential feature, which precludes the analysis of growth as a steady phenomenon.

- The explanation of cyclical growth encompasses a much wider variety of possibilities than (e.g.) the Goodwin (1951) model. Especially, growth may be explained with capital using as well as with capital saving technical change, depending on the rate of labour saving that goes along with it.

Literature

R.G,D. Allen (1968), Macro economic Theory, London.

R. Eisner (1972), "Components of Capital Expenditures: Replacement and Modernization versus Expansion", Review of Economics and Statistics, Vol. 54, pp. 297-306.

M.S. Feldstein, D.K. Foot (1971), "The Other Half of Gross Investment: Replacement and Modernization Expenditures", Review of Economics and Statistics, Vol. 53, pag. 49 ff.

R.M. Goodwin (1951), "The Non-linear Accelerator and the Persistence of Business Cycles", Econometrica Vol. 19, nr. 1.

R.M. Goodwin (1953), "The Problem of Trend and Cycle", Yorkshire Bulletin of Economic and Social Research, Vol. 5, nr. 2.

both cited from:

R.M. Goodwin (1982), Essays in Economic Dynamics, London.

N. Kaldor, Essays on economic stability and growth, London 1960.

M. Kalecki (1954), Theory of Economic Dynamics, London.

M. Kalecki (1971), Selected Essays on the Dynamics of the Capitalist Economy, 1933-1970, Cambridge.

M. Kalecki (1972), Selected Essays on the Economic Growth of the Socialist and the Mixed Economy, Cambridge.

K.B.T. Thio (1983), "A Non-linear model of cyclical growth with endogenous technical change", Research Memorandum of the Department of Economics, University of Amsterdam, no. 8328.

J. Tinbergen, P. de Wolff (1939), 'A Simplified Model of the Causation of Technological Unemployment', Econometrica, vol. 7, p. 139 ff.

SOME NEW TECHNIQUES FOR MODELLING NON-LINEAR ECONOMIC FLUCTUATIONS: A BRIEF SURVEY

F. Cugno

Laboratorio di Economia
Università di Torino
10124,Turin,Italy

L. Montrucchio

Dipartimento di Matematica
Politecnico di Torino
10129,Turin,Italy

1. Introduction

Despite the dynamic nature of classical theories (Smith, Ricardo, Marx), for many years the mathematical tools employed in economics have been essentially static. It is plain that in such a way it is not possible to get beyond equilibrium analysis. However, when we try to understand the nature of the equilibria (substantially of their stability), the inadequacy of this approach becomes apparent (Hicks (1939),Samuelson (1947)).

A first attempt to avoid this has been the introduction of some functions of reaction against disequilibria. Of course, these functions are essentially dynamic.

At first, efforts were addressed to studying local stability around equilibrium points. As a result, only linear models were regularly used.

Generally speaking, one can distinguish various stages in the path toward "realism".

First stage: static models and equilibrium analysis.

Second stage: linear dynamic models and analysis of local stability in non linear models.

These stages do not deal with certain relevant problems such as economic fluctuations and global stability of the system attractors.

Clearly, one can answer these new questions only by escaping from linearity to investigate the richer possibilities of non-linear dynamics. This requires some new stages.

Third stage: non-linear dynamic models and analysis of the global property of equilibria and the problem of the existence of periodic so lutions.

Although the third stage is important (see the pioneeristic and seminal work of Goodwin (1982)), its analysis is not yet completely practicable due to the analytical difficulties of studying non-linear dynamics (especially in large dimensions). Furthermore, it is well known that an extremely large variety of phenomena arises in a non-linear context.

What we have just said has a twofold consequence. The positive aspect is the increased possibility of modelling accurately real phenomena. The negative one is the great analytical difficulty involved in analyzing it.

The tension between these two antagonist poles generates a fourth stage in which both qualitative analysis of complex phenomena and analytical description of the non-linear phenomena must be simultaneously considered.

Without claiming to be exhaustive, we can say that bifurcation theory, catastrophe theory, qualitative and generic theories, exotic dynamics analysis and structural stability theory belong to this fourth stage.

In this paper we explore the above subjects and present some new ideas used recently by many authors and give some examples. While we are convinced of the importance of the new tools, we are quite sure that they must be coordinated with new economic concepts.

2. Bifurcation Theory

2.1. Some general concepts

Let $E(\lambda)$ be a family of "objects" parameterized by a point λ of a space of parameters L, where L is a topological space. Moreover, let $\approx$ be a certain equivalence relation between the objects $E(\lambda)$ of the family. So it is possible to state when two objects $E(\lambda_1)$ and $E(\lambda_2)$ are "equivalent": $E(\lambda_1) \approx E(\lambda_2)$ (i.e., when $E(\lambda_1)$ has a same form as $E(\lambda_2)$; see Thom (1975)).

The relation $\approx$ has to be precisely defined in any specific case.

If $E(\lambda_1)$ is the object corresponding to a given point λ_1 in L, it can occur that, for any λ sufficiently close to λ_1 in L, the corresponding object $E(\lambda)$ is equivalent to $E(\lambda_1)$. In this case $E(\lambda_1)$ is said to be a <u>structurally stable</u> or <u>generic</u> object of the family. Formally, $E(\lambda_1)$ is structurally stable if $\exists\, U(\lambda_1)$ in L such that $\forall\, \lambda \in U(\lambda_1)$ implies $E(\lambda) \approx E(\lambda_1)$.

Let S be the subset of L formed by the points λ such that $E(\lambda)$ is generic. The complementary set, $K = L \setminus S$, is called the set of <u>bifurcation points</u>. So a general statement is found in Thom (1975) (see also Arnold (1980), Smale (1980), Hale (1981)). For some discussion concerning bifurcation theory and structural stability in economics see Medio (1979), Cozzi (1982), Cugno and Montrucchio (1982a), Vercelli (1982).

2.2. One has got to the concepts expressed in 2.1. by taking into account a certain variety of problems which were met in mathematics in the last century. Therefore, many subjects (rather independent) are included under the headline "theory of bifurcation". For instance,the catastrophe theory, i.e. the study of jets of functions depending on parameters, the singularity theory in algebraic geometry, the bifurcation theory of the solutions of equations depending on parameters, fall into the bifurcation theory.

In this paper we will above all outline the dynamic aspects of this theory. In our case the objects $E(\lambda)$ are dynamical systems and $\lambda \in L$ is a vector of parameters and $\backsimeq$ is a certain equivalence relation between dynamical systems (for instance, as that of Andronov-Pontryagin).On this subject see Abraham and Robbin (1967), Smale (1980), Arnold(1980), Irwin (1980).

We should also clarify the notion of dynamical system. On this subject we refer to Bathia and Szegö (1967), Abraham and Robbin (1967),La Salle (1976), Nitecki (1971), Arnold (1974), Smale (1980), Geymonat (1981) and, in an economic context, Gandolfo (1971) and Varian (1981).

We limit our work to the following systems:

$$\dot{x} = f(x,\lambda),\ x_{t+1} = f(x_t, \lambda),\ x \in \mathbb{R}^n,\ \lambda \in \mathbb{R}.$$

The former represents the usual modelling of continuous dynamical systems and the latter the modelling of discrete dynamical systems.

2.3. Here we list the most important bifurcational aspects that can be found in dynamical systems.

A) Continuous Case.

a) Bifurcation of equilibrium points. This concerns the study of the number of equilibrium points (and their nature) as parameters vary.

Classical tools are: implicit function theorem, topological degree theory, transversality theory, Poincaré-Hopf index and so on. For some macroeconomic applications see Varian (1979), Cugno and Montrucchio (1982).

b) Hopf Bifurcation ($n \geqslant 2$). This concerns the study of the rising of periodic solutions around an equilibrium point when it changes its stability as a parameter varies. We will treat again this subject in more details in the next section.

c) Bifurcation of Invariant Tori ($n \geqslant 3$). This is the case of the rising of an invariant torus around a cyclical orbit, when it loses its stability as a parameter varies. We will not deal with it here (see Iooss (1979)).

B) Discrete Case.

a) Bifurcation of fixed points. This is analogous to A.a. Substantially this happens when an eigenvalue crosses the unit circle at the point +1 (tangential bifurcation; see Iooss (1979)).

b) Flip Bifurcation. We have this case when an eigenvalue of the linearized map, at the fixed point, crosses the unit circle at -1. In this way we have, generally, the generation of an orbit of period two, bifurcating from the fixed point. See Guckenheimer (1977, 1978) and Iooss (1979). For economic applications see Montrucchio (1982a) and Benhabib and Nishimura (1982).

c) Hopf Bifurcation. This happens when two complex eigenvalues cross the unit circle. In this case we have, generally, the creation of a closed orbit (invariant circle) around the fixed point. The Hopf theorem, in the discrete case, has been stated by several authors (see Ruelle and Takens (1971) and Iooss (1979)). This subject will be developed in section 4.

d) Successive Bifurcations and Transition to Chaos. See section 5.

3. Hopf Bifurcation in the Continuous Case.

There exist several variants which generalize the classical Hopf theorem (see Marsden and McCracken (1976), Ize (1976) and Hale (1981)). Here we give the "homotopic" version of Alexander and Yorke (1978) (we quote only the local part of the theorem and not the global part which is not possible to mention here, although is more important from the conceptual point of view).

Theorem (Alexander and Yorke). Let $\dot{x} = f(x,\lambda)$, $x \in \mathbb{R}^n$, $\lambda \in \mathbb{R}$, f of C^1-class. Let $f(0,\lambda) = 0$, i.e., $x = 0$ is an equilibrium solution for any λ. Let $\partial f(0,\lambda)/\partial x = L(\lambda)$, and $i\beta_0$, $-i\beta_0$ ($\beta_0 \neq 0$) be two purely imaginary eigenvalues of $L(\lambda)$ for $\lambda = \lambda_0$. Denote with $\omega_1(\lambda)$, $i = 1,2,\ldots,r$, the eigenvalues of $L(\lambda)$ such that $\omega_i(\lambda_0)$ are positive integer multiples of $i\beta_0$. Under the assumptions:

real part

i) $Re\,\omega_i(\lambda) \neq 0$ for $\lambda \neq \lambda_0$;

ii) the number of $\omega_i(\lambda)$ whose real part, $Re\,\omega_i(\lambda)$, is zero at λ_0 changing sign, is odd;

then there exist some periodic solutions bifurcating from $x = 0$, at $\lambda = \lambda_0$ and the period of the solutions is close to $2\pi/\beta_0$.

Notice that the great generality of the theorem does not assure us of the local uniqueness of the cyclical orbit nor of its attactivity. In practice, two cases are important: the supercritical bifurcation and the subcritical bifurcation (see Fig. 1) but there are other cases (an example of transcritical bifurcation can be found in Montrucchio (1982a).

In supercritical bifurcations the periodic orbit arises on the si de where the stationary solution is unstable and the orbit is attracting. In the subcritical case, the periodic orbit arises on the side where the stationary solution is stable and the orbit is repelling.

In practice it is not easy to recognize the different kinds of bifurcation. If f is smooth enough, the nature of bifurcation is related to the third order jet of $f(x,\lambda)$. The calculations are very complicated (see Marsden and McCracken (1976) and Hale (1981)). Moreover, the discriminant conditions are generally meaningless from the economic point of view.

As an example, here we apply the method to a model based on the dynamic multiplier, the Phillips curve and the adaptive expectations assumption (for other applications in economics see Torre (1977), Benhabib and Nishimura (1979), Benhabib and Miyao (1981), Galeotti and Gori (1982), Cugno and Montrucchio (1982a, 1983). The equations of the model are the following:

$$\dot{y} = \mu(D - y) \qquad \mu > 0 \tag{3.1}$$

$$D = D\{y + (\delta - \pi)m, R(y,m) - \pi\} \qquad 1 > D_1' > 0,\ D_2' < 0 \tag{3.2}$$

$$R_1' > 0,\ R_2' < 0$$

$$\dot{m}/m = \delta - \nu(y - \bar{y}) - \pi \qquad \nu > 0 \tag{3.3}$$

$$\dot{\pi} = \lambda\nu(y - \bar{y}) \qquad \lambda > 0 \tag{3.4}$$

where y = GNP, D = the demand for goods, m = the real money supply, δ = the rate of expansion of the nominal money supply, π = the expected rate of inflation, R = the nominal interest rate, $\bar{y}$ = the potential output and where μ, ν and λ are reaction parameters.

Equation (3.1) represents the dynamic multiplier. The effective demand function in (3.2) is obtained assuming that: (i) the demand for goods depends positively on the expected disposable income y^d and negatively on the real interest rate $R - \pi$; (ii) R depends positively on y and negatively on m (liquidity preference theory); (iii) the expected disposable income consists of y plus transfer payments m minus expected capital losses on money holdings $\pi \cdot m$, that is $y^d = y + (\delta - \pi)m$ (see Fischer (1972)).

Equation (3.3) says that $\dot{m}/m$ is equal, by definition, to $\delta - \dot{p}/p$, where $\dot{p}/p$ is the actual rate of inflation which is equal, for hypothesis, to $\gamma(y - \bar{y}) + \Pi$ (expectations augmented Phillips curve).

Finally, equation (3.4) is obtained assuming that people adjust the expected rate of inflation to the actual one with a speed measured by λ, that is $\dot{\Pi} = \lambda(\dot{p}/p - \Pi)$ (adaptive expectations hypothesis).

Setting $\dot{y} = \dot{m} = \dot{\pi} = 0$, we get the equilibrium solution $E^* = (y^*, m^*, \pi^*)$, where $\pi^* = \delta$, $y^* = \bar{y}$ and m^* is the unique solution of $D(y^*, R(y^*, m) - \pi^*) = y^*$.

The characteristic equation of the system linearized at the equilibrium point is

$$\rho^3 + a\rho^2 + (\lambda b + c)\rho + \lambda c = 0$$

where

$$a = \mu\left\{1 - D_1'(E^*) - D_2'(E^*)\, R_2'(E^*)\right\} > 0,$$
$$b = \gamma\mu\left\{D_1'(E^*)\, m^* + D_2'(E^*)\right\} \gtrless 0,$$
$$c = \gamma\mu\, m^*\, D_2'(E^*)\, R_2'(E^*) > 0\,.$$

Remembering that necessary and sufficient conditions for local stability are $a > 0$, $\lambda c > 0$, $a(\lambda b + c) - \lambda c > 0$, we can distinguish two significant cases.

1) $b = \mu\gamma\left\{D_1'(E^*)\, m^* + D_2'(E^*)\right\} > 0$, that is at the equilibrium point D decreases when π increases, since the effected capital losses on money holdings exceeds the effect of the real interest rate. In this case the necessary and sufficient conditions for local stability always hold.
2) $b = \mu\gamma\left\{D_1'(E^*)\, m^* + D_2'(E^*)\right\} < 0$, that is at the equilibrium point D increases when π increases, since the effect of the real interest rate exceeds the effect of the expected capital losses on money holdings. Of course, this behavior represents a tendentially destabilizing force. By means of simple calculations we can see that there exists a critical level of λ, i.e. $\lambda_0 = ac/(c - ab)$, such that for $\lambda = \lambda_0$ the linearized system has one negative real eigenvalue and two complex eigenvalues whose real part is zero (in fact, $a > 0$, $\lambda_0 c > 0$, $a(\lambda_0 b + c) - \lambda_0 c = 0$).

   For λ increasing at λ_0, the real part of the complex eigenvalues changes from the negative to positive sign and so the equilibrium point E* loses its stability and we have the rising of cyclical solutions from the equilibrium point itself (see Alexander-Yorke theorem above). Of course, the bifurcation may be supercritical or subcritical, but not only the first case is interesting. In fact, as Benhabib and Miyao (1981) have pointed out, the subcritical case seems to have something in common with the corridor of stability concept formulated by Leijonhufvud (1973).

4. Hopf Bifurcation in the Discrete Case

In section 2 we have quoted the bifurcations of "invariant circles". Here we give the theorem of Iooss (1979) for them.

Theorem: Let $x_{t+1} = \Phi(x_t, \lambda)$, with $x_t \in \mathbb{R}^2$, $\lambda \in \mathbb{R}$ and Φ of class C^6 near $(0, \lambda_0)$ and $\Phi(0, \lambda) = 0$. In other words, $x = 0$ is a fixed point for each λ. Let $L(\lambda) = \partial\phi(0,\lambda)/\partial x$ and $\mu_1(\lambda)$, $\mu_2(\lambda)$ be the two eigenvalues of $L(\lambda)$. Suppose furthermore:

H_1) $\mu_1(\lambda_0)$ and $\mu_2(\lambda_0)$ are complex number ($\mu_2(\lambda_0) = \overline{\mu_1(\lambda_0)}$) and $|\mu_1(\lambda_0)| = 1$ and $\mu_1(\lambda_0) \neq \pm 1$;

H_2) $\frac{d}{d\lambda}|\mu(\lambda)|_{\lambda=\lambda_0} > 0$ (transversal condition);

H_3) $\{\mu_1(\lambda_0)\}^n \neq 1$, for $n = 1, 2, 3, 4$;

then, if $\alpha^* > 0$, where α^* is a computable quantity depending on the third order jet of ϕ, there exists a rigth neighborhood of $\lambda = \lambda_0$ in which there is an invariant attractive circle of the map $\Phi(\cdot,\lambda)$ in $\mathbb{R}^2$, bifurcating from O. In this case there is an exchange of the stability of the fixed point O and the invariant circle (supercritical case).

If $\alpha^* < 0$, there exists a left neighborhood of $\lambda = \lambda_0$ in which there is an invariant repelling circle for the map ϕ, bifurcating from the fixed point 0 which is stable here. For $\lambda > \lambda_0$ the fixed point 0 is unstable (subcritical case).

The calculation of α^* is very complex (see Iooss (1979) for details).

Here we give an application of such a technique in an economic context (for another example, concerning an atomistic market with traders, see Montrucchio (1982a)).

We deal with a discrete version of Goodwin's 1967 model to which we add an assumption on the behavior of output money price like that introduced by Desai (1973) (for a first-order discrete version of Goodwin's model, see Pojhola (1981)).

The assumptions are the following:

(i) labor productivity π and labor force N increase at constant rate, that is

$$\pi_{t+1}/\pi_t = 1 + \alpha \ , \ N_{t+1}/N_t = 1 + \beta \ , \ \alpha > 0 \ , \ \beta > 0;$$

(ii) the variation rate of the money wage is an increasing function of the employment rate (Phillips curve); then

$$w_{t+1}/w_t = 1 + f(L_t/N_t) \ , \quad f' > 0,$$

where w = the money wage and L = employment;

(iii) the capital-output ratio is constant, that is

$$k_t = \sigma \pi_t L_t \qquad , \sigma > 0,$$

where k is the capital stock;

(iv) wages are fully consumed and a constant percentage of profits is saved and invested; so, we have

$$k_{t+1} = k_t + \rho(\pi_t - w_t/p_t)L_t \ , \quad 1 > \rho > 0,$$

where ρ is the capitalists's propensity to save and p is the money price of output;

(v) the money price of output desired by capitalists, p*, equals m times the unit cost of output in money terms, that is

$$p_t^* = mw_t/\pi_t \qquad , \quad m > 1$$

and the actual price adjusts to the desired one in the following way (see Desai (1973)):

$$p_{t+1}/p_t = (p_t^*/p_t)^{\mu} \qquad , 1 > \mu > 0,$$

where μ measures the adjustment speed. Note that if $\mu = 0$ we have a discrete version of the original Goodwin model.

Setting $L_t/N_t = v_t$ (employment rate) and $w_t/p_t\pi_t = u_t$ (labor share in national income) and having to be $0 \leq v \leq 1$, $0 \leq u \leq 1$, we get

$$
\text{(G)}\quad
\begin{cases}
v_{t+1} = \min\left[1;\ \dfrac{v_t}{(1+\alpha)(1+\beta)} + \dfrac{\rho}{\sigma}\dfrac{v_t(1-u_t)}{(1+\alpha)(1+\beta)}\right] \\[2ex]
u_{t+1} = \min\left[1;\ \dfrac{(1+f(v_t))u_t}{(1+\alpha)(mu_t)^{\mu}}\right] .
\end{cases}
$$

We now add the following assumptions:

A_1) $(\alpha+\beta+\alpha\beta)\,\sigma/\beta < 1$,

A_2) f is a strictly increasing function and $f(0) < \alpha < f(1)$ and $f(0) + 1 > 0$.

Under these assumptions, we get:

(i) a continuous mapping $F: [0, 1] \times [0,1] \to [0, 1] \times [0, 1]$ associated with the system (G);

(ii) furthermore, F has a unique fixed point in $(0, 1) \times (0, 1)$:
$u^* = 1 - \sigma(\alpha+\beta+\alpha\beta)/\rho$, $f(v^*) = (1+\alpha)(mu^*)^{\mu} - 1$.

It is easy to verify that there are three significant cases:

a) $m > 1/u^*$ (equilibrium with inflation): v^* increases as μ increases;

b) $m = 1/u^*$ (equilibrium without inflation): v^* is independent of μ and $v^* = f^{-1}(\alpha)$;

c) $m < 1/u^*$ (equilibrium with deflation): v^* decreases as μ increases.

By easy calculation, we get the following characteristic equation at the point (u^*,v^*):

$x^2+(\mu-2)\,x + 1 - \mu + E = 0$, where $E = u^*v^*\rho\, f'(v^*)/ / \{\sigma(1+\alpha)(1+\beta)(1+f(v^*))\}$.

In this paper we only examine the case $m = 1/u^*$ (case b) and with $0 < E \leqslant 1$. By simple considerations, we find the location of the roots as μ varies. Precisely:

$0 < \mu < E$, two roots outside the unit circle;

$E < \mu < 1$, two roots inside the unit circle.

So, for $\mu = E$, <u>there is generally a Hopf bifurcation</u> (it is easy to verify that H.1 and H.2 of Iooss theorem hold). We also assume that f is of class C^6 and it has the expansion:

$f(v) = \alpha+\alpha_1(v-v^*) + \alpha_2(v-v^*)^2 + \alpha_3(v-v^*)^3 + O(v-v^*)^4$, near v^*.

We can finally conclude that if $\alpha^* = \alpha^*(\alpha,\beta,\sigma,\rho,m,\alpha_1,\alpha_2,\alpha_3) > 0$ then there is an invariant attracting circle bifurcating from (u^*,v^*) for $\mu < E$ (supercritical case). While, if $\alpha^* < 0$, there is a repelling circle bifurcating for $\mu > E$ (subcritical case).

The explicit expression of α^* is very complicated (as it is a function of eight parameters). We give here some estimations on α^* making strong simplifications. However, all this gives us the possibility of observing some interesting phenomena. For example, if $\alpha_2 \to 0$, $\alpha_3 \to 0$ (i.e. f is "almost" linear) and $E \to 1$ (i.e. Phillips curve with a sufficiently high slope), then $\alpha^* \to \rho^2 / \{4\sigma^2(1+\alpha)^2 (1+\beta)^2\} > 0$.

On the other hand, if α_1 is small enough (i.e. Phillips curve with a small slope), then $\alpha^* \to -5\rho^2 / \{16\sigma^2(1+\alpha)^2(1+\beta)^2\} < 0$.

So, we see that subcritical and supercritical phenomena can coexist in the same model. We want to recall that the theorem of Iooss is only a local one. However it follows reasonably that in the supercritical case we may have, for some values of parameters, an attracting circle also for $\mu = 0$ (i.e. the classical Goodwin model).

5. Chaotic Dynamics

It is well known that the very simplest non-linear difference equations can possess an extraordinarily rich spectrum of dynamical behavior, through cascades of stable cycles, to a regime in which the behavior, although fully deterministic, is, in many respects, "chaotic", or indistinguishable from the sample function of a random process (we use indifferently the terms: chaotic , strange, erratic, exotic or complex dynamics).

The same phenomena happen in the continuous dynamic systems when the space dimension is greater than 2. So, the phenomena of transition to chaos, via successive bifurcations, are quite general and one must take them into account when studying non-linear dynamic systems. For enlightening examples see May (1976).

From the mathematical point of view, the chaotic dynamics have been sufficiently clarified thanks to the Sharkovskii (1964) and Li-Yorke (1975) theorems (see also Stefan (1977)) in the first order discrete case. On the other hand, for non-linear discrete dynamics of the higher order, little theoretical information is available and many problems remain open (see Diamond (1976), Guckenheimer et al. (1977), Marotto (1978,1979), Pounder and Rogers (1980), Benhabib and Day (1981)).

There are already a lot of works on chaotic dynamics in economics. We quote the following: Rand (1978), Stutzer (1980), Benhabib and Day (1981), Day (1981, 1982a,b), Pohjola (1981), Dana and Malgrange (1981), Simonovits (1982), Montrucchio (1982a,1983).

This viewpoint in the domain of economic modelling seems to us very stimulating expecially in the theory of economic fluctuations. This approach can explain in an endogenous way the cyclical and erratic behavior of systems without resorting to exogenous shocks. So, the rich spectrum of contingencies depends on the values of the parameters of the model.

Some other "philosophical" implications derived from this approach could be the following:

1) Chaotic dynamics are extremely sensitive to initial conditions. Evidently, the "future" behavior of a model solution cannot be anticipated from its patterns in the "past". This implies <u>impredictability</u> and so it is possible to predict the future only by statistical methods (see the ergodic theory, Lasota (1977), Boyarsky (1980)).
2) Generally, chaotic dynamics present a certain degree of robustness, i.e., they appear as "structurally stable" phenomena (see Smale and Williams (1975)).

We can distinguish the emergence of chaos in two different kinds of models, that is, models with "free dynamics" and models with "controlled dynamics". We end this paper by giving two examples covering both the above mentioned aspects.

5.1. <u>Free dynamics in an agricultural market</u>

The long story of the cobweb model is well known. Its simplest version is

$$q_t = f(p_{t-1}), \quad p_t = F(q_t)$$

where q_t is the quantity at time t, p_t is the price at time t, f is the supply function and F is the Marshallian demand function.

Such a simple framework cannot capture some phenomena that we meet in empirical data such as cyclical and erratic movements (for an empirical study based on Italian data see Garoglio (1983)). This is linked to the fact that the equation regulating the dynamics, $q_{t+1} = f(F(q_t))$, is monotonic under usual assumptions.

If we modify the supply function f by taking into account an upper bound for the variation rate of q, say ρ, we get

$$q_{t+1} = \min \left\{ (1+\rho)\ q_t;\ f(F(q_t)) \right\}$$

(we can find such a device in Day (1978)).

In order to present more specific results we will set

$f(p_{t-1}) = -a + bp_{t-1}$, $F(q_t) = c - dq_t$.

Thus, we have

$$q_{t+1} = \min \left\{ (1+\rho)\ q_t;\ \ bc - a - bdq_t \right\} . \tag{5.1.1}$$

By the cobweb theorem we know that the equilibrium point, $\bar{q} = (bc-a)/(1+bd)$, is stable when at the margin the supply is less sensitive to changes in p_{t-1} than the demand to changes in p_t, i.e. when $bd < 1$.

At $bd = 1$ we have the first bifurcation and we get the rising of two-period solutions.

As bd increases beyond 1 orbits of period 2^n arise. At a certain point a first orbit of odd period appears and at last for $bd = (2+\rho)/(1+\rho)$ we have a three-period orbit. This implies chaos (see Lii and Yorke (1975)). Summarizing, if

$$\frac{1+\rho}{\rho} > bd \geqslant \frac{2+\rho}{1+\rho} ,$$

then the time paths of q_t and p_t of (5.1.1) are chaotic and the solutions are meaningfull from the economic point of view (for more details see Cugno (1983)). In Fig. 2 we show an example of chaos generated by 5.1.1.

5.2. Dynamics under optimal control

The case of dynamics in optimally controlled systems (i.e., the case in which the decision makers act rationally by planning economic va riables over time) is of some interest. We can have a new insight into the above dynamics by the bifurcation theory and chaos theory. Some papers about the existence of cyclical paths in models of intertemporal optimization already exist (see Sutherland (1970), Benhabib and Nishimura (1979, 1982), Montrucchio (1982,b)).

By the "turnpike theory" it is well known that these phenomena tend to disappear as the discount factor, λ, tends to 1 (see McKenzie(1976) and Scheinkman (1976)). Thus, we will generally observe all strange dynamics only for λ not too close to 1.

Here we briefly discuss a general over time decision model (for more details see Montrucchio (1983)).

Let us consider the following optimal programming $P(x_0,\lambda,T)$.

$$\text{Max} \sum_{t=1}^{T} V(x_{t-1},x_t)\, \lambda^{t-1} \quad \text{subject to}$$

$x_t \in \Gamma(x_{t-1})$, x_0 fixed, under assumptions:

A.1) X is a compact and convex subset of $\mathbb{R}^n$;

A.2) V: X x X $\to$ $\mathbb{R}$ is a continuous and strictly concave function(short -run utility function);

A.3) $x \to \Gamma(x)$ is a set-valued continuous function from X into X with non-empty compact and convex images;

A.4) the graph of Γ in $X \times X$ is convex;

A.5) $1 \leqslant T \leqslant +\infty$ is the lenght of the time horizon;

A.6) $0 < \lambda < 1$ is the "discount parameter" of the future.

It is easy to give many examples of $P(x_0,\lambda,T)$ producing chaotic time paths. Here we mention only a global problem when $T = \infty$.

We notice that, for $T = \infty$, the optimal sequences $(x_0^*,x_1^*,x_2^*,....)$of $P(x_0,\lambda,\infty)$ are generated by the one-parameter family of discrete dynamic systems $x_t^* = \Theta_\lambda\ (x_{t-1}^*)$, $x_0^* = x_0 \in X$ and where $\Theta_\lambda: X \to X$ is a continuous map (under assumptions A.1 - A.6). Thus, to understand the behavior of $(x_0^*,x_1^*,...)$ it will be sufficient to analyse the global nature of Θ_λ's coming from $P(x_0,\lambda,\infty)$ problems.

The next theorem gives some global information on Θ_λ's.

<u>Theorem</u>: Under assumptions A.1,....A.6 and with additional assumptions:

A.7) $X = \bar{A}$, where A is open in $\mathbb{R}^n$;

A.8) $\dim \Gamma(x) = n$ for each $x \in X$;

the set of Θ_λ's coming from all the programmings $P(x_0, \lambda, \infty)$ is <u>dense</u> in $C^0_\Gamma(X;X)$, the space of all the continuous functions

$f: X \to X$, with $f(x) \in \Gamma(x)$, endowed with the uniform topology.

Namely, dynamics coming from infinite programmings are of all kinds. As a by-product, we can easily deduce the existence of chaotic motions (see Montrucchio (1983)).

It is obvious that, for $T < +\infty$, the dynamical behavior will be also more various. Any way not all the aspects are completely clarified. For instance, it is difficult to understand how <u>myopia</u> (i.e. the horizon lenght T) and <u>impatience</u> (measured by λ) work.

Generally, as myopia decreases dynamical complexity decreases. In the same way, as impatience decreases dynamical complexity decreases. In such problems bifurcational tools play a central role.

We end by giving one of the simplest examples producing chaotic motions.

Let $X = [0, 1]$ and $V(x,y) = -a\,x^2y + axy - (1/2)y^2 - (A/2)x^2$ and $\Gamma(x) = X$, for each $x \in X$. V turns out to be strictly concave on X x X for $A > a^2$. For small λ and for a near the value 4, the maps Θ_λ are chaotic. For $\lambda_0 \leqslant \lambda < 1$ the map Θ_λ has the unique globally attracting fixed point $x = 0$, where $\lambda_0 = (a-1)/(A-a) < 1$.

So, the Θ_λ family of maps gives rise to a cascade of bifurcational phenomena as the λ discount parameter runs from 0^+ to 1^-.

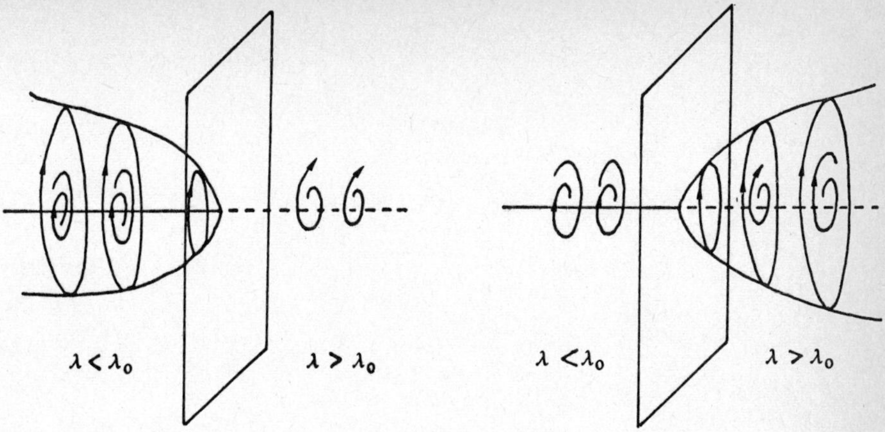

subcritical bifurcation supercritical bifurcation

Fig. 1

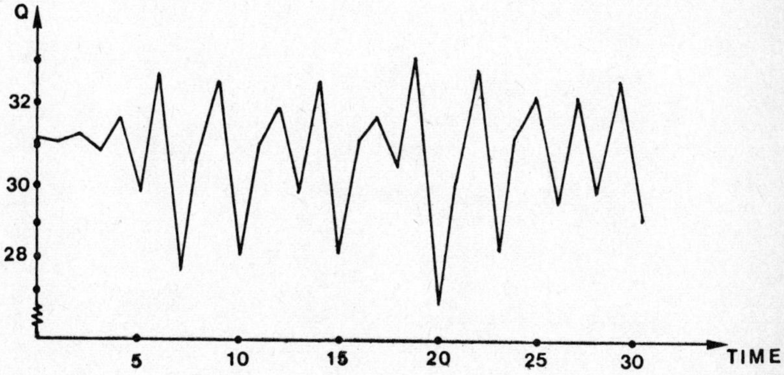

bd = 2.1 bc-a = 96 ρ = 0.1 q_0 = 31

Fig. 2

REFERENCES

Abraham, R., and J. Robbin (1967), Transversal Mapping and Flows, Benjamin, New York.

Alexander, J.C., and J.A. Yorke (1978), "Global Bifurcation of Periodic Orbits", American Journal of Mathematics, 100, 263-292.

Arnold, V. (1974), Equations Differentielles Ordinaires, MIR, Moskow.

Arnold, V. (1980), Chapitres Supplementaires de la Theorie des Equations Differentielles Ordinaires, MIR, Moskow.

Benhabib, J., and R.H. Day (1981), "Rational Choice and erratic Behaviour", Review of Economic Studies, XLVIII, 459-471.

Benhabib, J., and T. Miyao (1981), "Some New Results on the Dynamics of the Generalized Tobin Model", International Economic Review 22, 589-596.

Benhabib, J., and K. Nishimura (1979), "The Hopf Bifurcation and the Existence and Stability of Closed Orbits in Multisector Models of Optimal Economic Growth", Journal of Economic Theory, 21,421-444.

Benhabib, J., and K. Nishimura (1982), Sufficient Conditions for the Existence of Periodic Cycles in Discrete-Time Intertemporal Optimization Models and Applications to Optimal Growth and the Adjustment-Cost Theory of Investment, Preprint, New York University.

Bhatia, N.P., and G.P. Szegö (1967), Dynamical Systems: Stability Theory and Applications, Springer-Verlag, Berlin and New York.

Boyarsky, I. (1980), "Randomness Implies Order", Journal of Mathematical Analysis and Applications, 76, 483-497.

Cozzi, T. (1982), "Marco Fanno e la Teoria Moderna del Ciclo", Rivista Internazionale di Scienze Economiche e Commerciali, 1-2, 87-88.

Cugno, F. (1983), Modello della Ragnatela e Comportamenti erratici , Working Papers, Laboratorio di Economia Politica Cognetti de Martiis, Torino.

Cugno, F., and L. Montrucchio (1982), "Stability and Instability in a Two Dimensional Dynamical System: a Mathematical Approach to Kaldor's Theory of the Trade Cycle", in Szegö, G.P. (ed.), New Quantitative Techniques for Economic Analysis, Academic Press, New York.

Cugno F., and L. Montrucchio (1982a), "Cyclical Growth and Inflation:a Qualitative Approach to Goodwin's Model with Money Prices", Economic Notes, 11, 93-107.

Cugno, F., and L. Montrucchio (1983), "Disequilibrium Dynamics in a Multidimensional Macroeconomic Model: a Bifurcational Approach" Ricerche Economiche, forthcoming.

Dana, R. A., and P. Malgrange (1981), The Dynamics of a Discrete Version of a Growth Cycle Model, Preprint, C.E.P.R.E.M.A.P., Paris.

Day, R.H. (1981), "Complex Dynamics in Recursive Economizing Models", The 20th Conference on Decision and Control, 1387-1392.

Day, R.H. (1982a), "The Emergence of Chaos from Classical Economic Growth", Quaterly Journal of Economics, 201-213.

Day, R.H. (1983b), "Irregular Growth Cycles", American Economic Review, forthcoming.

Day R.H. (1978), "Cobweb Models with Explicit Suboptimization", in R. H. Day and A. Cigno (eds), Modelling Economic Change: the Recursive Programming Approach, North Holland, Amsterdam.

Desay, M. (1973), "Growth Cycles and Inflation in a Model of Class Struggle", Journal of Economic Theory, 6, 527-545.

Diamond, P. (1976), "Chaotic Behavior of Systems of Difference Equation", International Journal of Systems Science, 7, 953-956.

Fischer, S.R. (1972), "Keynes-Wicksell and Neoclassical Models of Money and Growth", American Economic Review, LXII, 880-890.

Galeotti, M., and F. Gori (1982), "Forma e Stabilità degli Insiemi di Equilibrio in un Modello di Crescita Monetaria", Atti del Convegno AMASES.

Gandolfo, G. (1971), Mathematical Methods and Models In Economic Dynamics, North Holland, Amsterdam.

Garoglio, P. (1983), L'Andamento del Mercato di Alcuni Prodotti Agricoli a Prezzi Amministrati, IRES, Torino.

Geymonat, G. (1981), Lezioni di Matematica, Levrotto e Bella, Torino.

Goodwin, R.M. (1982), Saggi di Analisi Economica Dinamica, La Nuova Italia Scientifica, Roma.

Guckenheimer, J. (1977), "Bifurcations of Maps of the Interval", Inventiones Math., 35, 165-178.

Guckenheimer, J. (1978), "Bifurcations of Dynamical Systems", in Dynamical Systems, corso CIME, Liguori, Napoli.

Guckenheimer, J., Oster, G., and A. Ipatchi (1977), "Dynamics of Density Dependent Population Models", Journal of Math. Biology, 4, 101-147.

Hale, J.K. (1981), Topics in Dynamic Bifurcation Theory, A.M.S., Providence, Rhode Island.

Hicks, J.R. (1939), Value and Capital, Oxford University Press.

Irwin, M.C. (1980), Smooth Dynamical Systems, Academic Press, New York.

Iooss, G. (1979), Bifurcation of Maps and Applications, North Holland, Amsterdam.

Ize, J. (1976), Bifurcation Theory for Fredholm Operators, A.M.S., Providence, Rhode Island.

Lasalle, J.P. (1976), "The Stability of Dynamical Systems", SIAM, Philadelphia.

Lasota, A. (1977), "Ergodic Problems in Biology", in Dynamical Systems, Asterisque 50, Societé Mathematique de France.

Leijonhufvud, A. (1973), "Effective Demand Failure", Swedish Journal of Economics, 75, 27-48.

Li, T.Y., and J.A. Yorke (1975), "Period Three Implies Chaos", American Math. Monthly, 82, 985-992.

McKenzie, L.W. (1976), "Turnpike Theory", Econometrica, 44, 841-865.

Marotto, F.R. (1978), "Snap-Back Repellers Implies Chaos in R^n", Journal of Math. Analysis and Applications, 72, 199-223.

Marotto, F.R. (1979), "Perturbations of Stable and Chaotic Difference Equations", Journal of Math Analysis and Applications, 72, 716-729.

Marsden, J.E., and M. McCracken (1976), The Hopf Bifurcation and its Applications, Springer-Verlag, Berlin and New York.

May, R.M. (1976), "Simple Mathematical Models with Very Complicated Dynamics", Nature, 261, 459-467.

Medio, A. (1979), Teoria Nonlineare del Ciclo Economico, Il Mulino, Bologna.

Montrucchio, L. (1982a), "Chaotic Dynamics in Economics", paper presented at the IXth Conference of Applied Economics, Budapest.

Montrucchio, L. (1982b), "Some Mathematical Aspects of the Political Business Cycle", Journal of Optimization Theory and Applications, 37, 251-275.

Montrucchio, L. (1983), "Optimal Decision Over Time and Strange Attractors", paper presented at the 11th Conference on System Modelling and Optimization, Copenhagen.

Nitecki, Z. (1971), Differentiable Dynamics, M.I.T. Press, Cambridge, Mass..

Pohjola, M.J. (1981), "Stable and Chaotic Growth: the Dynamics of a Discrete Version of Goodwin's Growth Cycle Model", Nationalökonomie, 41, 27-38.

Pounder, J.R., and J.D. Rogers (1980), "The Geometry of Chaos: Dynamics of a Non-Linear Second-Order Difference Equation", Bull.Math. Biology, 42, 551-597.

Rand, D. (1978), "Exotic Phenomena in Games and Duopoly Models", Journal of Mathematical Economics, 5, 173-184.

Ruelle, D., and F. Takens (1971), "On the Nature of Turbolence", Comm. Math. Physics, 20, 167-192.

Samuelson, P.A. (1947), Foundation of Economic Analysis, Harvard University Press. Cambridge, Mass..

Scheinkman, J.A. (1976), "On Optimal Steady-States of n-Sector Growth Models when Utility is Discounted", Journal of Economic Theory, 12, 11-30.

Simonovits, A. (1982), "Buffer Stocks and Naive Expectations in a Non-Walrasian Dynamic Macromodel: Stability, Cyclicity and Chaos", The Scandinavian Journal of Economics, 84, 571-581.

Sharkovskii, A.N. (1964), "Coexistence of Cycles of a Continuous Map of a Line into Itself", Ukr. Math. Z., 16, 61-71.

Smale, S. (1980), "Differentiable Dynamical Systems", in Smale, S.,The Mathematics of Time, Springer-Verlag, Berlin and New York.

Smale, S., and R. Williams (1975), "The Qualitative Analysis of a Difference Equation of Population Growth", Journal of Mathematical Biology, 3, 1-4.

Stefan, P. (1977), "A Theorem of Sharkovskii on the Existence of Periodic Orbits of Continuous Endomorphism of the Real Line", Comm.Math. Phisics, 54, 237-248.

Stutzer, M. (1980), "Chaotic Dynamics and Bifurcation in a Macro-Model", Journal of Economic Dynamics and Control, 2, 253-276.

Sutherland, W.A. (1970), "On Optimal Development in Multi-Sectoral Economy: the Discounted Case", Review of Economic Studies, 37, 585--589.

Thom. R. (1975), Structural Stability and Morphogenesis, Benjamin, New York.

Torre, V. (1977), "Existence of Limit Cycles and Control in Complete Keynesian System by Theory of Bifurcation", Econometrica, 45, 1457 -1466.

Varian, H.R. (1979), "Catastrophe Theory and the Business Cycle", Economic Inquiry, XVII, 14-28.

Varian, H.R. (1981), "Dynamical Systems with Application to Economics", in Arrow, K.J., and M.D. Intrilligator (eds), Handbook of Mathematical Economics, Vol. I, North Holland, Amsterdam.

Vercelli, A. (1982), "Is Instability Enough to Discredit a Model?", Economic Notes, 11, 173-190.

SYNERGETICS AND DYNAMIC ECONOMIC MODELS

A. Medio
Department of Economics
University of Venice

1. Dealing with complex dynamic systems, economists must face two difficult problems simultaneously. On the one hand, they have to study the interrelations among the elements of the system at a given moment of time, on the other hand they have to describe their evolution in time, as determined by external forces and internal reaction-mechanisms. Whereas the former area of investigation is well developed and is dealt with by general equilibrium theories of one type or another, the study of the latter problem is still in its infancy, partly owing to formidable mathematical difficulties.

Most dynamic economic models are indeed characterized by "heroic" aggregation, which of course makes their results of little relevance. Detailed description of very complicated systems is likely to lead to unintelligible conclusions where the answer to any question is "it depends". A more promising approach would be to find certain synthetic indicators which may represent the working of the system *in nuce*, without destroying its multidimensional character.

The present paper is an attempt to provide a contribution in this direction.

2. The starting point of our discussion will be a standard dynamic input-output model of the type

$$x = Ax + B\dot{x}, \qquad (1)$$

where the (n x 1) vector x indicates the levels of production of the n commodities; A is the (n x n) flow matrix; B the (n x n) stock matrix and dots over variables indicate derivatives with respect to time, t. The model represented by equation (1) suffers from two major drawbacks. First of all, it implicitly assumes that demand for and supply of commodities, as well as desired and actual investment [1/], are always in equilibrium. Secondly, the model is linear, i.e. the consumption and investment coefficients - represented by the elements of the matrices A and B - are constant and in particular they do not depend on the levels and rates of variation of output.

In order to improve the realism of the model, we shall modify it as follows:

(i) discrepancies are permitted between demand for and supply of commodities, as well as between desired and actual investment, and the relevant equilibrium conditions are replaced by adjustment mechanisms of the tâtonnement type (i.e. by simple exponential lags);

(ii) a nonlinearity is introduced by allowing the accelerator coefficients to vary when outputs (or their rate of change) vary. To make things simple, the nonlinearity will take a semilinear form, i.e. only a finite number of values of the coefficients will be considered.

For each commodity i, therefore, we shall have

$$(T_i^{(y)} D + 1) x_i = x_i^D$$

$$x_i^D = x_i^C + x_i^I$$

$$x_i^C = \sum_{j=1}^{n} a_{ij} x_j$$

$$(T_i^{(i)} D + 1) x_i^I = \sum_{j=1}^{n} b_{ij}(x_1, x_2, \ldots, x_n) \dot{x}_j$$

where $T_i^{(y)}$ and $T_i^{(i)}$ indicate, respectively, the lengths of the demand-supply and desired investment-actual investment lags (or, equivalently $[1/T_i^{(y)}]$ and $[1/T_i^{(i)}]$ indicate the speeds of adjustment of the same

---

[1/] Desired investment is here determined by means of a simple accelerator mechanism, i. e., for any commodity i, demand for investment is equal to

$$x_i^{(I)} = \sum_{j=1}^{n} b_{ij} \dot{x}_j, \qquad i = 1, \ldots, n.$$

mechanisms); x_i^D, x_i^C, x_i^I indicate, respectively, demand consumption and investment with regard to commodity i; finally, $D \equiv (d/dt)$, t being time. For the entire system, in matrix form we shall thus have the following equations:

$$[\hat{T}^{(y)} \hat{T}^{(i)}]\ddot{x} + \{\hat{T}^{(y)} + [\hat{T}^{(i)}][I - A] - B(x)\}\dot{x} + [I - A]x = 0, \quad (2)$$

where $\hat{T}^{(y)}$ and $\hat{T}^{(i)}$ are the (n x n) diagonal matrices composed by the element $T_i^{(y)}$ and $T_i^{(i)}$, respectively; $\ddot{x}_j \equiv (d^2x_j/dt^2)$; and of course I is the identity matrix. It will be observed that the stock matrix is no longer constant but a function of the output levels x. More specifically, we shall assume that for each commodity the nonlinearity in the accelerator function is of the "saturation" type, i.e. the relevant coefficients take larger positive values when the levels of outputs are in a certain neighborhood of equilibrium and smaller (possibly zero) values outside (either above or below) that area.

3. Quite evidently, the structure of (2) looks like that of the aggregate nonlinear models of business cycles produced in several versions since the 1950's, most of them inspired by the early works of Richard Goodwin. The present writer has discussed such models in a book [Medio, 1979] where both the economic assumptions and the techniques of analysis are dealt with extensively. And yet our model (2) differs from most previous formalizations of business cycles in the vital respect that it describes the evolution in time of a multisector economy.
Dynamic multidimensional nonlinear models are enormously difficult to treat in general and even when nonlinearities are very simple as in (2), they do not lend themselves to any easy conclusions. In the sequel we shall tackle this problem by combining two techniques of analysis not very well known in economic literature. The first one may be labelled "synergetics" and has recently received increasing attention by scholars belonging to different fields, mainly physicists, chemists and biologists [1/]. The second technique we shall make use of is called "point

1/ An introduction to synergetics can be found in H. Haken [1978], from whose analysis this author has greatly benefited.

transformation" and will be discussed later on (Cf. AVK, 1966 , pp. 443-582; Medio, op. cit., pp. 61-122).

Synergetics studies dynamic systems composed of many subsystems. The basic idea is that certain critical values of parameters exist near which the evolution of the whole system can be described by very few variables which are sometimes called "order parameters". At those critical points, order parameters, so to speak, "slave" the other variables whose behaviour is therefore determined by that of the former. This principle contains certain procedures of elimination of stable modes which are also called "adiabatic approximation".

The idea is not entirely new and can be found in the analysis of the so-called relaxation oscillations [1/]. The prerequisite for its application is that, when the speed of adjustment of certain variables is much greater than that of the others, it is possible to split the system in two parts, "slow motion" and "rapid motion" and, if the difference in speed is sufficiently great, one can assume that the "rapid" variables are always in equilibrium, the latter being defined in terms of the "slow" variables. Of course, when the conditions exist, the same procedure can be repeated so that the system may be ordered in a hierarchy of variables, each group of them controlling the next (faster) one.

The interest of this approach is twofold. On the other hand, it allows one to simplify enormously the analysis of multidimensional systems and to apply to them certain known methods of investigation, previously limited to aggregate models. Secondly, in a number of specific cases belonging to vastly different areas of research, by the synergetic approach it has been possible to simulate at least qualitatively certain interesting phenomena occuring in multidimensional systems, by means of a system of differential equations of much lower order.

This should not be surprising, though. In essence, synergetics studies the behaviour of systems in which instability appears only in relation

---

[1/] Cf. AVK, op. cit., pp. 645-788; for an economic application, see Medio, op. cit., pp. 123-137.

to very few variables. This is presumably the only case in which the dynamics of complex systems is intelligible, i.e. in which it produces recognizable patterns.

If one thinks of that, synergetics makes explicit and rigorous a method of investigation which is routinely applied in a more or less conscious manner in all fields of analysis, including economics. Indeed in most dynamic models one studies the evolution in time of a limited number of variables, whereas the others are implicitly or explicitly assumed to take their equlibrium values. In formal terms, for some ("slow") variables the solution of the model gives us certain functions of time, while the other ("fast") variables are determined by algebraic equations as functions of the former. The rationale for this procedure must be that, while the slow variables evolve in time, the fast ones adjust instantaneously to their (changing) values.

This is nothing but the aforementioned "adiabatic approximation" which in most cases, however, is adopted without the author discussing its conditions and implications. For example, hardly ever in the literature is it indicated that, in order for the approximation to be acceptable, it is required that (i) the "fast" variables be stable and (ii) their speed of adjustment be sufficiently high with respect to the motion of the "slow" ones. This is particularly important in nonlinear models where stability is not determined once and for all over the entire domain of the relevant variables.Sudden changes from stability to instability of "fast" variables, which may occur at certain critical values of the "slow" variables, may give rise to catastrophe and discontinuous (relaxation) oscillations. (Cf. Medio, op. cit.; Haken, op. cit.).

The main purpose of this paper is to attempt an application of synergetics to a well known economic problem, with a view to a better understanding of the power (and the limits) of this method when applied to social sciences.

Before resuming our formal analysis, one final caveat. When we speak of dividing the variables into "order parameters" (or "slow" variables) and "slave parameters" (or "fast" variables) we should not assume that these should necessarily correspond to the variables of the original problem. Indeed this is an exceptional occurence. As we shall see, in most cases stable and unstable modes take place in relation to certain derived variables which are (linear) combinations of the original ones. In geometric terms this means, for example, that in unstable systems, motion away from equilibrium takes place only along a certain line (when only one order parameter exists), or over a certain plane (when only two order parameters exist), and so on and so forth. The direct economic interpretation of these new variables may or may not be possible. It is always possible, however, to derive the evolution of the original variables by performing backward the transformation which has generated the new ones. This procedure is very akin to that followed by Goodwin in a number of recent works in which he makes use of "normalized coordinates" [1/].

4. Let us now return to the system of equations (2). We want first of all to transform it into a system of first order differential equations. This is done by introducing the 2n auxiliary variables $z_i^{(1)}$, $z_i^{(2)}$, $i = 1, \ldots, n$, such that

$$\begin{aligned} z_i^{(1)} &= x_i \\ z_i^{(2)} &= \dot{x}_i . \end{aligned} \qquad (3)$$

Substituting (3) into (2), we have

$$\begin{aligned} \dot{z}^{(1)} &= z^{(2)} \\ \dot{z}^{(2)} &= \{-[\hat{T}^{(i)}]^{-1} - [\hat{T}^{(y)}]^{-1}[I - A] + [\hat{T}^{(y)}\,\hat{T}^{(i)}]^{-1} \, . \\ &\quad . \, B(x)\}z^{(2)} - [\hat{T}^{(y)}\,\hat{T}^{(i)}]^{-1}[I - A]z^{(1)}, \end{aligned} \qquad (4)$$

where $z^{(1)}$, $z^{(2)}$ are (n x 1) vectors with elements $z_i^{(1)}$, $z_i^{(2)}$, respectively.

In a more compact manner, (4) can be re-arranged thus:

1/ Cf. Goodwin, [1976].

$$\begin{bmatrix} \dot{z}_1^{(1)} \\ \cdot \\ \cdot \\ \cdot \\ \dot{z}_n^{(1)} \\ \dot{z}_1^{(2)} \\ \cdot \\ \cdot \\ \cdot \\ \dot{z}_n^{(2)} \end{bmatrix} = \left[\begin{array}{c|c} 0 & I \\ \hline G_1 & G_2 \end{array} \right] \begin{bmatrix} z_1^{(1)} \\ \cdot \\ \cdot \\ \cdot \\ z_n^{(1)} \\ z_1^{(2)} \\ \cdot \\ \cdot \\ \cdot \\ z_n^{(2)} \end{bmatrix} \tag{5}$$

where the matrices 0, I, G_1, G_2 are square of order (n x n), 0 is the null matrix and

$$G_1 = - [\hat{T}^{(y)} \hat{T}^{(i)}]^{-1}[I - A],$$

$$G_2 = - [\hat{T}^{(i)}]^{-1} - [\hat{T}^{(y)}]^{-1}[I - A] + [\hat{T}^{(y)} \hat{T}^{(i)}]^{-1} B(x), \tag{6}$$

or, still more simply,

$$\dot{z} = G^* z,$$

$$G^* = \left[\begin{array}{c|c} 0 & I \\ \hline G_1 & G_2 \end{array} \right] ; \; z = [z_1^{(1)}, \ldots, z_n^{(1)}; z_1^{(2)}, \ldots, z_n^{(2)}]. \tag{7}$$

Next we want to discuss the stability of the matrix G^*, or equivalently we want to study the sign of its eigenvalues. Before doing that, however we must specify better the form of the function B(x). We assume that, for any pair of commodities (i, j), the accelerator coefficients b_{ij} take only two distinct values, i.e.: they are equal to zero, for values of x_j sufficiently far from the equilibrium point; for values of x_j near equilibrium, none of the accelerator coefficients is smaller and some of them are greater then the corresponding far-from-equilibrium values.

We can think of the elements of B as lights that are on near equilibrium but are switched off far from it. In general, the switches do not have to take place at the same distance from equilibrium, but we assume that the differences are so small vis-à-vis the speed of the motion of x(t) that the thresholds may be assumed to be equally located. Formally we have

$$B(x) = \begin{cases} 0 & \text{for } |x| > x_0 \\ \tilde{B} \geq 0 & \text{for } |x| < x_0 \end{cases}$$

5. Let us now consider the matrix G^*. By simple inspection it can be shown that system (7) has only one equilibrium point at which $\dot{z} = 0$ and it is located at the origin of the coordinates where $z = 0$. Furthermore, we observe that $\det(G^*) > 0$ always. To see this consider that, in general, [1/]

$$\det \left[\begin{array}{c|c} A & B \\ \hline C & D \end{array}\right] = \tag{8}$$

$\det(D) \,.\, \det(A - B D^{-1} C)$, if $\det(D) \neq 0$.

Applying this result to the matrix

$$G^* \left[\begin{array}{c|c} 0 & I \\ \hline G_1 & G_2 \end{array}\right]$$

we have

$$\det(G^*) = \det(-G_1) =$$

$$\det([\hat{T}^{(y)} \hat{T}^{(i)}]^{-1}) \,.\, \det(I - A).$$

We know that $\hat{T}^{(y)}, \hat{T}^{(i)} > 0$. Moreover, A is a standard input-output flow matrix and therefore, if the system is economically viable, $\det(I - A) > 0$. This completes the proof.

Since the order of G^* is even (2n), it follows that either all its roots have positive real part, or those that have negative real part must appear in even numbers.

By making use of the result (8), it can be proved that, for sufficiently small values of the elements of the matrix B, all the eigen values of the matrix G^* have negative real parts, and the equilibrium point $z = 0$ is therefore stable.

To see this, let us write the auxiliary equation of G^*, thus:

[1/] Cf. Gantmacher, [1966], pp. 46-47.

$$\det(\hat{\lambda} - G^{*}) = \left[\begin{array}{c|c} \hat{\lambda} & -I \\ \hline -G_1 & \hat{\lambda}-G_2 \end{array}\right] = 0 \qquad (9)$$

where $\hat{\lambda}$ is the diagonal matrix whose elements are the eigenvalues of G^{*}. From (8), and (9) we have

$$\begin{aligned} &\det(\hat{\lambda}) \;.\; \det[(\hat{\lambda} - G_2) - G_1 \hat{\lambda}^{-1}] = \\ &\det[(\hat{\lambda} - G_2)\hat{\lambda} - G_1] = 0. \end{aligned} \qquad (10)$$

Let us now consider that, for B = 0, from the definitions of the matrices G_1 and G_2, we have:

$$G_2 = \hat{T}^{(i)} G_1 - (\hat{T}^{(i)})^{-1}$$

Equation (10) can therefore be developed thus:

$$\begin{aligned} \det(\hat{\lambda}-G^{*}) &= \det\{[\hat{\lambda}+(\hat{T}^{(y)})^{-1}(I-A)+(\hat{T}^{(i)})^{-1}]\hat{\lambda} + (\hat{T}^{(y)}\hat{T}^{(i)})^{-1}(I-A)\} = \\ &= \det\{\hat{\lambda}^{2}+\hat{\lambda}(\hat{T}^{(y)})^{-1}(I-A)+\hat{\lambda}(\hat{T}^{(i)})^{-1} + (\hat{T}^{(y)}\hat{T}^{(i)})^{-1}(I-A)\} = \\ &= \det\{\hat{\lambda}[(\hat{T}^{(y)})^{-1}(I-A)+\hat{\lambda}] + (\hat{T}^{(i)})^{-1}[(\hat{T}^{(y)})^{-1}(I-A)+\hat{\lambda}]\} = \\ &= \det\{[\hat{\lambda} + (\hat{T}^{(i)})^{-1}][(\hat{T}^{(y)})^{-1}(I-A) + \hat{\lambda}]\} \end{aligned}$$

Therefore, when B = 0, the 2nd eigenvalues of G^{*} are as follows:

(i) n eigenvalues are equal to $[-(T_i^{(i)})^{-1}]<0$, where $T_i^{(i)}$ is an element of $\hat{T}^{(i)}$;

(ii) the remaining n eigenvalues of G^{*} are those of the matrix $[-(\hat{T}^{(y)})^{-1}(I-A)]$. Considering that all the diagonal elements of $\hat{T}^{(y)}$ are positive and that $[-(I-A)]$ is D-stable we can conclude that these eigenvalues too, have negative real parts [1].

1/ A matrix X is called D-stable if, for every diagonal matrix with positive elements D, DX is stable. On this and other related topics, see Magnani U.-Meriggi M.R.[1981], pp. 535-549. This author wishes to thank Prof. Magnani for his kind help in developing the proof above.

If the elements of B are now increased monotonically, sooner or later some of the eigenvalues of G^* will take positive real parts. That this must be the case can be seen by considering that, when all the elements b_{ij} increase so does the trace of G^* and that the latter is equal to the sum of the eigenvalues of G^*. For elements of $B \geq 0$, therefore, we have two possibilities. The first one occurs when $B \neq 0$ is such that all the eigenvalues of G^* still have negative real parts. In this case the system is globally stable.
The second possibilty occurs when, for $|z| < z_0$[1], B is such to produce eigenvalues with positive real parts and therefore instability. This is the case we are mainly interested in.
By applying the principle of synergetics discussed above, we assume that when certain basic parameters (the accelerators) are changed and the system moves from stability to instability, only few eigenvalues become positive (in real part) whereas all the others remain negative. Since our main interest is the behaviour of the system near a critical point - i.e. the point at which the value of the real part of a small number of eigenvalues passes through zero -, it is reasonable to assume that the negative eigenvalues are much greater in absolute value than the positive ones and the adiabatic approximation therefore holds.

6. Let us now procede to a convenient rearrangement of our system. Consider first the situation in which $B \geq 0$. Let P be the matrix whose j^{th} column ($j = 1, \ldots, 2n$) is f_j, where $\{f_1, \ldots, f_{2n}\}$ is a basis of eigenvectors of $G^*\big|_{|z|<z_0}$ and let P^{-1} be its inverse. We shall then have

$$P^{-1} G^* P = \hat{\lambda}, \tag{12}$$

where $\hat{\lambda}$ is a diagonal ($2n \times 2n$) matrix, whose elements are the eigenvalues of $G^*\big|_{|z|<z_0}$. If the matrix G^* has complex eigenvalues, along

---

[1] Notice that if the binding constraint only refers to the vector $[x_i]$ the relevant elements of z_0 will always be taken equal to $[z_i^{(2)}]$.

the diagonal of $P^{-1} G^{*} P$ there will be blocks D such that

$$D = \begin{bmatrix} \sigma & -\omega \\ \omega & \sigma \end{bmatrix}$$

where σ is the real part $j\omega$ the imaginary part of the eigenvalues, j being of course = $\sqrt{-1}$. In this case, the differential equations concerning the relevant ξ's will be paired as follows:

$$\dot{\xi}_1 = \sigma\xi_1 - \omega\xi_2$$

$$\dot{\xi}_2 = \omega\xi_1 + \sigma\xi_2$$

Let us now define a (2n x 1) vector ξ, such that

$$z = P\xi, \text{ or}$$

$$\xi = P^{-1} z. \tag{13}$$

By making use of (12) and (13), (7) can be transformed thus:

$$\dot{\xi} = \hat{\lambda}\xi + R\xi, \tag{14}$$

where [1/]

$$R = \begin{cases} 0, \text{ for } |z|<z_0 \\ P^{-1} \left[\begin{array}{c|c} 0 & 0 \\ \hline 0 & -\overset{\circ}{B} \end{array}\right] P, \text{ for } |z|>z_0 \end{cases}$$

and

$$\overset{\circ}{B} = \hat{T}^{(y)} \hat{T}^{(i)\,-1} \tilde{B}.$$

The ξ's are of course normalized coordinates in the sense of Goodwin. Suppose now that only few eigenvalues have positive real parts and let us call them λ_u; the others having negative real parts we shall call λ_s.

1/ Notice that the thereshold $|z|\gtrless z_0$ can be easily formulated in terms of the transformed variables ξ. Considering that $z = P\xi$, the inequalities $|z|\gtrless z_0$ are equal to $|P\xi|\gtrless\xi_0$, ξ_0 being a constant vector.

If the adiabatic approximation holds, i. e. if we can assume that [1/]

$$|\lambda_s| >> |\lambda_u|, \qquad (15)$$

system (14) can be partioned as follows:

$$\begin{bmatrix} \dot{\xi}_u \\ \hline \dot{\xi}_s \end{bmatrix} = \left[\begin{array}{c|c} \hat{\lambda}_u & 0 \\ \hline 0 & \hat{\lambda}_s \end{array}\right] + \left[\begin{array}{c|c} R_{uu} & R_{us} \\ \hline R_{su} & R_{ss} \end{array}\right] \begin{bmatrix} \xi_u \\ \hline \xi_s \end{bmatrix} \qquad (16)$$

where the subscripts to the (generally rectangular) submatrices R_{ij} indicate rows and columns pertaining to stable or unstable transformed variables.

Moreover, in virtue of (15) we can assume that,while the system moves slowly in a direction defined in terms of the coordinates ξ_u, any deviation in term of the coordinates ξ_s is rapidly corrected and can be ignored.

Formally, we have

$$\dot{\xi}_u = \hat{\lambda}_u \xi_u + R_{uu} \xi_u + R_{us} \xi_s, \qquad (17)$$

$$\dot{\xi}_s = \hat{\lambda}_s \xi_s + R_{ss} \xi_s + R_{su} \xi_u = 0 \qquad (18)$$

(where of course $R_e \lambda_u > 0$; $R_e \lambda_s < 0$), from which we have

$$\xi_s = - [\hat{\lambda}_s + R_{ss}]^{-1} R_{su} \xi_u. \qquad (19)$$

Replacing (19) into (17), we have

$$\dot{\xi}_u = \{\hat{\lambda}_u + R_{uu} - R_{us} [\hat{\lambda}_s + R_{ss}]^{-1} . R_{su}\} \xi_u. \qquad (20)$$

[1/] If the λ_s' have imaginary parts, in order for the adiabatic approxima tion to hold it must be

$$R_e \lambda_s >> R_e \lambda_u$$

and

$$R_e \lambda_s >> I_m \lambda_u$$

i.e. the imaginary part of λ_u must be much smaller than the real part of λ_s, (Cf. Haken, op. cit., p. 199). Since the imaginary part measures the frequency of oscillations, which is inversely correlated to their period, the second condition above requires that oscillations of the unstable variables have sufficiently low frequency (= long period) vis-à-vis the speed of adjustment of the stable variable, so that the latter may always be found very near equilibrium.

7. What we now have is a system of differential equations in which only the unstable variables appear (20), and a system of algebric equations in which the stable variables are given as functions of the unstable ones (19). The solutions of the former system consist of functions of time, defining the paths followed by the system out of equilibrium. For each point in time we can then solve the latter system and obtain the values of the "slaved" variables.

We are now in position to apply our method to the investigation of the disequilibrium dynamics of the system. For this purpose, suppose that for $|P\xi|<\xi_0$, only two unstable modes exist in the system and let us call the corresponding coordinates ξ_1 and ξ_2.

If the eigenvalues are real and positive, the corresponding differential equations are

$$\begin{bmatrix} \dot{\xi}_1 \\ \dot{\xi}_2 \end{bmatrix} = \begin{bmatrix} \lambda_1 & 0 \\ 0 & \lambda_2 \end{bmatrix} + F \cdot \begin{bmatrix} \xi_1 \\ \xi_2 \end{bmatrix} \tag{21}$$

where both λ_1 and λ_2 are >0 and real and F is a (2×2) matrix derived from (20), and is equal to zero for $|P\xi|<\xi_0$ and $\neq 0$ for $|P\xi|>\xi_0$.

If the two eigenvalues are complex with positive real part equal to $\sigma \pm j\omega$, we shall have

$$\begin{bmatrix} \xi_1 \\ \xi_2 \end{bmatrix} = \begin{bmatrix} \sigma & \omega \\ \omega & \sigma \end{bmatrix} + F \begin{bmatrix} \xi_1 \\ \xi_2 \end{bmatrix} . \tag{21.1}$$

The general features of the dynamics of the system can be described thus. (Cf. figs. 1, 2). Any path starting within the prescribed neighborhood, but out of equilibrium, will move away from it either with a definite direction (if $\lambda_{1,2}$ are real) or with an oscillating motion (if $\lambda_{1,2}$ are complex conjugate).

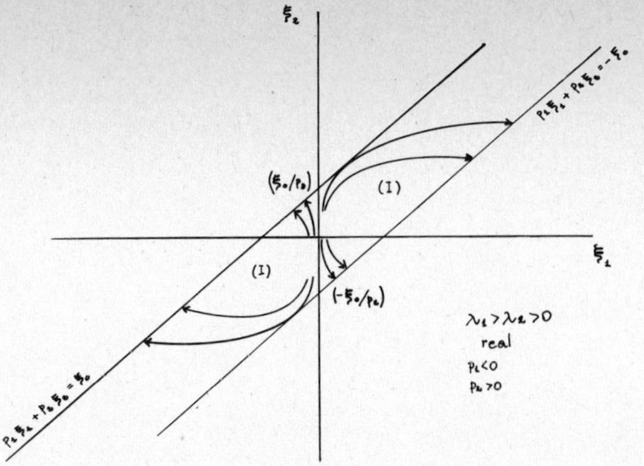

Fig. 1

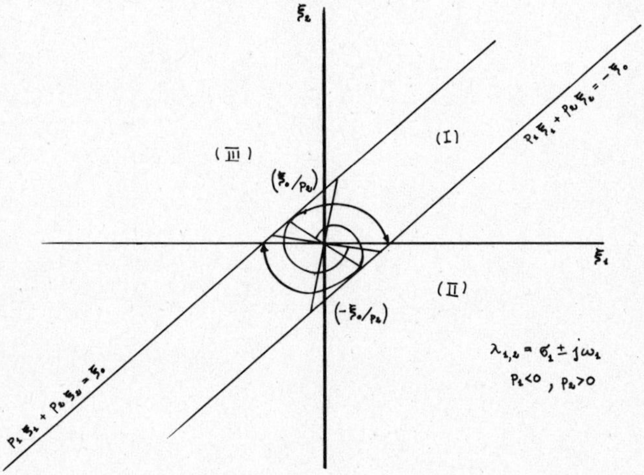

Fig. 2

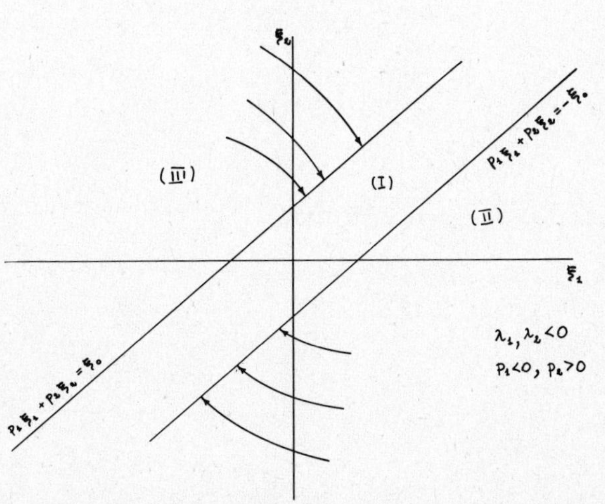

Fig. 3

Outside the threshold,we know that the motion is stable, i.e. any path will return towards the equilibrium point (fig. 3)). The conclusion can be verified considering for a moment the complete system (14)

$$\dot{\xi} = \hat{\lambda}\xi + R\xi .$$

By making use of (12), (14) and the definition of R, we have

$$(\hat{\lambda} + R) = P^{-1}\, G^{*}\big|_{|z|>z_0}\, P,$$

and therefore $(\hat{\lambda} + R)$ and $G^{*}\big|_{|z|>z_0}$ have the same eigenvalues. But we know that all eigenvalues of $G^{*}\big|_{|z|>z_0}$ have negative real parts. Q.E.D.

We can now write the solutions of systems (21) and (21.1) in the region (I)$(|P\xi|<\xi_0)$ thus:

$$\begin{aligned} \xi_1(t) &= \xi_1(0)\, e^{\lambda_1 t} \\ \xi_2(t) &= \xi_2(0)\, e^{\lambda_2 t} \end{aligned} \tag{22}$$

when the eigenvalues are real; and

$$\begin{aligned} \xi_1(t) &= k_1 e^{(\sigma+j\omega)t} + k_2 e^{(\sigma-j\omega)t} \\ \xi_2(t) &= -\, jk_1 e^{(\sigma+j\omega)t} + jk_2 e^{(\sigma-j\omega)t} \end{aligned} \tag{23}$$

when the eigenvalues are complex. k_i $(i = 1,2)$ are complex numbers depending on initial conditions, such that

$$(k_1 + k_2) = \xi_1(0)$$

$$j(k_2 - k_1) = \xi_2(0).$$

and, it will be remembered, $\sigma \pm j\omega$ are the complex eigenvalues.

In region (II) and (III) the solution will be instead:

$$\begin{aligned} \xi_1(t) &= l_1 q_{11} e^{\mu_1 t} + l_2 q_{12} e^{\mu_2 t} \\ \xi_2(t) &= l_1 q_{21} e^{\mu_1 t} + l_2 q_{22} e^{\mu_2 t}, \end{aligned} \tag{23.1}$$

where the matrix

$$Q = (q_{ij}), \quad i,j = 1,2,$$

is derived from the matrix P of $G^{*}\big|_{|z|>z_0}$ when all rows and columns but the first two are deleted; l_i are arbitrary constants depending on initial conditions, and μ_i are the roots of the auxiliary equation.

8. The phase diagram of our transformed system may be complicated and there exist several possibilities depending on the values of the coeffi cients of the original system and thereby on the elements of the matrices P and P^{-1}. Here we present only a specific simple case. It will be remembered that, independently of the matrix B, $\det(G^*) > 0$ and therefore roots with negative real part must always appear in even numbers. Since the order of G^* is even, this is also true of roots with a positive real part. It follows that, when the system moves from stabili ty to instability, two complex conjugate roots will simultaneously take a positive real part.

In particular we assume that:

(i) the eigenvalues pertaining to region (I) are complex conjugate equal to

$$\sigma_1 \pm j\omega_1, \quad \sigma_1 > 0, \quad \omega_1 < 0,$$

which means that the motion in that region is described by clockwise unstable spirals;

(ii) the eigenvalues pertaining to regions (II) and (III) are also complex conjugate equal to

$$\sigma_2 \pm j\omega_2, \quad \sigma_2 < 0, \quad \omega_2 < 0, \qquad ^{1/}$$

(iii) the switching line between region (I) and (II) or (III) has the form

$$|p_1 \xi_1 + p_2 \xi_2| \gtrless \xi_0,$$

where ξ_0 is a positive constant; it is assumed the $p_i < 0$, $p_2 > 0$, so that the lines are positively sloped.

1/ Stability depends on $\sigma_i \gtrless 0$ $(i = 1,2)$, the clockwise motion on $\omega_i < 0$ (Cf. Hirsch-Smale, [1974], p. 95). If we consider a sufficiently small interval, the cyclical motion (stable in region (II) and (III)), unstable in region (I)) must take place in the same direction, i.e. ω_1 and ω_2 must have the same sign.

In this case the phase-diagram will be as indicate by fig. 4.

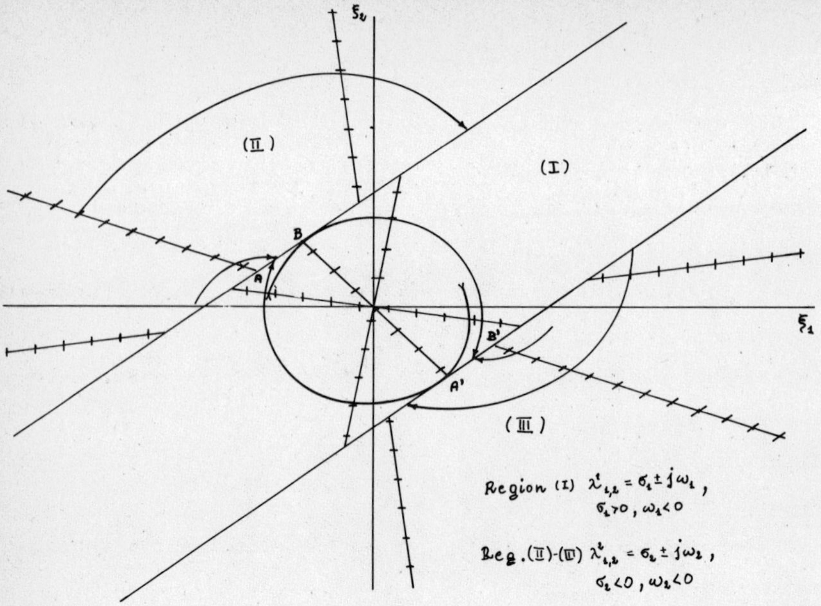

Fig. 4

The (BA') line and the similar (AB') line, are the loci of points at which trajectories pertaining to region (I) or (II)and (III), respectively, are parallel to the swîtching lines [1/], and therefore indicate

---

[1/] It can be easily shown that the (BA') has a negative slope. Consider that, for region (I) we have

$$\left[\frac{d\xi_2}{d\xi_1}\right]_I = \frac{\omega_1\xi_1 + \sigma_1\xi_2}{\sigma_1\xi_1 - \omega_1\xi_2} = -\frac{p_1}{p_2} > 0.$$

Assume now that $\omega_1 < 0$ - i.e. the spirals are clockwise. We can write the equation of the line (BA') thus:

$$\left[\frac{\xi_2}{\xi_1}\right]_I = \frac{\omega_1 - \sigma_1(p_1/p_2)}{\sigma_1 + \omega_1(p_1/p_2)} = \kappa_I \qquad (*)$$

Since the denominator is positive, $\kappa_I \gtrless 0$ if

$$\omega_1 - \sigma_1(p_1/p_2) \gtrless 0 \text{ or } -(\sigma_1/\omega_1) \gtrless -(p_2/p_1).$$

As, near the switching line, σ_1 is small the sign < prevails and therefore $\kappa_I < 0$. The same result applies if the spirals are counterclockwise, i.e. if $\omega_1 > 0$. In this case the numerator of (*) is > 0 and therefore

whether trajectories point inside or outside those lines.

If we now consider regions (I) to (III) together, there exist two main possibilities. The first one occurs when the trajectories point toward the switching lines on one side and away from them on the other side, so that the representative point moves from one region to the other. The second occurs when the switching lines are approached on both sides. In the former case the representative point of the system reaches a switching line, from, say, region (I), moves into region (II)(or (III))and then returns to region (I). In the latter case, the representative point moves into the switching line and then continues its motion along it, until it reaches a zone of the plane where the directions of the paths are compatible with each other.

The motion of the system along the switching line - which is sometimes called <u>slip-motion</u> [1/] - must be interpreted as a limit case of a situation in which the changes in the dynamic régimes (i.e. the changes in the

---

$$\kappa_I \gtrless 0 \quad \text{if}$$

$$\sigma_1 + \omega_1(p_1/p_2) \gtrless 0 \quad \text{or}$$

$$(\sigma_1/\omega_1) \gtrless -(p_1/p_2).$$

Since, for σ_1 small, the sign < prevails, $\kappa_I < 0$. With analogous reasoning it can be shown that the slope κ_{II} of the (AB') line is negative if $|\sigma_2 - \sigma_1|$ is small and (p_1/p_2) not too large, otherwise it may be positive.

[1/] Cf. AVK, <u>op.cit.</u>, pp. 501-512. A quick inspection of the phase-diagrams will suggest that, for the slip motion to occur, it must be

$$|\kappa_{II}| < |\kappa_I|$$

if the spirals are clockwise. On the contrary, if the spirals are counterclockwise, the condition of the slip motion is

$$|\kappa_{II}| > |\kappa_I|.$$

acceleration that occur when the system moves from region (I) to region (II) or (III) are not instantaneous but take time).

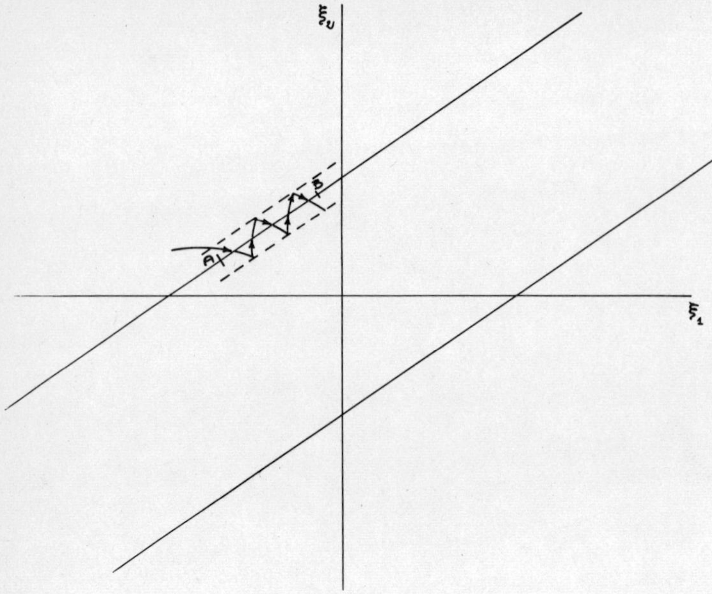

Fig. 5

This is described by fig. 5. When a trajectory moving from region (II) reaches the AB segment of the switching line, the motion continues into region (I) because of the delay in the switch. When the latter finally operates, a trajectory will start in region (I) directed toward AB and - owing to the delay - will cross it, reaching region (II) again. An oscillating motion will ensue around the segment AB, sometimes called "chattering".

The slip-motion along the trajectory can be conceived as the limit of the chattering as the delay in the switch tends to zero. To define rigorously the direction and speed of the slip motion we must make use of the "solution in the Filippov sense" of a system of differential equations including discountinuous nonlinearities.

The details of this solution can be found in Diljak [1969], pp. 542-544 and the literature quoted there, but we shall recall here the essential conclusions applicable to our model.

It can be shown that, as the delay in the switch tends to zero, limit motion and velocity along the switching line are determined by the following system:

$$\dot{\xi} = X^{o}\ \xi = \alpha\ X^{+}\ \xi + (1-\alpha)\ X^{-}\ \xi,$$

where

$$X^{+} = \begin{bmatrix} \sigma_1 & -\omega_1 \\ \omega_1 & \sigma_1 \end{bmatrix}, \qquad (24)$$

$$X^{-} = \lfloor X^{+} + F \rceil ,$$

and α is a number ($0 \lesseqgtr \alpha \leqslant 1$) such that ($d\xi_2/d\xi_1$) as defined by (24) is equal to ($-p_1/p_2$), i.e. the slope of the switching line.
To construct the vector (22) in practice we proceed thus. At any point ($\bar{\xi}_1$, $\bar{\xi}_2$) on the segment AB (or A'B') - where of course

$$\xi_2 = \pm (\xi_0/p_2) - (p_1/p_2)\ \xi_1,$$

we construct the vectors $X^{+}\xi$ and $X^{-}\xi$ and join their ends by a segment. The point of intersection with the switching line is the end of the required vector.
Simple geometrical considerations and the inspection of fig. 4, suggest that on the AB segment we have $\dot{\xi} > 0$ and $\dot{\xi}_2 > 0$, and on A'B' we have $\dot{\xi}_1 < 0$ and $\dot{\xi}_2 < 0$. In either case, therefore, the slip motion will continue on the switch lines until a point is reached where the trajectories moving from region (I), (II) or (III) are consistent, i.e. the switch lines can be crossed.

9. In order to investigate the existence of limit cycles with a minimum of complication we shall now consider the behaviour of the system outside the region of slip-motion. The analysis that follows, however, could be extended to the case of slip-motion with some obvious (although not necessarily simple) alterations.
We have postulated that the eigenvalues pertaining to regions (I) are complex conjugate with a positive real part and those pertaining to regions (II) and (III) are also complex conjugate with a negative real

part. This situation is described by fig. 6.

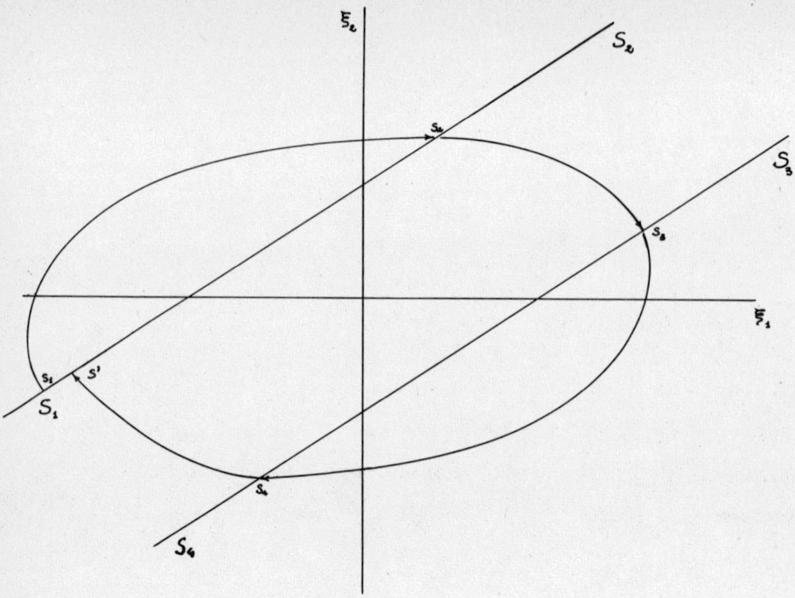

Fig. 6

We can now apply the point transformation technique. Omitting at this stage a number of mathematical details, we can procede as follows. Consider the sequence of point s_1, s_2, s_3, s_4, respectively on the half straight lines S_1, S_2, S_3, S_4.

Generally speaking a point in the (ξ_1, ξ_2) plane should be defined by two numbers corresponding to the two coordinates. However, since the points in question lie on the switching lines where we have

$$\xi_2 = \pm (\xi_0/p_2) - (p_1/p_2)\,\xi_1 \tag{25}$$

it is always possible to express points on those lines in terms of one co-ordinate only, say ξ_1.

For each arc of trajectory, equations (23) and (23.1) in conjunction with (25) will give us the "terminal" values of ξ_1 as functions of the initial values and the transit time. From these equations we can construct the following correspondence functions:

$$
\begin{aligned}
C_1 &: s_2 = \phi_1 (t_1); \quad s_1 = \psi_1 (t_1);\\
C_2 &: s_3 = \phi_2 (t_2); \quad s_2 = \psi_2 (t_2);\\
C_3 &: s_4 = \phi_3 (t_3); \quad s_3 = \psi_3 (t_3);\\
C_4 &: s' = \phi_4 (t_4); \quad s_4 = \psi_4 (t_4);
\end{aligned}
\tag{26}
$$

t_i being the time of transit over the relevant region.
Correspondence functions relate the initial and the terminal values of ξ_1 along each arc of trajectory, in a parametric form, time being the parameter.
Clearly the succession of transformations $C = C_1 . C_2 . C_3 . C_4$ constitutes a (linear) transformation of the half straight line S_1 onto itself.
The problem of studying the existence of the limit cycles over the entire region I-II-III amounts to finding the conditions for $s'=s_1$, or, equivalently, to finding the fixed point of the overall transformation C. For this purpose we have to solve the system of equations

$$
\begin{aligned}
\phi_1 (\bar{t}_1) &= \psi_2 (\bar{t}_2);\\
\phi_2 (\bar{t}_2) &= \psi_3 (\bar{t}_3);\\
\phi_3 (\bar{t}_3) &= \psi_4 (\bar{t}_4);\\
\phi_4 (\bar{t}_4) &= \psi_1 (\bar{t}_1),
\end{aligned}
$$

where $T \equiv \sum_{i=1}^{4} \bar{t}_i$ is the length of the cycle.

Considering that the relevant equations are symmetrical with respect to the origin of the co-ordinate axes, it will be sufficient to consider transformations C_1 and C_2 only. The existence of a limit cycle will be established if there exists an end point on the line S_3 whose co-ordinates are the same as those of the starting point on S_1, but with opposite sign.
The equations of the limit cycle will therefore be the following, simpler ones:

$$\phi_1(\bar{t}_1) = \psi_2(\bar{t}_2)$$

$$\phi_2(\bar{t}_2) = -\psi_1(\bar{t}_1)$$

where $2(\bar{t}_1 + \bar{t}_2)$ is the length of the cycle.

The study of the relevant functions that we omit here, shows that in our case, one and only one limit cycle exists. Proof of this can be developed along the same line as in this author's mentioned work [Cf. Medio (1979), pp. 77-104].

The stability of the cycle can be ascertained by means of Koenig's theorem, i.e. by establishing whether, at the fixed point

$$\frac{ds'}{ds_1} \lessgtr 1,$$

(the cycle being stable in the former case, unstable in the latter). In the present case it can be shown that, the cycle is indeed stable. [ibidem].

10. The interesting and new aspect of this analysis is that persistent fluctuations of the system are not defined in relation to two original variables, in our case two commodities, but to two <u>combinations of all the commodities of the system</u>. Goodwin (op. cit.) calls these "eigencommodities", but we must be careful in giving them economic interpretation. Indeed the eigencommodities may include negative quantities which cannot be directly interpreted as real commodities. The meaning of the co-ordinates ξ_u lies in that they indicate the directions in which disequilibrium manifests itself in the system, i.e. by producing in the different sectors various combinations of deviations from equilibrium of different sign (e.g. booms and recessions). Only in special cases, therefore, oscillations take the form of business cycles in the usual sense, i.e. with all (or most) sectors simultaneously experiencing a phase of prosperity or recession.

When complex eigenvalues occur, that means that the said discrepancies do not take a definite direction but oscillate in the relevant plane. Finally, it must be remembered that the overall state of the system at any given moment in time (not only in equilibrium but also along the cyclical path) may always be reconstructed, first by making use of equations (19) - which give us the stable eigencommodities ξ_s in terms of the unstable ones ξ_u, and then by transforming back the ξ_s into the original variables z's and x's.

11. So far we have considered the motion of the system with regard a stationary equilibrium ($\dot{z} = z = 0$) but most of the ideas developed in the preceding paragraphs could be easily refarred to a steady-state growth path, that is to a state in which the system grows at a uniform rate.

If we call this rate g, the equilibrium position can be described thus:

$$[I - A - gB]\, x = 0,$$

or (27)

$$gx = B^{-1}\,[I - A]\, x.$$

Assuming the nonnegative matrices A and B are connected (we shall call them **n.n.c.**) from (27) we deduce that a unique positive solution for x exists if and only if dom $(A + gB) = 1$ and accordingly, that for $x > 0$ and $g > 0$, it must be dom $(A) < 1$. This means that: (i) in order for the steady-state to be characterized by both positive quantities and a positive growth rate, the flow side of the economy must be efficient in the usual sense that for all commodities gross output must be sufficient to replace consumption and, for some of them, there must be a positive net output; (ii) since for any n.n.c. matrix X, dom(X) is a positive continuous function of X, the greater B the smaller is the growth rate g consistent with positive levels of output. This result is the multidimensional equivalent of the Harrodian proposition that the greater the accelerator v, the smaller the steady-state rate of growth $g = (s/v)$, for any given saving ratio s.

In order to incorporate steady-state growth, equation (7) must be rewritten thus:

$$\dot{z} = \tilde{G}^{*} z,$$

where

$$\tilde{G}^{*} = \left[\begin{array}{c|c} 0 & I \\ \hline \tilde{G}_1 & \tilde{G}_2 \end{array}\right],$$

$$\tilde{G}_1 = - [\hat{T}^{(y)}\hat{T}^{(i)}]^{-1} [I - A - gB],$$

$$\tilde{G}_2 = - [\hat{T}^{(i)}]^{-1} - [\hat{T}^{(y)}]^{-1} [I - A] + [\hat{T}^{(y)}\hat{T}^{(i)}]^{-1} [I + g\hat{T}^{(i)}] B(x).$$

If the function B(x) is the same as in the stationary case, we can conclude that, in a certain neighborhood of the equilibrium path, deviations from it may be self-sustaining, either in an oscillatory manner or not, depending on the matrix B and on the steady-state growth rate g. Beyond a certain threshold, however, (when $B \to 0$) the expansionary forces will cease to operate and - whatever the value of g may be - - the system will move back to the equilibrium path.

The resulting combined motion will be a cyclical growth of the system.

Bibliography

ANDRONOV, A.A.; VITT, A.A.; KHAIKIN, S.E., (AVK), Theory of Oscillators, Pergamon, 1966.

GANTMACHER, F.R., Théorie des matrices, Gunod, Paris, 1966.

GOODWIN, R., "The Use of Normalized General Coordinates in Linear Value and Distribution Theory", in POLENSKE, K.R.; SKOLKA, J.V. (eds), Advances in Input-Output Analysis, Cambridge, Mass., 1976

HAKEN, H., Synergetics, Springer Verlag, 1978.

HIRSCH, M.W.; SMALE, S., Differential Equations, Dynamical Systems and Linear Algebra, Academic Press, 1974.

MAGNANI, U.; MERIGGI, M.R., "Characterization of K-matrices", in Mathematical Programming and its Economic Applications, Castellani G. and Mazzoleni P. (eds), Franco Angeli, Milano, 1981.

MEDIO, A., Teoria nonlineare del ciclo economico, Bologna, 1979. (This is an Italian version of the author's Ph.D. dissertation, submitted to Cambridge University).

SILJAK, D.D., Nonlinear Systems, John Wiley and Sons, Inc., New York, 1969.

EMBODIED TECHNICAL PROGRESS IN A DYNAMIC ECONOMIC MODEL: THE SELF-ORGANIZATION PARADIGM

Gerald Silverberg

Institut für Sozialforschung
Universität Stuttgart
D-7000 Stuttgart 1/FRG

1. Introduction

A number of distinguished economists have pointed out that the theoretical approaches dominant today have yet to come to terms with the historical, irreversible, and heterogeneous nature of the industrial societies they purport to deal with.[1] Indeed, there seem to be fundamental reasons for this failure. Neoclassical theory, in aggregating capital and presupposing a very special equilibrium process, seems more to obscure than illuminate what is actually going on at the microeconomic level from which its concepts ostensibly are taken. And the post-Keynesian tradition deriving from Sraffa and von Neumann, by working exclusively with so-called long run equilibrium prices, implicitly assumes a single technique over all of history and thereby rules out the analysis of processes of transition (which indeed are the only ones we have known until now in the history of industrial society) involving the appearance and disappearance, the coexistance and differential reproduction (replacement) of distinct capital and consumer goods, natural resources, etc., which in dynamic terms is the ultimate justification for introducing heterogeneity in the first place. The deeper insights of Schumpeter on the disequilibrium process of industrial evolution, and of Keynes, particularly regarding the relationship between expectations and effective demand, have largely failed to find entrance into the mainstream of analytical economics.

In this paper we develop a simple economic model of embodied technical progress based on some ideas borrowed from the relatively new paradigm of self-organization. Although the model is quite simple and makes no claims to immediate empirical applicability, it already illustrates the basic principles of this explanatory approach and generates some very suggestive results. Its essential feature is the incorporation of structural fluctuations (innovations) into a nonlinear dynamic model to show how new configurations can emerge in a progressive, evolutionary way from a historical instability in the underlying dynamic

1. See e.g. Georgescu-Roegen (1971, 1976), Hicks (1976), and Robinson (1975).

system. After summarizing the workings of the model we go on to discuss some implications of the self-organization paradigm for economic modeling as well as some of the methods developed thus far by workers in this field. We also attempt to show how these analytical techniques fit into the evolutionary or ecological framework recently proposed by a number of authors.

2. The Model

Goodwin (1967) has developed a simple one-commodity nonlinear model of economic development which exhibits both trend and cyclic behavior and in which both the rate of profit (and hence also of growth) and the real wage are endogonously determined in a plausible, if highly simplified way. The model assumes neutral, exponential, disembodied technical progress, fixed coefficient production, full utilization of capital made possible by instantaneous disinvestment, but varying rates of labor unemployment as the determinant of changes in the level of real wages. Instead of disembodied technical progress the present analysis presupposes an economy with a fixed production process and then proceeds by examining the stability of the resulting equilibrium state when a second production process embodied in a new capital good (machine 2) with different technical coefficients is introduced as a "seed" industry. If the new technique destroys the stability of the old system it will grow and eventually replace it. This implies a nonuniform rate of profit between the two industries and thus differential rates of growth. This "disequilibrium" condition (in the sense of traditional economic thought) would appear to be the sine qua non for analyzing the process of economic development, i.e., the qualitative change of the nature of an economy over time as opposed to mere equal-proportional, "balanced" expansion as usually considered in growth models with a uniform rate of profit. Indeed, Schumpeter regarded the quasi-rents deriving from innovations to be the motor of the economic process.

Following Goodwin the following assumptions are made:

q is output, consisting of a consumption and a capital good produced in arbitrary proportions by the same production process (one unit of capital is defined to be the number of machines produced by the same amount of labor as required to produce one consumption good);

k is real capital stock;

w is the real wage rate (in units of q);

l is labor employed;

a is constant labor productivity characteristic of a given technique: $a = q/l$;
c is constant capital-output ratio: $c = k/q$;
$n = n_o \exp(\beta t)$ is labor supply, β constant.

Workers' share of product is clearly $wl/q = w/a$; the share of profits $1 - w/a$. Assuming all wages are consumed and all profits reinvested we clearly have

profits = investment = $\dot{k} = (1 - w/a)q$,

and thus

$$\dot{q}/q = \dot{k}/k = (1 - w/a)/c.$$

Taking logarithmic derivatives,

$$\dot{a}/a = \dot{q}/q - \dot{l}/l = 0$$
$$\dot{l}/l = (1 - w/a)/c.$$

Introducing $v = l/n$, $\dot{v}/v = \dot{l}/l - \dot{n}/n = \dot{l}/l - \beta$,

$$\dot{v}/v = (1 - w/a)/c - \beta.$$

Goodwin further assumes that real wages rise near full employment and takes a linear approximation:

$$\dot{w}/w = -m + nv.$$

Thus we obtain a coupled system of nonlinear differential equations of the Lotka-Volterra type:

$$\dot{v} = Av - Bvw$$
$$\dot{w} = -mw + nvw$$

where

$$A = 1/c - \beta \text{ and } B = 1/ac. \qquad (1)$$

The stationary values of the system are defined by the condition $\dot{v} = \dot{w} = 0$ and are

$$v = m/n, \quad w = A/B.$$

Away from the stationary values the orbits are closed and periodic. Hence the system is stable but not asymptotically stable and is known as a center in the qualitative theory of dynamic systems. Unfortunately, this system does not possess the property of structural stability, i.e., the topological character is not robust with respect to small perturbations in the form of the equations, and hence cannot realistically be thought to describe equilibrium or cyclic behavior of a real-world economy.[2]

Let us now assume the economy has evolved employing a production process embodied in a capital stock k_1 characterized by coefficients a_1 and c_1, and has settlednear equilibrium. Suppose a second process (k_2,a_2,c_2) is then introduced with k_2 initially small. This event - the "innovation" - must be thought of as emanating from outside the main economic sphere, being either the product of the heroic entrepreneur/inventor or the R&D sector, and not subject to the same profitability constraints as normal business. Capital good k_2 can be used to produce the basic consumption good q as well as itself, and as with k_1, output is freely adjustable between wage and capital goods. However, k_2 will be thought of as a distinct type of machine which can only be manufactured in the k_2 process. The possibility of manufacturing type 2 machines with the type 1 capital stock will be excluded here for simplicity. Realistically, some intermediate production process $k_1 \rightarrow k_2$ should be viable, but since the extent to which resources in k_1 will be diverted to manufacturing type 2 machines will also be a function of the relative profitability of type 2 machines, the assumption of autocatalytic self-reproduction is probably a good first approximation and has the virtue of making additional behavioral assumptions unnecessary. The possibility of imitation is of course very important in the innovation process, but it will undoubtedly effect the rate of replacement more than the general features of the replacement process itself.

A uniform wage rate serves to couple the two sectors. Denoting the employment level in each sector by $v_1 = l_1/n$, $v_2 = l_2/n$, the wage rate equation becomes

$$\dot{w} = - mw + nw(v_1 + v_2).$$

Continuing to assume that each sector expands in proportion to its own profitability we have

$$\dot{v}_1 = A_1v_1 - B_1wv_1 \quad (2a)$$
$$\dot{v}_2 = A_2v_2 - B_2wv_2, \quad (2b)$$

2. For a discussion of this point in an economic context see Medio (1975). We consider this a problem of secondary mathematical importance for our purposes since a center can be thought of as embedded in a family of differential equations undergoing a Hopf bifurcation as the transitional system between a stable focus and a stable limit cycle. This can be shown e.g. using a theorem due to Kolmogorov (see May (1974), pp. 86-87, 190 ff). The results obtained for the stationary point of the center can then be generalized to the two strucurally stable and economically relevant cases. This question will be ignored in the following. It also recedes in importance once the new process introduced into the model below begins to dominate the system. As the computer analyses show, oscillations due to non-stationary initial values are eliminated during the replacement process and only reassert themselves when it is over.

where A_1, B_1 and A_2 and B_2 are defined for technique 1 and 2 respectively as in (1).

Allen (1975, 1976) has investigated biological evolution in systems of interacting populations, in particular, the predator-prey system in terms of the instability of the system to the appearance of mutant species with higher selective potential. His method is fully applicable to the above description of technical innovation, and we believe the analogy with biological evolution to be more than merely formal, as has also been pointed out using a stochastic model of technical change by Jimenez Montaño and Ebeling (1980). The method is straightforward. The eigenvalues of the expanded system (with mutant species/new process included) are evaluated at the stationary point of the original system with mutant population/new capital stock zero. If this results in an eigenvalue with positive real part the previous equilibrium is unstable to the appearance of any population level of the new species/process, however small, so that the mutant/process will begin to multiply exponentially. A new equilibrium will be established in which the new species/process has completely driven out the old one and is stable with respect to the latter's reappearance (but not to the appearance of a species/process with yet higher selective potential).

Linearizing the above 3x3 system of equations around the stationary point $v_1 = m/n$, $w = A_1/B_1$, $v_2 = 0$ and evaluating the determinant for the eigenvalues, one clearly sees that it is the product of subdeterminants. Hence the first two eigenvalues remain unchanged (and are the purely imaginary roots $\pm i(A_1 m)^{1/2}$) while the third eigenvalue is $A_2 - B_2 w = (A_2 B_1 - A_1 B_2)/B_1$. This is positive (negative) according to

$$A_2/B_2 \gtrless A_1/B_1.$$

The new process will begin to replace the old one if it raises this ratio. Applying this criterion in reverse to the other stationary point $w = A_2/B_2$, $v_1 = 0$, $v_2 = m/n$, one sees that the new technique, once it has established itself, is also stable to the reintroduction of the old one. Thus its evolutionary superiority is not dependent on prevailing wage and profit rates at the time of its introduction; rather, these themselves are endogonously determined by prevailing technology.

Recalling the definitions of A and B we obtain the following criterion of technical change: the quantity

$$T = A/B = a(1 - \beta c)$$

must increase. If the rate of labor force growth is zero this criterion reduces to a near triviality, but perhaps the best established fact about economic growth: technical progress entails a constant secular increase in labor productivity. This holds regardless of the direction of change of the capital-output ratio. This is no longer the case if the labor force is growing; techniques increasing the capital-output ratio will be selected against unless they engender offsetting gains in labor productivity. The tradeoff relation becomes increasingly steep as βc approaches unity. This can be seen by examining the contours of constant T in the a-c plane in Figure 1a. However, the tradeoff relationship is weak for realistic values of β and c. The retarding effect of increasing c is more apparent when we come to consider the <u>rate</u> of replacement below.

Letting M = ac = capital/worker = "degree of mechanization", the selection criterion can be rewritten

$$T = a - \beta M.$$

Thus a new technique increasing M by ΔM must compensate with a labor productivity gain Δa of at least $\beta \Delta M$ (see Figure 1b).

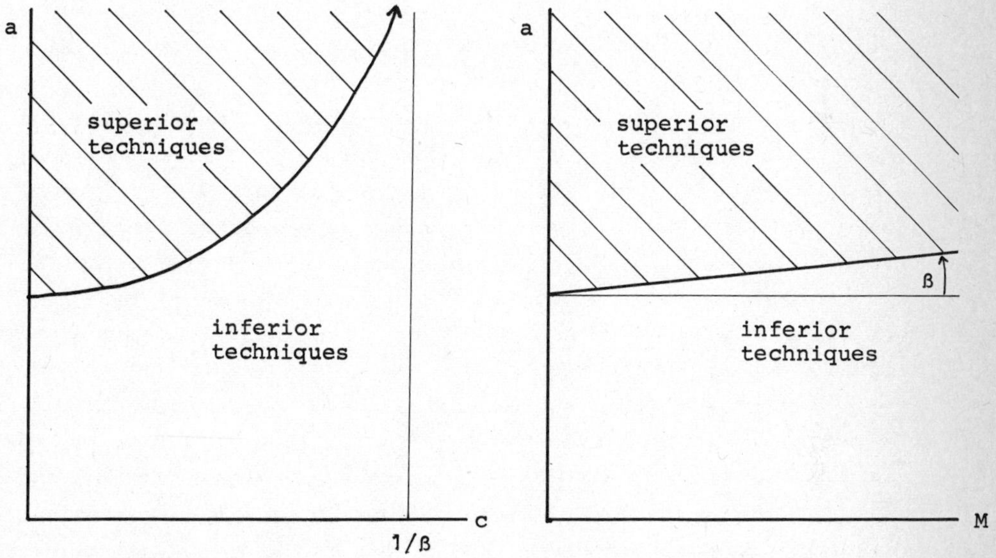

Figure 1a   Figure 1b

Figure 1a. Contour of equal selective potential in the a-c plane.

Figure 1b. Contour of equal selective potential in the a-M plane.

Summing up these observations, technical progress will generally lead to progressive increases in a while being neutral to or slightly biased against upward changes in c, depending on the rate of labor force growth. This accords completely with Kaldor's so-called stylized facts of economic growth.

As one technology replaces another the associated wage rate averaged over the cycle, which is also $A/B = a(1 - \beta c)$, will also secularly increase, whereas the average rate of profit will remain constant at β, the rate of labor force growth. During the substitution disequilibrium process itself, however, this need no longer be the case. The rate of profit may well increase or decline depending on the ability of the wage rate to track the increase in productivity. As opposed to the exponential increase in real wages Goodwin derives for exponential disembodied technical progress, the exact course of wages will depend on the historical sequence in which innovations are introduced and the detailed dynamics of the substitution process. In consequence, a real-world economy passing through a sequence of such instabilities will always find itself undergoing a process of substitution of greater or lesser intensity as long as the rate of basic innovation is comparable to the rate of replacement derived below, and thus will never come to rest at the equilibrium values. Rather, these should be thought of as the proverbial "moving target" towards which the economy is constantly striving.

This becomes clearer when we examine the results of numerical solutions of the model. Figure 2 plots the time course of the rate of total employment v as well as the rates of employment in each sector, v_1 and v_2, and the wage rate w. The following values were assumed for the parameters: $m = .96$, $n = 1$, $a_1 = 1$, $c_1 = 4$, $a_2 = 2.5$, $c_2 = 4$, $\beta = .01$. The initial values were $v_1 = .95$, $v_2 = .01$, $w = .95$. A succession of innovations in historical time would lead to a sequence of (possibly) overlapping wag curves of this type building upon each other.

Figure 3 shows the time course of the rate of profit r, the rate of growth of productivity g_{prod} and the rate of growth of the real wage rate g_w, as well as the rate of unemployment u. It can be seen that the increase in productivity initially accrues to profits, which rise steadily and very quickly cease to show cyclical fluctuations. Wages on the other are slow to respond to the increase in productivity and continue to fluctuate around a slowly rising trend. Late in the "replacement cycle", however, wages begin to accelerate more sharply and lose their last traces of the "Goodwin" cycle. After 28 years the rate of wage increase very definitely (and not just cyclically) exceeds that of productivity, but by this time the rate of productivity increase is about to peak and

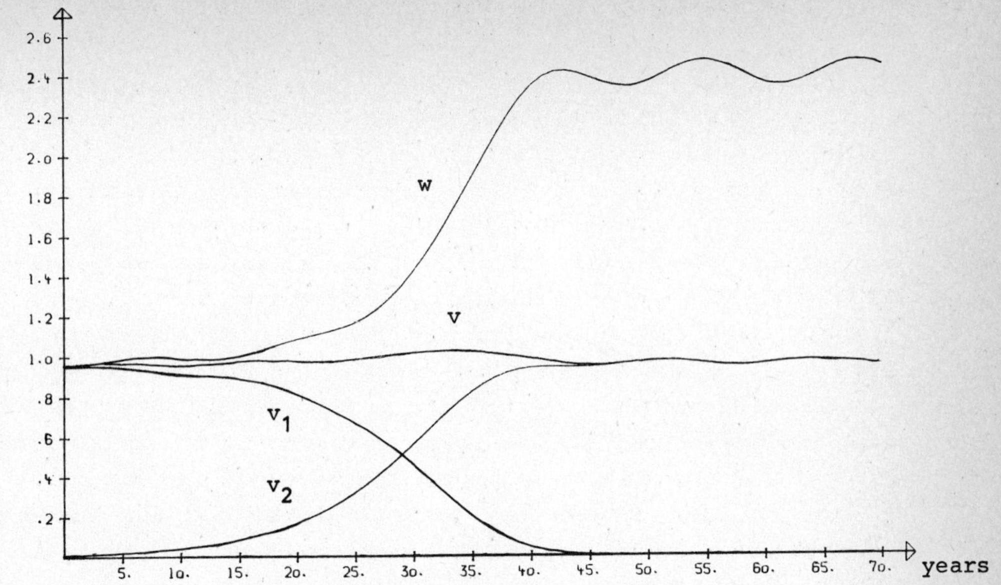

Figure 2. Typical time series for v, v_1, v_2, and w.

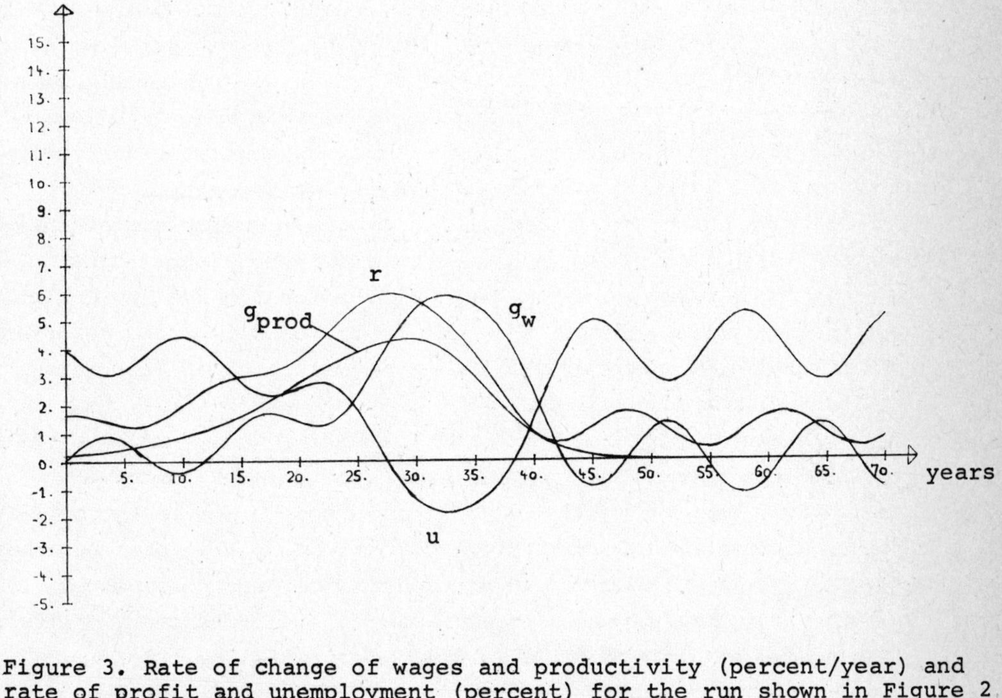

Figure 3. Rate of change of wages and productivity (percent/year) and rate of profit and unemployment (percent) for the run shown in Figure 2 ($m = .96$, $n = 1.0$).

r = rate of profit

g_w = rate of growth of wages

g_{prod} = rate of growth of productivity

u = rate of unemployment

and then declines sharply, so that profits begin to be squeezed from both sides at once. The wage rate is now on a firmly rising trend and only turns around and plunges after the rate of profit has been toppled from almost 30 years of uninterrupted prosperity. At this point the replacement process is practically over and the system reverts to Goodwin cycles, profits fluctuating about the rate of labor force growth and wages about their new equilibrium value.

Varying the parameter values in the simulation does not change the essence of this parable, with the exception of a proportionate increase in m and n. Increasing n to 2 results in a very steep final increase in g_w, followed immediately by a very precipitous fall or crash rather evoking a whiplash (Figure 4).

Are we witnessing the elusive Kondratieff wave? This depends of course on how literally one chooses to interpret the model. The short-term Goodwin cycles obviously have a different status than the long-term replacement cycle. The latter is not very sensitive to changes in model parameters or initial values (the chief effects being a stretching or compression of the time scale and the degree of wage overshooting); the former are directly dependent on initial values. Perhaps the reversion to the Goodwin cycle should be interpreted as general instability in the absence of a renewed surge of technical progress. The wage rate whiplash and the precipitious fall in the rate of profit, which can no longer be restored to its previous high level even by falling real wages, could very well provoke a crisis of confidence which subsequently inhibited investment, so that this instability would manifest itself as a chronic depression rather than short-term cycles. And of course technical change has an autonomous aspect as well. But if we consider economic history to be a sequence of major "paradigmatic" innovations (the steam engine, iron and steel, electrical power, the internal combustion engine, mass production, electronic communications and control, etc.) followed by improvements and "mopping up", as Kuhn (1962) has suggest for the history of science, then this picture is not all that far-fetched. It would have to be modified to incorporate continuous and anticipated improvement along basic lines (something like a vintage model) but would continue to single out the major innovations opening up whole areas of investment and expansion. The same would apply to new consumer products, where an Engel curve income dependence of demand would lead to analogous S-shaped expansion curves. That the history of technology provides support for distinguishing between continuous improvements characterized by a given exponential rate of change and "species" replacement along a different curve is borne out in a study by Lienhard (1979).

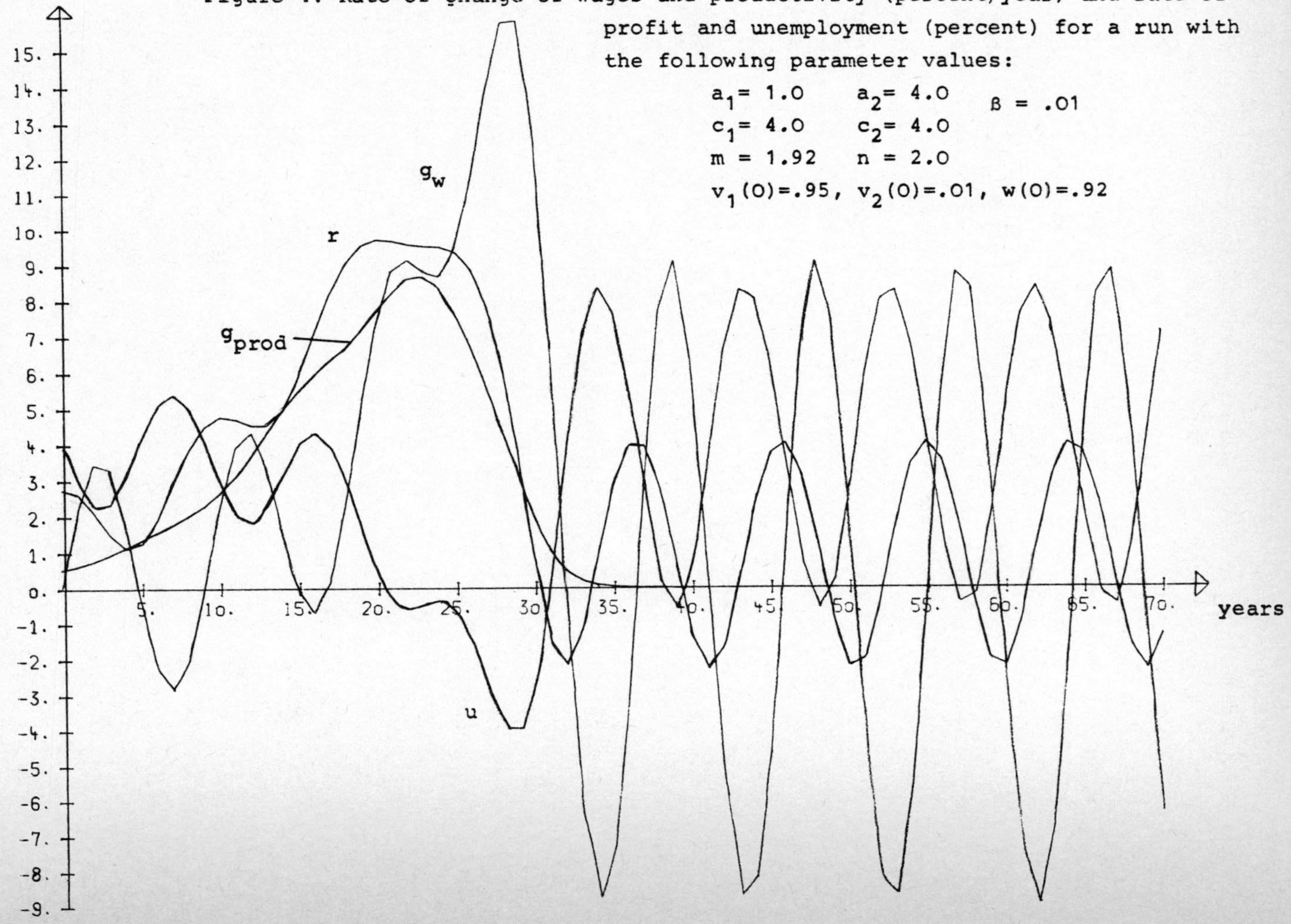

Figure 4. Rate of change of wages and productivity (percent/year) and rate of profit and unemployment (percent) for a run with the following parameter values:

$a_1 = 1.0$ $a_2 = 4.0$ $\beta = .01$
$c_1 = 4.0$ $c_2 = 4.0$
$m = 1.92$ $n = 2.0$
$v_1(0) = .95$, $v_2(0) = .01$, $w(0) = .92$

One salient feature of the model which comes out in all of the simulations is the fact that the real wage rate lags behind the growth in productivity for more than half of the replacement process (except for brief cyclical periods depending on initial conditions) but thereafter remains considerably above it until the system collapses back to Goodwin cycles. This trend crossing of the growth of productivity curve simultaneously marks the end of the high profit plateau and is thus a watershead in the replacement cycle. On the basis of suitable extensions of the model to include a monetary sphere this fact might well be relevant to a long-wave theory of class struggle and inflation.

The process of replacement can be described by eliminating w from the two equations for the sectoral employment levels. Multiplying (2a) by B_2 and (2b) by B_1 and subtracting, one obtains

$$B_1 \dot{v}_2/v_2 - B_2 \dot{v}_1/v_1 = A_2 B_1 - A_1 B_2.$$

Integrating with respect to time and introducing initial values $v_1(0)$ and $v_2(0)$,

$$v_2^{B_1}/v_1^{B_2} = v_2^{B_1}(0)/v_1^{B_2}(0) \cdot e^{(A_2 B_1 - A_1 B_2)t}.$$

Recalling the definitions of the A's and B's, this can be rewritten as

$$v_2^{M_2}/v_1^{M_1} = v_2^{M_2}(0)/v_1^{M_1}(0) \cdot e^{\Delta T \cdot t}$$

where M_i is the degree of mechanization of process i and $\Delta T = (a_2 - a_1) - \beta(c_2 - c_1)$ is the difference in selective potential of the two techniques. This should be compared with the well-known Fisher-Pry model of industrial replacement in individual economic sectors.[3] Should $M_1 = M_2 = M$, the Fisher-Pry equation is exactly obtained with rate constant $\Delta T/M$. In general, however, one expects $M_2 > M_1$. At the beginning of the replacement process with $v_1 \sim 1$ and $v_2 \ll 1$ we have approximately

$$v_2/v_1 = v_2(0)/v_1(0) \cdot e^{\Delta T \cdot t/M_2},$$

whereas at the end of the process with these conditions reversed we have

$$v_2/v_1 = v_2(0)/v_1(0) \cdot e^{\Delta T \cdot t/M_1}.$$

The rate of replacement thus accelerates with time if the degree of mechanization increases. The effect of an increase in the capital-output ratio c on the rate of replacement, in addition to its effect via the term $\beta(c_2 - c_1)$ in the numerator, is compounded in the initial phase by the amplification of the damping effect of the increase in labor productivity via M_2 in the denominator ($= a_2 c_2$). The net effect is to signifi-

---

3. Fisher and Pry (1971). For a further discussion of substitution models see Montroll (1978).

cantly retard the replacement process even if it does not prevent the selection of this technique altogether. This is shown in Figure 5a for a number of parameter values. The retarding effect of an increase in the rate of labor force growth from 1% to 2.5% is shown in Figure 5b.

3. The Self-Organization Paradigm

The self-organization approach to the explanation of structure and change differs in a number of important respects from the theoretical paradigms implicit in most current economic thinking, all of which hinge in one way or another on the notion of equilibrium.

In recent years it has been shown that in many physical, biological, and chemical systems far from classical equilibrium, temporal and spatial structures can emerge which radically differ from and appear to be in contradiction with the tendency to uniformity associated with closed systems. At certain moments in the history of such systems fluctuations, which are normally held in check by restoring forces and the law of large numbers, can expand to the macroscopic level and drive the system to a new and often more highly ordered or differentiated state. The analysis of this process requires an explicit, though often only qualitative model of the dynamic interaction between the macrosystem and its component subsystems, which in general will be nonlinear. The mathematical methods of the qualitative theory of differential equations - in particular bifurcation and catastrophe theory and the concept of structural stability - have proven especially useful in this regard. In addition, the dynamic behavior of stochastic fluctuations, the other principal element, can be treated using the master or Fokker-Planck equations known to social scientists from the theory of stochastic processes. The combination of these two elements yields a number of by now more or less systematized analytical methods emphasizing the dialectic of whole and part on the one hand and chance and necessity on the other.

The most widely known and ambitious formulations of the theory of self-organization have been presented by Haken and his coworkers in Stuttgart ("synergetics") and Prigogine and his group in Brussels ("dissipative systems").[4] In Haken's formulation, the centerpiece of which is the so-called slaving principle, the analysis of the eigenvalues

4. Haken (1978) provides an introduction proceeding from first principles to advanced methods and applications. Prigogine (1976) and Prigogine, Allen and Hermann (1977) are directed at social scientists and biologists. Nicolis and Prigogine (1977) contains a review of work in this field at an advanced level.

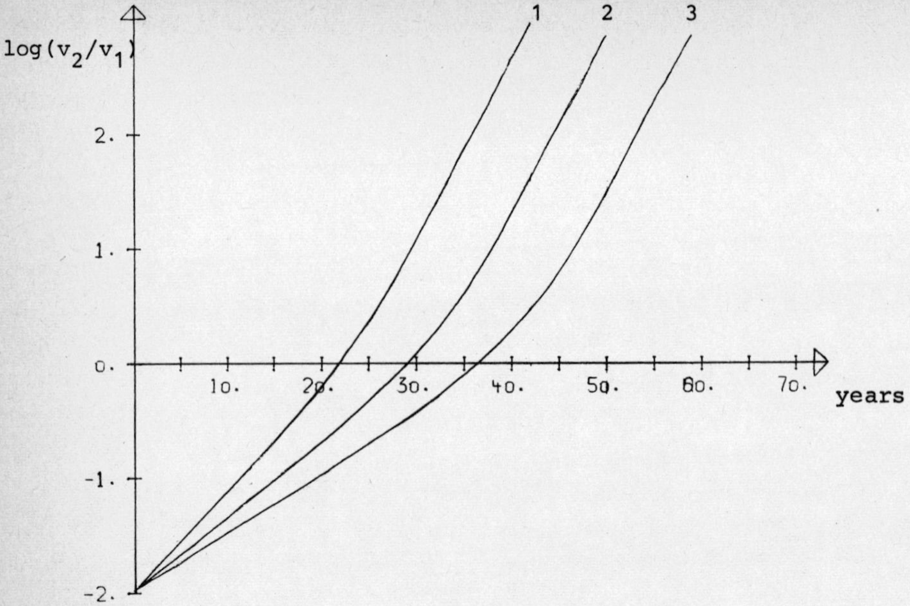

Figure 5a. Log(v_2/v_1) vs. t for various capital-output values: (1) $c_2 = 3$, (2) $c_2 = 4$, (3) $c_2 = 5$ ($a_1=1$, $a_2=2.5$, $c_1=4$, $\beta = .01$)

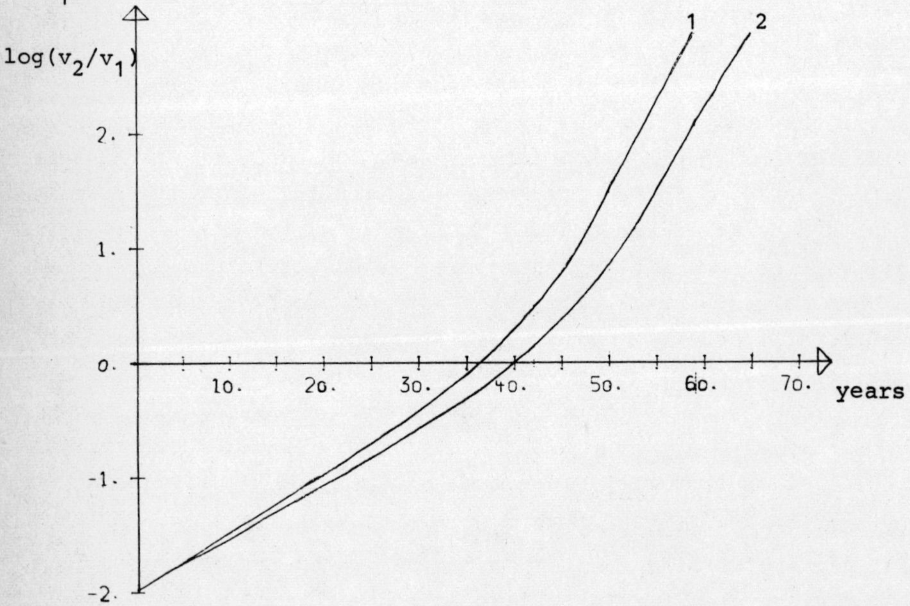

Figure 5b. Log(v_2/v_1) vs. t for (1) $\beta = .01$ and (2) $\beta = .025$ ($a_1 = 1$, $a_2 = 2.5$, $c_1 = 4$, $c_2 = 5$).

of a dynamic system in a (meta) stable regime will reveal that their real parts are negative and can be ordered. Fluctuations and/or changes in external conditions may drive the eigenvalue closest to zero into the positive, unstable region, at which point the associated variable becomes subject to positive feedback and proceeds to drag the other variables (as long as the real parts of their associated eigenvalues remain sufficiently negative - the so-called adiabatic approximation) with it into some new structurally stable dynamic state (or even "chaos"). The variable associated with the destabilizing eigenvalue is called the order parameter, and its analysis, via the slaving principle, enables the dynamics of a system with a great number of degrees of freedom to be reduced to a simpler and more manageable form. Examples include the transformation of a stable focus into a limit cycle (the Hopf bifurcation) or any of Thom's elementary catastrophes in systems admitting a potential function description.

Our model is a very simple illustration of these principles. Stochastic effects in the dynamic equations are not explicitly modeled, but this could be done along the lines used in a similar model by Jimenez Monataño and Ebeling (1980). (One advantage of such a procedure would be the derivation of minimum thresholds for technological change.) Stochastic fluctuations enter the system in the form of new machines and processes initially present in small quantities. These are stochastic because inventions are intrinsically unpredictable both as to their nature and date of introduction and because the entrepreneurs promoting them cannot be sure they will be accepted by the market for a number of reasons. For one, their technical and economic feasibility is uncertain until they are tried out on a large scale. Nor is it known how competitors will react, or how the wage rate and other costs and the state of global and partial demand will evolve, especially since these variables will themselves be influenced in the course of time by changing technology and entrepreneurial decisions. Thus, although there may be certain biases present in the innovation process, we may just as well conceive of innovations as practically randomly generated by Keynesian "animal spirits" and then set about determining what leads to their selection *ex post*, rather than second guess the emergent properties of a complex system by trying to specify "optimum" decision-making rules for individual entrepreneurs. Of course, feedback between the results of this selection process and the search procedures of economic agents may eventually be established, but this could at most distort, not contradict, the thrust of our argument.

This view practically mandates the simultaneous existence of a diversity of expectations, techniques, and rates of profit, a prospect which for the most part has been gingerly avoided by economic theorists until now. This does not necessarily imply an indeterminacy of the system, however; the interaction of its components as well as external constraints will usually impose a definite structure upon it, but a structure which will be characterized by an alteration between periods of a certain general stability and historical instabilities driving the system toward new basic technological conditions and institutions. The outcome of such a historical instability cannot be predicted with certainty but, as in our model, it may be possible to specify certain conditions it will have to satisfy (e.g. our selection criterion). And once the character of the dominant trend emerging from such an instability has been established, it will usually also be possible to provide a more or less deterministic description of its evolution (e.g. the replacment equation and numerical solutions to the dynamic equations).

This description will necessarily involve a dynamic interaction of the system's heterogeneous components (labor, various capital and consumer goods, energy, etc) and thus may rightly be termed an ecological one. Goodwin's growth cycle, which is formally equivalent to the well-known predator-prey model of mathematical ecology, is a prime example.[5] That socioeconomic development can be considered an ecological history of human artefacts and populations is the theme of Boulding (1978, 1981)

Of course, socioeconomic systems are characterized by such emergent properties as intentions and expectations - we are not advocating a sociobiological reductionism. But these features too can in principle be modeled within an ecological/evolutionary framework (dynamic models of the formation of expectations, directed innovation and imitation, etc.). The work of Nelson and Winter (1974, 1982), who among economists have been in the forefront in developing this approach, provides evidence of the practicability of this project. And recent work of Weidlich and Haag(1983) and Mensch, Weidlich, and Haag (1983) directly addresses these problems in a self-organization setting. Thus it appears that non-linearity, microeconomic heterogeneity, and macroeconomic disequilibrium rather than being insuperable obstacles to economic analysis, may well prove to be essential ingredients in furthering our understanding of the historical unfolding of modern industrial society.

---

5. This analogy had already been hinted at by L. von Bertalanfy in 1962: "One may, for example, suspect that the laws governing business cycles and those of population fluctuation according to Volterra stem from similar conditions of competition and interaction in the system." (Bertalanfy (1962), p. 13)

References

Allen, P.M. (1975), "Darwinian Evolution and a Predator-Prey Ecology," *Bulletin of Mathematical Biology*, 37, pp. 389-405.

Allen, P.M. (1976), "Evolution, Population Dynamics, and Stability," *Proc.Nat.Acad.Sci.USA*, 73, 3, pp. 665-668.

Bertalanfy, L.v. (1962), "General System Theory - A Critical Review," *General Systems*, VII, pp. 1-20.

Boulding, K.E. (1978), *Ecodynamics: A New Theory of Societal Evolution*, Beverly Hills-London.

Boulding, K.E. (1981), *Evolutionary Economics*, Beverly Hills-London.

Fisher, J.C. and R.H. Pry (1971), "A Simple Substitution Model of Technological Change," *Technological Forecasting and Social Change*, 3, pp. 75-88.

Georgescu-Roegen, N. (1971), *The Entropy Law and the Economic Process*, Cambridge, Ma.

Georgescu-Roegen, N. (1976), "Dynamic Economic Models and Economic Growth," *Energy and Economic Myths*, New York, pp. 235-253.

Goodwin, R.M. (1967), "A Growth Cycle," in *Socialism, Capitalism and Economic Growth*, edited by C.H. Feinstein, London.

Haken, H. (1978), *Synergetics: An Introduction*, 2nd. ed., Berlin-Heidelberg-New York.

Hicks, J.R. (1976), "Some Questions of Time in Economics," in *Evolution, Welfare, and Time in Economics*, edited by A.M. Tang *et. al.*, Lexington, Ma.

Jimenez Montaño, M.A. and W. Ebeling (1980), "A Stochastic Evolutionary Model of Technological Change," *Collective Phenomena*, 3, pp. 107-114.

Kuhn, T.S. (1962), *The Structure of Scientific Revolutions*, Chicago-London.

Lienhard, J.H. (1979), "The Rate of Technological Improvement before and after the 1830s," *Technology and Culture*, 20, 3, pp. 515-530.

May, R.M. (1974), *Stability and Complexity in Model Ecosystems*, Princeton.

Medio, A. (1975), *Nonlinear Models of Economic Fluctuations*, unpublished Ph.D. thesis University of Cambridge.

Mensch, G.O., W. Weidlich, and G. Haag (1983), *The Schumpeter Clock*, Cambridge, Ma. (forthcoming).

Montroll, E.W. (1975), "Social Dynamics and the Quantifying of Social Forces," *Proc.Nat.Acad.Sci.USA*, 75, 10, pp. 4633-4637.

Nelson, R. and S. Winter (1974), "Neoclassical vs. Evolutionary Theories of Economic Growth: Critique and Prospectus," *Economic Journal*, 84, pp. 886-905.

Nelson, R. and S. Winter (1982), *An Evolutionary Theory of Economic Change*, Cambridge, Ma.

Nicolis, G. and I. Prigogine (1977), *Self-Organization in Non-Equilibrium Systems*, New York.

Prigogine, I. (1976), "Order through Fluctuation: Self-Organization and Social System," in *Evolution and Consciousness*, edited by E. Jantsch and C.H. Waddington, Reading, Ma., pp. 93-133.

Prigogine, I., P.M. Allen, and R. Hermann (1977), "Long Term Trends and the Evolution of Complexity," in *Goals in a Gloabal Community*, vol. 1, edited by E. Laszlo and J. Bierman, New York.

Robinson, J. (1975), "The Unimportance of Reswitching," and "Reswitching: Reply," *Quarterly Journal of Economics*, 89, pp. 32-39, 53-55.

Weidlich, W. and G. Haag (1983), *Concepts and Methods of a Quantitative Sociology*, Berlin-Heidelberg-New York.

FLUCTUATIONS AND GROWTH: KEYNES, SCHUMPETER, MARX AND THE STRUCTURAL INSTABILITY OF CAPITALISM

Alessandro Vercelli
Istituto di Economia, Facoltà di S.E.B. — Università di Siena
Piazza S. Francesco, 17 — 53100 Siena (Italy)

Keynes, Schumpeter and Marx contributed, perhaps more than anybody else, to the understanding of the inherent instability of a monetary economy and of the connected essential relation between cycles and growth. The analysis of economic cycles cannot be severed from the analysis of growth, because cycles and growth crucially interact in a structurally unstable economic structure, which is typical of any monetary economy and especially of developed capitalism. Each of our three authors reacted, though in different ways, to the traditional mainstream view according to which we may distinguish two sets of economic forces, respectively determining cycles and growth. The first set of forces should, in this view, explain disequilibrium cyclical movements around equilibrium trends whose dynamics is explained by the second set of forces. Disequilibrium dynamics is conceived as not affecting equilibrium trends so that we may study separately cycles and growth. The relation between the two sets of forces is then often rationalized through the distinction between short-period and long-period where short-period precisely excludes growth from the scope of analysis, while long-period excludes business cycles and all other disequilibrium movements. We will try to show that the relation between short-period and long-period as well as between cycle and growth has to be considered in a completely different perspective in the theory of our three authors. The structural instability of a monetary economy implies an unavoidable feed-back between short-period and long-period as well as between cycle and growth.

We will now analyze our three authors in the following order: Keynes, Schumpeter and Marx, progressively broadening the scope of the analysis from a shorter to a longer period. However, for the sake of brevity, we will here almost completely neglect the well-known features that sharply distinguish the "visions" and the theoretical systems of these three authors.

1. Structural and dynamical (in)stability

Before entering in medias res we will briefly recall a few basic concepts which we will define in the most elementary way.

We have, first of all, to make a clear distinction between dynamic and structural instability. Both definitions are founded on the observation of the behaviour of a system perturbed by a disturbance. A disturbance is simply any transformation, endogenous or exogenous, impinging on a system. Dynamic (in)stability, as it is well-known, is about convergence (or divergence) of the behaviour of a perturbed system to (or from) equilibrium. This concept is by now well-established in economic theory and does not need, for our purposes, any further comment.

Structural (in)stability is about qualitative (or structural) change of the behaviour of a perturbed system. If qualitative change in the behaviour of the system exceeds a certain preassigned minimum standard, the system is said to be structurally unstable. This depends on a) the kind and size of the disturbance; b) the standard chosen to define the change induced in the system as qualitative (or structural) rather than merely quantitative. Clearly enough, a system may have different degrees of structural instability according to the relation between the size of the disturbance and the qualitative characteristics of the system's response (in the formal model this depends on the definition of a) the admissible perturbations, b) the concept of equivalence between systems, c) the topology adopted).

We will find it useful in this paper to think of the economic system as represented by a flow-diagram. The economic structure is then given by a) the structure of flows, b) the "functional structure" of the system, that is the ordered set of functions contained inside the blocks. Any discontinuous change of the flow-structure and/or the functional structure of the system implies a qualitative change of the system's behaviour. In this case we are, in principle, bound to find a sizable change in its equilibrium properties, which may involve its uniqueness and determinateness, and a sizable change in disequilibrium behaviour (see Vercelli, 1981, appendix 3).

The rigorous definition of structural (in)stability is rather recent. It was first formulated by Andronov and Pontryagin in a seminal paper of 1937 (the history of the concept, its precise meaning and its methodological implications are analized in some detail in the appendix to this paper). A conscious and explicit application of the concept to economics is much more recent and not altogether satisfactory (see Vercelli, 1982). Still, I believe that the concept of structural (in)stability, suitably mended and worked out, will play a very important role in economics as well as in other social science, where the main problem is often that of explaining and forecasting structural changes. Unfortunately, the modern formalized version of the concept has not yet been reshaped to fit the specific problems of economics. This is a research target of the greatest importance. As a preliminary step in this direction, we will try to show, first of all, that the analysis of capitalistic instability suggested by Keynes, Schumpeter and Marx may be better modelled, in many crucial steps of the analysis, as structural instability rather than dynamic instability. Moreover, we will find in these classical texts a few useful suggestions for working out a revised version of the concept of structural (in)stability more suitable for economics.

2. Keynes

One of the main interpretative paradoxes in the General Theory of Keynes is about the instability of capitalism. He vigorously challenges the "classical" vision of capitalism (actually of any "monetary economy") as a system able to self-adjust to a stable full employment equilibrium. He contends that only a barter economy may have this property. On the contrary, a monetary economy is defined, already in the introduction, as "essentially one in which changing views about the future are capable of influencing the quantity of employment and not merely its direction" (Keynes, 1936, p. xxii).

All that has led part of the interpreters to stress the Keynesian views on the instability of capitalism by modelling them in terms of dynamic instability. So, for example, Minsky contends that "during each short-period equilibrium, in Keynes's view, processes are at work which will disequilibrate the system. Not only is stability an unattainable goal; whenever something approaching stability is achieved, destabilizing processes are set off" (Minsky, 1975, p. 61). Keynesian economics is then interpreted as the "economics of permanent disequilibrium" (ibid., p. 68), owing mainly to the influence of "financial instability". The trouble with this kind of interpretation is that Keynes, although stressing in a loose but compelling way the instability of capitalism, takes some pain in explaining why capitalism is after all "substantially stable":

> "it is an outstanding characteristic of the economic system in which we live, that, whilst it is subject to severe fluctuations in respect to output and employment, it is not violently unstable. Indeed it seems capable of remaining in a chronic condition of sub-normal activity for a considerable period without any market tendency either towards recovery or towards complete collapse" (Keynes, 1936, p. 249).

A monetary economy is thus characterized by an area, reasonably limited, of real and monetary values inside which dynamic instability may play a role, even an important one, but this area — considered as a whole — is dynamically stable. These observations by Keynes have till now severely jeopardized all the interpretations centered around the instability of capitalism. Mainstream interpretations of Keynesian theory (first of all, "neoclassical synthesis") were able to exploit these arguments to rebutt the heterodox interpretations. But their view of full employment equilibrium as dynamically stable (although admitting, at the same time, that the adjustment process may be very slow) does in its turn unduly neglect the recurrent insistence by Keynes on the instability of a monetary economy.

I think that we may find a way out of this paradox. Dynamic instability is not the only possible way of modelling actual instability. A deeper analysis of Keynesian contribution suggests a different specification in terms of structural instability.

We tried elsewhere (Vercelli, 1981) to develop at some length the outlines of an interpretation of this kind. We will only try here to recall briefly a few points without any attempt to demonstrate them.

Each element of the set of admissible equilibria (full employment equilibrium and unemployment equilibria) may be considered in itself as a dynamically stable equilibrium. The main analytical targets of General Theory are: a) to show what determines one of these possible equilibria and b) what determines the shift from an equilibrium to another one. He is able to show that each equilibrium is associated with different economic policy rules and that a change in them determines a shift of the equilibrium position. The reason must be found in the influence exerted by different economic policy rules on the functional structure of the economy (mainly characterized by consumption propensity, marginal efficiency of capital and liquidity preference). So, for example, a change in monetary policy is liable to shift the liquidity preference function and/or the marginal efficiency of capital. We do not mean here either stochastic shifts, or cyclical shifts around an unchanging average, but shifts in their "long-run" position. We may thus understand why Keynes feels allowed to repeat that:

> "On my view, there is no unique long-period position of equilibrium equally valid regardless of the character of the policy of the monetary authority. On the contrary there are a number of such positions corresponding to different policies" (Keynes, C.W. XXIX, p. 54-55).

An alteration of monetary policy rules would affect the functional structure of the system in a "permanent" way, until another modification in monetary policy rules will intervene to change it again.

The same kind of reasoning is developed with reference to the repercussions of a change in money wages, mainly analysed in the famous passages of ch. 19, which are crucial for a proper understanding of the entire General Theory. A reduction of money wages in a situation of unemployment equilibrium is not enough, generally speaking, to restore full employment and is not anyway preferable to a policy of money inflation, because it would affect in a decisive way the functional structure of the economic system:

> "The reduction in money-wages will have no lasting tendency to increase employment except by virtue of its repercussion either on the propensity to con-

sume for the community as a whole, or on the schedule of marginal efficiencies of capital, or on the rate of interest" (Keynes, 1936, p. 262).

The induced shifts of the three psychological functions displace the equilibrium position but probably in a perverse direction.

To sum up the preceding discussion, we may observe, first of all, that we could interpret a change in economic policy rules as a change of the environment in which a market economy happens to operate. We may thus consider such an event as a disturbance, or better, a change in the structure of disturbances affecting the economic system. We are thus allowed to apply rigorously to the preceding Keynesian arguments the modern concept of structural instability. We may then observe that a capitalist economic system is structurally unstable because even a small disturbance, either endogenous or exogenous, affecting over-sensitive and conventional expectations, is liable to generate a considerable qualitative change in its behaviour.

3. Schumpeter

We have seen in the General Theory a sort of short-term structural instability mainly connected with different economic policy rules. Its relevance is not only restricted to its crucial influence on the choice of the best economic policy rules, but applies also to the longer-term structural influence on production conditions through technical change embodied in investment decisions. This topic is only hinted at in the General Theory, but it is not systematically analyzed because of the self-imposed bounds implied by short-period assumptions.

The nexus between entrepreneurial investment, business cycles and development is, on the contrary, at the center of Schumpeter's contribution. We are of course compelled, from the very outset, to break the strait-jacket of short-period, because the main object of Schumpeterian analysis, innovation, cannot be even defined without dropping the assumption of constant capital stock. Clusters of innovations here explain, as it is well-known, at the same time cycles and development. Any boom induced by a swarm-like wave of innovations is characterized by a discontinuous structural change setting the pace and direction of growth. These recurring structural changes are "the only fundamental cause of instability inherent to the capitalist system" (Schumpeter, 1928, p. 385).

But what does Schumpeter mean by instability? Certainly not dynamic instability, in the usual meaning of the word. The effects of a wave of innovations should not be described, according to Schumpeter, as a progressive divergence from equilibrium but as a destruction of equilibrium. The old equilibrium does not rule any more the economic behaviour and a new one is not yet established. Any autonomous structural change displaces endogenously the equilibrium position. However, in the boom endogenous structural change is so rapid and discontinuous that the equilibrium position is unable to exert any detectable influence on economic behaviour. This means that, during a boom, while a swarm of innovations makes the economic structure to implode, there is no much point in using the equilibrium concept:

> "we will not postulate the existence of states of equilibrium where none exist, but only where the system is actually moving toward one. When, for instance, existing states are in the act of being disturbed, say, by a war financed by government fiat, or by a 'mania' of railroad building, there is very little sense in speaking of an ideal equilibrium coexisting with all that disequilibrium. It seems much more natural to say that while such a factor acts there is no equilibrium at all. When it has ceased to act, and when we observe that readjustment sets in which we interpret as a movement toward equilibrium, then and only then the ideal equilibrium becomes the goal of an economic process, the nature of which can be elucidated by reference to it. Then and only then the equilibrium becomes what we have called it before, the 'theoretical norm' of the economic variables. Hence, we will, for our purpose, recognize existence of equilibrium only at those discrete points on the time scale at which the system approaches a state which would, if reached, fulfill equilibrium conditions" (Schumpeter, 1939, pp. 70-71).

As we can see, we cannot interpret Schumpeter's instability as dynamical instability. On the contrary, we may today naturally reappraise his instability concept as an early and particularly lucid definition of structural instability. He could not, of course, refer to the mathematical definition of the concept which was then not yet worked out in a rigorous way. Schumpeter's concept may be found at least since the first edition of <u>The theory of economic development</u> (1911), while the first rigorous mathematical definition has been given, as we have seen, only much later. Still the concept expressed by the great Austrian economist is surprisingly similar, even in the language, to the modern mathematical concept. As a matter of fact, Schumpeter means by instability a radical and discontinuous qualitative change in economic structure (or, what is the same thing, in economic behaviour), induced by inherent disturbances.

This definition may be clearly understood as a specification of the current standard definition of structural stability. The specific traits requiring a comment are the following:

a) qualitative change is defined as a discontinuous "change in the channels of economic routine or a spontaneous change in the economic data arising from within the system" (Schumpeter, 1926, p. 82). We may notice the analogy, even in the language, with the definition of structural change given in the second paragraph. In our language the change of channels becomes a change in the flow diagram and the change in economic data a change in the parameters (appearing in the blocks).

b) The conceptual "topology" put forward for identifying qualitative change is not too "fine". Schumpeter is careful in excluding from his instability concept minor and/or continuous qualitative changes:

> "what we are about to consider is that kind of change arising from within the system <u>which so displaces its equilibrium point that the new one cannot be reached from the old one by infinitesimal steps</u>. Add successively as many mail coaches as you please, you will never get a railway thereby" (Schumpeter, 1926, p.64, n.1).

On the contrary, a relevant qualitative change is often defined as "destruction" of the preceding equilibrium or structure.

c) The trigger-mechanism of structural change is always defined as a <u>disturbance</u>, exactly as in the modern definitions of structural instability:

> "innovations cluster densely together. So densely, in fact, that the resultant disturbance produces a distinct period of adjustment — which precisely is what the depression phase of the business cycle consists in" (Schumpeter, 1928, p. 382).

d) In most of his contributions, he restricts the class of relevant disturbances to "inner" or "economic" disturbances only, because he is interested first of all in analyzing the inherent structural instability of the economic system.

e) Inner disturbances of the economic system induce structural change in two distinct phases. In the boom structural change is accompanied, as we have seen, by an absence of equilibrium, while in the depression structural change is accompanied by the reappearance of a new stable equilibrium, i.e. it goes together with dynamic stability. We have thus in both phases structural instability but of a different kind: in the boom a "creative" structural instability, in the depression an "adaptive" structural instability (not to be confused with dynamic stability).

f) The well-known results springing from Schumpeterian analysis of structural instability of Capitalism are that "there is, though instability of the <u>System</u>, no economic instability of the <u>Order</u>" (1928, p. 384), where by capitalist <u>order</u> is meant "the institutional survival of capitalism" and by capitalist <u>system</u> is meant "business conditions" (ibid., p. 363). Moreover, as a consequence of "trustified" capitalism, swarm-like innovations, that is "the only fundamental cause of instability inherent to the capitalist system, is losing in importance as time goes on, and may even be expected to disappear" (ibid., p. 385). Capitalist <u>order</u> "whilst economically stable, and even gaining in stability" is unstable for other non-economic reasons too well-known to be recalled here.

The preceding observations suggest <u>inter alia</u> that not only Schumpeter may be considered as a lucid forerunner of the concept of structural instability, but that he also began a much needed effort of adaptation of the concept to the specific exigences of economic and social analysis.

We may particularly appreciate the following suggestions:

a) the current concept of structural stability, defined — broadly speaking — as structural change induced by a disturbance, is too generic a concept for economic analysis. We have to distinguish between different categories of disturbances not only of various intensity but also of various qualitative kind (external, internal, affecting the flow diagram or the functional structure, etc.). Engineers and mathematicians who worked out the modern version of the concept do not care because their problem is very often that of maximizing the stability of an optimal behaviour (we may think, for instance, to the performance of an airplane), so that any structural change, whatever the nature of the disturbance, might be disruptive and has to be avoided. Unfortunately economic problems are much more complex and need a much more sophisticated concept of structural instability.

b) Economic reality may be considered as a hierarchical system articulated in many subsystems, of which the lower is strongly affected by the higher and weakly affecting it in its turn, so that it could change even radically without disturbing considerably the higher system. This is the case, for example, of the Schumpeterian distinction between capitalistic order and capitalistic system, the first being the higher system and the second the lower. A hierarchical system may have a different degree of structural instability in each of its subsystems whose interactions, which may be very complex, should never be neglected.

4. Marx

Nobody would deny that structural change is at the center of Marxian analysis. Still, to be able to relate his contribution to the modern concept of structural instability, we lack, apparently, the other ingredient: disturbances. Structural change is typically related not to disturbances but to internal contradictions.

We cannot even try to propose here a satisfactory interpretation of Marxian notion of contradiction. We are then compelled to begin by an assumption (which we tried to argue elsewhere: Vercelli, 1973 and 1979): in many instances Marxian dialectical language may be reasonably well translated in the more usual language of system dynamics. We may then interpret a "latent" contradiction as an equilibrium and an "open" contradiction as "disequilibrium". Structural change is typically related to the concept of adequacy. A "metamorphosis" occurs when a form (a structure) happens to become intolerably inadequate to fulfill one of its vital targets. Adequacy may be simply modelled as an equilibrium between a certain performance norm and actual performance, a growing inadequacy as a growing disequilibrium. When a cumulative disequilibrium process goes beyond a certain threshold, structural change is induced: "merely quantitative differences beyond a certain point pass into qualitative changes" (K. II., p. 309).

We cannot, here, try to argue the plausibility of the interpretation so briefly outlined, but we may examplify. Let us consider the following statement:

"the exchange of commodities implies contradictory and mutually exclusive conditions. The differentiation of commodities into commodities and money does not sweep away these inconsistencies, but develops a modus vivendi, a form in which they can exist side by side. This is generally the way in which real contradictions are reconciled. For instance, it is a contradiction to depict one body as constantly falling towards another, and as, at the same time, constantly flying away from it. The ellipse is a form of motion which, while allowing this contradiction to go on, at the same time reconciles it" (K. I., p. 103-104).

If the dynamical forces of the system, centripetal and/or centrifugal, change, also the ellipse has to change in a different kind of ellipse or, more radically, in an altogether different kind of form: a parabola or a hyperbola, for example. Structural change is here related with easily identifiable thresholds in the relation between the dynamic forces of the system. We may thus interpret disequilibrium (typically when it exceeds a certain threshold) as a sort of endogenous disturbance inducing structural change. We are then put not only in the position of applying to the Marxian theory the modern concept of structural instability, but also of coordinating it with the concept of dynamic instability. The internal disturbance leading to structural change is typically induced by dynamic instability itself.

Our interpretative hypothesis has been till now examplified by an exceedingly simple case, drawn from the natural world. As soon as we consider an economic structure, dynamic and structural characteristics become so complex to make it difficult, even for Marx, to be as clear as he was in the preceeding example. Still, we believe that we can find the same basic concepts also in the more complex analysis of the capitalist world. We will try to exemplify again. For the sake of comparison with Schumpeter but also with Keynes, we choose the process of technical change under capitalism.

First of all, Marx knows very well that technical change is a crucial aspect of modern capitalism:

"Modern Industry never looks upon and treats the existing form of a process as final. The technical basis of that industry is therefore revolutionary, while all earlier modes of production were essentially conservative" (K. I., p.486).

But to allow this continuous process of structural change, capitalism needs the highest degree of flexibility for:

a) labour: "Modern Industry, by its very nature, therefore necessitates variation of labour, fluency of function, universal mobility of the labourer" (K. I., p.487).

b) capital as is already clearly shown by the process of centralization which "intensifies and accelerates the effect of accumulation" and "simultaneously extends and speeds those revolutions in the technical composition of capital which raise its constant portion" (K. I., p. 628). Capitalism needs, in other words, a high degree of structural instability.

This is assured for labour by the reserve army mechanism and for capital by the development of credit:

> "with capitalist production an altogether new force comes into play — the credit system, which in its first stages furtively creeps in as the humble assistant of accumulation, drawing into the hands of individual or associated capitalists, by invisible threads, the money resources which lie scattered, over the surface of society, in larger or smaller amounts; but it soon becomes a new and terrible weapon in the battle of competition and is finally transformed into an enormous social mechanism of centralization of capitals" (K. I., p. 626).

The third major factor assuring the necessary degree of structural instability to capitalism is the State whose principal function in this respect is exactly that of assuring the good performance of the reserve army mechanism, the credit mechanism and thus the process of centralization and accumulation of capital (see, e.g., K. I., ch. XXVIII and XXXI).

5. Money, credit and structural instability

As we have seen, money and credit induce in a monetary economy a certain degree of structural instability, which is crucial in explaining simultaneously cycle and growth. All the three authors agreed on the fundamental role played by the development of monetary and financial relations in explaining the high degree of structural instability of the capitalism as compared to the substantial structural stability of the economic system in all the preceding modes of production.

In Keynes this crucial role is played not so much by money and credit as quantities but by money as institutional structure. The peculiar structure of a monetary economy explains both cyclical fluctuations of marginal efficiency of capital, which are considered as the major determinant of business cycles, and long -term consequences of short-term dynamics. Keynes knew very well the role of money in the process of redistribution of income (as it is witnessed, e.g., by his concept of "income inflation" best analyzed in the Tract on Monetary Reform) and, analogously, its crucial role in allowing the continuous change of the structure of relative prices, notwithstanding all the rigidities characterizing the actual capitalistic market. Unfortunately in the General Theory the aggregative point of view necessarily clouds these important aspects of the role played by money in fluidifying the economic structure. But an important aspect is left. The attention is focused on money as a store of wealth. A monetary economy is defined as one in which the main target of economic process is the accumulation of wealth. This makes expectations about an uncertain future play an important role:

> "The whole object of the accumulation of wealth is to produce results, or potential results, at a comparatively distant, and sometimes at an indefinitely distant, date. Thus the fact that our knowledge of the future is fluctuating, vague and uncertain, renders wealth a peculiarly unsuitable subject for the methods of the classical economic theory" (C.W. XIV, p. 113).

That is why a monetary economy:

> "being based on so flimsy a foundation, (it) is subject to sudden and violent changes. The practice of calmness and immobility, of certainty and security, suddently breaks down. New fears and hopes will, without warning, take charge of human conduct. The forces of disillusion may suddenly impose a new conventional basis of evaluation. All these pretty, polite techniques, made for a well -panelled board room and a nicely regulated market, are liable to collapse" (C.W. XIV, p. 114-115).

These quotations, chosen among many similar ones, should be enough to recall why and in which sense Keynes believes that a monetary economy is structurally unstable. Even a small disturbance, either exogenous or endogenous, affecting oversensitive and conventional expectations, is liable to generate a big qualitative change in the behaviour of the economic system.

Schumpeter, differently from Keynes, perceived the crucial role of money in producing structural change, mainly in the form of credit creation. This is, in his opinion, not only the differentia specifica of capitalism, but also and foremost the necessary condition of the process of redistribution of resources allowing innovation and thus all the implied structural changes. Credit creation gives the system the necessary structural instability:

> "the essential function of credit in our sense consists in enabling the entrepreneur to withdraw the producers' goods which he needs from their previous employments, by exercising a demand for them, and thereby to force the economic system into new channels" (Schumpeter, 1926, p. 106).

We may consider structural instability as a "dispositional" concept (structural change dunàmei). Innovation is then the internal disturbance which has the crucial role of "actualizing" structural change. Without credit, structural change would be much slower, which is the main explanation of the pronounced dynamism of the Capitalist system as compared to preceding economic systems:

> "while granting credit is not essential in the normal circular flow, because in it no necessary gap exists between products and means of production ... it is certain that there is such a gap to bridge in the carrying out of new combinations. To bridge it is the function of the lender, and he fulfills it by placing purchasing power created ad hoc at the disposal of the entrepreneur ... Thus the gap is closed which would otherwise make development extraordinarly difficult, if not impossible in an exchange economy where private property prevails" (Schumpeter, 1926, p. 107).

In Marx, both money as institutional structure and credit creation play an important role in explaining structural change under capitalism. We cannot even understand capital if we do not start from money and analyze the process of development of monetary and financial relations:

> "if we abstract from the material substance of the circulation of commodities, that is, from the exchange of the various use-values, and consider only the economic forms produced by this process of circulation we find its final result to be money: this final product of the circulation of commodities is the first form in which capital appears" (K. I., p. 146).

In the simplest monetary form of circulation, Commodity-Money-Commodity, there is already _in nuce_ the possibility of both crisis and structural change, i.e. of both capitalistic fluctuations and accumulation. Money spatially and temporally separates purchase and sale which is the root of the structural instability of capitalism. We cannot here follow the development of this basic contradiction which implies the development of structural instability up to the specific form characterizing capitalism: "the historical progress and extension of exchanges develops the contrast, latent in commodities, between use-value and value" (K. I., p. 86). We would only like to observe that besides this genetic or "diachronic" point of view we may find in Marx another one which we may call "synchronic" in that it assumes as given the basic institutional structure of capitalism (but not its economic structure). In this second perspective, credit is considered fundamental in explaining structural change and in providing a crucial link between cycle and growth:

> "the credit system accelerates the material development of the productive forces ... at the same time credit accelerates the violent eruptions of this contradiction — crises — and thereby the elements of disintegration of the old mode of production" (K. 3., p. 441).

We may now appreciate the analogy between i) Marx's "diachronic" point of view, which focuses on money as an institutional structure, and the Keynesian point of view (this is partially admitted by Keynes himself in private notes and correspondence); ii) between Marx's synchronic point of views, which focuses on credit as a crucial control mechanism of structural change under capitalism, and the Schumpeterian point of view (this is openly admitted by Schumpeter himself).

6. Short-period, long-period and structural instability

We utilized, at the beginning of this paper, the traditional distinction between short and long period to settle the order of exposition. Any perceptive reader has by now understood that this distinction cannot be conceived in the usual way with Keynes, Schumpeter and Marx. All of them would agree that we may recognize in economic reality more or less permanent forces and relations. This is why they conceive of the economic structure as a hierachical system articulated in different subsystems characterized by different degrees of permanence, i.e. of structural instability. There is no harm in using the long-term concept for designating the more permanent relations, and short-term for designating the more structurally unstable, apart from the minor and easily mendable inconvenience that a dychotomy may not be enogh (especially with Marx) to adequately indicize the different levels of the hierarchy. The important point is that we have thus to consider the relation between short and long period in a way radically different from the usual one.

Long-term parameters affect short-term dynamics and vice-versa. If we consider first of all Keynes, we may see that long-term expectations affect short-term equilibria as well as disequilibrium dynamics. So, for example, speculative demand for money (M_2) crucially depends on long-term expectations about "what is considered a fairly safe level of r", the long-term rate of interest:

> "a given M_2 will not have a definite quantitative relation to a given rate of interest of r; — what matters is not the absolute level of r but the degree of its divergence from what is considered a fairly safe level fo r" (Keynes, 1936, p. 201).

The safe level of long-term rate of interest is regulated by long-term expectations which are highly conventional:

> "the rate of interest is a highly conventional, rather than a highly psychological, phenomenon. For its actual value is largely governed by the prevailing view as to what its value is expected to be. Any level of interest which is accepted with sufficient conviction as likely to be durable will be durable; subject of course, in a changing society to fluctuations for all kind of reasons round to expected normal" (ibid., p. 203).

As we can see, not only long-term expectations may affect short-term variables, but the influence may be so strong to auto-realize themselves as self-fulfilling prophecies. Unfortunately (for the stability of capitalism) short-term values affect in their turn long-term parameters (and then also long-term equilibria). So, for example, a reduction in money-wages associated to unemployment would likely affect the functional structure of the system, shifting the three "psychological" schedules: propensity to consume, liquidity preference, marginal efficiency of capital. Generally speaking, according to Keynes, short-term shocks could shift long-terms expectations:

> "a conventional valuation which is established as the outcome of the mass psychology of a large number of ignorant individuals is liable to change violently as the result of a sudden fluctuation of opinion due to factors which do

not really make much difference to the prospective yield; since there will be no strong roots of conviction to hold it steady" (ibid., p. 154).

Turning now to the point of view of Schumpeter, we may observe — first of all — that in his opinion the distinction between short and long period is unsatisfactory (see, e.g., Schumpeter, 1939, p. 45). Still he doesn't altogether rule out the use of this distinction but only a use implying independent layers of reality. First of all, he often stresses that equilibrium, even long-run equilibrium, depends on short-term disequilibrium dynamics:

"ultimate equilibrium, even if reached and even if nothing has occurred to change the situation, will in general depend on the path by which it is reached, i.e., on the whole series of transactions that are usually carried out at varying prices as the situation unfolds" (Schumpeter, 1939, p. 49).

Moreover we could add that short-term influences on entrepreneurs' behaviour will probably exert a long-term influence on the structure of capital stock because of the induced change in the pace and direction of innovations. Finally we should remember that Schumpeter is fully aware that long-term structural characteristics of capitalistic order (for instance the credit creation process) affects the functioning of a capitalistic system (for instance the process of innovation) and, inside the capitalistic system, the long-term equilibrium affects short-term processes of adjustment, mainly in the depression phase of business cycle.

Turning now our attention to Marx, we may observe that short-term disequilibrium dynamics, after a certain threshold, induces structural change. So, for example, a fall in the rate of profit under what capitalists believe to be as acceptable, not only "breeds over-production, speculation, crises, and surplus-capital alongside surplus-population" (K. 3., p. 242), but also induces counteracting influences affecting economic structure (ch. XIV of K.3.). At the same time, the long-term structure determines the rules of the game for short-term dynamics. So, for example, the "law of value" — as it is well-known — works in different ways in different phases of capitalism, not to mention different modes of production.

We could now ask ourselves whether our three authors' points of view may be reciprocally co-ordinated. Keynes focused on the structural instability of financial circulation in a monetary economy, Schumpeter on the structural instability of production process in relation to financial circulation in competitive capitalism, Marx on structural instability of different phases of capitalism and of capitalism itself in relation to structural instability of production and circulation in each of these phases. This does not imply that the broader scope of Schumpeterian analysis makes the contribution of Keynes superfluous or the even broader scope of Marxian analysis gets rid of "burgeois economics", particularly in the Keynesian and Schumpeterian version. Many analytical details provided by Keynes on financial circulation cannot be found either in Schumpeter or in Marx and many analytical details provided by Schumpeter on production processes cannot be found either in Keynes or in Marx. Their contributions could be then coordinated and developed according to the preceding lines.

7. Summary and conclusions

We have tried to show in this paper that instability of capitalism as analyzed by Keynes, Schumpeter, Marx cannot be properly understood in terms of dynamic instability only. On the contrary, the crucial instability concept worked out by these authors has to be properly modelled in terms of structural instability.

This paper was not meant to clarify the differentiae specificae which, as it is well known, divide and contrast the theories of the authors here considered. Our aim was that of picking-up a few common ideas which we may try to summarize in the following way:

a) to understand properly the instability of a capitalist economy a crucial concept of instability is that of structural instability;

b) a system is defined as structurally unstable if it is liable to undergo a structural change when disturbed;

c) the disturbances inducing structural change may be endogenous or exogenous to the economic system. Our three authors considered the role of external disturbances as trivial for economic theory (not of course for economic history). That is why they limited themselves, in their theoretical contributions, to analysing the relation between endogenous disturbances and structural change of economic system;

d) the attribute of structural instability is conferred on the economic system mainly by financial relations (money and credit);

e) capitalistic fluctuations are intimately related not only to the dynamic instability of the economic system but also to its structural instability;

f) internal disturbances, which are cause and effect of fluctuations, necessarily induce a structural change and thus produce development and growth;

g) as a consequence of the preceding points we cannot conceive fluctuations as independent of growth and viceversa, or short-term as independent of long-term and viceversa.

APPENDIX

STRUCTURAL STABILITY: THE RECENT EVOLUTION OF THE CONCEPT AND METHODOLOGICAL IMPLICATIONS

I will sharply distinguish between the mathematical meaning of structural stability and the philosophical meaning. Only studying their interrelations as distinct concepts we may satisfactorily understand:

a) the genesis and evolution of the different mathematical formalizations of the concept;
b) the methodological implications of employing structurally stable (from now on: s-stable) or structurally unstable (from now on: s-unstable) models in empiric research.

1. The modern philosophical view of structural stability

The modern philosophical view of a s-stability may be traced back to the turn of this century, when:

> "a simple description of physical theory evolved, especially among continental physicists — Duhem, Poincaré, Mach, Einstein, Hadamard, Hilbert — which may still be quite close to the views of many mathematical physicists. This description — most clearly enonciated by Duhem (1906) — consisted of an experimental domain, a mathematical model, and a conventional interpretation. The model, being a mathematical system, embodies the logic, or axiomatization, of the theory. The interpretation is an agreement connecting the parameters and therefore the conclusions of the model and the observables in the domain.
> Traditionally, the philospher-scientists judge the usefulness of a theory by the criterion of adequacy, that is, the verifiability of the predictions, or the quality of the agreement between the interpreted conclusions of the model and the data of the experimental domain" (Abraham and Marsden, from now on AM, 1980, XIX).

Duhem himself goes on to clarify in a brief example that the adequacy implies the stability of the model, when the model is slightly perturbed. Otherwise, however precise the instruments quantifying the conditions of our experience we might always deduce from practically determined experimental conditions, infinite different practical results (Duhem, 1906, p. 154). An unstable model would thus be useless for describing the empirical evidence. In addition it would be useless for predictions, as Maxwell had already pointed out a few decades earlier:

> "when an infinitely small variation of the current state may cause a finite difference in a finite spell of time, the condition of the system is said unstable. It is obvious that the existence of unstable conditions prevents any forecasting of future events" (Maxwell, 1876, p. 400).

Although the basic concept of "structural stability" as expressed by Maxwell and Duhem is fairly intuitive, a full understanding of its implications is quite tricky because it involves many complicated epistemological issues. Unfortunately these unsettled questions have been almost completely neglected in this century, also because "the traditional mutuality of mechanics and philosophy has declined in recent years, because of the justifiable interest in the problems posed by relativity and quantum theory" (AM, xix). This is one of the reasons why, notwithstanding the extensive and rapidly growing literature on the topological criterion for structural stability, "it is safe to say that a clear enonciation of this criterion in the correct generality has not yet been made" (AM, xx). We should never forget that the formalization of the concept so far worked out strictly refer to "the model only, the interpretation and domain being fixed. Therefore, it concerns mainly the model, and is primarily a mathematical or logical question" (AM, xix-xx). Unfortunately, the methodological significance of s-stability depends also on other considerations, interrelated with the logical features of the model but partially independent of them, and in particular:

a) the qualitative characteristics of the empirical domain,

b) the specific ends of the scientific investigation.

2. The topological definition of structural stability

A rigorous and successful formalization of the modern notion of structural stability has been offered only in 1937 by Andronov and Pontryagin on the basis of modern differential topology.

The intuitive notion of s-stability underlying this research program is the following: a sistem is said to be structurally stable if for any small change, induced by a perturbation, in the vector field the system thus obtained is equivalent to the initial system (Arnold, 1978, p. 88). The concept underwent a considerable evolution first of all by the "Gorki school" founded by Andronov (Smale, 1980, p. 147), and in a second time also outside Russia as soon as the classical book by Andronov, Vitt, Khaikin (1937) was translated into English by Lefschetz (1949).

The attention concentrated first of all on the definition of "equivalence". The finest classification of dynamical systems should consider as equivalent only diffeomorphic systems which "are indistinguishable from the point of view of the geometry of smooth manifolds" (Arnold, 89). However, a classification up to diffeomorphisms is much too fine in the sense that "too many systems turn out to be inequivalent" (Arnold, 89). That is why a coarser equivalence has been introduced, the so-called topological equivalence: "two systems are topologically equivalent if there exists a homeomorphism of the phase space of the first system onto the phase space of the second, which converts the phase flow of the first system into the phase flow of the second" (Arnold, 90). Unfortunately, even topological equivalence is too fine. The main reason is that the period of motion on the cycle is a continuously changing invariant (modulus) with respect to topological equivalence as well. To avoid that, a new notion of equivalence has been worked out:

> "two systems are said to be topologically orbitally equivalent if there exist a homeomorphism of the phase space of the first system onto the phase space of the second, converting oriented phase curves of the first system into oriented phase curves of the second. No co-ordination of the motions on corresponding phase curves is required" (Arnold, 90).

This is considered by Arnold "the final definition of structural stability". This opinion seems to me very naive. Even this definition is very demanding. Moreover, to appraise its validity, we have to consider it in the context of the history of differentiable dynamics. The succession of three definitions of s-stability that we have just examined may be thus understood as part — perhaps the prologue — of the so-called "yin-yang" parable:

> "At one point in the history of differentiable dynamics, it was hoped that even though an arbitrary phase portrait was too complicated to classify, at least the typical garden variety would be manageable. And so began the search for generic properties of vector fields ... Since then, most properties proposed eventually fell to a counterexample, and the ever-widening moat between the generic and the classifiable became known as the yin-yang problem (AM, 531) ... we may think of the generic vector fields G_4 as heaven (yin) and the Morse -Smale systems Σ_M as earth (yang). Differentiable dynamics attempts to build a tower from earth to heaven, in spite of warnings from Puritan poets and others" (AM, 536).

An early candidate for genericity was structural stability. Genericity is of course a very important concept. According to topologists, only a theory of generic systems may be simple, powerful and manageable. Moreover, the knowledge of the behaviour of generic dynamical systems would be enough to approximate the behaviour of any dynamic system since a deformation as small as we wish would be enough to transform a non-generic case in a generic one (Arnold, 1978, chap. 6). We may well understand why the dream of differential topology in its infancy has been the genericity of structural stability. This dream seemed to be about to materialize when Peixoto (1962) was able to prove that s-stable dynamical systems are generic in a 2-dimensional compact manifold (Smale, 1980, 88). Unfortunately, Smale soon discovered that s-stability is not a generic property for compact differential manifolds of dimension 3 or more. This theorem acted as a gelid shower on the mathematical community. According to Arnold:

> "for the qualitative theory of differential equations this result has approximately the same significance as Liouville's theorem on the impossibility of solving differential equations by quadrature for the integration theory of differential equations. It shows that the problem of the complete topological classification of differential equations with high-dimensional phase space is hopeless" (Arnold, 1978, 87).

We may now fully understand the yin-yang parable. In the beginning we had Heaven on Earth, i.e. both genericity and s-stability, but Smale ate the apple and we have been suddenly driven away from our Earthly Paradise. A hiatus opened between earth and heaven and from then on mathematicians are striving to build a tower able to reduce at least the extent of this hiatus, building-up weaker and weaker notions of s-stability progressively more generic.

Important weaker concepts have been proposed, first of all, by Smale himself: λ-stability and ω-stability (1970, b). λ-stability is weaker than ω-stability, which is weaker than s-stability. Unfortunately, within days of proposal of these weaker notions of stability, the first counterexample was constructed (Abraham-Smale, 1970), killing hopes that they might be generic properties of vector fields. Smale has then tried to build-up a parallel tower, the A-tower, based on his "Axiom A" of 1966:

> "Although it subsequently turned out to be a little shorter than the tower of stability, it has wonderful features ... reasonable bounds for numbers of critical elements and so forth" (AM, 537).

Unfortunately, even the construction of this tower had to stop very far from heaven (a very lucid account by the chief-architect himself may be found in Smale, 1980, 90-94). Other towers have been recently built-up (for the tower of absolute stability, see MA, 541), but heaven seems farther than ever. Maybe that eventually, as AM still hope, a generic notion of stability will be found. It will certainly be much weaker than the weakest till now worked out.

3. A few reflections on the multiplying zoo of structural stability concepts: relativity and degree

We have described the main evolutionary tree of the notions of structural stability (in the topological sense). We may now try to develop a few considerations on the family of concepts so far generated.

First of all, we would like to point out that each notion of structural stability is relative to a series of conditions: equivalence concept, qualitative and quantitative characteristics of perturbations, the topology and the metric chosen (see Cugno, Montrucchio, 1982). The set of structurally stable systems changes its boundaries whenever we change any of the above conditions. As we have seen, the evolution of s-stability concepts has been mainly the result of the reiterated attempt of finding out weaker notions of equivalence. The attention has been much less concentrated so far on the other conditions. This should not be taken as if they were less important. On the contrary, I believe that they will play a major role in the future evolution of the concept, specially for empirically oriented applications. I will here limit myself to show through simple examples why the definition of the admissible perturbations matters.

We should, first of all, draw the attention of the reader on the basic difference between perturbations arbitrarily small or just small. Obviously enough we may have very different results. A system may be s-stable for arbitrarily small perturbations and s-unstable for small perturbations beyond a certain threshold. This is so obvious to appear superfluous. But there is a problem in the literature. The current topological definitions consider arbitrarily small perturbations only, while the philosophical concept (of which topological concepts may be considered a formalization) is generally stated (even by topologists) in reference to small perturbations. Moreover, small but finite perturbations are very important in applications. We should thus turn our attention to thorough formalizations of structural stability in the case of small but finite perturbations.

The second distinction about perturbations which is very important to make is between perturbations that do not alter the order of the system (the dimension of the phase-space) and those which may have this disgraceful effect. Standard definitions exclude implicitely this second kind of perturbations (only Andronov, Khaikin, Vitt, 1937, make explicit the existence and the scope of this hidden assumption). This makes life much simpler for supporters of structural stability, highly increasing its "likelyhood". In fact, as we have seen, the "likelyhood" of structural stability decreases as the order of the system increases. In particular, even the genericity of structural stability in the compact manifold of dimension two would be jeopardized for such a kind of perturbation. Unfortunately the excluded case may be of the utmost scientific interest. This is the case, for example, of so-called parasitic parameters which play an important role in many fields of physics and engineering (e.g. electric circuit theory and design). The widespread existence of this sort of disturbance greatly undermines the plausibility of structural stability analysis, in which

> "we cannot help being 'naive', for, otherwise, we should have to verify that all possible small parasitic parameters, increasing the order of the equation, shall not disturb the stability of a given state. However, we can never carry out this verification exhaustively, since the number of such parasitic parameters in every system is very large. In addition, as will be shown, it may happen that these parameters act in different directions, so that, in order to verify their influence we have not only to assume the presence of these parameters but also to know the quantitative relations between them" (Andronov, Vitt, Khaikin, 1937, xxx).

My third and last observation about perturbations refers to the so-called "structural perturbations", that is perturbations altering the interrelations between the elements of a system (Siljak, 1978). Their influence has been extensively studied on dynamic stability (ibid.). An extension to structural stability is possible because a structural perturbation does not necessarily alter the qualitative dynamic behaviour of the system. This is because the word "structural" has different, although strictly related, meanings as modifier of perturbation and stability. A notion of structural stability relative to specified families of structural perturbations, would be of course a very strong requirement. Still it would be precious for describing and designing structures which have to be very reliable (as electric-power nets, airplanes, etc.), as well as for clarifying the concept of structural stability.

The relativity of the concepts of s-stability which we have documented in relation to different definitions of equivalence and admissible perturbations, leads us naturally to put some order between weaker and stronger notions, defining a hierarchy. We have already considered a few attempts at defining hierarchies of structural stability notions through yin-yang towers. A different, though in part symmetrical, approach is that of defining a hierarchy of s-instability degrees.

This is the way followed by Andronov, who introduced the concept of degree of s-instability in 1938, which has been developed by his "Gorki school". According to this school:

> "structurally unstable systems can be divided into 'less structurally unstable' and 'more structurally unstable'. This leads to a classification according to the degrees of structural instability ... the least structurally unstable systems in this classification are the systems of the first degree of structural instability: under small changes, these systems either go to a structurally unstable system or retain their topological structure ... A dynamic system of the first degree of structural instability was found to have one and only one structurally unstable singular path, i.e., it has either a multiple equilibrium state, or a multiple limit cycle, or a saddle-to-saddle separatrix. To establish the bifurcations of a system of the first degree of structural instability, it suffices to consider the changes in its topological structure in the neighborhood of its structurally unstable singular path" (Andronov, Leontovich, Gordon, Maier, 1967, xiii).

These excerpts may be enough to get the flavour of this approach. It puts the problems, both methodological and applicative, in the most promising perspective. Structural stability, which may be now properly defined in a strong version, appears as a limit-case of a spectrum, i.e. the zero degree of s-instability. Systems with a low degree of s-instability have good stability properties, although not strong enough to be classified as s-stable. Stability and instability lose here any emotional connotations, which on the contrary are not altogether absent in the yin-yang mainstream. For the sake of application, we only need to know which the characteristics and the specific conditions of application of each degree of s-instability are.

4. Structural (in)stability and the methodology of empirical science

We are now in a position to discuss the methodological use made of s-stability in the recent and current practice of model-building. As it is well-known, on the grounds of the modern philosophical notion of s-stability, s-instability (defined in whichever way) has been almost universally considered as a sufficient reason for rejecting a model as useless if not misleading (among the very few exceptions, see Andronov et al., 1967, and Vercelli 1982). A s-unstable model is generally considered as hopeless for both descriptive and forecasting purposes.

I believe that, in the light of the preceding conceptual reconstruction, this methodological prescription is to be considered as ungranted. We have first of all to clarify to which notion and degree of s-instability we are referring to. A model s-unstable according to a certain definition may turn out to be s-stable under another one. This already raises strong doubts on the ordinary simplistic version of the prescription.

Anyway, for the sake of argument, let's suppose that we have only one possible definition of s-stability (and consequently of s-instability) and only one possible degree for both concepts. Our methodological prescription would then be acceptable only in the hypotheis that reality is structurally stable. This obvious condition of validity is almost never made explicit. However, R. Thom admits occasionally that "the a priori need for structural stability [is only valid] when dealing with a process that is empirically stable" (1975, 19) and that "qualitatively indeterminate phenomena may be described by structurally unstable dynamical systems" (ibid.). Still he believes that only s-stable systems, processes and catastrophes are really intelligible although he never explains why.

At any rate, how likey may we consider the hypothesis that systems, processes, catastrophes are generally s-stable? Unfortunately, it is very unlikely whenever the relevant phase space has dimension 3 or more. We know in fact that in this case the set of catastrophe points is likely to be locally dense which will force us "to consider the process in the neighborhood of some points as chaotic and turbulent, when the idea of structural stability loses most of its significance" (ibid., 18). Moreover, the interaction between two s-stable systems generates s-instability, because generally "the topological product of two structurally stable dynamical systems is not structurally stable" (ibid., 130). This offers an important key to understand why the more complex is a system the more likely is that its dynamical behaviour is s-unstable.

Thom has recently admitted that the topological notion of structural stability may be considered adequate only for experimental sciences (physics, chemistry and biology) and not for observative sciences: geology, paleontology, ethnography, history, psychology, social sciences etc. (Thom, 1980, 4-5). But even in the so-called experimental sciences — even in physics which has always been considered the queen of hard sciences — there are wide and relevant areas of stubborn inadequacy. The most blatant case is Hamiltonian mechanics, whose models are typically s-unstable, even according to the weakest definition so far worked out for non-Hamiltonian systems. There have been many recent attempts at working out a much weaker notion of s-stability suitable for Hamiltonian systems, but they proved to be very soon extremely far from genericity. We are bound to observe:

> "an appropriate notion of structural stability for Hamiltonian dynamics must be extremely vague and fuzzy, if not downright statistical. This is a real obstacle to a reasonable philosophy of stability in the Hamiltonian context, and no relief is visible on the horizon" (MA, 595).

Notwithstanding all the preceding considerations which leave little hope for the hypothesis that reality is, generally speaking, s-stable, we will assume, for the sake of argument, that it is so. Even in this case, not always s-stability has to be considered as a necessary condition for a useful scientific effort. It depends on the specific aims of the research. In particular, there may be a trade-off between a higher degree of s-stability of the model and a higher degree of satisfaction of another specific end of scientific research. A case in point is the trade-off between s-stability and computability:

> "structural stability and computability are, to a certain extent, contradictory demands, because all quantitative and effectively computable models must necessarily appeal to analytic functions [whose structural stability is problematic], while a function that is differentiable, and no more, rarely lends itself to explicit evaluation. ... There seems to be a time scale in all natural processes beyond which structural stability and calculability become incompatible. In planetary mechanics this scale is of such an extent that the incompatibility is not evident, whereas in quantum mechanics it is so short that the incompatibility is immediately felt, and today the physicist sacrifices structural stability for computability" (Thom, 1975, 29).

It is absolutely clear from this example that we may wish to sacrifice to some extent s-stability in order to better satisfy other targets of our scientific inquiry. Other examples may be found. I choose to mention one that I consider particularly emblematic because it is relative to the explanation of structural change itself. I believe that an important key to understand structural change in many fields (and first of all in social sciences like economics), consists in seeing it as a stabilization process meant to preserve certain desired qualities of the existing structure. We have already an abstract theory of stabilization of s-unstable systems which may be very useful for pursueing this line of thought (Petitot, 1979). I think that the application of this theory to the evolution of biological and social structures would offer a lot of analytical and methodological insights. For example, we could better understand the deapest reasons of the irreversibility of evolution and historycal time:

> "The notion of stabilization (partial or total) defines a preordering among singularities. The asymmetry of this relation, somehow expressing the irreversibility of stabilization processes, may appear slightly paradoxical. It de-

pends on the fact that the property of stability is an open one. Thus, whenever through the 'explosion' of a critical point or through the separation of critical values of f, we stabilize f in f' by infinitesimal deformation, we cannot come back from f' to f unless by finite deformations. By infinitesimal deformations we may only, as soon as we reach f', get f' again, because f' is stable" (Petitot, 1979).

We may now conclude our critical analysis of the recent debate on s-stable versus s-instability, observing that the widespread claim that only s-stability models may be useful in empiric research must be considered by now completely ungranted.

The received view claims that only s-stable models may assure the observability and predictability of empirical phenomena. I believe that s-stability is neither necessary nor sufficient condition for either observability or predictability. It is not a necessary condition of observability, because "it is an everyday experience that many common phenomena are unstable" (Thom, 1975, 126), and because many models successfully employed in empirical science, are, as we have seen, s-unstable. It is not a sufficient condition of observability as it is clarified by the classical analysis of observability offered by System Theory (see, e.g., Marro, 1979). It is not a sufficient condition for predictability because the topological notion of s-stability cannot rule out the possibility that "the perturbed system may have a completely different structure from the original system after sufficient time has passed" (Thom, 1975, 26) since "it is not required that the homeomorphism h commute with time" (ibid.). It is not a necessary condition for predictability because, e.g., for the sake of forecasting the results of a stabilization process we have to analyze first the characteristics of the s-unstable system which undergoes the stabilization process.

I do not wish to question, with these skeptical observations, that in many cases, ceteris paribus, we should try to minimize the degree of s-instability of our model, but this methodological rule should never become a dogma. We should always take account of the specific aims of the research and of the characteristics of the empirical evidence.

REFERENCES

Abraham R., Marsden J.E. (1980), Foundations of Mechanics, Benjamin/Cummings, Reading (Mass.), 2nd ed., 2nd print.

Abraham R., Smale S. (1970), Nongenericity of Ω-stability, in Chern, Smale, 1970.

Andronov A.A., Vitt A., Khaikin (1937), Theory of oscillations, Princeton Un. P., Princeton, N.J., ed. 1966.

Andronov A.A., Leontovich E. (1938), Sur la variation de la structure qualitative de la division du plan en trajectoires, Dokl. Akad. Nauk. SSSR, 21: 427-430.

Andronov A.A., Leontovich E., Gordon I, Maier A. (1971), Theory of bifurcations of dynamical system in the plane, Israel Program of Scientific Translation, Jerusalem.

Andronov A.A., Pontryagin L. (1937), Systèmes grossiers, Dokl. Akad. Nauk SSSR, 14: 247-251.

Arnold V.I. (1978), Geometrical Methods in the Theory of Ordinary Differential Equations, Springer, N.Y., 1983.

Chern S.S., Smale S. (eds.) (1970), Proceedings of the Symposium in Pure Mathematics: Global Analysis, Am. Math. Soc., Providence, R.I.

Cugno F., Montrucchio L. (1982), "Cyclical growth and Inflation: a qualitative approach to Goodwin's model with money prices", Economic Notes, Vol. XI, n. 3.

Duhem P. (1906), The aim and structure of physical theory, Princ. Un. Press, Princeton, N.J.

Keynes J.M. (1923), A Tract on Monetary Reform, Macmillan, London.

Keynes J.M. (1936), The General Theory of Employment, Interest and Money, Macmillan, London.

Keynes J.M., The Collected Writings of John Maynard Keynes, Vol. XIII, 1973, Vol. XIV, 1973, Vol. XXIX, 1979.

Lombardini S. (1982), Economics: Past and Future, in Szegö, ed., 1982, 29-75.

Marro G. (1979), Fondamenti di teoria dei sistemi, Patron, Bologna, 3a ed.

Marx K., K.1, K.2 and K.3, Capital, Voll. I, II and III, Progress, Moscow.

Minsky H.P. (1975), John Maynard Keynes, Macmillan, London.

Palis J., Smale S. (1970), Structural stability theorems, in Chern, Smale, eds., 1970.

Peixoto M. (1959), On structural stability, Ann. Math. 69: 199-222.

Peixoto M. (1962), Structural stability on two-dimensional manifolds, Topology, 2: 101-121.

Peixoto M. (ed.) (1973), Dynamical Systems, Academic, N.Y.

Petitot J. (1979), Locale/globale, in Enciclopedia, vol. VIII, Einaudi, Torino.

Schumpeter J.A. (1911), The Theory of Economic Development, Oxford. Un., N.Y.

Schumpeter J.A. (1928), The instability of capitalism, The Economic Journal, sept.

Schumpeter J.A. (1939), Business Cycles, McGraw-Hill, N.Y.

Siljak D.D. (1978), Large-Scale Dynamic Systems, North Holland, N.Y.

Smale S. (1959), Diffeomorphisms of the two sphere, Proc. Am. Math. Soc., 10: 621-626.

Smale S. (1966), Structurally stable systems are not dense, Am. J. Math. 88: 491-496.

Smale S. (1980), The Mathematics of Time, Springer, N.Y.

Szegö G. (1982), New Quantitative Techniques for Economic Analysis, Academic, N.Y.

Thom R. (1975), Structural Stability and Morphogenesis: an Outline of a General Theory of Models, Benjamin-Cummings, Reading (Mass.).

Thom R. (1980), Parabole e Catastrofi, il Saggiatore, Milano.

Vercelli A. (1973), Teoria della Struttura Economica Capitalistica, Fondaz. Einaudi, Torino.

Vercelli A. (1979), Equilibrio e dinamica del sistema economico, Quad. n. 4, Ist. di Ec., Siena.

Vercelli A. (1981), Equilibrio e disequilibrio nella Teoria Generale di Keynes, in AA.VV., Studi di Economia Keynesiana, Liguori, Napoli.

Vercelli A. (1982), In instability enough to discredit a model?, Economic Notes, 11: 173-90.

Vicarelli F. (1977), Keynes, l'instabilità del capitalismo, Etas, Milano.

CYCLICAL GROWTH IN A NON-LINEAR MACRODYNAMIC MODEL OF THE ITALIAN ECONOMY (*)

G. Gandolfo and P.C. Padoan
Facoltà di Economia e Commercio
Università di Roma
Via del Castro Laurenziano 9, 00161 Roma/Italy

1. Introduction

Cyclical growth is usually analyzed at the theoretical level by means of very small models (normally not exceeding two dynamic equations, to enable the theoretician to use phase-plane techniques). Although these models may give important theoretical insights (Goodwin's well-known models are an excellent example), they are far too small to be of any practical use. On the other hand, the problems of cyclical growth are all too easily lost in the labyrinth of huge econometric models.
This unsatisfactory state of things is no more than a reflection on the problem at hand of the fact that, at macroeconomic level, there is a discrepancy between theoretical and econometric modelling. Theoretical modelling proceeds by means of complete qualitative analyses of very small models (with all the limitations inherent in the oversimplification made necessary by this smallness). Econometric modelling on the other hand proceeds by means of numerical analyses of much larger models (with all the limitations inherent in this approach, such as the validity for the single numerical case and not in general). This discrepancy is definitely not favourable to the advancement of both scientific knowledge and knowledge of the behaviour of actual economic systems. Also, such a discrepancy is particularly annoying to those —ourselves among them — who believe that econometrics is not a mere armoury of methods, but ought to conform to Frisch's (1933, p. 2) original defini-

(*) Research support by the University of Rome and the Ministry of Public Instruction is gratefully acknowledged.

tion: "...each of these three view points, that of statistics, economic theory, and mathematics, is a necessary, but not by itself a sufficient, condition for a real understanding of the quantitative relations in modern economic life. It is the unification of all three that is powerful. And it is this unification that constitutes econometrics".

To eliminate this discrepancy it is not sufficient to start from a theoretical model of the usual type and estimate its parameters, for the oversimplification inherent in a two-or three-equation model does not commend it for practical applications, such as are required in policy analysis.

In our opinion, small econometric models may help to eliminate this discrepancy, on the one hand by maintaining all the advantages of a well-founded and consistent theoretical structure and amenability to qualitative analysis, and on the other by allowing the estimation of their parameters as well as their use for policy analysis.

We also believe that such models are better specified as systems of non-linear stochastic differential equations and estimated in continuous time. The specification of a macrodynamic model as a differential equation system is more appealing to the economic theorist for a number of reasons, that it would be impossible to go into here[(+)] (for a treatment see, for example, Gandolfo, 1981). But once one has a differential equation system, the problem arises of estimating its parameters. Now, current econometric techniques are based on discrete time: therefore in order to estimate such a model it was hitherto necessary to approximate it with a discrete model (and approximations which have been used in the past are not acceptable once the problem is formulated rigorously). Fortunately, in the last few years new methods (see, for example, Bergstrom (ed.), 1976; Gandolfo, 1981; Wymer, 1976) have been developed which allow a rigorous estimation of the parameters of a system of sto-

---

(+)We would like, however, to recall that the first theorist to explicitly advocate the formulation of economic models in continuous time was Richard M. Goodwin (1948). On the econometric side, the first who set forth the idea of formulating econometric models in continuous time was T.C. Koopmans (1950); however — except in occasional works — his suggestions were not followed up and the topic was taken up again and gone into more deeply only in the seventies.

chastic differential equations on the basis of samples of discrete observations such as are available in reality.

In general, a continuous time model will be of the type

$$Dy(t)=H[y(t),z(t),\theta]+u(t),$$

where D is the differential operator d/dt, y(t) the vector of endogenous variables, z(t) the vector of the exogenous variables, θ a vector of parameters (consisting of a subvector α of adjustment speeds and a subvector β of other behavioural parameters), H a vector of non-linear differentiable functions, and u(t) a vector of disturbances with classic properties. We would like to stress the fact that <u>all</u> equations are formulated as <u>disequilibrium</u> equations, in which <u>each</u> endogenous variable is assumed to adjust with a certain speed α to its partial equilibrium or desired level. Therefore, the empirical analysis will also give the estimates of these adjustment speeds, and this is a very important feature, because economic theory alone is <u>not</u>, in general, sufficient to determine a precise ordering of these speeds.

The qualitative analysis of the model proceeds by examining four main points:

1) steady state,
2) comparative dynamycs,
3) stability,
4) sensitivity.

There is not sufficient time to talk about each of these points in general (these will be illustrated with reference to our model), but we would like to draw the reader's attention to sensitivity analysis. By sensitivity analysis we here mean the analysis of the effects of changes in the parameters on the characteristic roots of the model. This can be performed in a general way by computing the partial derivatives of these roots with respect to the parameters. If we call $\underline{A}$ the matrix of the linear approximation to the non-linear system written above, we can compute $\partial\mu_j/\partial A$, where μ_j denotes the $\underline{j}$-th characteristic root of $\underline{A}$. This is very important not only at the theoretical level (for example to determine bifurcations, structural stability and the like), but also for policy purposes.

As regards the econometric estimation, we can repeat what we said above, namely that these new methods allow a rigorous estimation of the parameters of the stochastic differential equation system, for they are based on a stochastically equivalent discrete analogue to the continuous model.

The model that we present in this paper belongs to such a category(").

It is the third version — and by no means the last — of a model that we started to build a few years ago(+) according to the general principles illustrated above. Although we did not build it for the specific purpose of analyzing cyclical growth, it did turn out that our model gives rise to a stable cyclical growth path; this is why we think that it is worthwhile presenting here.

2. An overview of the model

The model considers stock-flow behaviour in an open economy in which both price and quantity adjustments take place. Stocks are introduced with reference to the real sector (in which adjustments of fixed capital and inventories to their respective desired levels are present) and to the financial sector which includes the stock of money, the stock of commercial credit, the stock of net foreign assets and the stock of international reserves. Real and financial feed backs are, therefore, largely considered in the model. Government expenditure and revenues

(")For other continuous time econometric models see, e.g., Bergstrom and Wymer (1976); Reserve Bank of Australia (1977); Knight and Wymer (1978); Jonson and Trevor (1981).

(+)Earlier versions of this model are to be found in Gandolfo (1981) and in Gandolfo and Padoan (1982). In the present version the financial sector is more highly developed, for it includes bank advances, interest rate, money demand and supply, capital movements, international reserves (all these variables are endogenously determined); interrelationships between real and financial variables are better specified; government expenditure and taxation are explicitly considered in addition to the monetary authorities' reaction function.

(taxation) are also present so that the effects of endogenous public deficits are included.

TABLE 1

EQUATIONS OF THE MODEL[a]

Private consumption

$$D\log C=\alpha_1 \log(\hat{C}/C)+\alpha_2 \log(M^d/M^s), \tag{1}$$

where

$$\hat{C}=\gamma_1 e^{\beta_1 D\log Y} e^{\beta_2 (r_{TIT}-D\log P)} \left[\frac{P}{PMGS}\right]^{\beta_3} (Y-T/P), \quad \beta_1 \gtrless 0, \beta_2 \gtrless 0, \beta_3 \gtrless 0, \text{ and}$$

$$M^d=\gamma_2 r_{TIT}^{-\beta_4} P^{\beta_5} Y^{\beta_6}, \tag{1.1}$$

Rate of growth in fixed capital stock

$$Dk=\alpha_3 [\alpha' \log(\hat{K}/K)-k]+\alpha_4 D\log A, \tag{2}$$

where

$$\hat{K}=\gamma_3 \tilde{Y}, \quad \gamma_3=\kappa/u, \tag{2.1}$$

Expected output

$$D\log\tilde{Y}=\eta \log(Y/\tilde{Y}), \tag{3}$$

Imports

$$D\log MGS=\alpha_5 \log(M\hat{G}S/MGS)+\alpha_6 \log(\hat{V}/V), \tag{4}$$

where

$$M\hat{G}S=\gamma_4 P^{\beta_7} PMGS^{-\beta_8} Y^{\beta_9}, \quad \hat{V}=\gamma_5 Y, \tag{4.1}$$

Exports

$$D\log XGS=\alpha_7 \log(X\hat{G}S/XGS), \tag{5}$$

where

$$X\hat{G}S=\gamma_6 (PXGS/PF)^{-\beta_{10}} YF^{\beta_{11}} (\gamma_3 Y/K)^{-\beta_{12}} \tag{5.1}$$

Output

$$D\log Y=\alpha_8 \log(\tilde{Y}/Y)+\alpha_9 \log(\hat{V}/V), \tag{6}$$

Price of output

$$DlogP=\alpha_{10}\log(\hat{P}/P)+\alpha_{11}m, \tag{7}$$

where

$$\hat{P}=\gamma_7 PMGS^{\beta_{13}}W^{\beta_{14}}PROD^{-\beta_{15}}, \tag{7.1}$$

Price of exports

$$DlogPXGS=\alpha_{12}\log(P\hat{X}GS/PXGS), \tag{8}$$

where

$$P\hat{X}GS=\gamma_8 P^{\beta_{16}}PF^{\beta_{17}}, \tag{8.1}$$

Money wage rate

$$DlogW=\alpha_{13}\log(\hat{W}/W), \tag{9}$$

where

$$\hat{W}=\gamma_9 P^{\beta_{18}}e^{\lambda_5 t}, \tag{9.1}$$

Interest rate

$$Dlogr_{TIT}=\alpha_{14}\log(M^d/M^s)+\alpha_{15}\log(\gamma_{10}r_f/r_{TIT}), \tag{10}$$

Rate of growth in bank advances

$$Da=\alpha_{16}[\alpha''\log(\hat{A}/A)-a], \tag{11}$$

where

$$\hat{A}=\gamma_{11}r_{TIT}^{\beta_{19}}M^s, \qquad \beta_{19}\gtrless 0, \tag{11.1}$$

Net foreign assets

$$DlogNFA=\alpha_{17}\log(N\hat{F}A/NFA), \tag{12}$$

where

$$N\hat{F}A=\gamma_{12}r_{TIT}^{-\beta_{20}}r_f^{\beta_{21}}(PY)^{\beta_{22}}(PF\cdot YF)^{-\beta_{23}}Q^{\beta_{24}}, \quad \beta_{24}\gtrless 0, \tag{12.1}$$

Monetary authorities' reaction function

$$Dm=\alpha_{18}[\delta_1\log(R/\gamma_{13}PMGS\cdot MGS)+\delta_2(DlogY-\lambda_y)$$

$$-\delta_3(DlogP-DlogPF)-m]+\delta_4 Dlog(PG/T), \qquad \delta_2\gtrless 0, \tag{13}$$

Taxes

$$DlogT=\alpha_{19}log(\hat{T}/T), \quad (14)$$

where

$$\hat{T}=\gamma_{14}(PY)^{\beta_{25}}, \quad (14.1)$$

Public expenditure

$$DlogG=\alpha_{20}log(\gamma_{15}Y/G), \quad (15)$$

Inventories

$$DV=Y+MGS-C-DK-XGS-G, \quad (16)$$

International reserves

$$DR=PXGS\cdot XGS-PMGS\cdot MGS+(UT_a-UT_p)-DNFA, \quad (17)$$

Fixed capital stock

$$DlogK=k, \quad (18)$$

Bank advances

$$DlogA=a, \quad (19)$$

Money supply

$$DlogM^s=m. \quad (20)$$

---

[a]For economy of notation, the disturbance terms are omitted and the model is described in deterministic terms. A hat (ˆ) refers to the partial equilibrium level or desired value of the hatted variable, a tilde (˜) to expectations; the symbol D denotes the differential operator d/d*t* and log the natural logarithm. All variables are defined at time *t*. All parameters are assumed positive, unless otherwise specified.

TABLE 2

VARIABLES OF THE MODEL[a]

Endogenous

C = real consumption of the private sector

K = stock of fixed capital in real terms

k = proportional rate of increase of K

$\tilde{Y}$ = expected real net domestic product and income

MGS = real imports of goods and services

XGS = real exports of goods and services

Y = real net domestic product and income

V = stock of inventories in real terms

P = domestic price level

PXGS = export price level

W = money wage rate

r_{TIT} = domestic nominal interest rate

M^s = domestic nominal money stock (M2)

A = bank advances

a = proportional rate of increase of A

NFA = nominal stock of net foreign assets

m = proportional rate of increase of M^s

R = nominal stock of international reserves

T = tax receipts in nominal terms

G = public expenditure, in real terms

Exogenous

PMGS = import price level

PF = foreign competitors' export price level

YF = real world income

PROD = labour productivity

r_f = foreign nominal interest rate

Q = ratio of the forward to the spot exchange rate

(UT_a-UT_p) = net unilateral transfers in nominal terms

t = time

---

[a]Details of the variables and sources of data are available on request.

Quantity behaviour equations are considered for the traditional macroeconomic variables in real terms (private consumption, net fixed investment, imports and exports of goods and services, inventories, net domestic product). Expectations are present through an adaptive mechanism concerning expected output.

A price block is included, which determines the domestic price level, the nominal wage rate, and the export price level. Endogenous determination of the last was considered crucial for an export-led economy such as Italy's, while wage-price spiral effects are explicitly taken into account. The specification of a financial sector was completed by the inclusion of an interest-rate determination equation.

Although the model is a closely interlocked system of simultaneous differential equations, the following causal links may be singled out. Their description makes also possible a better understanding of the "vision" of the economy which underlies the model itself. Let us start with the real side.

The growth process is both export-led and expectations-led. Given foreign demand and prices, real exports grow according to domestic competitiveness and to supply constraints. Export growth enhances output growth which in turn modifies expectations and, consequently, real capital formation. Output growth also influences real imports, aggregate public consumption, direct taxes and the level of private consumption through the determination of disposable income. Changes in inventories, whose desired level is linked to expected output, act as a buffer in output determination.

The performance of real aggregates is also deeply influenced by price behaviour based essentially, but not exclusively, on cost push mechanisms. Prices also enter into the determination of financial variables whose behaviour is closely connected with that of real variables.

A central place in the model is occupied by credit, whose expansion, as determined by the behaviour of the banks, influences real capital accumulation. A crucial role is also played by the rate of interest as it influences real consumption, credit expansion, and accumulation of net foreign assets. Given the foreign rate of interest and the demand for money, the rate of interest is determined by the supply of money whose expansion is determined by the monetary authorities, account being taken of the performance of the balance of payments (and hence of the stock of foreign reserves), of inflation (which is determined by both external and internal factors), of real growth and of the rate of change of the public deficit.

In sum, our model stresses the central role of real and financial accumulation in an advanced open economy in which aggregate demand and expectations on the one hand, and liquidity (i.e. money and credit availability), on the other, play crucial roles.

We should now note that the exchange-rate is not explicitly present as an endogenous variable in the model. It is, of course, indirectly present through Q and the two foreign price variables (PMGS and PF): the latter are defined in domestic currency terms, but they could be defined as follows

$$PMGS=rPMGS_f, \qquad PF=rPF_f,$$

where r is the exchange rate (defined as units of domestic currency per unit of foreign currency) and the subscript f denotes magnitudes in foreign currency.

As our sample period covers both fixed exchange rates and managed float the fact that the exchange rate is not explicitly considered reflects the assumption that the behavioural functions present in the model have not been significantly altered by the change-over from the fixed exchange rate regime to the managed float (+). If the empirical analysis rejects this assumption, then the switch in the exchange rate regime will have to be dealt with. This can be accomplished either by introducing dummy variables or by means of more sophisticated methods, such as the switching function suggested by Wymer (1979) as a general method of coping with models which contemplate two different states of the economy, each described by different behavioural functions.

We can anticipate that the empirical analysis did not refute our assumption. Therefore the model can also be used, if the case, for simulations which involve the exchange rate.

(+) In other words, and by way of example, economic agents react to PMGS as such rather than to r and $PMGS_f$ separately.

3. Steady-state, stability, and sensitivity

Since this is a medium-term model, it is important to check that it possesses an economically meaningful steady-state solution. This also helps as a check on the mathematical consistency of the model itself and as a source of cross-equation restrictions on the parameters which may prove useful during estimation.

The results concerning the steady-state growth rates of the endogenous variables are summarized in Table 3, where λ_1=growth rate of PMGS, λ_2= growth rate of PF, λ_3=growth rate of YF, λ_5=time trend in W. Space limitations prevent us from discussing these results, the steady-state

TABLE 3

STEADY-STATE GROWTH RATES

Variable	Growth rate
C,K,$\tilde{Y}$,MGS,XGS,Y,V,G,T/P	$\beta_{10}(\lambda_2-\lambda_1)+\beta_{11}\lambda_3$
P,PXGS	λ_1
W	$\beta_{18}\lambda_1+\lambda_5$
M^S,A	$\beta_5\lambda_1+\beta_6[\beta_{10}(\lambda_2-\lambda_1)+\beta_{11}\lambda_3]$
R,NFA	$\lambda_1+\beta_{10}(\lambda_2-\lambda_1)+\beta_{11}\lambda_3$
k,r_{TIT},a,m	0

levels and the comparative dynamics of the model. We can only emphasize two points. The first is that all the real variables grow at a rate which, given the elasticities, depends only on the rest of the world variables, namely on the rate of growth of world output (term $\beta_{11}\lambda_3$), account being taken of the behaviour of the home country's competitiveness [term $\beta_{10}(\lambda_2-\lambda_1)$]. This is consistent with the "export-led" way of looking at growth. The second point is that M^S and A on the one hand, and R and NFA on the other, may grow at different rates. Therefore if one wishes all the financial variables to grow at the same rate, one must impose the additional constraint $\lambda_1+[\beta_{10}(\lambda_2-\lambda_1)+\beta_{11}\lambda_3]=\beta_5\lambda_1+\beta_6[\beta_{10}(\lambda_2-\lambda_1)+\beta_{11}\lambda_3]$ (a particular case of which would be $\beta_5=\beta_6=1$), but this is not required for the existence of the steady-state.

We now turn to the empirical part of our study("). Some of the parameters included in the model were restricted during estimation (either according to *a priori* information or because the value of the parameter obtained in earlier stages of estimation did not differ significantly from the value to which it was eventually constrained), and cross-equation constraints were imposed according to steady-state analysis results. All these restrictions increased the efficiency of the estimates.

TABLE 4

ESTIMATED ADJUSTMENT PARAMETERS

Parameter	Entering equation number	Point estimate	Asymptotic standard error	Mean time lag (quarters)	Standard error of mean time lag
α_1	(1)	0.945	0.186	1.06	0.21
α_2	(1)	0.330	0.078		
α_3	(2)	1.350	0.242	0.74	0.13
α_4	(2)	0.151	0.063		
α_5	(4)	1.285	0.189	0.78	0.11
α_6	(4)	0.881	0.154		
α_7	(5)	0.712	0.123	1.41	0.24
α_8	(6)	1.909	0.323	0.52	0.09
α_9	(6)	0.531	0.084		
α_{10}	(7)	0.073	0.030	13.61	5.65
α_{11}	(7)	0.495	0.183		
α_{12}	(8)	0.279	0.068	3.59	0.87
α_{13}	(9)	0.517	0.179	1.93	0.67
α_{14}	(10)	0.120	0.051		
α_{15}	(10)	0.076	0.019	13.11	3.30
α_{16}	(11)	4.429	1.009	0.23	0.05

(")The model was linearized in the logarithms about sample means in its non-linear parts [pertaining to eqs. (12) and (14)]. The continuous log-linear model was then reduced to a stochastically equivalent discrete analogue according to the procedure explained in Gandolfo (1981, ch. 3, especially §3.3.2), which was estimated by using the FIML program "RESIMUL" developed by Wymer. The subsequent stability and sensitivity analyses were performed by means of his "CONTINEST" program.

α_{17}	(12)	0.077	0.027	12.97	4.64
α_{18}	(13)	3.524	0.752	0.28	0.06
α_{19}	(14)	1.398	0.299	0.72	0.15
α_{20}	(15)	0.238	0.067	4.20	1.19
α'	(2)	0.059	0.004	16.99	1.15
α''	(11)	0.009	0.003	106.96	33.69

TABLE 5

OTHER ESTIMATED PARAMETERS

Parameter	Entering equation number	Point estimate	Asymptotic standard error
β_1	(1)	-1.292	0.340
β_2	(1)	-2.442	0.835
β_3	(1)	0^*	—
β_4	(1),(10)	-0.564	0.146
β_5	(1),(10)	0.998	0.098
β_6	(1),(10)	1.454	0.173
β_7	(4)	0.723	0.113
β_8	(4)	0.701	0.092
β_9	(4)	0.890	0.126
β_{10}	(5)	0.245	0.135
β_{11}	(5)	0.678	0.013
β_{12}	(5)	1.018	0.059
β_{13}	(7)	0.404	0.178
β_{14}	(7)	0.536	0.130
β_{15}	(7)	0^*	—
β_{16}	(8)	0.758	0.133
β_{17}	(8)	0.260	0.105
β_{18}	(9)	0.583	0.085
β_{19}	(11)	-4.997	0.611
β_{20}	(12)	0.409	0.289
β_{21}	(12)	-0.030	0.127
β_{22}	(12)	0.755	0.256
β_{23}	(12)	0.403	0.195

β_{24}	(12)	3.149	1.233
β_{25}	(14)	0.396	0.064
η	(3)	0.107	0.042
λ_5	(9)	0.021	0.002
λ_y	(13)	0.0058	0.0001
δ_1	(13)	-0.004	0.005
δ_2	(13)	-0.155	0.090
δ_3	(13)	-0.025	0.027
δ_4	(13)	-0.025	0.018
$\log\gamma_1$	(1)	-0.478	0.059
$\log\gamma_2$	(1),(10)	-7.907	1.726
$\log\gamma_3$	(2),(5)	2.230	0.109
$\log\gamma_4$	(4)	-0.536	1.252
$\log\gamma_5$	(4),(6)	-2.717*	—
$\log\gamma_6$	(5)	0*	—
$\log\gamma_7$	(7)	0.358	0.145
$\log\gamma_8$	(8)	0.097	0.028
$\log\gamma_9$	(9)	-0.425	0.038
$\log\gamma_{10}$	(10)	0*	—
$\log\gamma_{11}$	(11)	-23.391	1.674
$\log\gamma_{12}$	(12)	-5.568	2.309
γ_{13}	(13)	1.046	0.035
$\log\gamma_{14}$	(14)	-3.287	0.628
$\log\gamma_{15}$	(15)	-1.827	0.026

*Value imposed

On the whole, estimation results (sample period: 1960-I to 1980-IV) are satisfactory. Of 64 estimated parameters, 56 are significantly different from zero on asymptotic tests (10 at the 5% level and 46 at the 1% level); only three have an incorrect sign. It is also noteworthy that these results were obtained by constraining only five out of sixty-nine parameters to a given value. The Carter-Nagar system R_w^2 statistic

(Carter and Nagar, 1977) is 0.483, and the associated χ^2 value is 1046 with 66 df: therefore, the hypothesis that the model as a whole is not consistent with the data is rejected.

Space limitations preclude a full discussion of parameter estimates; in any case, these are preliminary and subject to revision. However, we should like to make two considerations. The first is that most unsatisfactory results (in the sense that parameter estimates have incorrect signs and/or are not significantly different from zero) are concentrated in eq. (13), the monetary authorities' reaction function. This is not surprising, as the Italian monetary authorities have been burdened with the care of a large number of targets, although obviously not always at the same time and with the same weights (represented by the δ's). In other words, it is very likely that the "true" δ's have taken on different values in different unknown periods of our sample. But in eq. (13) they are forced to have a constant value over the whole sample period, and this might explain why their estimates turn out not to be significantly different from zero. This is a serious problem, and work is under way on this issue.

The second consideration concerns the α's. The higher (lower) α is, the faster (slower) will the variable adjust to its desired or partial equilibrium value. To have an idea of the empirical meaning of "fast" and "slow" one can refer to the mean time-lags (defined as $1/\alpha$), which give the time needed to eliminate about 63 percent of the divergence between actual and partial equilibrium values (Table 4).

The point estimates of the adjustment speeds allow a ranking of the variables between "high motion" and "slow motion" ones('). Also note that such a ranking can be tested by using the usual statistical tests on the significance of a difference; for instance we can test the hypothesis that $\alpha_j > \alpha_i$ by testing whether $\alpha_j - \alpha_i$ is significantly greater than zero.

The lowest adjustment speed (α") is that of the stock of bank advances

---

(')If one wishes to refer to the "adiabatic approximation" discussed by Medio (1983), one could refer to "slaved" (high motion) and "ordering" (slow motion) variables, assuming that the former are always near equilibrium and that the motion of the model is determined by the latter.

A to its desired value. The mean time-lag is extremely high (over 26 years), although highly significant. However, as sensitivity analysis suggests (see later), the two-stage adjustment hypothesis for bank advances embodied in eq. (11) is probably to be rejected and so not much weight should be attached to this result.

If we discard α'', estimation results show that there is a group of three variables — price of output, net foreign assets, fixed capital stock (^) — whose mean time-lag is considerably larger than those of the other variables (over four years). If we concentrated our attention on the last two we would obtain the information that real and financial accumulation variables "slave" (to use the "adiabatic" terminology) all the others. A result which is certainly realistic and consistent with the medium term approach followed in our model.

We now give a summary of the stability and sensitivity properties of the model; these are particularly important when the model is to be used for policy simulations.

Table 6 presents the estimates of the characteristic roots of the model (previously log-linearized about its steady state), together with their asymptotic standard errors. The damping period is the time required for about 63 per cent of the initial deviation to be eliminated (of course the damping period is defined only for stable roots). The period of the cycle corresponding to the complex roots is defined in the usual way.

TABLE 6

CHARACTERISTIC ROOTS OF THE MODEL

Root	Asymptotic standard error	Damping period (quarters)	Period of cycle (quarters)
-1.373	0.320	0.728	

(^)Also α_{15} shows a mean time-lag of a similar magnitude. In our opinion α_{15} may be considered an adjustment speed since it indicates the speed at which the interest rate adjusts to the partial equilibrium value $\gamma_{10}r_f$, the latter being determined by the monetary authorities in order to keep the domestic rate in line with the foreign "representative" rate. However, eq. (10) contains also a term depending on excess demand for money, to show that the interest rate is only partially policy determined and, for this reason, α_{15} cannot be a "pure" adjustment speed.

-0.744	0.170	1.344	
-0.819	0.166	1.221	
-0.429	0.080	2.331	
-0.194	0.031	5.159	
-0.236	0.078	4.234	
-0.099	0.025	10.115	
-0.007	0.002	139.475	
-1.088 ±0.994	0.391 ,0.628	0.919	6.321
-1.033 ±0.168	0.234 ,0.130	0.968	37.487
-0.499 ±0.091	0.128 ,0.058	2.005	69.182
-0.0028±0.040	0.0008,0.108	359.217	136.528
-0.077 ±0.002	0.386 ,0.0005	13.016	3986.526
0.0029±0.004	0.0088,0.0132	—	1429.355

All the real characteristic roots are negative, and all the complex roots have negative real parts, except the last pair. This, however, gives rise to a cycle so mildly undamped and having so long a period as to be negligible for all practical purposes. Also, the real part of this pair of complex roots is not significantly positive on the usual tests at any reasonable level of significance(¨). This indicates that the hypothesis that the steady state is asymptotically stable cannot be rejected.

Therefore we can conclude that our model gives rise to a stable cyclical growth behaviour, which is certainly the type of movement which Italy (and most other industrialized countries) experienced in the period under consideration. It should also be pointed out that, depending on the conditions determining the arbitrary constants in the general solution of the linearized model, in certain cases the cyclical components may also bring about a decrease in the level of the relevant variables (real output, for instance). This would not be inconsistent with the most recent past and with the possible future behaviour of some indus-

(¨)As a matter of fact also the real part of the last but one pair of complex roots is not significantly different from zero. It would be interesting to examine the reasons and implications (for example for the study of critical points) of this fact more deeply, but this lies outside the scope of the present paper.

trialized countries.

The importance of <u>sensitivity analysis</u> has already been stressed in the introduction. Among its possible applications, one seems to be of interest to the supporters of the synergetics principle (Medio 1983, Silverberg 1983, and references therein). According to this principle, when one assumes that certain critical parameters are changed and the system moves from stability to instability, only a few characteristic roots become positive in real part. By means of sensitivity analysis one can find out whether such parameters exist (instead of simply assuming that they do) and establish which they are; furthermore one can also determine the change in the characteristic roots which is determined by a given change in the parameter.

Since there are 20 characteristic roots and 64 estimated parameters, the complete sensitivity matrix, which contains the partial derivatives of each characteristic root with respect to each parameter, is a 20x64 matrix. We therefore decided at this stage to concentrate on the search for the causes of the possible instability discussed above. This search, if fruitful, could suggest ways to reformulate the model, for the presence of unstable roots in a model of this type may also be due to a structural defect or mis-specification (Gandolfo, 1981).

Now, the parameters which appeared to have a crucial effect on the last pair of complex conjugate roots turned out to be α_{14} and α'' (Table 7)

TABLE 7

SENSITIVITY ANALYSIS WITH RESPECT TO SELECTED PARAMETERS

Characteristic root (μ)	Partial derivative with respect to α_{14} ($\partial\mu/\partial\alpha_{14}$) Real, imaginary	Partial derivative with respect to α'' ($\partial\mu/\partial\alpha''$) Real, imaginary
-1.3728	0.0279	0.5498
-0.7439	0.0016	0.0668
-0.8190	-0.0003	0.0008
-0.4290	0.0011	0.0142
-0.1938	0.0027	0.0663
-0.2362	0.0014	0.0168

-0.0989	-0.0407	-0.9273
-0.0072	0.0038	-0.0080
-1.0876±0.9940	-0.0036, 0.0182	-0.1558, 0.2375
-1.0331±0.1676	-0.0225,-0.1371	0.2323,-1.1847
-0.4986±0.0908	0.0196, 0.0100	0.2880, 0.1575
-0.0028±0.0400	0.0836, 0.1515	-0.7185, 0.8926
-0.0768±0.0016	0.0049, 0.0051	0.0990,-0.1459
0.0029±0.0044	0.1990,-0.3620	0.3283,-0.0106

As regards α_{14}, a decrease in this parameter from 0.120 to 0.106 (namely -0.014 in absolute terms and -12% in relative terms) would be enough to bring the real part of the last pair of complex roots into the stable region. Note also that this decrease would not appreciably affect the stable nature of the other roots, for these would remain in the stable region. Therefore one of the causes of the possible instability would seem to be too high a reaction of the rate of interest to the excess demand for money.

As regards α'', a 94% decrease in this parameter (from 0.009 to 0.0005, namely almost to zero) would be required to bring the real part of the last pair of complex roots into the stable region. However, this decrease would cause the real part of the last but two pair of complex roots to pass from the stable to the unstable region (all the other roots would remain in the stable region). Since the presence of α'' is due to the assumption of a second-order adjustment process in the supply of bank advances(") , the suggestion that seems to derive from sensitivit analysis is that such an assumption might be unwarranted and, consequently, that the specification of eq. (11) ought to be carefully investigated.

(") The assumption is that the gap between $\underline{\hat{A}}$ and $\underline{A}$ does not give rise directly to the actual rate of change in bank advances, but rather is the determinant of their desired rate of change $\underline{\hat{a}}$, namely $\hat{a} \equiv D\log\hat{A} = \alpha''\log(\hat{A}/A)$. We then assume that banks adjust the actual rate of change in bank advances $\underline{a} = D\log\underline{A}$ to the desired rate $\underline{\hat{a}}$ according to the partial adjustment equation $Da = \alpha_{16}(\hat{a}-a) = \alpha_{16}[\alpha''\log(\hat{A}/A)-a]$, which is eq. (11) in Table 1. If, on the contrary, one assumed the usual first order adjustment process, then the equation would simply be $D\log A = \alpha_{16}\log(\hat{A}/A)$.

4. Conclusion

Once one has a satisfactory model at hand, one can use it for simulating different policies. Since the model is expressed as a system of non-linear differential equations, the simulations can be performed either by using the linearized discrete analogue that has been employed for estimation or by using the original non-linear continuous model. For the reasons expounded at some length in Gandolfo (1981, ch. 3, section 3.4) we think that the second alternative is preferable.
Although we have performed several policy simulations, we decided not to burden this paper with them[^], for its main purpose was to show how the gap between theoretical modelling and econometric modelling can be eliminated by means of macrodynamic medium-term econometric models, with a small number of equations but embodying much more economic theory than is usually possible, specified and estimated in continuous time. We hope to have been able, if not to convince the reader, at least to illustrate our point clearly.

References

Bergstrom, A.R., ed., 1976, Statistical Inference in Continuous Time Economic Models (North-Holland, Amsterdam).

Bergstrom, A.R. and C.R. Wymer, 1976, A Model of Disequilibrium Neoclassical Growth and its Application to the United Kingdom, in A.R. Bergstrom (ed.), 1976, pp. 267-327.

Carter, R.A.L. and A.L. Nagar, 1977, Coefficients of Correlation for Simultaneous Equation Systems, Journal of Econometrics 6, 39-50.

Gandolfo, G., 1981, Qualitative Analysis and Econometric Estimation of Continuous Time Dynamic Models (North-Holland, Amsterdam).

Gandolfo, G. and P.C. Padoan, 1982, Policy Simulations with a Continuous Time Macrodynamic Model of the Italian Economy: A Preliminary Analysis, Journal of Economic Dynamics and Control 4, 205-24.

(^)A few simulations with our model are presented in Gandolfo and Padoan (1983).

Gandolfo, G. and P.C. Padoan, 1983, Inflation and Economic Policy in an Open Economy: Some Simulations with a Dynamic Macroeconometric Model paper presented at the 4th IFAC-IFORS Conference on "The Modelling and Control of National Economies" (Washington, D.C., June 17-19, 1983), forthcoming in the Proceedings (Pergamon Press).

Goodwin, R.M., 1948, Secular and Cyclical Aspects of the Multiplier and the Accelerator, in: Income, Employment and Public Policy: Essays in Honor of A.H. Hansen (Norton, New York); reprinted in R.M. Goodwin (1982).

Goodwin, R.M., 1982, Essays in Economic Dynamics (Macmillan, London).

Jonson, P.D. and R.G. Trevor, 1981, Monetary Rules: A Preliminary Analysis, Economic Record **57**, 150-67.

Knight, M.D. and C.R. Wymer, 1978, A Macrodynamic Model of the United Kingdom, IMF Staff Papers **25**, 742-78.

Koopmans, T.C., 1950, Models Involving a Continuous Time Variable , in: Koopmans, T.C., ed., Statistical Inference in Dynamic Economic Models, Cowles Commission for Research in Economics, Monograph 10 (Wiley, New York).

Medio, A., 1983, Synergetics and Dynamic Economic Models, in this volume.

Reserve Bank of Australia, 1977, Conference in Applied Economic Research, (RBA, Sydney).

Silverberg, G., 1983, Embodied Technical Progress in a Dynamic Economic Model: The Self-Organization Paradigm, in this volume.

Wymer, C.R., 1976, Continuous Time Models in Macro-economics: Specification and Estimation. Paper presented at the SSRC-Ford Foundation Conference on Macroeconomic Policy and Adjustment in Open Economies (Ware, England, April 28-May 1).

Wymer, C.R., various dates,TRANSF, RESIMUL, CONTINEST, PREDIC, APREDIC computer programs and relative manuals; Supplement No. 3 (Oct. 1979) on solution of non-linear differential equation systems.

Wymer, C.R., 1979, The Use of Continuous Time Models in Economics, unpublished manuscript.

AN ECONOMETRIC MODEL OF THE SHARE OF WAGES IN NATIONAL INCOME: UK 1855-1965

Meghnad Desai
London School of Economics
Houghton Street, London WC2A 2AE

Earlier versions of the paper were presented to the World Congress of the Econometric Society at Toronto (1975) and to the AUTE meeting at Exeter (1979) as well as at seminars in Cambridge, Southampton and Leeds. I am grateful to David Blake for much research help, to Stephen Glaister, Steve Nickell and Malcolm Pemberton for clarification on questions of theory. This research was supported over its long gestation period by the UK SSRC in a series of programmes to the LSE econometrics group - SEPDEM (1973-1976) PQE (1976-1979) MIME (1979-1982) and DEMEIC (1982-1985).

A piece of conventional wisdom in economics for about fifty years up to the beginning of the 1970's was that the share of labour in national income in developed capitalist economies was constant. Keynes called it 'a well-known statistical phenomenon...', '... one of the most surprising, yet best-established, facts in the whole range of economic statistics' and 'a bit of a miracle'. (Keynes (1939)).

Keynes was citing Bowley's statistical findings for the UK and similar work by Paul Douglas and Simon Kuznets for the US. This conistancy inspired much theoretical work to explain it. Thus the Cobb-Douglas production function in a competitive neoclassical framework or Kalecki's work on the degree of monopoly are alternative explanations of this constancy. Both the neoclassical explanation, involving the assumption of an aggregate production function, and Kalecki's theory have elicited scepticism.[1] But as an empirical fact, constancy of shares was accepted by neoclassical growth theorists, as well as Keynesian and post-Keynesian macroeconomists.

The upsurge of inflation in the 1960's and 1970's has brought to our notice the possibility that it is perhaps the changes in the share of wages which may account for recent price and income trends. Thus Glyn and Sutcliffe brought to general attention the declining share of profits, now admitted to be a more widespread phenomenon for the developed countries (Glyn and Sutcliffe (1972)). It is to the merit of Mr Goodwin that his is perhaps the only theoretical model which takes the variations in the share

---

1 On the aggregate production function controversy the literature is large and well known. As to Kalecki's theory, early doubts were expressed by Keynes (1939). See also Mitra (1981) which is a reprint of his 1952 book.

of labour as the central variable and explains a cycle in the share and in aggregate economic activity in the context of a growing economy. (Goodwin (1967), see also Desai (1973) for an extension).

The actual experience of the UK economy, summarised in Table 1, shows much greater variability than was noticed previously. In terms of quinquennial averages, the share of wages (u) does show cycles around an upward trend. The share seems to move sluggish but if we look at the percentage change in the share (Dln u) we are able to discern the variability much more clearly. Thus starting from around 50% in the 1850's, it declines to 48% in the 1870's and then recovers in the long depression of 1873-1896. By the outbreak of World War I, a figure of around 55% is typical for the wage share. In this period which was thought to epitomise stability, the percentage change in U ranges from -3.8 to 6.2, the range being a fifth of the mean value. World War I, with the experience of full employment for the first time since the 1870's and the lowest recorded unemployment until then for three years consecutively, gave a distinct upward push (+13%) to the wage share. In the interwar period, despite the high unemployment of the 1920's and the Great Depression of the 1930's, the share remains around 60%. Percentage variations in the share show a smaller range between -3.7 and 1.8 (excluding the 1915-19 quinquennium). The low range of variation in the share contrasts with the tremendous variation in unemployment in the interwar period. World War II restored ful employment and gave another five percent boost to the share. The postwar years added to this high level and correspondingly low variation in unemployment. King has recentl estimated the share as being well in the 70% range in the 1970's (King (1975)). (Our data are from Feinstein (1972), See also Phelps-Brown and Weber (1953), Phelps-Brown and Browne (1972)).

Having established the variability in the share of wages as an empirical fact, let us look at Goodwin's theoretical model which purports to explain it in terms of the struggle for shares in total income between capital and labour along the lines of Marx's model of the class struggle.

Goodwin proposes a Phillips-curve-type bargaining equation in <u>real</u> wages (w) and uses the employment rate (v) rather than the unemployment rate as the independent variable. The equation is then a <u>linearised</u> version of the Phillips curve as follows

$$D \ln w = -\gamma + \rho v \qquad (1)$$

[D = d/dt. All variables are in continuous time, eg, w(t), v(t) but the (t) will be omitted]. The share of wages in national income (u) can then be defined in the context of this one-good model as the ratio of real wage (w) to the average product per worker (a). The average product is assumed to grow at an exogenous rate α_1. So we get

$$D \ln u \;=\; D \ln w - \alpha_1 = -(\gamma+\alpha_1) + \rho v \qquad (2)$$

Equation (2) is one of the two basic equations of the model. The proportion of the labour force employed (v) is arrived at by making the assumptions that (i) the capital-output ratio σ is constant (ii) there is no depreciation of capital (iii) all profits are invested. Thus if q is output and k is capital stock, we have

$$D \ln q \;=\; D \ln k \;=\; (1-u)/\sigma \qquad (3)$$

Let the labour force (n) grow at a constant proportion α_2, and let actual employment be denoted by ℓ, then we have

$$D \ln v \;=\; D \ln \ell - D \ln n \;=\; D \ln q - D \ln a - D \ln n$$

$$= [1/\sigma - (\alpha_1+\alpha_2)] - 1/\sigma\, u \qquad (4)$$

Equations (2) and (4) form a <u>closed, nonlinear dynamic</u> model of the growth cycle in the share of wages in national income and employment. It has a steady-state which is given by setting (2) and (4) equal to zero. Using asterisks to denote steady state values, we get

$$v^* \;=\; (\gamma+\alpha_1)/\rho; \qquad u^* = 1 - \sigma(\alpha_1+\alpha_2)$$

The actual trajectories of the system form a closed cycle around the singular point - a centre - given by the u*, v* coordinates. This is easily checked by relabelling the variables as $z_1 = \ln u$, $z_2 = \ln v$. Then we can rewrite (2) and (4) as

$$Dz_1 \;=\; -a + b \exp(z_2) \qquad (2a)$$

where $a \;=\; (\gamma+\alpha),\; b = \rho$

$$Dz_2 \;=\; c - d \exp(z_1) \qquad (4a)$$

where $c \;=\; [1/\sigma - (\alpha_1+\alpha_2)], \qquad d = 1/\sigma$

Equations (2a) and (4a) can be compared with the classic predator-prey model of fish populations well known in mathematical biology. The only qualification to make, an important one as we shall see later, is that Goodwin's variables are defined to be in the (0,1) interval.

There are only five parameters $\gamma, \rho, \sigma, \alpha_1, \alpha_2$ in the two equations. The dynamics of the model can be analysed by expanding (2) and (4) around the steady-state. The economy has a steady growth rate equal to the natural growth rate $(\alpha_1+\alpha_2)$ and wages grow at the same rate as productivity in the steady-state. As Figure 1 shows the steady-state is never reached if the economy starts at an initial point other than u^*, v^*.

The pair of nonlinear differential equations (2a) and (4a) has imaginary roots. Thus while $u = 0$, $v = 0$ is one solution of the system, the singular point (u^*,v^*) in the positive orthant is a centre. But this qualitative property of the system, ie, that there will be cycles everywhere in the positive orthant around (u^*,v^*), is not a robust one. The Volterra-Lotka system is structurally unstable in the sense that small variations in the parameters will alter the properties of the system. Thus it is clear that in equation (1) if we add a term in $\ln w$ (say, to incorporate real wage resistance then equation (2) ((2a)) will have non-zero coefficients for $\ln u(z_1)$. Similarly if the constancy of the capital-output ratio is relaxed to incorporate the effects of employment variation on output growth, equation (4)((4a)) will have non-zero terms for say $\ln v\ (z_2)$. These two modifications will radically alter the qualitative properties of the system and the singular point may change from being a centre to being a stable or unstable focus depending on the coefficients.

From an econometric point of view, the structural instability means that one should tes the prior zero restrictions imposed on the equations by Goodwin as a test of the validity of the model. If the data do not reject the zero restrictions, then one may u the parameter estimates to generate predictions of the length of the growth cycle impli by the model, which was shown by Atkinson (1969) to be

$$\theta = 2\pi[\rho/\sigma\ v^*u^*]^{-1/2} \tag{5}$$

To allow us to test the prior restrictions, it is best to take a slightly generalised version of the Goodwin model proposed in an earlier paper (Desai (1973)). But econometric investigation also compels the introduction of stochastic terms to the equations. Indeed once we move to an econometric specification, the structural instability of the Volterra-Lotka system becomes a liability since the probability of certain parameters being exactly zero is negligible. While there has been some simulation work in a stochastic version of the predator-prey scheme (Bartlett (1959)), a full stochastic specification will take us into the abstruse area of Ito processes which we wish to avoid. A compromise would therefore be to take the 1973 version and augment it by adding error terms. But before we do that there are some further considerations to be taken into account.

First, as we have already mentioned, the Goodwin model in its original version as well as in the Desai extension, is a closed, nonlinear, dynamic (CND) model. This makes it econometrically a challenging one to estimate. Since the model is closed, there are no exogenous variables in the model (except implicitly the time trend). The model is nonlinear, nonlinear in parameters as well as in variables. It is dynamic in that its constituent components are nonlinear differential equations. If it were not closed, the parameters of the model could be estimated by nonlinear maximum likelihood methods. If it were not nonlinear, then it would be the continuous analogue of the closed bivariate models of the Box-Jenkins type. Its dynamic nature creates further estimation problems. The lack of exogenous variables implies that we only have lagged endogenous variables available as instruments. But their admissibility depends on the absence of high order vector autoregressive processes in the error terms. If the zero restrictions imposed by Goodwin were valid, then the ability of the system to generate closed cycles will depend crucially on the errors behaving in a self-correcting fashion to keep the variables closed to the deterministic trajectory, ie, they would be required to be vector autoregressive with stable roots. But then this is of no help in testing the validity of the restrictions since if errors were vector autoregressive there are no admissible instruments. The only ways to escape the horns of the dilemma is to ignore the problem, or to modify the model to incorporate some outside influences. We shall see that the adaptation of the theoretical scheme for econometric estimation suggests some natural modifications.

Our first modification allows for the fact that wage bargains are in money terms and not in real terms. This leads to the addition of a variable measuring inflation. But here again to capture an important feature of the real world, we have to allow for a distinction between the rate of growth of retail prices (p_r) and the rate of growth of the price of output (p_q). Another modification has to be that while the theoretical model assumes labour to be homogeneous, we have observations on employment ratio in terms of persons but not hours. To measure total labour income, we need to explain earnings (e) rather than wages. Lastly we have to allow for price expectations in the wage bargain. These three modifications lead to an econometric version of equation (1).

$$\Delta \ln e_t = -\gamma_1 + \rho_1 v_t + \eta_1 \Delta \ln p^e_{rt} + \varepsilon_{1t} \tag{6}$$

$$\Delta \ln p^e_{rt} = \lambda_1 \Delta \ln p_{rt} + (1-\lambda_1)\Delta \ln p^e_{rt-1} + \varepsilon_{2t} \tag{7}$$

In equations (6) and (7), we have already approximated the differential equations by difference equations using a naive approximation. (Alternative methods of approximation do not make much difference to the estimates). Equation (6) explains the growth of money earnings ($\Delta \ln e_t$) in terms of employment and the expected rate of inflation of consumer goods. Equation (7) then specifies an adaptive expectations scheme. If $\eta_1 = 1$ and $\lambda_1 = 1$ then (6) and (7) collapse to a discrete version of equation (1). So this specification allows us to test those restrictions. Combining (6) and (7) we get

$$\Delta^2 \ln e_t = -\gamma_1\lambda_1 + \rho_1\Delta v_t + \rho_1\lambda_1 v_{t-1} + \eta_1\lambda_1\Delta \ln p_{rt} - \lambda_1\Delta \ln e_{t-1} + \varepsilon_{3t} \qquad (8)$$

In equation (8) $\varepsilon_{3t} = (\Delta\varepsilon_{1t} - \lambda_1\varepsilon_{1t-1} + \varepsilon_{2t})$. Apart from the specification of employment rather than unemployment and its presence in a linear rather than a nonlinear form (8) is the expectations-augmented Friedman-Phelps Phillips curve.

To get to the share of labour, we have to obtain an estimate of α, the rate of growth of labour productivity. Since this is taken to be exogenous, we approximate it by a trend

$$\ln a_t = \alpha_o + \alpha_1 T + \varepsilon_{4t} \qquad (9)$$

where a_t is output per worker and T is trend taking a value of 1 in 1855 and 111 in 1965.

The price variable is endogenised by distinguishing between retail price p_r, output price p_q and import price p_m. Cheap imports of wage goods played a crucial part in maintaining a high standard of living in the UK economy during this period. So we captured this feature by taking p_r to be a weighted sum of p_q and p_m. Then we explain output price determination in a cost plus mark-up equation following the work of Godley and Nordhaus, Sargan et al. (Godley and Nordhaus (1972), Sargan (1980)).

Thus we have

$$\ln p_{rt} = \delta_o + \delta_1 \ln p_{qt} + \delta_2 \ln p_{mt} + \varepsilon_{5t} \qquad (10)$$

$$\Delta \ln p_{qt} = \lambda_2[\ln \xi + \ln(e/a)_t - \ln p_{qt-1}] + \varepsilon_{6t} \qquad (11)$$

ξ is the mark-up factor and e/a unit labour cost. Thus equation (11) says that in equilibrium $p_q^* = \xi e/a$.

We also modify the employment generating side of the model by allowing for excess capacity to take form of a variable capital-output ratio. This is done by making the capital output ratio a function of the level of employment

$$\ln \sigma_t = \ln \sigma^* - \mu \ln v_t + \varepsilon_{7t} \qquad (12)$$

The introduction of these additional equations makes the model much larger and much less elegant than the original Goodwin model. We still retain the assumptions that all profits are invested for simplicity since the specification of an investment function would vastly complicate the model.

In our econometric model, we now have five equations (8), (9), (10), (11) and (12) and the modification that we have made give us two exogenous variables $\ln p_m$ and T. We may be able to use lagged endogenous variables as instruments if the errors are not autoregressive and if we can reject the Goodwin restrictions.

Our data series come from Feinstein's National Income, Expenditure and Output of the United Kingdom 1855-1965 (Feinstein (1972)). We have to somehow pretend that our highly aggregative model with one good, homogeneous labour, malleable capital stock, constant rates of growth of labour force and productivity, no government sector is in some sense an approximation to the UK economy for this long period. Data on average weekly wage rates (m) and average weekly wage earnings (e) both in nominal terms and after deflating by retail prices are given in Feinstein, Table 65 (T140-141). Other variables such as output per worker, capital-output ratio (Table 20, T51-53), unemployment (Table 57) and GDP deflator and import price indices are also available from the same source.

With these qualifications, let us look at the scatter diagram for v and u in Figure 2 for the 111 observations. The period up to World War I somewhat resembles a compressed version of Figure 1. There is a steady shift to the right (rising u) even during these years. But in this period, there are comparable movements in both the variables. In the inter-war period the movement in u is very small compared to the yo-yo like swing in v. The post-war period shows little movement in v and a horizontal shift in u. (Recent years would show greater movement in v.)[2]

The diagram appears to indicate that the first sixty years form a separate subsample with regular cycles in u and v, with a different economic structure in the subsequent period. So we estimated the parameters of our model for five different combinations of our sample. These are

(0)	The Entire Sample	1855-1965
(1)	Nineteenth Century	1855-1913 (Subsample 1)
(2)	Twentieth Century	1914-1965 (Subsample 2)
(3)	Inter-War Period	1914-1947 (Subsample 3)
(4)	Post-War Period	1948-1965 (Subsample 4)

No observations were dropped and no dummy variable added for the war or postwar years. This is because the war years, especially those of World War I, crucially affected the

2 The solution of the Goodwin model, using estimates of equations (2) and (4), restricting u and v to lie in the interval (0,1) and beginning with the 1855 actual values of u and v mimics the actual historical path (Figure 2) quite well, giving a cycle of 30 years about an equilibrium solution $u^*=.93$, $v^*=.93$.

context of industrial bargaining in the UK. This was because the trade unions were granted official acceptance in the tripartite committees as a part of the mobilisation effort and also because these years 1916-1918 were the first years, since recorded data became available to have an unemployment rate consistently below 1%. Our data period overlaps considerably with that used by Phillips in his 1958 paper so we tried to follow as far as possible his grouping. Thus the third subsample 1914-1947 is the same as Phillips' second period and so is the fourth subsample except that we have eight more observations. We have similarly a few more observations in the period before World War I which is the period over which Phillips estimated his famous curve. This will facilitate comparison with the results of Phillips (1958) and Lipsey (1960).[3]

Estimation was by OLS as well as by ALS which allowed for a possible first order autoregressive (1AR) process in the errors. In the latter case we use the likelihood ratio (LR) test for the autoregressive restrictions (χ_1^2). Where we detect possible simultaneous equations bias, we use instrumental variable (IV) estimation and also allow for a 1AR process using the GIVE program of Hendry (Hendry and Srba (1978)). In this case we test for the overidentifying restrictions using again the LR test (χ_2^2). (These econometric techniques are now well known so no further explanation seems necessary. See Desai (1976) for details). Since the presentation of results for five samples and four estimation methods is somewhat tedious, we present only the relevant estimate in each case. Thus if OLS (IV) estimates allow us to reject the hypothesis of 1AR then we do not present the ALS (AIV) results. If however the 1AR parameter (labelled β_i for the ith equation) is significantly different from zero, we give both OLS (IV) and ALS (AIV) results. We provide β_i estimates in each case whether they are significant or not. Where β_i are nonsignificant but there is simultaneity we give both OLS and IV estimates.

With these preliminaries we are ready to present our estimates. We first present the results for the restricted version of (6) and (7) where we impose the restriction $\lambda_1 = 1$ ie, replace p_r^e by p_r. The estimated equation is then

$$\Delta \ln e_t = -\gamma + \rho v_t + \eta \Delta \ln p_r + \varepsilon'_{1t} \tag{13}$$

We test for the autoregressive error process

---

3 I have earlier discussed the difference in Phillips' estimation method for his curve (which I therefore label the 'classic' Phillips curve) which was fitted to 1861-1913 and Lipsey's method, which was OLS and by which he fitted an equation to each of three subperiods 1861-1913, 1924-1947 and 1948-1957. In that paper, I fitted equations using Phillips' method of transforming the data. Now I am using untransformed data using methods similar to Lipsey's. (Desai (1975)).

$$\varepsilon'_{1t} = \beta_1 \varepsilon'_{1t-1} + \zeta_{1t} \tag{14}$$

Equations (13) and (14) were estimated by OLS for the five subperiods and the results are presented in Table 2. We can see that for the entire sample and the period before World War I (which incidentally coincides except for the first eight observations with the sample which Phillips used to fit his curve), we have evidence of the influence of the state of excess demand in the labour market on wage income outcomes. Thus $\hat{\rho}$ has a t value of 1.9 in the whole period and 3.5 in the Subsample 1. Notice also the contrast in the coefficient $\hat{\eta}$ of the inflation term. It is not significantly different from 1 in the entire sample at 95% level but it is barely so ie, very little of the distribution lies above the value of 1. In subsample 1, $\hat{\eta}$ is definitely significantly less than 1. The second subsample resembles the entire sample in the $\hat{\eta}$ is now not significantly different from 1 and $\hat{\rho}$ is not significantly different from zero. Thus the two subsamples present a contrast with the Phillips relationship holding for the period before World War I but the curve becoming horizontal in the period after World War I. The possibility that the Phillips curve may be <u>horizontal</u> has been advanced by the post-Keynesian school associated with Kalecki and Joan Robinson but not seriously entertained or tested in the literature. The Phelps-Friedman prediction of a vertical Phillips curve requires not only that η be unity but that ρ be non-zero ie, that there be a short run trade-off but no long run trade-off. Normally the effect of excess demand in the labour market on money (and real) wage growth has been taken so much for granted that if such an effect is not found, this is blamed on unemployment being a poor proxy for the excess demand for labour. In our case, using the same variable throughout, we see that it is still possible to have contrasting results for the various periods. The hypothesis of a horizontal Phillips curve is one that needs to be examined much more closely in future work.

Further subdivision of the second subsample reveals a surprising pattern. The first 'half' which includes the observations for the war years and immediate post war years (for both World Wars) shows a horizontal Phillips curve but the post Second World War period shows strong evidence of the Phillips relationship. Once again $\hat{\eta}$ is significantly less than unity and $\hat{\rho}$ is significantly different from zero and indeed very high in numerical terms compared to earlier periods.

For each of the samples except the first subsample, the $\bar{R}^2$ figures are fairly high and the Durbin Watson Statistic indicates the presence of some autocorrelation in the residuals. Before we discuss the ALS estimation, there are three aspects relating to equations (13) which are worth mentioning.

1) <u>Wages as against earnings as the dependent variable</u>: For each subsample we also fitted an equation using wages as the dependent variable. The results uniformly showed

a lower value for $\hat{\rho}$ and $\hat{\eta}$ compared to the earnings equation. (The only exception was $\hat{\eta}$ for the fourth subsample where it was higher in the wage equation compared to the earnings equation). Also the $\bar{R}^2$ as well as the DW was low in the wage equation. As an example, we had for the entire sample

$$\Delta lnm_t = 0,1076 + 0.1236 v_t + 0.7577\, \Delta lnp_{rt} \qquad \bar{R}^2 = 0.6521 \quad DW = 1.24$$
$$\qquad (1.08) \quad (1.18) \qquad (11.21) \qquad s = 0.0315 \tag{15a}$$

$$\Delta lne_t = 0.1493 + 0.1727 v_t + 0.8751\, \Delta lnp_{rt} \qquad \bar{R}^2 = 0.767 \quad DW = 1.45$$
$$\qquad (1.70) \quad (1.87) \qquad (14.64) \qquad s = 0.0278 \tag{15b}$$

Since the difference the growth rates of earnings and wages reflects hours worked, the implication is that hours worked have procyclical behaviour. While this is well known, the interesting implication is that in inflationary conditions, faced with a decline in the real wage rate a worker may recoup earnings by adjusting hours worked. Thus the presence of some money illusion in the wage equation ($\eta<1$) is not as irrational as it may seem, since this gap can be restored and this is reflected in real earnings growth.

2) <u>Nonlinear specification for the employment variable</u>: Following Phillips, one may wish to explore a nonlinear form for the influence of v on Δlne. This was done by respecifying (13) as

$$\Delta lne_t = -\bar{\gamma} + \bar{\rho}\,(lnv_t)^{-1} + \bar{\eta}\,\Delta lnp_{rt} \tag{13a}$$

(The bars over the parameters indicate an alternate specification and not their mean values). The results were again fairly similar to those for the linear case. Again, we cite for the entire sample,

$$\Delta lne_t = -0.0092 - 0.00014\,(lnv)^{-1} + 0.8694\, \Delta lnp_{rt} \qquad \bar{R}^2 = 0.711 \quad DW = 1.47$$
$$\qquad (2.51) \quad (2.28) \qquad (15.11) \qquad s = 0.0276 \tag{15c}$$

3) <u>Real earnings specification</u>: Relative to our specification (13), the Goodwin model imposes the restriction that $\eta=1$. We estimated the restricted version of (13) and by a likelihood ratio test of the restricted against the unrestricted version, we were unable to reject the restriction for the entire sample, for subsample 2 and subsample 3. We were able to reject it for subsamples 1 and 4. This is entirely consistent with the t values for $\hat{\eta}$ in Table 2 which is an equivalent Wald Test for the restriction. For the entire sample, we have

$$\Delta ln(e/p_r)_t = -0.0478 + 0.0647\, v_t \qquad \bar{R}^2 = -0.0029 \quad DW = 1.59$$
$$\qquad (0.64) \qquad (0.83) \qquad s = 0.0283 \tag{15d}$$

The ALS results are also given in Table 2 along side the OLS results. The $\chi^2(2)$ critical value for 95% confidence level is 5.99. Thus, we see that for the entire sample, there is an interesting conflict. Whereas $\hat{\beta}_1$ is significantly different from zero and so we can reject the null hypothesis $\hat{\beta}_1=0$, the implied restrictions are rejected. This indicates the need for dynamic respecification of equation (13) along the lines suggested in equations (6) and (7). The same is true of the second subsample 1914-1965 and of the third subsample 1914-1947. For the pre-World War I period, $\chi^2(2)$ is below the critical level and the t value for $\hat{\beta}_1 > 0$ and the implied restrictions are not rejected. In the last subsample, the likelihoods for the restricted and unrestricted were so similar (as can be seen from the S values) that we obtained a small negative χ^2 value. Here the t value for $\hat{\beta}_1$ is 1.43 and the evidence against β_1 is not so strong.

To summarise the ALS results on the earnings equation, it would seem that for the period of the classical Phillips curve, ie, the period before World War I on which Phillips based his curve, his results are still validated. There is an influence of (un)employment and the influence of prices is mild. This part of the nineteenth century was a period of deflation and UK terms of trade were improving making a gap between product wage and real wage in terms of wage goods. Thus an $\hat{\eta}$ coefficient of less than one is not merely due to money illusion but requires a more sophisticated interpretation. Surprisingly, the Phillips curve also fits well for the more recent years at least up to 1965 when much was made of it as a possible policy tool. The naive specification of (13) turns out to be validated by the data. While later observations are said to have departed from the Phillips curve pattern, its good fit for 1948-1965 is still remarkable.

By contrast, for the entire sample $\hat{\rho}$ is significantly different from zero and $\hat{\eta}$ not significantly less than one but the rejection of the autoregressive restrictions suggests dynamic misspecification. The 'interwar' period, which saw a much greater variation in prices and wages than either the first or the last subsample, yields a horizontal Phillips curve but again there is need for respecification.

The interwar result of a <u>horizontal</u> Phillips curve confirmed by the ALS result contrasts with the result for the interwar period obtained by Lipsey. In his 1960 follow-up of Phillips' work, Lipsey obtained similar wage-unemployment curves for the three periods 1862-1913, 1924-1947 and 1948-1957. This in a sense established the 'Phillips curve' as a constant relationship. As we pointed out before, using Phillips' method of transforming the data, the relationship between wage change and unemployment alters shape in each period. Lipsey's omission of the ten observations for 1914-1923 which saw tremendous variation in the wage change and price change led to distortion of the underlying relationship. By the same token, our own previous result failed to turn up the horizontal shape due to the transformation of the data. We now have a horizontal Phillips-Lipsey relationship for the interwar period which needs further examination (Lipsey (1960), Desai (1975). These extreme values for 1914-1923 are obvious in the scatter diagrams provided by Phillips (1958)).

As we mentioned above, the set of instruments available is small. Transformation of the differential equation to discrete form opens up the possibility of using lagged values of endogenous variables as instruments but given the evidence of autoregressive errors, the admissibility of these instruments is arguable. But for completeness, we did estimate equation (7) by IV methods treating both v_t and $\Delta \ln p_{rt}$ as endogenous. The instruments used were $\Delta \ln e_{-1}$, v_{-1}, $\Delta \ln p_{r-1}$, $\ln a_{-1}$, $\Delta \ln p_m$, $\Delta \ln p_{q-1}$.

The results were similar to OLS and ALS and AIV. The t values were in general lower as is to be expected but the broad pattern of size and significance of ρ and η across the subperiods remained. But when we carried out a test of the overidentifying restrictions implied by the availability of instruments, except in the case of 1855-1913 and 1948-1965, the tests rejected the restrictions. Thus to avoid proliferation of numbers in Table 2 we present only the χ^2 statistics for the LR test on over-identifying restrictions for IV and AIV. The test of these restrictions confirms what we know about the validity of the restrictions in this model already from ALS results.

The next stage then is to relax the restriction that $\lambda_1=1$. This brings us to equation (8) as a generalised version of equation (13). The estimates of equation (13) with an 1AR process for ε_{3t} are given in Table 3. The AR parameter is labelled $\hat{\beta}_3$. In its respecified form the equation residuals exhibited no autoregressive errors, whether the estimates were by OLS or by IV. We have thus confirmed that the observed residual serial correlation in estimates of equation (13) were not due to auto-regression in the errors but due to a dynamic misspecification. This is confirmed by the similarly of $\hat{\rho}$ and $\hat{\rho}_1$ in Table 2 and Table 3 as well as by a comparison of $\hat{\eta}$ and $\hat{\eta}_1$.

The pattern for $\hat{\eta}_1$ for OLS shows a steady rise from 0.76 in 1855-1913 to 0.9293 in 1948-65. The anomaly in Table 2 whereby $\hat{\eta}$ for 1914-47 was higher than that for 1948-1965 is now clarified. Thus there is a steady acceleration in the speed of adjustment of inflationary expectations over the years, as one would expect. The degree of money illusion $(1-\hat{\eta}_1)$ is much higher in the nineteenth century and the post-war period than in the interwar period. This difference in the estimated degree of money illusion may be systematically related to the experienced instability in the rate of growth of prices. As has been argued recently the variance of inflation may be itself induce behavioural changes. If price changes are mild (have low variance) then individuals will live with them rather than bear the extra cost of making the adjustments in their contracts. This is certainly true of our data. The (ex post) variance of $\Delta \ln p_r$ was more than ten times as high in the 1914-47 period than in either of the other two periods.

The IV estimates show a much higher value for $\hat{\lambda}_1$ in the nineteenth century and $\hat{\lambda}_1$ there is not significantly different from unity. In the 1948-65 period it is again not significantly different from unity. Apart from this, the only other notable difference between OLD and IV estimates in Table 3 is the low and nonsignificant value for $\hat{\rho}_1$ in the entire sample.

Thus in substantive terms, we have a short run Phillips-Lipsey relationship for 1855-1913 and for the 1948-1965 period. These results tally with those of Lipsey. In the middle period, $\hat{\rho}_1$ being nonsignificant we find no such relationship in contrast to Lipsey. As for a vertical long-run Phillips curve of the Friedman-Phelps hypothesis, we find that for the two periods where we have a short run Phillips curve, we do not have a long-run vertical Phillips curve. In the middle period, we have no short run Phillips curve ($\hat{\eta}$=1) but we have a long run horizontal Phillips curve ($\hat{\rho}_1$ is non-significant).

Our results for the postwar period agree with Parkin's results for the UK economy. He also found the η_1 coefficient less than unity although he was using quarterly data for 1948(3)-1967(2) (Parkin (1971)). For the US data 1904-65, Lucas and Rapping found a similar instability in the short run as well as the long-run Phillips curve. In their case there was a significant long-run trade-off in the New Deal period 1930-1945 but not in 1904-29 or 1946-65. They found a short-run trade-off in every period but with the coefficient being dissimilar across periods. (Lucas and Rapping (1969); their model tests also were different from ours).

Let us now turn to the other four equations noted in Table 4. Of these the equation for $\ln p_r$ is the most straightforward being almost an identity. In this case, the OLS $\bar{R}^2$ (not given in Table 4) was in four cases 0.99 and in one 0.98. There was a highly autoregressive error which is shown by the $\hat{\beta}_1$ estimates for ALS and GIVE. Only in the 1914-47 period was there no evidence of autoregression. Over the hundred and eleven years' span, the component of domestic output price in retail price (δ_1) has risen steadily showing the diminishing importance of foreign trade as well as of the favourable terms of trade. In the postwar period, $\hat{\delta}_2$=0.4 in the first subperiod. The overidentifying restrictions as well as the autoregressive restrictions are all accepted. The estimates for $\hat{\alpha}_1$ do not need much comment as they are self explanatory.

The parameter μ was estimated by first differencing equation (12) and a constant was added to test for any trend. This constant was always nonsignificant hence is not listed on the Table. The estimates of μ are volatile. They are not significantly different from 1 in 1855-1913 and 1914-47 but jump to 6 in the postwar period. This was a period of very little variation in lnv and a very slight downward movement in σ. Since the size of μ is crucial to stability of the model as shown in our previous paper, this large jump in σ is worrying.

For the pricing question, the cost-plus hypothesis works well though the speed of adjustment of prices to changes in unit labour costs seems to fall over the hundred odd years from 0.78 to 0.65 but the difference is by no means statistically significan The size of the markup itself shows an interesting pattern.

	1855-1913	1855-1913	1914-1965	1914-1947	1948-1965
$\hat{\xi}$	1.0356	1.0564	1.0476	1.0572	0.9868

These $\hat{\xi}$ are derived from the ALS estimates and they show a remarkably similar size of mark up factor except for the last period where $\hat{\xi}$ is below 1 but given the size of the standard-errors attached to the coefficient from which it is derived it is unlikely to be significantly different from unity or from the other $\hat{\xi}$'s. In this equation however the restrictions imposed by the autoregressive error process as well as by instrumental variables are rejected and there is a case for respecificatio This can be done perhaps by specifying import prices as well as relaxing the restriction that the coefficient of $\ln(e/a)$ and $\ln(p_q)_{-1}$ is identical.

An interesting aspect of the UK economy which has been emphasised often is the favourable terms of trade it enjoyed in the 19th century and indeed much later due to the availability of colonial sources of supply. This had the advantage that the wedge between the product price and the price of wage goods favoured the employers. Thus the wage in terms of wage goods could be kept high while at the same time the wage in terms of product price could be relatively low. Thus, if we define u in terms of product price as we should do we have

$$\Delta \ln u = \Delta \ln e - \Delta \ln p_q - \alpha_1 \tag{16}$$

$$= (\Delta \ln e - \Delta \ln p_r) + (\Delta \ln p_r - \Delta \ln p_q) - \alpha_1 \tag{17}$$

The first term is the growth of real wages in wage good terms. The second term being negative will go to the employers and the third term also favours the employers. This can be further explored by assuming for the time being $\lambda_1 = 1$ as seems justified by our results. Then we get

$$[1-(1-\lambda_2)L]\Delta \ln u = -\lambda_2(\gamma_1+\alpha_1)+\rho_1[1-(1-\lambda_2)L]v_t+(\eta\delta_1-1)\lambda_2(\ln\xi+\ln u)$$
$$+ \eta\delta_2[1-(1-\lambda_2)L]\Delta \ln p_m \quad (18)$$

The steady state of (18) gives

$$\ln u^* = -\ln\xi - \frac{(\gamma_1 + \alpha_1)}{(1-\eta_1\delta_1)} + \frac{\rho_1}{(1-\eta_1\delta_1)} v + \frac{\eta_1\delta_2}{(1-\eta_1\delta_1)} \Delta \ln p_m. \quad (19)$$

The significance of $(1-\eta_1\delta_1)$ is now clear in terms of the struggle for income shares. To the extent that $\eta_1\delta_1<1$ there is an additional advantage to the employers of making lnu-v relationship flatter since it is the bit they can concede to the workers without losing themselves. This is so even when the long run Phillips curve is vertical in terms of wage goods prices, ie, $\eta_1=1$ as long as there is an open economy and $\delta_1<1$ and $\delta_2>0$. As our pattern of estimates for δ_1 show, we see that over the one hundred and eleven years, this wedge has been eroded by δ_1 getting larger. (This like any other statement derived from econometric estimates is made subject to the usual qualifications). In the period before World War I both η_1 and δ_1 were well below 1 the product of their point estimates being 0.2365. In the interwar period 1914-1947, this rises to 0.69 and stays at this level in 1948-1965. Events since 1965 have seen a marked rise in inflation consciousness on the part of British workers, signifying a rise in η_1 and one presumes that $(1-\eta_1\delta_1)$ - the wedge advantage to the employers - is now practically zero. Thus simple though it is, our model sheds some light on the reasons behind the change from relatively docile worker behaviour in nineteenth century to rising militancy in the interwar and postwar periods.

Our other equation can be written as

$$(1-\mu)\Delta \ln v = -(\alpha_1+\alpha_2) + \sigma^{*-1}\{v^{\mu}(1-u)\} \quad (20)$$

The steady state then gives

$$v^* = [\sigma^*(\alpha_1+\alpha_2)/(1-u)]^{1/\mu} \quad (21)$$

We are now in a position to look at our system of equations together. We started with Goodwin's elegant model contained in equations (2) and (4) which had a pair of constant values for u* and v*. In examining the system of equations, we interpreted its structural instability as caused by the imposition of prior zero restrictions on certain variables. We were able to cast the model in econometric terms which allowed us to nest the Goodwin model within the Desai extension. But econometric estimation forced us to add exogenous variables such as $\Delta \ln p_m$ and add equations such as the one for $\Delta \ln p_r$ in terms of the component prices.

Our econometric results are mixed about the Goodwin model. In the light of our more general specification, the Goodwin model involves the prior restrictions that (a) $\eta_1=1$ (b) $\lambda_1=1$ (c) $\mu=0$. Now our results in Table 4 show that $\mu=0$ is always rejected except for the rather large estimated of 6.86 for 1948-65 which has a t value of 1.3. As for the restriction on η_1 and λ_1, Table 2 shwos that conditional upon $\lambda_1=1$, we reject $\eta=1$ in two subsamples 1855-1913 and 1948-65 but cannot reject them in 1914-65 and 1914-47. For the entire sample $\hat{\eta}=0.87$ with a standard error of 0.066 is just marginally nonsignificantly different from 1 if we use a t value of 2. Once we relax the restriction $\lambda_1=1$, which only causes dynamic misspecification, we see that in those cases where $\eta_1=1$ is accepted $\lambda_1=1$ is rejected and vice versa. In no case is $\eta_1=1$, $\lambda_1=1$ accepted as a pair. We cannot therefore use our parameter estimates to compute the predicted cycle length. With $\mu\neq0$ and λ_1 and η_1 not equal to one, the economy is more likely to be stable than to exhibit cycles.

Still the model as in our equations (8) to (12) captures many interesting features of the UK economy - increasingly faster adaptations of inflationary expectations as well as the declining size of money illusion and its correlation with the observed variance of inflation. We also confirmed the crucial role that the advantageous terms of trade played in giving a breathing space to capital in its struggle with labour and we also see that this breathing space was disappearing in the postwar period. The class compromise which accounted for the decline of revolutionary politic noticed by many socialists is thus accounted for by the dividend earned from the international spread of British capital and Empire.

In extending the Goodwin model, we lose its simplicity and elegance we cannot for example, solve the implied cycle length as in equation (5) for the Goodwin model. A combination of (18) and (20) gives a nonlinear third order equation. But despite these complications, it still reamins a simple model. Thus it has a very naive investment function whereby all profits are automatically invested. (See for a recent extension of the Goodwin model with a modified investment function Desai and Pemberton (1981)). It neglects international capital movements which were such an important feature of the nineteenth centure UK economy. It also treats technical change as exogenous while it is obvious that not only does technical change presuppose appropriate investment but also that the rate of adoption of new techniques is endogenous to the class struggle (see Desai and Shah (1981) for an extension of the Goodwin model to take account of induced technical progess).

For the present we can conclude that

(a) The estimation of the growth model, which is closed, nonlinear and dynamic in character, presents interesting econometric problems, but is feasible if we admit lagged endogenous variables as instruments and add appropriate assumptions about the error terms.

(b) The Goodwin model **and** its extension bring out the cyclical character of the wage share and the importance of such elements as the product price/wage goods price wedge, the benefits from terms of trade and the changing importance of money illusion in the wage bargain. This aspect of the model supplements and clarifies the Phillips-Lipsey results which relate to the same time period.

(c) There is a need to respecify the model to allow for the impact of international capital movement on employment and accumulation, as well as to endogenise technical progress.

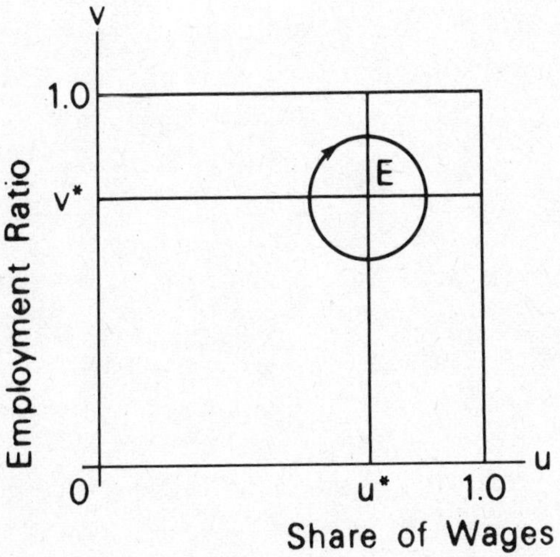

TABLE 1 - THE SHARE OF WAGES IN GDP AND UNEMPLOYMENT IN UK 1855-1965

	The share of wages in GDP %	% change in the share	Unemployment %
1855-59	50.52		4.20
1860-64	48.62	-3.77	3.62
1865-69	48.72	0.21	4.66
1870-74	48.28	-0.99	1.78
1875-79	51.28	6.21	5.38
1880-84	51.90	1.21	4.34
1885-89	52.38	0.92	6.82
1890-94	55.34 (21.0)	5.65	5.26
1895-99	53.82 (20.1)	-2.75	3.44
1900-04	54.78 (18.3)	1.78	4.10
1905-09	54.16 (18.1)	-1.14	5.56
1910-14	55.34 (17.7)*	2.18	3.28
1915-19	62.62 (n.a.)	13.15	1.26
1920-24	63.74 (15.6)	1.79	7.68
1925-29	61.40 (16.4)	-3.67	7.66
1930-34	62.48 (14.9)	1.76	13.58
1935-39	61.76 (13.9)	-1.15	8.66
1940-44	65.06 (12.2)	5.34	1.16
1945-49	66.38 (12.7)	2.03	1.26
1950-54	66.58 (11.0)	0.30	1.34
1955-59	67.74 (9.3)	1.74	1.44
1960-64	67.88 (10.1)	0.21	1.68

Source: Feinstein (1972) Table 18 (T44-46), Column 1 and Table 57 (T125-127) Column 6. Share of wages in GDP is taken to be the share of income from employment in GDP. Parentheses indicate the share of self-employed income in GDP for the same quinquennia.

* Average for 1909-1913

TABLE 2 - ESTIMATES OF THE EARNINGS EQUATIONS (EQUATION 13) 1855-1965

	1855-1965		1855-1913		1914-1965		1914-1947		1948-1965	
	OLS	ALS	OLS	ALS	OLS	ALS	OLS	ALS	OLS	ALS
γ	0.1493 (1.70)	0.1880 (1.82)	0.4626 (3.39)	0.4130 (2.83)	0.0765 (0.70)	0.1249 (0.85)	0.0023 (0.01)	0.0664 (0.32)	2.9804 (3.04)	3.4157 (2.92)
ρ	0.1727 (1.87)	0.2266 (1.98)	0.4942 (3.47)	0.4438 (2.91)	0.0998 (0.86)	0.1540 (0.99)	0.0183 (0.11)	0.0900 (0.40)	3.0680 (3.07)	3.5083 (2.95)
η	0.8751 (14.64)	0.7651 (11.78)	0.3447 (3.07)	0.3641 (3.47)	0.9523 (12.51)	0.8703 (10.13)	0.9978 (10.14)	0.9113 (8.07)	0.4623 (3.47)	0.5001 (3.43)
β_1	-	0.3424 (3.78)	-	0.2206 (1.68)	-	0.3382 (2.47)	-	0.3141 (1.79)	-	0.3956 (1.43)
$\bar{R}^2$	0.767	-	0.403	-	0.845	-	0.855	-	0.649	-
DW	1.45	-	1.49	-	1.43	-	1.50	-	1.32	-
S	0.0278	0.0260	0.0223	0.0209	0.0288	0.0279	0.0338	0.0335	0.0122	0.0122
$\chi_1^2(2)$	-	15.56	-	0.271	-	7.60	-	7.31	-	*
χ_2^2	22.00	13.45	3.70	0.50	13.98	10.86	10.40	8.83	4.84	3.81

Notes:

(1) * a small negative number was obtained here

(2) Figures in parentheses below the estimates are 't ratios'. The figure besides χ^2 is the appropriate degrees of freedom. χ_1^2 is the test of autoregressive restrictions. χ_2^2 is the LR test for over-identifying restrictions for the corresponding IV and AIV estimates. The df are 4 for IV and 3 for AIV

TABLE 3 - ESTIMATES OF THE EARNINGS EQUATION (EQUATION (8)) 1855-1965

	1855-1965 (1872-1965)		1855-1913 (1872-1913)		1914-1965		1914-1947		1948-1965	
	OLS	IV	OLS	IV	OLS	IV	OLS	IV	OLS	IV
$\gamma_1\lambda_1$	0.0284	-0,0042	0.2684	0.3262	-0.0176	-0.0309	-0.1008	-0.1363	0.5201	0.0835
	(0.34)	(0.42)	(1.53)	(1.49)	(0.17)	(0.28)	(0.69)	(0.83)	(0.51)	(0.07)
λ_1	0.6975	0.7309	0.7609	0.9145	0.7453	0.7681	0.7413	0.7692	0.9293	0.9150
	(12.13)	(10.66)	(5.95)	(5.85)	(10.17)	(9.03)	(8.52)	(7.81)	(6.71)	(6.00)
$\eta_1\lambda_1$	0.7213	0.8222	0.3327	0.2796	0.8212	0.8557	0.8698	0.9203	0.6353	0.6227
	(11.54)	(7.50)	(2.90)	(1.53)	(9.95)	(7.60)	(8.46)	(6.86)	(6.00)	(4.61)
$\rho_1\lambda_1$	0.0400	-0.0372	0.2888	0.3482	-0.0070	-0.0207	-0.0988	-0.1366	0.5601	0.1167
	(0.45)	(0.34)	(1.57)	(1.51)	(0.06)	(0.17)	(0.63)	(0.77)	(0.54)	(0.10)
ρ_1	0.2177	0.0409	0.4586	0.7528	0.1782	0.0354	0.0421	-0.1884	4.2689	3.3995
	(1.51)	(0.11)	(2.48)	(2.33)	(0.74)	(0.10)	(0.14)	(0.45)	(5.57)	(3.66)
$\bar{R}^2$	0.708	-	0.511	-	0.803	-	0.818	-	0.878	-
DW	1.92	1.79	1.91	1.70	1.86	1.83	1.98	1.95	1.82	1.44
S	0.0249	0.0235	0.0220	0.0196	0.0259	0.0263	0.0300	0.0308	0.0087	0.0095
$\hat{\beta}_3$	0.0347	0.1745	0.1729	0.0840	0.0869	0.1008	0.0134	0.0226	0.1469	0.2604
	(0.30)	(1.48)	(0.57)	(0.20)	(0.51)	(0.58)	(0.06)	(0.11)	(0.43)	(0.69)
$\chi^2(4)$	-	4.17	-	4.38	-	5.54	-	3.43	-	7.45

Notes:

(1) In each case $\hat{\beta}_3$ is quoted from the appropriate restricted transformed equation, ie, ALS in case of OLS and AIV in case IV.

(2) $\chi^2(4)$ is the Likelihood Ratio Test Statistic for the overidentifying restrictions Thus it is a test of validity of the specification. The degrees of freedom equal no. of instruments - number of included endogenous variables.

(3) The instruments used were Δ in p_{r-1}, Δv_{-1}, $\Delta \ln e_{-2}$, $\ln a_{-1}$, $\Delta \ln p_m$, $\Delta \ln p_{q-1}$. The price series p_q and p_m were available only 1870 onwards, hence the IV estimates in the entire sample and the first subsample relate to 1872-1965.

(4) Figures in parentheses below estimates are 't ratios' or their asymptotic equivalent in the IV case.

TABLE 4 - ESTIMATES OF EQUATIONS (9)-(12) 1855-1965

	1855-1965		1855-1913		1914-1965		1914-1947		1948-1965	
	OLS	ALS	OLS	ALS	OLS	ALS	OLS	ALS	OLS	ALS
	Growth of labour productivity equation									
α_0	4.1593	4.1430	4.1352	4.1796	3.9601	3.6901	4.1658	4.1752	2.9420	2.8872
	(415.0)	(44.87)	(534.0)	(115.77)	(92.07)	(12.57)	(68.49)	(26.39)	(43.77)	(13.10)
α_1	0.0091	0.1000	0.0104	0.0097	0.0113	0.0145	0.0085	0.0085	0.0007	0.0223
	(58.70)	(7.70)	(46.36)	(10.13)	(22.73)	(4.66)	(10.85)	(4.20)	(32.50)	(10.39)
β_4	-	0.9331	-	0.8410	-	0.8725	-	0.7009	-	0.6688
		(20.27)		(10.47)		(10.84)		(5.29)		(2.78)
$\bar{R}^2$	0.969	-	0.974	-	0.910	-	0.778	-	0.984	-
DW	0.21	-	0.35	-	0.31	-	0.60	-	0.77	-
S	0.0525	0.0238	0.0294	0.0169	0.0536	0.0290	0.0451	0.0332	0.0144	0.0123
	ALS	AIV	ALS	AIV	ALS	AIV	ALS	AIV	ALS	AIV
	Retail price equation									
λ_1	0.7538	0.8999	0.7283	0.7818	0.7650	0.9130	0.7656	0.8598	0.6616	0.6462
	(17.33)	(12.68)	(11.03)	(10.10)	(12.82)	(11.06)	(9.87)	(9.05)	(6.44)	(5.94)
$\lambda_1 \ln\xi$	3.4978	4.1713	3.3939	3.6459	3.5585	4.2118	3.5683	4.0000	3.0380	2.9681
	(17.36)	(12.69)	(10.98)	(10.07)	(12.84)	(11.01)	(9.92)	(9.07)	(6.53)	(6.02)
β_5	0.8644	0.8939	0.8895	0.9017	0.8586	0.8855	0.7690	0.8044	0.5894	0.5769
	(15.39)	(17.14)	(10.28)	(10.95)	(11.20)	(12.56)	(6.07)	(6.57)	(2.35)	(2.25)
S	0.0206	0.0218	0.0134	0.0135	0.0252	0.0268	0.0301	0.0309	0.01115	0.01117
$\chi_1^2(1)$	24.25	-	12.99	-	14.04	-	10.11	-	0.76	-
$\chi_2^2(5)$	-	32.89	-	22.15	-	18.98	-	18.23	-	12.31
	ALS	AIV	ALS	AIV	ALS	AIV	ALS	AIV	ALS	AIV
	Output price equation									
δ_0	0.2985	0.2566	-0.3503	-0.7656	0.4676	0.3050	0.7199	0.8588	-0.4011	-0.9012
	(3.52)	(2.85)	(0.88)	(1.73)	(2.63)	(1.49)	(8.36)	(10.13)	(0.99)	(1.22)
δ_1	0.7564	0.7889	0.6606	0.7737	0.7269	0.7894	0.6222	0.5875	0.9486	1.0280
	(25.04)	(22.42)	(6.44)	(6.52)	(13.80)	(12.21)	(27.67)	(26.54)	(17.30)	(9.25)
δ_2	0.1760	0.1510	0.4103	0.3893	0.1771	0.1419	0.2350	0.2441	0.0972	0.0974
	(6.39)	(4.92)	(10.04)	(9.36)	(5.05)	(3.46)	(14.81)	(17.52)	(2.97)	(2.99)
β_6	0.8298	0.8346	0.5224	0.4816	0.7940	0.8030	0.2228	0.2214	0.7827	0.8767
	(14.34)	(14.96)	(3.37)	(3.16)	(7.74)	(8.82)	(1.31)	(1.27)	(3.94)	(6.56)
S	0.0192	0.0193	0.0139	0.0141	0.0220	0.0223	0.0189	0.0191	0.0086	0.0091
$\chi_2^2(2)$	1.99	-	3.06	-	0.96	-	1.05	-	2.63	-
$\chi_2^2(4)$	-	0.3523	-	2.56	-	8.16	-	8.53	-	6.02

TABLE 4 (contd):

	1855-1965 OLS	1855-1965 IV	1815-1913 OLS	1815-1913 IV	1920-65 OLS	1920-65 IV	1920-47 OLS	1920-47 IV	1948-65 OLS	1948-65 IV
Capital output ratio equation										
μ	0.8479 (8.10)	*	0.6039 (5.44)	0.9282 (2.15)	1.2700 (7.46)	1.2576 (2.35)	1.2126 (5.89)	1.3440 (2.35)	5.1236 (7.02)	6.856 (1.31)
$\bar{R}^2$	0.376	-	0.307	-	0.475	-	0.497	-	0.736	-
DW	2.06	-	1.96	2.33	1.75	1.75	1.58	1.54	2.10	1.36
S	0.0231	-	0.0186	0.0198	0.0232	0.0230	0.0275	0.0272	0.0098	0.011
β_7	*	-	-0.0292 (0.21)	-	-0.0308 (0.22)	-	0.0131 (0.07)	-	-0.1095 (0.41)	0.185 (0.69)
$\chi_2^2(2)$	-	-	-	5.00	-	2.75	-	1.79	-	2.63

Notes:

(1) * indicates that due to a gap of five missing observations for 1915-1919, the computer program used (GIVE) was unable to estimate the parameters.

(2) As in Table 3 where β_i appears with OLS it gives the corresponding ALS estimate of β_i and AIV for IV. When it is with ALS and AIV, it is the joint restricted estimate along with the parameter estimates.

(3) χ_1^2 tests the validity of the AR restrictions. The appropriate degrees of freedom are given in parentheses alongside.

(4) χ_2^2 tests the validity of the overidentifying restriction. The appropriate degrees of freedom equal the number of instruments used less the number of included endogenous variables.

(5) Instruments used:-

For lnv (estimating): $\Delta \ln\sigma_{-1}$, $\Delta \ln v_{-1}$, $\ln a_{-1}$

For $[\log(e/a)-\ln p_{q-1}]$ (estimating λ_2): $\Delta \ln p_{q-1}$, $\ln a_{-1}$, $\ln e_{-1}$, T, $\ln p_m$, $\ln p_{r-1}$

For $\ln p_q$ (estimating δ_1): $\ln p_{r-1}$, $\ln p_{q-1}$, $\ln p_{m-1}$, T, $\ln a_{-1}$

(6) Figures in parentheses below estimates are 't values' or their asymptotic equivalent in the IV case.

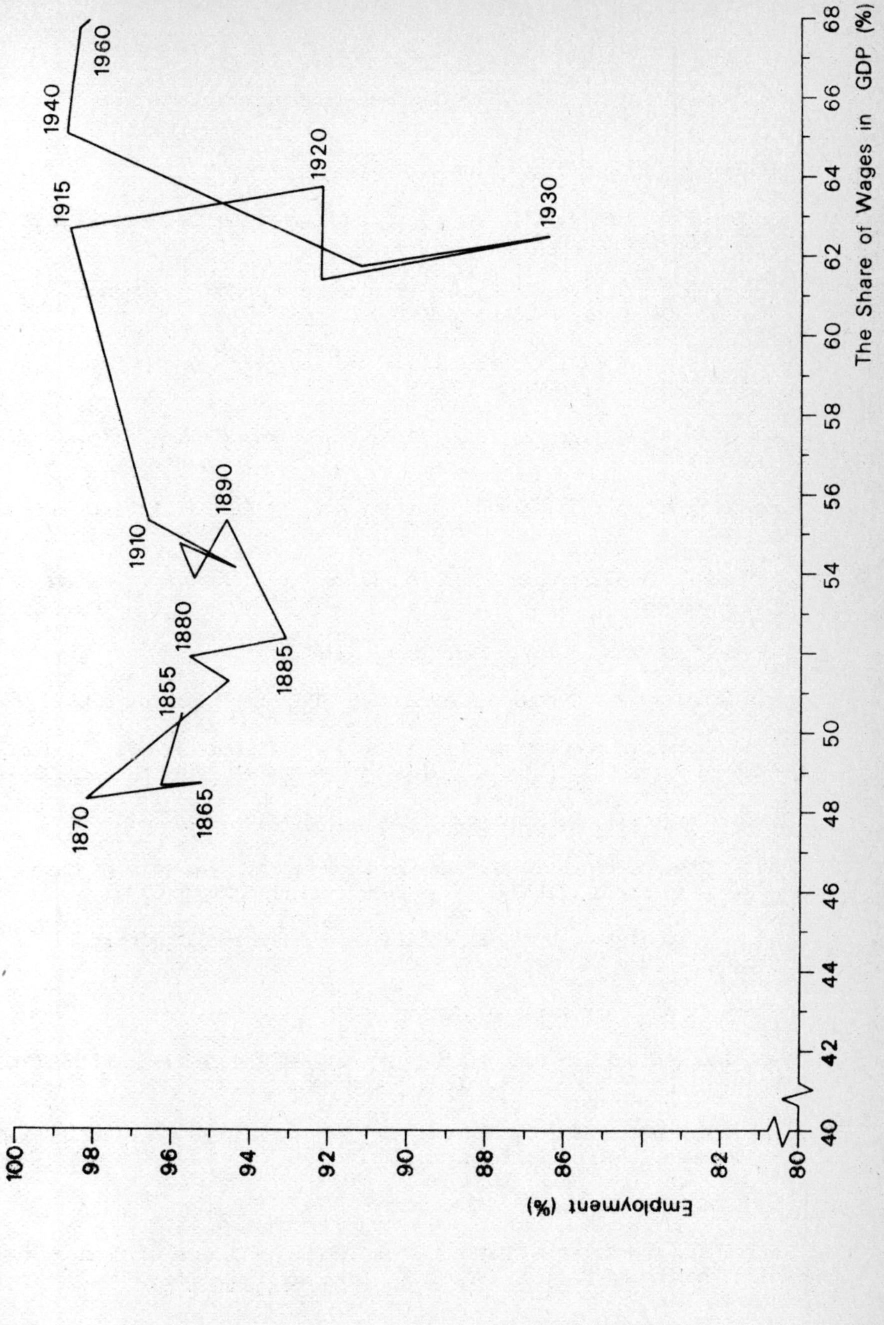

Employment (%)
100
98
96
94
92
90
88
86
82
80
The Share of Wages in GDP (%)
40
42
44
46
48
50
54
56
58
60
62
64
66
68
1855
1865
1870
1880
1885
1890
1910
1915
1920
1930
1940
1960

BIBLIOGRAPHY

ATKINSON, A B (1969), The Time Scale of Economic Models: How Long is the Long Run?, *Review of Economic Studies*, pp.137-152

DESAI, M (1973), Growth Cycles and Inflation in a Model of the Class Struggle, *Journal of Economic Theory*, Vol.6, pp.527-545

DESAI, M (1975), The Phillips Curve: A Revisionist Interpretation, *Economica*, February, pp.1-18

DESAI, M (1976), *Applied Econometrics*, (Philip Allan: Oxford)

DESAI, M and MALCOLM PEMBERTON (1981), On a Problem concerning the Goodwin Model of Growth Cycle (unpublished, LSE)

DESAI, M and ANUP SHAH (1981), Growth Cycles with Induces Technical Change, *Economic Journal*, December, pp.1006-1010

FEINSTEIN, C (ed), (1969), *Socialism, Capitalism and Economic Growth: Essays in Honour of Maurice Dobb*, (Cambridge)

FEINSTEIN, C (1972), *National Income, Expenditure and Output of the United Kingdom 1855-1965*, (Cambridge)

GLYN, A and R SUTCLIFF (1972), *British Capitalism, Workers and the Profit Squeeze* (penguin)

GODLEY, W and W NORDHAUS (1972), Pricing in the Trade Cycle, *Economic Journal*, September, pp.853-882

GOODWIN, R M (1967), A Growth Cycle in Feinstein C (1967)

HENDRY? D F and F SRBA (1978), Technical Manual for GIVE (unpublished, LSE)

KEYNES, J M (1939), Relative Movements of Real Wages and Output, *Economic Journal*, March (reprinted in the Collected Writings of J M Keynes, Vol. VII, pp.394-412).

KING, M (1975), The UK Profits Crisis, Myth or Reality, March, pp.33-34

LIPSEY, R G (1960), The Relationship between Unemployment and the Rate of Change of Money Wage Rates in the UK, 1862-1957, *Economica*, February, pp.1-31

LUCAS, R E and L RAPPING (1969), Price Expectations and the Phillips Curve: *American Economic Review*, June, pp.342-50

MITRA, A, The Share of Wages in National Income

PARKIN, M (1971), Incomes Policy: Some Further Results as the Determination of the Rate of Change of Money Wages, November, pp.386-401

PHELPS BROWN, E H and B WEBER (1953), Accumulation, Productivity and Distribution in The British Economy, 1870-1938, *Economic Journal*

PHELPS BROWN, E H and M BROWNE (1972), A Century of Pay

PHILLIPS, A W H (1958), The Relation between Unemployment and Rate of Change of Money Wage Rates in the United Kingdom 1861-1958, *Economica*, November, pp.283-99

SARGAN, J D (1980), The Consumer Price Equation in the Postwar British Economy, *Review of Economic Studies*, January, pp.113-136

VELUPILLAI, K (1979), Some Stability Properties of Goodwin's Growth Cycle, *Zeitschrift fur Nationalokonomie*, No.3-4, pp.245-257

Vol. 157: Optimization and Operations Research. Proceedings 1977. Edited by R. Henn, B. Korte, and W. Oettli. VI, 270 pages. 1978.

Vol. 158: L. J. Cherene, Set Valued Dynamical Systems and Economic Flow. VIII, 83 pages. 1978.

Vol. 159: Some Aspects of the Foundations of General Equilibrium Theory: The Posthumous Papers of Peter J. Kalman. Edited by J. Green. VI, 167 pages. 1978.

Vol. 160: Integer Programming and Related Areas. A Classified Bibliography. Edited by D. Hausmann. XIV, 314 pages. 1978.

Vol. 161: M. J. Beckmann, Rank in Organizations. VIII, 164 pages. 1978.

Vol. 162: Recent Developments in Variable Structure Systems, Economics and Biology. Proceedings 1977. Edited by R. R. Mohler and A. Ruberti. VI, 326 pages. 1978.

Vol. 163: G. Fandel, Optimale Entscheidungen in Organisationen. VI, 143 Seiten. 1979.

Vol. 164: C. L. Hwang and A. S. M. Masud, Multiple Objective Decision Making – Methods and Applications. A State-of-the-Art Survey. XII, 351 pages. 1979.

Vol. 165: A. Maravall, Identification in Dynamic Shock-Error Models. VIII, 158 pages. 1979.

Vol. 166: R. Cuninghame-Green, Minimax Algebra. XI, 258 pages. 1979.

Vol. 167: M. Faber, Introduction to Modern Austrian Capital Theory. X, 196 pages. 1979.

Vol. 168: Convex Analysis and Mathematical Economics. Proceedings 1978. Edited by J. Kriens. V, 136 pages. 1979.

Vol. 169: A. Rapoport et al., Coalition Formation by Sophisticated Players. VII, 170 pages. 1979.

Vol. 170: A. E. Roth, Axiomatic Models of Bargaining. V, 121 pages. 1979.

Vol. 171: G. F. Newell, Approximate Behavior of Tandem Queues. XI, 410 pages. 1979.

Vol. 172: K. Neumann and U. Steinhardt, GERT Networks and the Time-Oriented Evaluation of Projects. 268 pages. 1979.

Vol. 173: S. Erlander, Optimal Spatial Interaction and the Gravity Model. VII, 107 pages. 1980.

Vol. 174: Extremal Methods and Systems Analysis. Edited by A. V. Fiacco and K. O. Kortanek. XI, 545 pages. 1980.

Vol. 175: S. K. Srinivasan and R. Subramanian, Probabilistic Analysis of Redundant Systems. VII, 356 pages. 1980.

Vol. 176: R. Färe, Laws of Diminishing Returns. VIII, 97 pages. 1980.

Vol. 177: Multiple Criteria Decision Making-Theory and Application. Proceedings, 1979. Edited by G. Fandel and T. Gal. XVI, 570 pages. 1980.

Vol. 178: M. N. Bhattacharyya, Comparison of Box-Jenkins and Bonn Monetary Model Prediction Performance. VII, 146 pages. 1980.

Vol. 179: Recent Results in Stochastic Programming. Proceedings, 1979. Edited by P. Kall and A. Prékopa. IX, 237 pages. 1980.

Vol. 180: J. F. Brotchie, J. W. Dickey and R. Sharpe, TOPAZ – General Planning Technique and its Applications at the Regional, Urban, and Facility Planning Levels. VII, 356 pages. 1980.

Vol. 181: H. D. Sherali and C. M. Shetty, Optimization with Disjunctive Constraints. VIII, 156 pages. 1980.

Vol. 182: J. Wolters, Stochastic Dynamic Properties of Linear Econometric Models. VIII, 154 pages. 1980.

Vol. 183: K. Schittkowski, Nonlinear Programming Codes. VIII, 242 pages. 1980.

Vol. 184: R. E. Burkard and U. Derigs, Assignment and Matching Problems: Solution Methods with FORTRAN-Programs. VIII, 148 pages. 1980.

Vol. 185: C. C. von Weizsäcker, Barriers to Entry. VI, 220 pages. 1980.

Vol. 186: Ch.-L. Hwang and K. Yoon, Multiple Attribute Decision Making – Methods and Applications. A State-of-the-Art-Survey. XI, 259 pages. 1981.

Vol. 187: W. Hock, K. Schittkowski, Test Examples for Nonlinear Programming Codes. V. 178 pages. 1981.

Vol. 188: D. Bös, Economic Theory of Public Enterprise. VII, 142 pages. 1981.

Vol. 189: A. P. Lüthi, Messung wirtschaftlicher Ungleichheit. IX, 287 pages. 1981.

Vol. 190: J. N. Morse, Organizations: Multiple Agents with Multiple Criteria. Proceedings, 1980. VI, 509 pages. 1981.

Vol. 191: H. R. Sneessens, Theory and Estimation of Macroeconomic Rationing Models. VII, 138 pages. 1981.

Vol. 192: H. J. Bierens: Robust Methods and Asymptotic Theory in Nonlinear Econometrics. IX, 198 pages. 1981.

Vol. 193: J. K. Sengupta, Optimal Decisions under Uncertainty. VII, 156 pages. 1981.

Vol. 194: R. W. Shephard, Cost and Production Functions. XI, 104 pages. 1981.

Vol. 195: H. W. Ursprung, Die elementare Katastrophentheorie. Eine Darstellung aus der Sicht der Ökonomie. VII, 332 pages. 1982.

Vol. 196: M. Nermuth, Information Structures in Economics. VIII, 236 pages. 1982.

Vol. 197: Integer Programming and Related Areas. A Classified Bibliography. 1978 – 1981. Edited by R. von Randow. XIV, 338 pages. 1982.

Vol. 198: P. Zweifel, Ein ökonomisches Modell des Arztverhaltens. XIX, 392 Seiten. 1982.

Vol. 199: Evaluating Mathematical Programming Techniques. Proceedings, 1981. Edited by J.M. Mulvey. XI, 379 pages. 1982.

Vol. 200: The Resource Sector in an Open Economy. Edited by H. Siebert. IX, 161 pages. 1984.

Vol. 201: P. M. C. de Boer, Price Effects in Input-Output-Relations: A Theoretical and Empirical Study for the Netherlands 1949–1967. X, 140 pages. 1982.

Vol. 202: U. Witt, J. Perske, SMS – A Program Package for Simulation and Gaming of Stochastic Market Processes and Learning Behavior. VII, 266 pages. 1982.

Vol. 203: Compilation of Input-Output Tables. Proceedings, 1981. Edited by J. V. Skolka. VII, 307 pages. 1982.

Vol. 204: K.C. Mosler, Entscheidungsregeln bei Risiko: Multivariate stochastische Dominanz. VII, 172 Seiten. 1982.

Vol. 205: R. Ramanathan, Introduction to the Theory of Economic Growth. IX, 347 pages. 1982.

Vol. 206: M.H. Karwan, V. Lotfi, J. Telgen, and S. Zionts, Redundancy in Mathematical Programming. VII, 286 pages. 1983.

Vol. 207: Y. Fujimori, Modern Analysis of Value Theory. X, 165 pages. 1982.

Vol. 208: Econometric Decision Models. Proceedings, 1981. Edited by J. Gruber. VI, 364 pages. 1983.

Vol. 209: Essays and Surveys on Multiple Criteria Decision Making. Proceedings, 1982. Edited by P. Hansen. VII, 441 pages. 1983.

Vol. 210: Technology, Organization and Economic Structure. Edited by R. Sato and M.J. Beckmann. VIII, 195 pages. 1983.

Vol. 211: P. van den Heuvel, The Stability of a Macroeconomic System with Quantity Constraints. VII, 169 pages. 1983.

Vol. 212: R. Sato and T. Nôno, Invariance Principles and the Structure of Technology. V, 94 pages. 1983.

Vol. 213: Aspiration Levels in Bargaining and Economic Decision Making. Proceedings, 1982. Edited by R. Tietz. VIII, 406 pages. 1983.

Vol. 214: M. Faber, H. Niemes und G. Stephan, Entropie, Umweltschutz und Rohstoffverbrauch. IX, 181 Seiten. 1983.

Vol. 215: Semi-Infinite Programming and Applications. Proceedings, 1981. Edited by A. V. Fiacco and K. O. Kortanek. XI, 322 pages. 1983.

Vol. 216: H. H. Müller, Fiscal Policies in a General Equilibrium Model with Persistent Unemployment. VI, 92 pages. 1983.

Vol. 217: Ch. Grootaert, The Relation Between Final Demand and Income Distribution. XIV, 105 pages. 1983.

Vol. 218: P. van Loon, A Dynamic Theory of the Firm: Production, Finance and Investment. VII, 191 pages. 1983.

Vol. 219: E. van Damme, Refinements of the Nash Equilibrium Concept. VI, 151 pages. 1983.

Vol. 220: M. Aoki, Notes on Economic Time Series Analysis: System Theoretic Perspectives. IX, 249 pages. 1983.

Vol. 221: S. Nakamura, An Inter-Industry Translog Model of Prices and Technical Change for the West German Economy. XIV, 290 pages. 1984.

Vol. 222: P. Meier, Energy Systems Analysis for Developing Countries. VI, 344 pages. 1984.

Vol. 223: W. Trockel, Market Demand. VIII, 205 pages. 1984.

Vol. 224: M. Kiy, Ein disaggregiertes Prognosesystem für die Bundesrepublik Deutschland. XVIII, 276 Seiten. 1984.

Vol. 225: T. R. von Ungern-Sternberg, Zur Analyse von Märkten mit unvollständiger Nachfragerinformation. IX, 125 Seiten. 1984

Vol. 226: Selected Topics in Operations Research and Mathematical Economics. Proceedings, 1983. Edited by G. Hammer and D. Pallaschke. IX, 478 pages. 1984.

Vol. 227: Risk and Capital. Proceedings, 1983. Edited by G. Bamberg and K. Spremann. VII, 306 pages. 1984.

Vol. 228: Nonlinear Models of Fluctuating Growth. Proceedings, 1983. Edited by R. M. Goodwin, M. Krüger and A. Vercelli. XVII, 277 pages. 1984.